RESEARCHING
Interpersonal Relationships

RESEARCHING
Interpersonal
Relationships

Qualitative Methods, Studies, and Analysis

Jimmie Manning • **Adrianne Kunkel**

Northern Illinois University   University of Kansas

SAGE

Los Angeles | London | New Delhi
Singapore | Washington DC

Los Angeles | London | New Delhi
Singapore | Washington DC

FOR INFORMATION:

SAGE Publications, Inc.
2455 Teller Road
Thousand Oaks, California 91320
E-mail: order@sagepub.com

SAGE Publications Ltd.
1 Oliver's Yard
55 City Road
London, EC1Y 1SP
United Kingdom

SAGE Publications India Pvt. Ltd.
B 1/I 1 Mohan Cooperative Industrial Area
Mathura Road, New Delhi 110 044
India

SAGE Publications Asia-Pacific Pte. Ltd.
3 Church Street
#10-04 Samsung Hub
Singapore 048763

Acquisitions Editor: Matthew Byrnie
Editorial Assistant: Stephanie Palermini
Production Editor: Jane Haenel
Copy Editor: Mark Bast
Typesetter: Hurix Systems Pvt. Ltd.
Proofreader: Ellen Howard
Indexer: Terri Corry
Cover Designer: Candice Harman
Permissions Editor: Karen Ehrmann
Marketing Manager: Liz Thornton

Copyright © 2014 by SAGE Publications, Inc.

Printed in the United States of America

Library of Congress Cataloging-in-Publication Data

Manning, Jimmie.

Researching interpersonal relationships : qualitative methods, studies, and analysis / Jimmie Manning, Northern Illinois University, Adrianne Kunkel, University of Kansas.

pages cm

Includes bibliographical references and index.

ISBN 978-1-4522-0390-4 (pbk. : alk. paper)
1. Interpersonal relations--Research. I. Kunkel, Adrianne II. Title.

HM1106.M366 2013

302—dc23

2012046293

This book is printed on acid-free paper.

13 14 15 16 17 10 9 8 7 6 5 4 3 2 1

Brief Contents

Detailed Contents

8 Narrative Inquiry, Crystallization, and a Study of Workplace Relationships   175

9 Writing and Presenting Qualitative Interpersonal Communication Studies   199

Preface

This book is the result of our dialogues about the lack of resources for interpersonal communication scholars—or relationships researchers in general, really—who want to develop qualitative research studies. *Researching Interpersonal Relationships: Qualitative Methods, Studies, and Analysis* serves as the first book of its kind to offer interpersonal communication scholars a methodological primer specifically aimed at understanding interpretivist approaches to relationships research.

More than simply a research methods "how to" guide, this book is also a state-of-the-art review of literature related to qualitative interpersonal communication studies. It brings together multiple literatures—including philosophical readings, methodological primers, theoretical pieces, and research studies—that have never been considered as a coherent whole. Through that exploration of literature, we were able to theorize about interpretivist approaches to interpersonal communication studies, develop new methodological approaches for research, and encourage directions for future growth. We also wanted to try new approaches with this text, and so we invited other scholars to join us by contributing research reports that illustrate qualitative approaches in action. To help provide insights about their research practices, interviews with some of those scholars are included following each of the research studies. The candid words from the researchers allow for the messy elements of qualitative research practices—often erased in the writing process—to emerge and be considered. In addition to considering interpretivist theory, research design, common methodologies, research approaches, and analytical tools, the book also focuses on how good qualitative research can yield good theory and practical research understandings that can help people to make sense of their relational lives.

This book, we hope, is the tool interpersonal communication researchers need to balance interpretive and postpositivist approaches to interpersonal communication studies. Even for those who do not wish to engage interpretivist-oriented research, this book can serve as a source that allows for translation across paradigms and for postpositivist scholars to incorporate interpretivist research into their own studies. Our primary goals in writing this book were to provide a clear and grounded justification for the use of qualitative research methods, offer deep considerations about qualitative research designs, and highlight implications for the development of interpersonal communication theory from an interpretivist perspective. More than that, we wanted to infuse this writing with our voices and encourage those reading the book to consider how they may use their own voices in their research practices. As we hope readers can tell, our love for qualitative research methods is honest and unabashed, and we hope this enthusiasm provides for a contagious and exciting reading experience.

This book would not have been possible without contributions from and the support of a community of many interpersonal communication scholars. First, we thank Laura Ellingson, Patty Sotirin, Laura Stafford, Rachel Price, Molly Reynolds, Erin Sahlstein, Jennifer C. Dunn, Victoria Jennings-Kelsall, Denise Haunani Solomon, Rebecca Dohrman, Colleen Arendt, Patrice M. Buzzanell, and Natalie Litera, who contributed their excellent work to this project. We are especially happy that some of these scholars agreed to try their hand at qualitative analysis when their work is primarily quantitative. Of course we also were fortunate to have the guidance, support, and encouragement of Matt Byrnie, senior acquisitions editor of communication, media, and cultural studies at Sage, as well as the support from Stephanie Palermini, his editorial assistant. We also thank the reviewers who offered helpful feedback and kept us energized about this book's potential: Michael Irvin Arrington (University of Kentucky), David Boromisza-Habashi (University of Colorado at Boulder), Dawn Braithwaite (University of Nebraska-Lincoln), Karen Daas (University of Texas at San Antonio), Laura Ellingson (Santa Clara University), Rebecca Hains (Salem State University), Gretchen Norling Holmes (University of Memphis), Janice Kelly (Molloy College), Corey Jay Liberman (Marymount Manhattan College), Susan Millsap (Otterbein University), Kesha Morant Williams (Eastern University), and Kandi Walker (University of Louisville). The intellect and care in your feedback were beneficial.

Finally, as interpersonal communication scholars, it would be wrong for us not to acknowledge how our own relationships came into play with the creation of this book. Jimmie thanks Adrianne for her friendship, her commitment to this project, and her uncanny organizational abilities. As anyone who has worked with her can attest, she brings intellect, dedication, passion, a solid work ethic, and support to what she does. He dedicates this book to Adam, who has helped him grow into a nicer and happier person; to his father, who passed just as this project was beginning and who always told him, "If you think you know so much then why don't you write a #^@%ing book" (and who gave Jimmie his sense of humor); and Melody Tatum, who in high school talked him into conducting interviews with her for her science fair project. That was his first interpersonal qualitative research experience, and if he told you what it was about you wouldn't believe him.

Adrianne thanks Jimmie for his original, brilliant idea to write this book as collaborators. Our combined backgrounds and research styles have served this project better than could have ever been imagined. Jimmie's energy, passion, and ongoing friendship kept this book alive and kicking and at the forefront of all other projects. Adrianne dedicates this book to her incredibly supportive father, who has always encouraged her to work and write on that which she truly loves and cares about; to her mother, whose unquenchable appetite for knowledge is inspirational; to her partner, Mike, who listened to many stories and who has always been there as this book became a reality; and to her graduate students (of which Jimmie was one, a long time ago). Adrianne has always tried to be careful, thoughtful, and encouraging as her graduate students have embarked on new research journeys, some of which have truly helped develop her further as a scholar.

Introduction

*Embracing a Full Spectrum of Interpersonal
Communication Research*

We had to write this book. We had no choice. If we want to keep doing the kind of research we want to do, then this book is critical. We're not alone in our need, either—and we know that. Countless colleagues have told us their stories. Countless colleagues have made it clear: *when it comes to doing qualitative research, especially in the realm of interpersonal communication, we have a burden*. It is a burden of proof. It is a burden of explanation. It is a burden of colleagues not knowing, even when they think they know. They say things like, "Qualitative research is a great way to tell us about survey items." Or, "I respect that qualitative research helps to find themes we can do real research about later." Journal reviewers join in, too. "Couldn't you at least do some basic statistics?" they ask. Or they say, "Is this valid or reliable research, and how do you know? The sample is awfully small."

We've heard the comments. We've experienced the misunderstandings. But in spite of it all, we remain committed—and so we had to write this book. We hope these statements and the rest of this introduction make it clear why. We start by sharing our own personal stories of how we came to appreciate and love qualitative inquiry.

JIMMIE'S STORY

I'm hesitant to share the story of how I came to qualitative research, mostly because personal stories are sometimes pointed to as one of the things supposedly wrong with qualitative research. "It's so self-centered," I heard a fellow interpersonal communication scholar say during a panel session at a National Communication Association meeting. "Writing up other people's stories isn't science. Go write a biography if you want to do that. We need to do real, objective work here." I quickly scribbled down these words, shocked at his direct damnation and almost smiling at his arrogance. *Every bit of science*, I thought to myself—and back to the recent readings about positivism from my comparative communication theory seminar taught by Joann Keyton—*has at least one common limitation*. How can subjective, world-experienced people claim that what they know is wholly and fully objective? Sure, assigning numbers to meaning may allow some sense of uniformity and, consequently, a stronger sense of certainty. At the same time, all science—from the hardest of the hard to the softest of the soft—*is someone's interpretation*. Whether it is a person choosing a number on a survey or a researcher making a decision about a coding category when working through a quantitative content analysis, someone is interpreting. Someone is transforming a communicative life into a number. Someone is also making a decision about what that communication means and why. Social science is all an interpretation.

So why can't interpretation be through words? Why can't I, as a scholar, let people tell their stories, share their perceptions, and bring a sense of reflection to their own lives? Why can't I take the words they give me and work through them in an intuitive and iterative way to offer up some kind of empirical understanding? Why do the understandings I find have to be placed into some kind of already-existing box rather than considering how those understandings might make their own box—or a bag, or a bucket, or a blender, or a bathtub, or something that doesn't even vaguely resemble a container at all? Why can't a domain of understanding based in words (and, sometimes, images) be a big part of my scholarly path?

Undoubtedly, it can be. Even in interpersonal communication, an area of communication studies slower in embracing qualitative research than other contextual areas of the discipline, scholars have opened the door to how qualitative research can be a part of communication studies about relationships—even if only a few brave interpersonal communication researchers have blazed the path. In many ways, it is these heroes who have inspired me in intellectual *and* emotional ways about the potential qualitative studies have for developing interpersonal communication theory and practical understandings of how we do relationships.

I find myself with scholarly models in the series of studies conducted by Leslie Baxter, Dawn Braithwaite, and colleagues (e.g., Baxter & Braithwaite, 2002; Baxter et al., 2009) exploring wedding vow renewals and how interviews with those renewing their vows as well as with their stepchildren help show deep understandings of values found in rituals. I consider my own life stories and my part in them—and I know my students do, too—when I read the narrative work of Art Bochner (2002) or Carolyn Ellis (2004). I feel—as opposed to merely observing—the data so carefully collected by Paige Toller (2005, 2008, 2011) about parents coping with their child's death or people's accounts of the closet as they were captured and considered by Tony Adams (2011). I am energized by the methodological playfulness and the many possibilities of dissemination encouraged by the works of Ron Pelias (2011a, 2011b) and Laura Ellingson (2009). I *see* and *feel* and *think* these scholars—and so many others who study interpersonal communication through interpretive-oriented lenses—and I am inspired!

While I continue to be inspired by my disciplinary colleagues and the great work they are doing, I also find myself inspired by those with whom I have interacted while engaging my own studies. This was true from the very first qualitative study I engaged, one conducted while in a qualitative research methods seminar taught by Nancy Baym at the University of Kansas. I was frustrated by quantitative empirical work that suggested there may be little, if any, harm in anti-GLBT pejoratives (e.g., "Hey dyke!" or "Stupid queer!") because those using them did not mean them to literally refer to those they perceived as GLBT. The same research contended that GLBT people could rationalize that those using anti-queer pejoratives did not literally mean them to be against GLBT people, and so harm was minimized. I had a hunch that it couldn't be that simple. How could people *not* be affected by words that were probably used to demean and dehumanize them in other contexts? Even if someone could come to understand that a pointed word such as *fag* wasn't being used to literally call out a gay male, surely the word would have at least an initial reactive sting. In Rawlins's (2007) words, I was suspicious that the statistics used in the research were playing into "worldviews where detachment, objectivity, and the reduction of human activities and feelings to countable indicators are valued over persons' embodied performances and narrations of their lived experiences" (p. 61).

The focus groups I conducted with GLBT people soon confirmed my hunch. Speaking about his high school experiences with antigay language used toward him, one man shared, "I was always scared someone found out. Like, even if they couldn't be sure they knew who I was. That I had been found out and that my life was going to get even worse." One woman shared, "Every time someone uses *dyke*, unless it is another gay person, you still feel it. Because when people say it so much in a hateful way, especially men, how could it not?" More than confirm my questions based on another research study, though, the personal stories shared in the focus groups—as well as the interaction among participants—helped me to learn so much more. Instead of the possibility of one focus group paper giving context to the quantitative findings posited by the original article through a new form of data, I soon realized that numerous papers might be offered that built on existing interpersonal communication theories (such as a paper on relational dialectical tensions involving potentially offensive comments said by straight friends in gay-straight friendships) or offered new ideas or theoretical concepts of their own (such as a paper on how decentered symbols used in masculine social interaction have the possibility to continue to reify the centrality of the symbol). This discovery—that using qualitative methods allowed for multiple analytical decisions based on context, experience, consideration of past research, and continued reflection—convinced me of the great value of this "alternate" way of knowing.

The more I continued to do qualitative research, the more I realized that it shouldn't be an "alternate" way of knowing; but it should be a central way of knowing in the communication discipline and especially in the context of interpersonal relationships. This research makes a palpable and profound difference for the participants who come to reflect upon and develop a greater understanding for their own relationships (Manning, 2010b) but also for communities where the research is enacted. I've seen organizational cultures change as workplace relationships are reconsidered based on qualitative data collected from small-businesses or nonprofit organizations. I've seen communities rebuild as they examine their interpersonal interactions during crisis management situations (Manning, 2010a). And I've offered advice to people about how they might come out to family members (or how family members might react when loved ones come out to them) based on narratives shared by those who experienced coming out as lesbian, gay, or bisexual (Manning, in press-a). For me, qualitative research is a way of feeling, a way of knowing, and a conduit for difference making in a world that responds to and understands stories and dialogue. Moreover, it is a force for developing, extending, understanding, and creating theoretical bodies—both overarching and localized—that will ultimately enhance our understanding of interpersonal communication. In addition to interpretivist-oriented qualitative studies, I also engage studies of relationships that involve both cultural-rhetorical and quantitative paradigms; but it is in the interpretivist-oriented qualitative research I do where I continue to find my scholarly passion and heart.

ADRIANNE'S STORY

My journey as a qualitative researcher has been both fascinating and complicated, with more than its fair share of bumps, glitches, and stumbles. As a new MA student at Purdue University, my temporary advisor enrolled me in classes, including interpersonal communication theory, nonverbal communication, and a quantitative research methods course named Descriptive and Experimental Methods for Communication Research. While I was overjoyed and incredibly excited about the first two selections, I was also startled—if not intimidated—by the third. I had not had a class in research methods at my undergraduate institution, the University of Colorado at Boulder, which was just developing its major in communication. Moreover, both of my parents were artists, and my father, who ultimately raised me, is a very successful painter to this day. He literally "sees" the world in visual and narrative terms. My mother, on the other hand, has always been one of the most voracious and avid readers I know, so she is consistently filled with stories and words. Thus, my entire world had always been comprised of words, stories, images, and paintings. I was not a "numbers person" (at least, not at that point). I had no idea why it would be important to take a class focusing on a quantitative approach to inquiry.

As it is not in my nature to just sit back and be told what to do, I marched down the hall to my department chair's office and asked about my little surprise. He recognized, and sympathized with, my discomfort before explaining that all beginning graduate students in interpersonal communication *were expected* to take the course, and I would be, too. I reasoned that if the chair of the department told me to do it, then it must be the right thing to do. I did not question the class too much after that . . . at least until it began. I soon realized that the objectives included not only learning the basics about quantitative methods but also designing a study using one of the methods we covered. I decided to do a simple survey study investigating why people tell lies in romantic relationships that would require me to perform only minimal statistical analysis on the data.

Though the project was completed satisfactorily, I was left with questions about the class and the methods—big questions. Was I, as a young interpersonal scholar, destined to do quantitative work? Did interpersonal communication and quantitative research methods naturally go hand in hand? I thought about these questions a lot as my graduate career continued.

Early on in that first semester at Purdue, I decided to seek out research opportunities. My temporary advisor asked me if I wanted to help him with his research. As a super-motivated and truly excited graduate student, I agreed. I told myself it did not matter what kind of research I got involved in, as long as I got involved. The research turned out to be highly quantitative, and again, my questions about the marriage of interpersonal communication and quantitative methods filled my waking moments. When I told my father what I was working on and, even more so, how I was going about it, he seemed surprised. He asked if that was the kind of work I wanted to do, perhaps for the rest of my life? He did not see how distilling experience into statistical information fit my worldview at all. While I tried to defend what I was learning to do, quite frankly it was too early to tell. I did not know enough about research to be able to address the concerns.

As time went on that first semester, I found that my passion for interpersonal communication and its associated theories grew stronger and stronger. I decided that the person who first taught me about communication theory, the late and amazing Brant Burleson, was going to be my permanent advisor. Every time I left his class, questions (and more questions) about interpersonal communication theory bubbled up and diffused my consciousness. My journey continued as I collaborated with Brant, studying topics that thrilled me: attraction, romantic relationships, communication skills, cognitive complexity, emotional support, and sex differences and similarities in communication. Fulfilling as this was, the pattern was elongated. All of the investigations pursued answers to questions that called for quantitative research methods.

Eventually (for the most part), I accepted that the precision and rigor of the quantitative approach led to the most valid data and conclusions. I learned a ton from Brant about how to conduct top-notch research. My MA thesis won a dissertation award, even though it was only a thesis. The work was eventually published in *Human Communication Research* (Kunkel & Burleson, 1999), and other, smaller parts of it were published in the *Journal of Social and Personal Relationships* (Burleson, Kunkel, Samter, & Werking, 1996) and in various book chapters (Burleson & Kunkel, 2006; Kunkel & Burleson, 1998). I was on top of the world and had survey and experimental design to thank, along with dear Brant (of course).

Nonetheless, I never abandoned my puzzlement. I continued to feel as though something was missing. Where were the stories, images, lived experiences, and voices of the people whose communication and psychology I was studying? I talked to Brant about these questions. The great thing about having such a wonderful advisor and mentor was that, despite his firm positivist groundings, he allowed me to explore and venture out into new territory—in fact, he encouraged me to do so. So, out I went . . . and found others in Purdue's Department of Communication, such as Bill Rawlins (one of my all-time favorite professors of interpersonal communication) and Robin Clair (who was teaching primarily in the realm of organizational communication). I took every class Bill offered and most of Robin's classes. They really opened my eyes to an entirely disparate world of research approaches—including new ways of asking questions.

In one of my first classes with Robin, The Sexuality of Organization, I completed an interview study of our class on how we had become a completely socially supportive entity. I interviewed everyone in the class, and they told me their stories about how they felt they were able to open up in ways within the class context that truly surprised and astonished them. So my interests in social support continued, but I was able to pursue unique ways of discovering answers to my new kinds of questions. I later presented this work at a National Communication Association conference.

As my graduate work continued, I developed a special bond and friendship with Robin. We were both elementary school art teachers at an earlier point in our lives and both had the experience of teaching a child whom we knew had been abused in some way. We went on to explore this common interest and did a study using qualitative methods wherein we interviewed retired schoolteachers who had suspected child abuse. We presented this work at an International Communication Association conference and eventually published it in *Communication Monographs* (Clair & Kunkel, 1998). I also collaborated with Robin and another graduate student on a paper eventually published in the *Journal of Applied Communication Research* (Clair, Chapman, & Kunkel, 1996) about narrative approaches to sexual harassment. Our team then joined forces with Marifran Mattson of Purdue and published a chapter for Patrice M. Buzzanell's (2000) book, *Rethinking Organizational and Managerial Communication From Feminist Perspectives* (Mattson, Clair, Sanger, & Kunkel, 2000). Once again, I was enthralled! I loved these new ways of knowing and learning. To me, they were equally valid as research approaches, and I savored the richness and complexity of the data we gathered. Not to mention, I had developed new friendships with incredible mentors and eventual colleagues.

Throughout my MA and PhD programs at Purdue, Brant supported me fully. As long as I was doing high-quality work, he did not constrain me and say that I had to do only quantitative research as an interpersonal scholar, though that was his predominant way of doing research. He always reminded me that my research questions should drive my research methods. He motivated me to take as many classes in as many different kinds of methodologies as possible. I did this with blazing enthusiasm and full vigor! I took research methods classes in education, anthropology, psychology, and linguistics. I felt like I could do and be whatever kind of scholar I wanted to be—graduate school became a candy store filled with immense possibilities and options. I also knew in my heart that I would never want to be labeled as either a quantitative or qualitative scholar. I let my research questions continue to direct my path, as they do today.

Ironically, as part of my interview process to become an assistant professor of communication studies at the University of Kansas, I presented quantitative work, for which I was best known. It featured the very postpositivist approaches and data central to my examinations of social support and the associated differences (or rather, to be precise, the many similarities) between the sexes (Kunkel & Burleson, 1999). Consequently, upon my hiring and the onset of my experiences as a teacher and researcher at KU, I was known very much as a "quantoid." Though I often professed my devotion to using appropriate methods for particular questions asked, the first impressions of my new colleagues were difficult to dispel. On the tenure track, I also did what anyone would expect: I pulled out all of the data and research projects that had not yet been published and began working on them furiously as fuel for my tenure case. I had a ton of quantitative data collected from my years at Purdue. I analyzed it. I wrote it up. I published it. As more lines appeared on my CV, I naturally felt more assured.

But something else continued to evolve. At Purdue, while taking a required class on rhetorical theory, I was also dating Michael Dennis, a graduate student colleague in the department who would eventually become my collaborator in research and in life. When his father, a wonderful and funny veterinarian in Texas, was killed by a drunk driver, Mike struggled to write and perform his eulogy, despite his many semesters of teaching public speaking. In addition, my grandmother had recently passed, and I was pained as my father delivered a beautiful, heartfelt, and loving eulogy. These events sparked an idea for my rhetorical theory project, and eventually we went on to publish a series of investigations in the journal *Death Studies* about the communicative relief of grief and the specific comforting aspects of the eulogy (Dennis & Kunkel, 2004; Dennis, Ridder, & Kunkel, 2006; Kunkel & Dennis, 2003). We worked deductively from the known properties of social support to identify them, by way of thematic analysis, in contemporary eulogia. It was wonderful to share in this passion and make our contributions to understanding a grim but vital psychological and interpersonal context. Most importantly here, this work was purely qualitative.

Soon after receiving tenure, and long after realizing that I had learned an awful lot from my education and research, I also recognized that I could now devote myself purely to whatever kind of research most interested me. With some intense post-tenure self-reflection, I decided that the work that truly made my heart beat was the work I had done on child abuse, sexual harassment, and how people cope with and navigate the grief process. Before long, I was emerged in projects that encompassed my true passions. I went through a rigorous training process and became a domestic violence shelter volunteer, thus pursuing my lifelong interest in helping women and children to deal with, if not escape, domestic violence and abuse. I had always wanted to make a difference with the work I did, and now I was assisting people in changing their lives for the better.

I joined forces with a like-minded colleague at KU, Suzy D'Enbeau (now at Kent State University). As volunteer advocates, we developed a large-scale, multimethodological, purely qualitative research project (ethnographic, interview-based case study) to unravel the challenges and constraints facing domestic violence advocates and survivors. Over a 2-year period, and with the help of a fabulous graduate student at KU, Jennifer Guthrie, we garnered almost 60 interviews with advocates and survivors, transcribed and analyzed them, and formally presented our findings—some of which have been accepted for publication in the *Journal of Applied Communication Research*.

Hearing and learning about the life stories of domestic violence survivors and their advocates has been life changing. I have learned that the best way to truly understand the depth and richness of another human being is to listen to his or her stories. I have located the kinds of questions I now seem to predominantly ask as revolving around others' personal experiences. I have come to believe that, as an interpersonal scholar embracing qualitative methods, I can truly and forever affect lives positively. I hunger and crave to learn even more, though it also feels like the learning has just begun . . .

OUR GOALS IN WRITING THIS BOOK

Our stories are undoubtedly spirited with a love and respect for qualitative approaches to studying interpersonal communication. Although we argue here on behalf of qualitative research and interpretivist-theoretical approaches, we do so with a respect for the wide spectrum of research methods and theoretical approaches that constitute the field of communication studies (Craig, 1999). As many scholars continue to embrace qualitative social scientific research approaches, we hope this book can work especially to assist scholars in interpersonal communication—an area that has been particularly slow to embrace qualitative studies (Baxter, 2011; Levine, 2011; Tracy & Muñoz, 2011). To that end, we seek to create a resource that assists and encourages those who raise questions best answered by interpretivist-oriented approaches. We envision this book as a primer for doing qualitative interpersonal work as well as a resource to invoke when writing up or otherwise disseminating research studies. As such, we have three particular goals in writing this text. The goals are grounded in a large body of interpretivist metatheory and qualitative methodology and are articulated with a respect for the rich history of interpersonal communication research as well as a deep hope that the book may be practically used by those embarking upon qualitative research studies.

Our first goal is to alleviate issues of translation that often accompany qualitative studies of interpersonal communication. As those who have submitted qualitative research manuscripts to communication journals have probably experienced, illustrating and justifying methodological choices (including analysis) can often be a difficult task. Some words used in the methods sections of qualitative manuscripts (such as *triangulation*) may have a different meaning in a quantitative context and, as such, may lead to confusion for a reviewer who traditionally does quantitative work. Writing up a qualitative definition of triangulation takes valuable resource space, and it places a burden on a researcher who likely already has a results section filled with thick description that quickly helps to fill page limits. Even when valuable space is used to thoroughly explain methods, it can still lead to confusion. For example, many qualitative researchers have shared that when they write about using a coding method with their data, it may lead to a quantitative researcher asking for intercoder reliability or how many other people were engaged in the coding process. Further, some reviewers are shocked that one person and only one person may be coding the data. Yet we have never heard a story indicating the opposite—that a quantitative researcher was asked why he or she had multiple coders or did not take an interpretive approach. As this book details, manuscript space is often limited. The space to explain what *snowball sampling* or *interpretive validity* or any of the many other uniquely qualitative terms mean should not be within research manuscripts, just as research manuscripts currently do not demand at-length explanations for quantitative terms such as *varimax rotation* or *structural equation modeling*. Our hope is that interpersonal scholars—whether they are doing their own research or evaluating the work of others—can use this guide to help them consider what qualitative research is about and whether or not the research choices made (from data collection to analysis to write-up) seem to be good, solid choices for that particular study. Cross-paradigmatic literacy will allow for increased understanding of interpersonal communication studies and the potential for scholars to be inspired to do research in their home paradigms.

Second, and in line with our first goal, we seek to provide guiding considerations for doing qualitative interpersonal communication research. Whereas many who do quantitative research studies enjoy doing so because it provides a sense of certainty (and often a rigid sense of what comes next in the research process), many who enjoy qualitative research are intrigued by the messiness inherent in any social situation and the joy that comes from making sense of that messiness. Qualitative research methods are undoubtedly guided by logical choices, but these choices can lead to many different paths, and these many paths can each lead to reliable and valid results. As that assertion reflects, doing qualitative work is so much more than doing a particular type of method. It also involves a different type of thinking—thinking not geared toward absolutes or a strong sense of *this is what you will always find.* Instead, qualitative research, in so many ways, is about possibilities mined from particular social situations and the potential of those possibilities for similar social situations. In that sense, qualitative research is quite similar to statistical postpositivist research. Much of the difference comes from the presentation of the data and how data are used to build or enhance theory. To that end, we seek to move beyond simple directions about how to employ a particular research method. By doing so, we seek to demonstrate how conceptualizing research studies and analyzing collected data are dynamic and often inductive processes.

Finally, and perhaps most importantly, we hope to encourage a sense of community for interpersonal communication scholars across qualitative traditions (as well as across methodological paradigms in general). One of the biggest surprises we have encountered as teachers in the classroom is that many believe qualitative researchers are all of the same ilk and hold the same common assumptions and approaches. On the contrary, qualitative research is not a singular tradition but is instead a collection of many rich traditions. Some qualitative researchers, often those who also do statistical research, tend to have a more scientific approach that blends statistical findings with qualitative data to tell a multilayered story. Other qualitative researchers completely eschew statistics and instead argue that localized narratives offer a stronger sense of reality for those who are experiencing their social worlds. Whether you are on one end of the spectrum or somewhere in the middle, we hope you will feel welcome in reading and responding to this book *and* that you are open to others who may have different views about qualitative work and what it can mean. That means accepting a wide range of interpretivist views (we'll get more into those in the first chapter), as this book uses interpretivism and other nonpostpositivist paradigms as its guiding principles. If you do not typically approach research with an interpretivist attitude, fret not. We try to take special care to explain what it is, how it functions, and some of its paradigmatic relatives. We try even harder to show that everyone who congregates under the nonpostpositivist empirical umbrella—from grounded theorists to narrative enthusiasts to dialogic thinkers—has differences and commonalities that can be compared and contrasted to understand interpersonal communication.

THE ORGANIZATION OF THIS BOOK

In line with our three goals, the first chapter of this book explores how interpretive-oriented theories (across many traditions) and qualitative research can work hand in hand to generate localized research findings that allow for sensitization and increased understanding in a variety of interpersonal communication contexts. In addition to explaining differences between the more positivistic theories that often dominate interpersonal communication research and interpretivist-oriented theories that undergird qualitative inquiry, the chapter also explores some of the current limitations of a singular metatheoretical paradigm. The chapter then explores reasons those researching interpersonal communication may want to use qualitative research methods, including possible commitments for qualitative researchers. That leads into the second chapter where some of the most common qualitative research traditions are reviewed, as is a model for designing a qualitative research study. Other topics covered in the second chapter include concerns for conducting quality research, some of the paradoxes qualitative researchers may encounter as part of the research process, and research ethics.

After the opening chapters set up an understanding of what qualitative studies of interpersonal communication are and can be, the next six chapters offer considerations for the application of specific research methods to the study and analysis of particular relationships. We asked six different researchers or research teams to do a study using the elements presented in each chapter. Although most of the scholars who participated are established and well-versed with interpersonal communication research, they were not all well-versed with social scientific *qualitative* interpersonal communication research. This means that some of them, like many who will read this book, were grappling with new methods and analytical tools in a new paradigm. To capture their thoughts and feelings about their work, and to gain a better sense of what it entailed, we interviewed a researcher from each study (or, in one case, offered a survey) and included pieces of that conversation at the end of their chapters.

Overall, what this means is that each chapter contains some introductory text about a context, method, and analytical tool; a representative research project from a guest researcher or team that uses that same context, method, and tool; and then a candid interview that allows more insight about methods and process. Chapter 3 is on family communication and covers interviews, perhaps the most commonly used qualitative method for the study of interpersonal communication. Laura Ellingson and Patty Sotirin, two scholars quite familiar with using qualitative research methods to study interpersonal communication, use a modified version of emotion coding to come to deeper understandings of aunting relationships. Chapter 4 then presents a study that questions romantic relationship activities and uses focus groups as its method. Laura Stafford, who employs mostly postpositivist methods in her research, leads a research team that uses values coding to consider friends with benefits. Chapter 5 is a friendship study using open-ended surveys. Erin Sahlstein, who frequently uses both quantitative and qualitative methods for her studies, uses taxonomic coding (sometimes called typology development) to explore views of long-distance relationships.

Chapter 6 moves into ethnographic field studies and considers interpersonal identity. Jennifer C. Dunn, a scholar who often employs media criticism techniques for her research, observed workers at the Moonlight Bunny Ranch and used dramaturgical analysis to consider how identity may be negotiated. Next is Chapter 7 where Denise Solomon—whose work is squarely based in postpositivist paradigms—was invited to contribute a qualitative study exploring computer-mediated communication. She and Victoria Jennings-Kelsall use discourse analysis to consider the experiences of military spouses in a time of war. In the final research-oriented chapter, Chapter 8, qualitative research veteran Patrice M. Buzzanell, qualitatively trained Rebecca Dohrman, and their colleagues do a study of workplace relationships through a collection of narratives that is presented as a reader's theater piece. And, finally, in Chapter 9 we offer some closing considerations for writing up qualitative research, including checks for reliability and validity. Our hope is that by considering the various discourses concerning interpersonal communication and qualitative research, as well as getting up close to several studies, you will leave this book with new ideas for how you can use interpretive approaches in your work. We also hope the book is one you want to return to as a resource for your research and theorizing and to reinvigorate your qualitative spirit.

CONSIDERING POSSIBILITY

Before we move into the first chapter and begin this book in earnest, we want to offer one more consideration: Good qualitative research cannot be replicated. Sure, qualitative researchers steal ideas or learn techniques or become sensitive to how people will respond in a given situation, but a lot about qualitative research methods is learned by *doing* the work. With that in mind, we do not claim to have all the answers. What we do present is based on our experiences and through exploration of others' qualitative interpersonal communication research and their assertions about qualitative methodology—and, really, that is a relatively small body of literature. So we are not, by any means, asserting the methods or approaches found here are the *only* ways to go about doing your research. Instead, we hope to start a conversation about interpretive possibilities so that qualitative research studies of interpersonal communication continue to expand in innovative, diverse, and exciting ways. One of the reasons we invited such a wide array of researchers to join us in writing this book is because we want to recognize that interpretive qualitative research has so many possible directions. So as you read, and as you think about what it is in the wide world of interpersonal communication that you want to study, think about the possibilities for your work. What possible approaches can you take? What possible ways can you engage others? What possibilities lie ahead for analysis or writing up your data? What are the possible implications for theory and practice?

With each step of your research process, it is entirely possible that the answers to those questions may change. Once you have an answer, it is entirely possible that you can go back to your data set and find new questions, answers, and insights. *Possibility* is a big part of qualitative inquiry. As Jimmie recently noted,

> Undoubtedly, one of the largest explosions of rich and fruitful research findings will come from increased and diversified use of qualitative methods. Relationships researchers are sorely in need of research guides and strong educative materials to aid them in finding and using qualitative approaches that allow for deeper understandings of interpersonal interaction and how relationships are constituted through communication. (Manning, 2009b, p. vii)

We hope this book is a big step toward the possibility of making that happen.

Understanding Personal Relationships Through an Interpretivist-Oriented Lens

We spend considerable time in this opening chapter identifying and unpacking the metatheoretical elements that come together to make up an overarching body of interpretivist theory. *Interpretivist theory* collectively refers to the metatheoretical elements of interpretivism in all of its various traditions, much like *communication theory* is an umbrella used to collectively describe the various traditions that come together to constitute communication studies. We also make use of the term *interpretivist-oriented qualitative research* to acknowledge the full range of metatheoretical perspectives associated with qualitative research and to recognize that qualitative data can also be considered through realist paradigms such as postpositivism. As that indicates, the forms of qualitative analysis we examine in this book tend to align with interpretivism. To make all of these ideas clearer, this chapter explores some of the most common research traditions and approaches that fall into an interpretivist orientation. The chapter then considers how interpretivism can be used in interpersonal communication research studies and what such studies may offer to the development of interpersonal communication theory. We begin with a brief history of interpretivism.

INTERPRETIVISM EXPLAINED

Interpretivism, as a methodological paradigm, focuses on understanding individuals' interpretations of social actions and their social worlds (Baxter & Braithwaite, 2008; Lindlof & Taylor, 2011). Given that both communication and interpersonal relationships are fraught with meaning and action, it makes sense that studying relationships through an interpretivist-qualitative lens allows deeper insight into how meaning and action work together to constitute relationships. To do that, a deeper understanding of interpretivist theory is in order. This exploration begins with the presentation and discussion of Blumer's (1969) three core premises of symbolic interactionism that constitute a canonical understanding of interpretivism.

The pragmatist work of William James, John Dewey, Charles Sanders Peirce, and George Herbert Mead was moving toward symbolic interactionism for decades, but the idea crystallized with Herbert Blumer's (1969) *Symbolic Interactionism: Perspective and Method*. Blumer's monograph offered 12 chapters exploring what would come to be called an interpretivist paradigm, and the ideas explored across the book all rested on three foundational premises. Blumer's first premise theorizes that "human beings act toward things on the basis of the meanings which these things have for them" (p. 2). Such an idea is intuitive, as Blumer notes in presenting it—but even so, the idea that action is purposeful and based on meaning was ignored or played down by social sciences at the time. Blumer felt psychological studies especially missed the mark, noting that researchers took meaning for granted and had a tendency to

> treat human behavior as the product of various factors that play upon human beings; concern is with the behavior and with the factors regarded as producing them. Thus, psychologists turn to such factors as stimuli, attitudes, conscious or unconscious motives, various kinds of psychological inputs, perception and cognition, and various features of personal organization to account for given forms or instances of human conduct. (p. 2)

Psychology, then, was treating meaning as an *effect* instigated by different internal or external factors.

Although sociology (the other dominant social science at the time) took a slightly different approach using rigidly conceived notions of construct variables such as social roles, status demands, or norms, meaning was still accounted for by causal explanations (Blumer, 1969). As such, both psychology and sociology largely ignored meaning in designing and interpreting their studies. Rarely, and at best, meaning was accommodated for by either conflating it with or embedding it into initiating factors and any resulting behaviors or by treating it as a neutral link that intervenes between any initiating factors and the alleged behaviors they produce, almost as if it were a sort of transmitter (Blumer, 1969). In short, possibilities for meaning to be central to social interaction (or, more precisely, social action in general) were not considered in the social sciences; and as such, the idea that people act purposively based on the meaning they assign things—as intuitive as that seems—was ignored or dismissed.

The reframing Blumer (1969) offers with his first premise alone allows meaning to be laden *across a social scene and the action in it* rather than conceptualized as a simple effect in one's mind or as located solely within an object. That is not to suggest that people do not bring meaning to objects, but that the meanings people assign to objects in a social scene are not given. As Blumer articulates with his second premise, meanings come from "the ways in which other persons act toward the person with regard to the thing" (p. 4). Simply put, interaction creates meaning for an object. Objects, as defined by Blumer, include the physical (e.g., doors, trees, cars, hydrants), the social (e.g., friend, preacher, cousin, neighbor), and the abstract (e.g., justice, philosophies, marriage, virginity). Again, Blumer's notions were in opposition to dominant academic understandings that conceived meaning as "emanating from the intrinsic makeup of the thing that has meaning" or as "arising through a coalescence of psychological elements in the person" (p. 4). In other words, interpretivism holds that meaning is not innate or even inevitable for any object. Further, meaning is not dependent on a person's psychological traits or tendencies; instead, it is learned, shaped, and negotiated (even if it still feels static and tangible to a person) even as it continues to be reproduced and, consequently, reshaped.

As such, Blumer's third and final premise theorizes that meanings are understood in and modified through a process used by a person to understand and act toward objects he or she encounters. This third premise not only makes interpretivism distinct as a philosophy but also is a key link to how interpretivist theory can undergird interpersonal communication research. As the premise implies, meaning happens through an interpretive process dependent upon interaction. Blumer points out two steps in this *process of interpretation* (p. 5). First, an actor notices an object toward which she or he is acting. This is not simple psychological interplay, but is more of a person talking to herself or himself in order to make meaning about a perception in a social situation. Second, the social actor "selects, checks, suspends, regroups, and transforms the meanings in the light of the situation in which he is placed and the direction of his action" (p. 5). The first part of this formative process may seem highly internal, and in many ways it is. The second part of the process, however, makes a clear connection to understanding social interaction. Actors in a social scene are purposefully interacting in consideration of each other, constantly reassessing and renegotiating both meaning and action. This process should not suggest that one is always rational and in complete control of the meanings he or she makes. In fact, it is quite the opposite—meanings people bring to a social scene can be complex and deeply emotionally laden. An interpretive approach to interpersonal communication studies should carefully consider the communication inherent in such a scene.

A Family of Interpretivist Theories

As anyone who has studied interpretivism or any of its related concepts can probably attest, theorists across these spectra (some that precede interpretivism) have developed rich, nuanced, and oftentimes complex philosophical inquiries into the differences, similarities, evolving assumptions, controversies, and driving forces undergirding each paradigm (see Lincoln, Lynham, & Guba, 2011, for an excellent overview; or Miller, 2004, for an understanding of the historical development relevant to the communication discipline). Some of the identified differences between paradigms can have profound effects upon how research is conceptualized and data are interpreted (Ellingson, 2009, 2011); other disagreements about these philosophies likely have more impact at a metatheoretical level rather than a level that threatens the validity of the research (Lindlof & Taylor, 2011). Theory textbooks often place these various approaches or paradigms together into a *sociocultural tradition* of communication studies (Craig & Muller, 2007; Griffin, 2012; Littlejohn & Foss, 2008) based on Craig's (1999) essay identifying dominant traditions of the field, although rhetoric, semiotics, phenomenology, and critical theory—traditions Craig sets apart from a sociocultural tradition—may also have interpretivist leanings. The different branches of interpretivism, and the traditions contained within them, often lend ideas to each other, and this generally works as long as the ideas are meaningful to the context and situation of a given study and can be clearly explained (Maxwell, 2009). As such, many researchers have focused on the shared and least contested operational elements of these theoretical bodies to use in qualitative research studies.

Because of these overarching similarities across these paradigms, we use the term *interpretivist-oriented approaches* to note all of the nonrealist research paradigms involved with the qualitative research family. Like others in the past who have used umbrella terms to describe this family of qualitative approaches (e.g., Denzin & Lincoln, 2011; Lincoln et al., 2011; Tracy & Muñoz, 2011), we mean no disrespect by grouping these approaches together. Of course, we also realize that this muffles some of the qualities of the diverse and vibrant approaches that are interpretivist oriented but have considerable differences from traditional interpretive studies. As such, we review some of the most common variants here.

Phenomenological and Dialogic Approaches

Phenomenology is a body of diverse philosophical perspectives initiated by German philosopher Wilhelm Dilthey in the 19th century. When phenomenology was introduced to communication studies, three key uniting principles were noted: individual consciousness is where knowledge is found, not from external experience; the potential for a particular experience or object in a person's life is what allows meaning; and meaning is developed from language, the channel through which the world is largely experienced (Deetz, 1973). Beyond those key principles, phenomenological approaches largely depend on whether they involve a transcendental (where the taken-for-granted is considered) or social (where how people typify constructs is considered) phenomenological background (Miller, 2004). Although phenomenology has played an important role in the development of qualitative research (see Lindlof & Taylor, 2011, for a detailed overview), it has played a small role in interpersonal communication studies. Perhaps what is more important is how scholars involved with the movement—especially Max Weber, Edmund Husserl, and Alfred Schutz—helped to illustrate how *dialogue* is a key communicative tool for experiencing others (Craig & Muller, 2007). Dialogue has been explored often in consideration of relationships, especially by philosophers such as Buber, Gadamer, Habermas, and Bakhtin (see Anderson, Baxter, & Cissna, 2004). Collectively, their theoretical musings have made an ally to or even constituted the *dialogic approach* often used in interpersonal communication research. A dialogic approach to qualitative work focuses on discourse, but rather than examining effects of discourse or even how two people come to make meaning through discourse, the focus is instead on participation (Deetz, 1992) and how the "play of discourses constructs meaning" (Baxter, 2011, p. 13).

In a dialogic approach, meaning is not in the minds of those involved with the discourse but rather found *in the discourse itself.* This play of discourses allows the notion that "the selves in communication are not preformed, autonomous entities but instead are constituted in communication" (Baxter, 2011, p. 12). In other words, it moves beyond a person's perception of self and motivations for communicating to focus solely on the discourse produced by that person. And so unlike most interpretivist-oriented approaches, a dialogic approach does not focus on intersubjectivity or how people negotiate understanding with each other but instead on how the discourses themselves allow meaning. A key consideration for a dialogic approach (which, as discussed in Chapter 7, is not exactly the same as a discourse analytic approach) is the utterance chain. Simply put, an utterance chain suggests that many forces (e.g., time, presence) impact the production of a discourse, and examining a discourse through this lens moves interpersonal communication studies beyond the idea that a discourse is created by two all-controlling actors in a social situation (see Baxter, 2011, for a full explanation). Researchers should be careful in labeling all dialogic approaches as interpretive, as some scholars (including Baxter, 2011) seem to draw a line between interpretivism and dialogism. For an excellent exemplar of how dialogism can be used in qualitative interpersonal research, see Norwood's (2012) examination of trans-identity. The study uses relational dialectics theory (Baxter, 2011; Baxter & Montgomery, 1996), a respected theory in interpersonal communication based on the dialogic perspective, to understand how families negotiate a sense of loss when a family member comes out as transgender.

Critical Approaches

Critical approaches to qualitative research are those that seek to analyze and critique unjust social structures and perhaps offer a sense of restitution and emancipation (Lincoln et al., 2011). As Lindlof and Taylor (2011) note, in the communication discipline *critical* is often an umbrella term that includes multiple approaches related to social justice and the elimination of hegemonic assumptions. As evidenced by critical theory's overwhelming lack of representation in Tracy and Muñoz's (2011) state-of-the-art account of qualitative methods in interpersonal communication, as well as critiques from scholars that point out the subdiscipline's lack of exploring marginalized voices (Fassett & Warren, 2006; Foster, 2008; Manning, 2009b), it is evident that critical theory itself is being silenced in interpersonal communication studies. As discussion panels at communication conferences continue to explore the roles critical research can play in interpersonal communication studies (e.g., Eckstein, 2012; Eckstein & Frey, 2011), it is also evident that many critical approaches to personal relationships may also be finding other subdisciplines in communication more friendly to the research's axiological motives: namely, performance studies, language and social interaction, or generalist qualitative outlets. We suspect that, just as Bochner's (1985, 1994) arguments regarding the value of qualitative research methods for interpersonal communication have gained traction and allowed for an expanded—if not necessarily level—playing field for qualitative inquiry in the subdiscipline, critical theory will soon see its own transformation.

Whether such transformation will emerge primarily based on approach (engaging minoritized or stigmatized people and communities) or both approach and theory (engaging critical theories in conjunction with interpersonal concepts) remains to be seen, but a move forward holds potential for allowing voices into interpersonal communication research that may not otherwise be heard or embraced. This is not to be confused with the increased sense of voice qualitative research generally allows. Many interpretivist interpersonal communication studies, especially those using interview or survey methods, will allow for or encourage some form of voice that participants may not always feel they have—especially those frustrated with their relationships (Manning, 2010a). Although this sense of voice can be an important and illuminating way of emancipating people from unsatisfactory relationships, it would not likely be seen as a critical emancipation by many of the scholars committed to critical research stances. Rather, critical approaches often allow voice to those with *marginalized identities*, and in interpersonal communication research that especially applies to people whose marginalized identities may hamper or even dehumanize their relationships.

Examples of interpersonal communication studies using a critical approach include Castle Bell and Hastings's (2011) study interviewing 19 interracial couples about how they negotiate face threats; Manning's (in press-a) survey-driven study of positive and negative communicative behaviors in coming-out conversations; and Eckstein's (2004) study of adolescent-to-parent domestic abuse that used 20 in-depth interviews to consider, in part, communication's role in the escalation and progression of abuse episodes. For some good examples of studies that use critical theory in addition to a critical approach, one might consider viewing Allen, Orbe, and Olivas's (1999) use of feminist standpoint theory (and clever method of using their own e-mails to each other as data) as they explore perceptions of difference, especially race; and Endres and Gould's (2009) use of document analysis to consider how students perform whiteness in service-learning situations.

The majority of this text does not hone in on critical theory or approaches, but the methods and analytical tools demonstrated in the later chapters are metatheoretically compatible with the tenets of critical research. As is evident in the later chapters of this book, some of the studies have a critical edge to them. Laura Ellingson and Patty Sotirin's study on aunting is influenced by their feminist leanings, taking an analytical tool (emotion coding) that is quite rigid and loosening it up to value fluidities in understanding—something many feminist scholars strive for in their work. The study would not likely be considered a critical qualitative study, however, because aunts are not typically viewed as a marginalized group (although one could certainly make the argument that women family members are sometimes disadvantaged or advantaged in particular situations and contexts). Jennifer C. Dunn's study involving women from the Moonlight Bunny Ranch has a critical sexualities–studies edge, allowing insight into the women behind a commonly constructed identity of "sex worker." Dunn does not directly embrace critical sexuality theories, but the spirit of those theories can be felt in her work. The study in our book most indicative of a critical approach is Dohrman, Buzzanell, and colleagues' study involving women engineers. This study is certainly emancipatory, as it examines how mentoring relationships for women in engineering workplaces help to alleviate some of the sexist attitudes and behaviors that can permeate such dwellings. This particular study is also the only one to take on an explicitly postmodern edge.

Postmodern Approaches

For interpersonal communication scholars—or, perhaps, for most social scientific communication scholars in general—postmodern approaches to qualitative research seem to be met with the most suspicion. Critiques against postmodernism in the communication discipline tend to conflate postmodern tenets with other theoretical traditions (particularly critical approaches; Mumby, 1997), and many reduce postmodernism to a simple claim that there are no truths (or realities) to be found (Leslie, 2010). While a few postmodern scholars may claim absolute relativism or an inability to have any form of meaning, this vantage point does not seem to characterize most published or presented postmodern qualitative work. Sweeping dismissals of postmodernism should, like most sweeping dismissals, be taken with a grain of salt, as postmodernism as a philosophical approach is much too diverse (and fractured) to be characterized by any simple statements that define or reduce it to core criteria (Best & Kellner, 1997; Leslie, 2010). Perhaps it is the embracing of uncertainty and openness that many find to be so frustrating about trying to grasp postmodernism as a concept or approach.

Rather than trying to describe the numerous aspects of postmodern research here (see Leslie, 2010, for a fuller understanding), we instead explore three common tenets of postmodernism to provide a sense of what it tends to entail in the communication discipline. In doing so, we are not trying to reduce postmodernism to these three ideas; rather, we are introducing three ideas common to postmodern theorists that may be helpful in considering interpersonal communication studies. First, postmodernism tends to reject any sort of totalizing theory and instead suggests that perceptions of truth are localized and fragmented. As such, postmodern studies tend to be highly contextual and consider that researchers and participants are politically charged. *Politically charged*, in this sense, suggests that reality is loaded with unavoidable assumptions that vex any hopes of truly knowing. Depending on how that last sentence is read, it may either seem a lot like interpretivism or like it is implying that it is futile to try to understand any kind of truth—and neither is the case. Rather, this aspect of postmodernism is more of a sensibility, one that encourages suspicion toward what is known (or claimed to be known). As such, a postmodernist critique of knowledge is often used as a way to explicate political assumptions in any data or evidence, a reason that many scholars (e.g., Lindlof & Taylor, 2011) place postmodernism in the same realm as critical approaches. For example, in an interpersonal communication study, politicized views may lead researchers toward prima facie assumptions that it is natural for a married couple to have at least one child, that happiness is a result of having what one wants, or even that people should pursue a romantic relationship.

Sometimes to consider or demonstrate these politicized views, scholars embracing postmodernism find creative ways to play with meaning in a context. As such, a sense of playfulness is another common tenet of postmodernism (Best & Kellner, 1991; Fahy, 1997; Gergen, 1992). *Playfulness* here does not connote frivolity or a lack of serious scholarly contribution; rather, it asserts that postmodern scholarship often plays with form or function in meaningful, profound, and sometimes silly ways. These different ways of "doing" allow for different ways of knowing. Later in this book, Dohrman, Buzzanell, and colleagues use qualitative crystallization (Ellingson, 2009), one way of playing with how scholarship is presented. Rather than writing up their findings in a traditional research report, they chose to present it as a theater piece. Presenting the scholarship in such a way allows people reading or receiving the research different opportunities for using their senses, perhaps experiencing the women whose stories are shared as more fully human. Performance scholarship has revealed many insights into interpersonal communication concepts. Other examples include Olson's (2004) one-woman show that unpacks abuse in violent romantic relationships; Kaufman's (2000) play based on multimethod ethnographic research that explores how Laramie, Wyoming, town members coped and related following the death of Matthew Shepard; and Goltz's (2012) multimedia-enhanced stage show that unpacks how relational and sexual identities play out across time.

These performances all contain some autoethnographic elements. Autoethnography is another form of qualitative interpersonal research that plays with ideas about how research should look as well as the role of the researcher in his or her studies. A form of research that involves storytelling, autoethnography "shows people in the process of using communication to achieve an understanding of their lives and their circumstances" (Bochner & Ellis, 2006, p. 111). Instead of researching others, however, one researches himself or herself in consideration of life experience (Ellis, 2004). Stories are what allow knowledge and theorizing in this form of research because stories—different from a simple retelling, accounting, or journaling of what happened—are presented with some kind of moral that, in many ways, constitutes the theorizing that occurs (Bochner & Ellis, 2006). Writing—especially evocative writing—is key to this method (Denzin, 2006). As Bochner and Ellis (2006) note, in autoethnography readers can witness authors "learning how to live, struggling to make sense of their lives and their losses, healing their wounds, trying to move on from and survive the unnerving blows of fate to which all of us are vulnerable," qualities they explicitly link to the study of interpersonal communication (p. 118).

Exemplars of exquisite autoethnographic work abound, including Ellis's (1995) heartbreaking story of negotiating caretaker/wife and patient/husband roles in the face of her husband's illness; Pelias's (2006) beautifully written and deftly theorized story of how he experienced interpersonal relationships throughout his life in the unique space that is Bourbon Street; and Fox's (2007) harrowing telling of how waiting for the results of an HIV test made him consider his own and others' critiques of his skinny body. Both autoethnography and performances are highly reflexive, highly personal approaches to research that allow for an intriguing blurring between modernist forms of understanding (e.g., interviews, ethnography) and traditionally art-oriented forms (e.g., theater, performance, literature). Although some have been critical of whether or not these forms constitute scholarship (e.g., Parks, 1998), those critiques themselves play into the larger questions about how objective researchers can be and what they bring to a social scene. This reflexive aspect of postmodernism has instigated palpable and lasting consequences for all interpretivist-oriented qualitative research studies (Lindlof & Taylor, 2011).

Thus, the third aspect of postmodernism we explore is a crisis of representation that permeates all qualitative research (or all research, period, for that matter). Simply put, *the crisis of representation* came from the work of sociologists (e.g., Brown, 1977) and anthropologists (Ruby, 1982) who developed a series of monographs that indicted the fiction of an objective view in qualitative—particularly ethnographic—fieldwork. For many scholars who embrace qualitative work, it may seem unfathomable that anyone would even think about claiming objectivity in a field study—but such a view was not uncommon for many researchers prior to these revolutionary volumes. In many ways, the concept of "the crisis of representation" illuminates the assumptions of multiple, sometimes competing, always subjective truths present within the first characteristic of postmodernism we offered. It also suggests that exoticizing a participant or culture can be dangerous (and even justify cultural domination) and is more a result of a researcher producing that idea than an essential quality of the culture under view (Clough, 1995). Meaning, then, is considered in view of how the method plays with its conception (Clough, 1995) as well as the identity of the researcher (Clifford & Marcus, 1986) and how it interplays with knowledge claims. Such a view does not mean that knowledge claims cannot be made but that, when they are presented, they must be considered as a representation.

Rhetorical Approaches

In discussing interpretivism, we would be remiss to exclude rhetorical approaches, a foundation of the communication discipline and still one of the most common interpretive approaches to research. Rhetorical criticism, rather than embracing social science, takes a humanistic approach to examining texts such as speech transcripts, television programs, or even physical spaces and inductively considers rhetorical qualities of those texts (Burgchardt, 2010). These observations lead to using a particular rhetorical criticism method to analyze the text and consider its implications for rhetorical theory (Foss, 2009). Beyond this section, this book does not explore rhetorical criticism approaches to interpersonal communication research, but recent studies such as McAlister's (2011) exploration of the reconfiguration of marriage and the American family home; Arrington's (2002) study that examines how interpersonal interaction in the form of television interviews serves as apologia; or Dennis, Ridder, and Kunkel's (2006) social support–infused analysis of eulogies indicate that there is value for interpersonal scholars to explore this form of research. Indeed, other scholars are using interpersonal communication theories as makeshift tools for rhetorical criticism. For example, Meyer (2003) used relational dialectics theory (Baxter & Montgomery, 1996) for narrative criticism of *Dawson's Creek* and then considered her findings in conjunction with ethnographic understandings from past research to make assertions about relational identity; Manning (2010b) used social exchange theory (Thibaut & Kelley, 1978) to guide criticism of *Gilmore Girls* and compared those findings with discourse analysis of discussion about the show on Internet fan forums to unpack tendencies of social control and relationships.

Social Approaches

Throughout this book we explicitly and implicitly refer to the social elements of interpretive research using terms such as *social scene, social understandings*, or *social interaction*. We are careful to avoid using the term *social approaches*, however, because it connotes a particular brand of social constructionist research and theorizing. It is not uncommon for an interpretive approach to be clustered with other social constructionist paradigms (Craig & Muller, 2007; Lindlof & Taylor, 2011), and as such it will share vocabularies with those other perspectives. That may be especially true with a *social approaches* metadiscursive vocabulary, as it was developed as an alternative to interpretive theorizing in interpersonal communication (see Bartesaghi & Castor, 2008). Leeds-Hurwitz (1995) offered 11 themes to help characterize a social approach: theorizing as social, not cognitive; communication as process and product; assumptions of social constructed reality; social meanings as created; identity as socially constructed; culture; context as significant; direct observation used in research; symbols; research reflexivity; and holistic approaches.

These themes are not exclusive to the perspective and, in fact, are often a part of interpretive research. Lucaites and Fitch (1997) criticize that the various elements included under the rubric of social approaches may lose some of their unique elements when combined under such a perspective and caution that the differences across the elements are important. This alternative to an interpretive approach has yet to gain traction, but we present it here to acknowledge another effort to advance qualitative studies of interpersonal communication and to complete our list of notable approaches.

Embracing Multiple Paradigms

The approaches presented in the preceding section of this chapter have much more in common than their interpretivist leanings—they also all bring new and exciting ideas to the table for studying interpersonal communication across all of its paradigms. As qualitative research continues to become more prevalent in communication studies (Lindlof & Taylor, 2011), scholars from all paradigmatic vantage points should begin to understand that the work others do will allow insights or even radical reconceptualizations of their own work. The methodologies supporting all qualitative work, from realist orientations used with post-positivist studies to the more artistic forms of scholarship such as autoethnography and performance, can inform the entire body of interpersonal communication scholarship. Ellingson (2009, 2011) noticed this not only for interpersonal work but for all qualitative research when she developed a continuum approach to considering qualitative approaches. Placing science at the right end of the continuum and art on the left, Ellingson (2011) seeks not to use "the methodological 'other' to legitimate our particular methodological and paradigmatic preferences" (p. 596) but instead to emphasize the middle spaces of the continuum that "embody infinite possibilities for blending artistic, expository, and social scientific ways" (p. 595).

Unfortunately, and as noted by numerous scholars (including Baxter, 2011; Lindlof & Taylor, 2011; Manning, 2009a; Tracy & Muñoz, 2011), interpersonal communication scholars have been slow to embrace any qualitative research paradigms or traditions that stray too far from the realist end of the continuum. A recent surge in autoethnographic work (see Tillmann, 2009, for a discussion) has allowed extraordinary strides toward embracing the artistic end of the continuum for interpersonal communication studies, as have advances in performance (Pelias, 2009) and poetry (S. L. Faulkner, 2009; Pelias, 2011a). In many ways, it is the middle ground of the continuum that seems malnourished. Some scholars have made inroads, particularly those with language and social interaction approaches (Tracy, 2002), whose work features dialogue (Baxter, 2011) and those studying narratives (Bochner, 2002). The presence of feminist studies and feminine voices in the discipline as a whole has also loosened up paradigms that privilege objectivity, even if there has been backlash (Blair, Brown, & Baxter, 1994). In interpersonal communication studies, that often manifests as critical feminist theories (Wood, 2008). Despite these advances, middle-ground growth for interpersonal communication studies is not up to par with the rest of the communication discipline. If we are to believe Lindlof and Taylor's (2011) speculation that "it is now the discipline's *dominant* methodology" (p. 12, emphasis in original), then interpersonal communication as a subdiscipline has a lot of catching up to do in order to maintain its role as a thriving and innovative segment of communication studies.

Confusing Normative and Interpretive Approaches

In commenting on the state of metatheoretical and methodological diversity in interpersonal communication studies, Baxter and Braithwaite (2008) speculate that "interpretive scholars—and especially critical scholars—perceive that interpersonal communication is not the right place for their work, given the metatheoretical balance" (p. 15). Baxter and Braithwaite based this assertion not only in their many years of involvement with interpersonal and family communication studies but also their analysis of 19 core communication-oriented journals from 1990 to 2005. In examining articles related to interpersonal communication studies, they found that 83.2% of the articles were embedded in post-positivism. Only 13.9% were interpretive (with 2.9% being critical oriented). We agree with Baxter and Braithwaite's (2008) assessment of hesitancy, and we believe a key reason for this caution is that when interpretive work is submitted to journals, its values and assumptions tend to be misunderstood by reviewers who attempt to place postpositive worldviews upon it. This is not to suggest that reviewers are hostile toward interpretivist work (although some may be). Rather, it speaks to the oft-misunderstood idea that what makes data interpretive is the open-ended nature of their collection. The open-ended nature is what makes the data *qualitative*; the body of theory underlying its analysis and guiding its collection is what makes its analysis, and not the data itself, *interpretive*. Unfortunately, *interpretive* and *qualitative* are often conflated or treated as synonyms.

The confusion associated with mislabeling is not nearly as harmful as the confusion of practice. It is clear from our experiences over the years—and hearing the experiences of others—that many who use an inductive approach to interpersonal communication research are using some sort of realist paradigm to guide analysis. We are not arguing that this itself is always bad. Most mixed-methods research seems to use a realist approach, and that has allowed considerable developments in understanding interpersonal communication. What we are arguing is that inductive does not automatically equal interpretivist and that this misunderstanding or conflation holds the possibility for those who tend to embrace realist traditions to use (or even push) their paradigm—and the different senses of rigor, validity, and reliability it embraces—when trying to understand interpretive analysis. Because many interpretivist-oriented interpersonal communication researchers (and researchers in the communication discipline in general) research inductively, analyze interpretively, and then write up the results in a deductive form that mirrors realist styles (a practice that Tracy [2012, p. 109] labels as "toxic"), this potential for paradigmatic misunderstanding is also embedded in the way actual interpretivist qualitative research is expected to be presented.

What Interpretivist-Oriented Qualitative Research Is Not

To help undo the confusions so often involved with interpretivist qualitative research (and to consider how qualitative research can continue to spread along the qualitative continuum), here we identify many things that interpretivist-oriented qualitative research is assumed to be but *is not*. Examining some key areas of confusion, we hope, will allow the rest of the book—that looks in depth at what interpretivist-oriented qualitative research *is*—to do its job in a straightforward and nondefensive manner. In the spirit of qualitative inquiry, at times we turn to comments we recall from students and peers about interpretivist-oriented interpersonal communication research, as well as our own personal accounts and observations.

Interpretivist-Oriented Qualitative Research Is Not a Subset of Quantitative Research

In one of the author's graduate seminars on qualitative research methods, one article, above any other, seems to blow students' minds as it busts open how they consider the theoretical underpinnings of qualitative research: Jaan Valsiner's "Data as Representations: Contextualizing Qualitative and Quantitative Research Strategies" from the journal, *Social Science Information* (2000). The article does a beautiful job of articulating how the ongoing debate about qualitative versus quantitative research "is an organizational limitation that directs discussion of the topic away from the main issue—the adequacy of any kind of data in respect to the phenomena they represent" (Valsiner, 2000, p. 99). More than that, Valsiner (2000) questions some of the disdain exhibited by quantitative researchers toward qualitative research, especially because *quantitative research is a subset of qualitative research* in social science and therefore is rooted in qualitative practice. It is the italicized portion of the previous sentence that seems to blow students' minds.

"Is he actually right about that?" one student will always ask.

"Well, what do you think?" The question is turned back to the class.

"But if that's the case, then why do you see qualitative telling more about the quantitative in mixed-methods studies?"

"That's a good question—but do you believe they are mixing paradigms, or are they simply mixing methods?"

"It doesn't make sense, though," an especially skeptical student will respond. "Quantitative is based in something real, and qualitative is more like people's opinions."

That last assertion is key to why so many people reject interpretivism or believe it needs a quantitative backbone. The majority of interpersonal communication studies rely on surveys or questionnaires, and, reduced to simplest form, the choices people make are number oriented (meaning they actually select a number or make a mark that will later be transformed into a number). In this form of research, just as with interpretivist research, people are reflecting upon their lives and assigning meaning through symbols. Only instead of words, numbers are used to make that assessment. While these numbers provide a sense of certainty for analyzing the results, they are just as open to misinterpretation by those participating in the study as well as those analyzing it, and that gets back to Valsiner's (2000) point. It is not as much about whether or not quantitative or qualitative approaches to generating data are inherently better; it is more about whether or not the data presented truly represent what they claim. To borrow an old cliché, realist and interpretivist research methods *are* apples and oranges, but instead of asking which fruit tastes better, it is more a matter of making sure the fruit is appropriate for the meal ("Does this method make sense for what I want to learn?") and not rotten ("Am I making good choices in using this method?"). It is inspiring to know that many people—including the authors of this book—find both apples *and* oranges delicious!

Interpretivist-Oriented Qualitative Research Does Not Rely on Statistics

Perhaps the most frustrating feedback to find in a peer review of an interpretivist manuscript is that statistics are missing from the study. "Why have you not given percentages for your categories?" one reviewer asked. "Even qualitative research involves counting the specific number of occurrences in a case and presenting them with measures of reliability and validity," a reviewer offered for a different manuscript. Some become flat-out hostile, such as the reviewer who shared this:

It is UNACCEPTABLE to not include the VERY BASICS, and I am suggesting it REJECTED [*sic*]. WHERE do your findings come from? HOW many people were involved with making these categories? WHAT are your intra-rater [*sic*] reliability scores? WHY did you not include them? It makes me believe you are hiding something.

Nothing was being hidden—it is simply that statistics are not part of the interpretive-analytical process. This is not to suggest that claims in interpretivist research are not related to how often they occur or how salient they appear to be in data. Even claims about *dominant themes* or *types* are not unusual—but instead of being based on counting, they are based on whether or not it would be unusual to not find a particular quality within a given case. Dominance then is not necessarily a percentage indicating what chance there may be but instead how common a quality is to a lived experience. If statistics are included in a study, it is most likely either using a postpositivist/realist approach or using *quasi-statistics,* a validity check discussed in the next chapter.

Interpretivist-Oriented Qualitative Research Is Not Claiming to Be Objective

As the last section on statistics implies, interpretivist-oriented research does not seek to provide objective assessments of social situations. This is true in terms of epistemology, as the various paradigms and approaches in the interpretivist family already discussed in this chapter suggest. From an interpretive perspective, a given social world has multiple potentials for reality depending on the subject positions of those involved in that social world (Baxter & Braithwaite, 2008). This notion of multiple potentials for reality suggests a lack of objectivity in ontology as well. As Blumer's (1969) assertions suggest, people may see the same given objects, but it is the meaning negotiated for those objects that becomes central to understanding a social scene. So while it can be assumed that there is some sort of object-oriented common ontology, it is the meaning of those objects that shape their reality to people. So the reality in an interpretivist approach is the one actors create socially. Finally, lack of objectivity is assumed axiologically and, thus, methodologically too. Rather than getting at some objective truth about what is in a social scene, interpretive approaches celebrate the idea that understanding comes through negotiation in all aspects of a social scene, including researchers embracing that social scene (Denzin, 1992). The language choices and perspectives of participants in the scene (including scenes such as interviews or interacting through open-ended surveys) are honored, and their social realities become the basis for research findings. Ultimately, this reflects values for interpretive researchers grounded in meaning and meaning-making (Baxter & Braithwaite, 2008).

Interpretivist-Oriented Qualitative Research Is Not in the Service of Quantitative Research

Based on how qualitative research is often presented in interpersonal communication studies—as supplementary data to statistics—it is often considered that *mixed methods* means a quantitative study where open-ended explanations are allowed with a Likert scale–type item or where, at the close of a primarily quantitative survey, some open-ended items are included as support to statistical analysis. As countless guides for research methodology will confirm (e.g., Cresswell & Plano Clark, 2010), mixed-methods approaches can be a great way of understanding insights that may not be revealed by numbers alone. When used as described here, however, the open-ended segments are not interpretivist—they are realist. As such, it is realist qualitative research—and not interpretivist—at the service of quantitative approaches.

That may seem like splitting hairs, but it is an assumption that adds to confusion caused by realist-dominated worldviews in interpersonal communication studies. Another of these assumptions is that the primary use for stand-alone (i.e., not mixed methods) qualitative inquiry is to provide themes or categories that will later be tested in quantitative studies. After presenting a typology at a conference a few years ago, one of the authors of this book was simultaneously pleased and frustrated when that work was complimented by a much-respected scholar who said, "Looks like you've got a good setup to finish out your study. It'll be interesting to see what happens when you reapproach, run some numbers, and find out what's really there." These words were not meant to be insulting; in fact, the way they were delivered indicated excitement about the research project. It was the underlying assumption that quantitative research was the true end of the road that was somewhat disheartening. We do not deny that using interpretivist research findings to create, enhance, or otherwise consider a quantitative study is one of the many possibilities that can come from qualitative inquiry. In fact, we celebrate the idea that all research paradigms in communication studies can use each other's work to inspire their own. Our point is that interpretivist-oriented research findings still lead to the creation and development of theories as well as helpful understandings for people in both their personal and professional lives. Interpretivist-oriented research is not only a precursor to quantitative studies; it is meaningful, valuable, and empirical in and of itself.

Interpretivist-Oriented Qualitative Research Is Not Easy to Do

The labor and intellectual energy that often go into producing qualitative research are often undervalued. Those who teach research methods are probably used to many students flocking toward qualitative methods with the assumption that learning statistics is tough, but "talking to some people and writing it up" (as one of our students phrased it) is not that difficult. They soon learn the error of their assumption as they struggle to design, complete, transcribe, analyze, and write up ten interviews (a modest number for many qualitative studies). Qualitative research takes time: to think carefully about design, to come up with meaningful interview questions, to interview and then transcribe, to observe a social environment and carefully write up field notes, to code, to write, to think and rethink, to rewrite, to negotiate access, to go back to the existing literature as part of the abductive process—lots of time is needed. Qualitative research takes resources: social connections to find people or a research space, equipment to capture data as effectively as possible, software to manage data and assist analysis, comfortable spaces to carry out tasks, and access to research libraries. Qualitative research also takes patience: in finding participants for a study, for transcribing, for that iterative process to kick in and allow focus or insights, for coding, for explaining to others what you are trying to do—and especially patience as these often long-term projects head toward publication. Qualitative research is by no means easy.

Interpretivist-Oriented Data Are Not Easy to Analyze

One particular aspect of interpretive qualitative research is rather tough: analysis. Many seem to believe that qualitative research analysis simply consists of finding themes. That assumed process goes something like this: qualitative data are collected; the person notices themes that interest him or her; the data are then intuitively divided (with authors frequently and erroneously labeling this process as using a grounded-theory approach); finally, a manuscript is written that presents those themes with data exemplars for each. Those steps (minus the claim of grounded theory) do comprise *one way* to do interpretivist qualitative research, and as countless publications of such projects confirm, it has its strengths. We have even included a thematic analysis study in this book to help demonstrate in more detail how it is done. Thematic analysis pieces are only one way to do qualitative research, though, and we hope that as qualitative research becomes more common in interpersonal communication studies, researchers continue to envision possibility beyond the production of themes.

In the next chapter, an overview is provided for how researchers can move from a first round of analysis (such as theme development) to a second round of coding that allows for deeper, sometimes highly sophisticated considerations not apparent in initial analysis. More than that, as qualitative interpersonal communication researchers continue to develop theories or concepts from their work, they may also consider how they can develop new methods or analytical tools geared toward those theories. One recent and noteworthy example of this is Baxter's (2011) development of contrapuntal analysis, an analytical tool that pairs with explorations of relational dialectical theory. Baxter (2011) took elements of the theory and considered how they might be best explored in a research process and as a result came up with a new analytical approach that fits the theory. Similarly, Tracy (1995) developed action-implicative discourse analysis (AIDA) in conjunction with grounded practical theory (Craig & Tracy, 1995) to explore how problems, strategies, and situated ideals are worked out via talk (making the analytical tool more of a theory-method package). These forms of analysis should serve as inspiration for interpersonal communication scholars to consider how they might develop their own methodological stances based on their theoretical inclinations.

What Interpretivist-Oriented Qualitative Research Is

Now that we have reviewed what interpretivist-oriented qualitative research is not, we use the rest of the book to help describe what it is and what it can be for interpersonal communication research. We start by turning to Tracy and Muñoz (2011), who articulate four commonalities across the "family of approaches" that constitute qualitative research in interpersonal communication (p. 64). First, they note that interpersonal qualitative research privileges an *emic* perspective over an *etic* perspective. The emic perspective is that of the participants in a study: how they see the world or their social reality (Pelto & Pelto, 1978; Pike, 1967). The etic perspective, in contrast, focuses on existing research or theory and is often drawn from scholarly literature (Lindlof & Taylor, 2011; Pike, 1967). This privileging of emic over etic should not suggest that the etic has no place in qualitative research. The development of a qualitative study involves reviewing existing literature for ideas about what might be included in the research protocol, and once data are collected, they are often abductively or iteratively considered in conjunction with past research and theory. Second, Tracy and Muñoz note a preference for naturally occurring data in interpersonal communication studies. Some data are more natural than others, such as the data gathered while in a social scene and taking notes, captured talk or interaction as it naturally occurs (such as in a meeting or via an Internet message board), or letters or artwork. Other times, data may be somewhat natural but still contrived, such as data collected from a scripted interview or open-ended surveys collected online. Of course, almost all data have some worth, but given that interpretivism values how people make sense of their social world, it makes sense that data occurring naturally in that social world would be especially helpful.

The third common feature identified by Tracy and Muñoz is that interpersonal qualitative researchers proceed inductively (in order to build claims) rather than deductively (so as to test an idea). That does not mean that qualitative researchers will not go into a research study with an idea of what to expect.

Instead, it suggests that they will continuously examine the data they are collecting and make decisions about how to continue. During data analysis, conclusions are gathered from looking across the data and narrowing them into ideas rather than using the data to confirm or deny a preconstructed hypothesis. Finally, Tracy and Muñoz note that interpersonal qualitative researchers value words and images in presenting their findings. Words and images serve as concrete examples from data that can help to illustrate elements of a social situation. Although they often must be placed into context by the researcher, they also allow direct insights into social meaning that can allow for a deeper understanding of the concepts and theories being proposed.

All of this comes in play at the service of generating some form of knowledge about interpersonal communication. This might be forms of *local knowledge* or how meanings are understood as negotiated in a particular setting or among a particular group. Philipsen's (1975) classic Teamsterville study that explored talk among working-class men in Chicago is not easily generalized to the population at large, but it provides intriguing and thought-provoking insights into how language functions. Other considerations might involve *sensitized knowledge*, such as Thompson, Petronio, and Braithwaite's (2012) study that analyzed interviews with academic advisors to consider their communication with college athletes. To help make sense of the data, a communication privacy management framework (Petronio, 2002) was used, allowing the researchers to make better sense of the social scene (academic advising at colleges and universities) as well as a better sense of how the theory may be used (its scope and openness). Of course, *emergent knowledge* may also come into play—the development of theories or concepts elucidated from data in a given study or created across multiple studies. An interpretivist backdrop allows for many possibilities in studying and developing interpersonal communication concepts and theories. With these possibilities in mind, the second movement in this chapter considers interpretivist qualitative research's place in interpersonal communication studies.

A FUTURE OF METHODOLOGICAL PLURALITY IN INTERPERSONAL COMMUNICATION STUDIES

The diverse methods and perspectives used for scholarship in the communication discipline is one of its strengths. It would appear that a growing number of interpersonal communication scholars are moving toward the idea that methodological plurality should not only be tolerated, but celebrated (Baxter & Braithwaite, 2008). Still, there is much work to be done theoretically and methodologically in order to realize the full potential of interpersonal communication studies. We hope to inspire some of that work here by developing an understanding of how interpretivism fits into interpersonal communication studies and by offering a foundation that interpretivist-oriented scholars can use for their work. To do that, we begin by spotlighting how, in addition to the continuing stream of published interpretive qualitative research studies, three recent books are expanding perspectives of what interpersonal communication research can be. We especially focus on Baxter's (2011) "reworkings" of interpersonal communication theory (p. 8), as they allow insight into some of the taken-for-granted assumptions about interpersonal communication embedded in postpositivist theories and research. We are also hopeful that Baxter's (2011) reworkings will inspire others to create reworkings of their own. Along those lines, we end this section with a focus on some of the commitments interpretivist scholars will likely have to make as they embrace interpretive interpersonal communication research and theorizing.

Reworking Assumptions in Interpersonal Communication Studies

The three recent books we spotlight here offer especially heartening visions of a methodologically plural future. These books help navigate interpersonal communication theory when doing qualitative work as well as provide material for citations that support alternate framings of interpersonal communication. The first is Baxter and Braithwaite's (2008) *Engaging Theories in Interpersonal Communication: Multiple Perspectives*. The collection contains 28 chapters, each offering an in-depth explanation of an interpersonal communication theory. The book's introductory chapter does a masterful job of not only advocating on behalf of methodological plurality but also articulating differences in metatheoretical assumptions across theories. Many theories featured have both postpositivist and interpretivist backgrounds and applications, something that may not be widely known by those not using the theories, and the short (and relevant) literature reviews in each chapter help to consider how others have used this work. Qualitative researchers can use this book not only as a resource for exploring interpersonal communication theories but also to gain a sense of how interpretive theories have developed in interpersonal communication studies. A second recent publication that plays with notions of what interpersonal communication can be is Duck's (2011) *Rethinking Relationships*. Duck's book offers two new considerations for thinking about relationships: *the presentational nature of communication* and *rhetorical visions*. The former concerns language and performance (providing a direct link to interpretive studies), and the latter involves a reappropriation of classical rhetorical theory for studying interpersonal communication. The distinctively (but not exclusively) interpretivist edge provided in the book allows choice opportunities for scholars to cite alternate ways of thinking about interpersonal communication studies and demonstrates one way that cross-paradigmatic theorizing is possible.

The third book we highlight takes a more direct approach in unpacking limitations of the current ways many interpersonal communication concepts and theories are conceptualized. In the first chapter of Leslie Baxter's (2011) *Voicing Relationships: A Dialogic Perspective*, five suggestions are offered for reworking interpersonal communication studies. Unveiling these assumptions also unlocks some of the difficulty associated with escaping a postpositivist approach to embrace interpretivism. As we review these reworkings, consider that Baxter is working from a dialogic perspective. We have tried to open these perspectives to a larger interpretivist family of approaches—something necessary because dialogism, especially as Baxter uses it, is not always interpretive in and of itself—so scholars should keep in mind that these reworkings may need appropriation when used for one of their particular studies. That said, we suspect that Baxter's reworkings will be both useful and inspiring for all interpretive scholars in a variety of ways.

The first reworking Baxter suggests eschews a false binary between what is public and what is private. She particularly points out that "sociocultural phenomena are constituted in the interactions of so-called private life as much as in the public discussions of the so-called public spheres" (p. 8). That is, the broader domains sometimes labeled as *society* and *culture* have a profound influence on what happens in private relationships, and private relationships undoubtedly play into larger discourses of societies and cultures. This idea flies in the face of conceptions of interpersonal communication that suggest individual psychological processes play into interpersonal interaction with limited—if any—focus on general social standing or cultural background. Further, any statement made in a private domain is undoubtedly influenced by public understandings, and statements made in public have indicators or links to so-called private relationships. Second, Baxter suggests that scholars must temper a bias against uncertainty. Such a move, she argues, will help to eliminate biases against uncertainty that suggest uncertainty should be reduced (e.g., Berger & Calabrese, 1975) or managed (e.g., Afifi & Weiner, 2004). This reworking allows the idea that "meaning making is an unfinalizable process—it is pregnant with potential for emergent meanings that have not been uttered before" (Baxter, 2011, p. 10) and that such possibility allows for many positive outcomes that may not need to be reduced or managed.

Baxter next asserts that the idea of a monadic individual actor—especially common to interpersonal communication studies using cognitive approaches—may be an illusion. In making her argument, she illustrates how her own work helps to establish that a person's communication with another is never in a vacuum but is in response to prior utterances and in anticipation of utterances to come. As such, a fully polished identity cannot be predetermined, as dialogue between people continues to constitute and reconstitute identities. Moreover, it is never a person's discourse in and of itself that makes that person; rather, it is a person's discourse as it interplays with others that provides or allows meaning. Considering how meaning circulates throughout discourse would help to decenter interpersonal communication's current privileging of individualism. Fourth, Baxter asserts that more attention must be paid to power. Although this critique of power largely plays into how relational dialectics theory has been used in past research, her points have relevance to a wider body of interpretive research and theory as well. She suggests reconsidering where power lies, shifting from a "power-in-the-individual" perspective to a "power-in-discourse" perspective (p. 14). That claim can be applied beyond discourse, too. Because interpretivist qualitative studies do not involve preconceptualized variables, power does not have to necessarily be theorized beforehand. As such, the location of power need not be predetermined or assumed but is open to anywhere within a social scene.

Finally, Baxter suggests that the *container metaphor* for relationships is faulty by pointing out how interplay (in the context of Baxter's studies, "discursive interplay") is what creates relationships (p. 126). As she explains the container metaphor, "Relating parties communicate within the container of their relationship, and different kinds of containers (friendships, long-distance relationships, marriages, etc.) can be compared with respect to how communication is enacted" (p. 15). Such a static notion of a given relationship belies that people have a variety of experiences with past relationships, and they surely bring those experiences into their current relationships (something also explored by Duck, 2011). Moreover, relationships change moment by moment and day by day—and so one way to consider relationships, and their communication, is as being viewed at a particular moment in time (Baxter, 2011). Beyond these temporal elements, relationships are often not a person's own—they belong to cultures almost as much as they belong to the people in them (see Baxter's first reworking, 2011; or Duck, 2011). Societal structures, cultural expectations, and close social influences all play into relationships—suggesting that if relationships are in a container at all, then that container is filled with their life experiences: their past, current, and anticipated future interactions; those that are in their lives; media representations of similar relationships; and laws and policies that dictate relational functions, among other things (Manning, 2009b). Interpretivist-oriented approaches lead researchers away from conceiving relational partners as in a vacuum and instead gravitate toward the possibility of a relationship being part of a social scene as meanings circulate through it to create a sense (or multiple senses) of that relationship.

Commitments for Interpretivist-Oriented Interpersonal Communication Studies

Inspired by Baxter's (2011) reworkings, we offer some considerations of our own that take on a different sensibility. Because interpersonal communication studies are so engrained into realist-oriented paradigms, it may feel counterintuitive at times to proceed with research in a way that does not neatly line up with a scientific method originally developed for natural sciences. That is, because interpersonal communication is almost naturalized as a postpositivist area of inquiry, researchers may feel that committing to an interpretive approach seems counterintuitive despite the intuitive nature of interpretivist theory itself. To help navigate these conflicting feelings (and to reinforce the possibilities for an interpretivist paradigm to shape interpersonal communication studies), we offer three commitments scholars can make to understand and work in an interpretivist paradigm. It is our hope that, just as Baxter (2011) has inspired us to articulate these commitments, others will offer more reworkings, commitments, and other considerations in an ongoing quest to extend (and thus strengthen) interpretivist-oriented explorations into interpersonal communication studies.

A Social Scene Holds Many Possibilities for Truths

Our first commitment comes directly from interpretivist philosophies but also from our experiences. Over our many years of teaching and presenting interpretivist-oriented qualitative research, one common concern raised by colleagues is how truthful participants are in a given social situation. Some question whether or not people are honest with sensitive topics such as infidelity or abuse, or they wonder if dialogue captured from meetings or phone conversations reflects people always telling the truth. Others point out how participants will sometimes contradict themselves as they talk about their communication practices, making their explanations or stories suspect. These concerns, and others like them, may be valid for realist-oriented qualitative researchers, as a common goal of that research is determining some sort of reliable truth about a given situation or concept. Interpretive research, however, decenters a focus from *what really happened* to instead consider *what people experience*. People's perspectives as they are articulated in social scenes "are not simply their accounts of these events and actions, to be assessed in terms of truth or falsity; they are a part of the reality you are trying to understand" (Maxwell, 2009). Pelias (1999) elaborates upon ideas of *what really happened* and *what people experience* by noting that the former "marks an event that occurred" while the latter "tells of its character" (p. x).

As part of this characterizing, people will almost undoubtedly engage in what Medford (2006) calls *slippage*, or the unintentional and intentional abbreviation, editing, and modifying of Truth (the big-T concept of what really happened) as they share stories of their lives (a little-t concept of lived experience) with others. It makes sense, then, that within a given social scene (or across multiple social scenes) many truths come into play. Although this statement may seem as if it is embracing postmodernist ideas of rejecting totalizing truths, it is not meant to do so. Rather, it shares a common observation that multiple truths come into play as people interact and create a sense of meaning and their own social realities. As H. L. Goodall so elegantly stated, people experience "multiple *copresent* realities" (1991, p. 213, emphasis in original). He explains, "The communicative dimensions of experience are socially construct*ing* as well as socially construct*ed*" and as such "[t]here is, strictly speaking, no one 'reality' available to the mutually constructed and constructing communicative dimensions of experience" (p. 213, emphasis in original). Consequently, it is probably not in the best interest of understanding a social situation for an interpretivist-oriented researcher to privilege one truth over another—even in studies where questions about privileging a particular narrative or identity come into play. Participants involved in a given social situation may indicate their acceptance or rejection of truth, and that element of a social scene *should* be considered as part of the analysis as it allows insights into how people are interacting to create a social world.

Feeling Is a Way of Knowing

Not only is truth a slippery concept in social realities, but so are ways that truth can be known. It is not uncommon in everyday talk to hear assertions that people should consider their situations and make decisions logically, not based on feelings. The logic driving such assertions suggests that facts or quality information should drive decision making and that emotions should be parsed out to allow a sense of rationality (Mumby & Putnam, 1992). Although the notion of removing emotion and operating based on logic holds appeal to many, it is probably in many ways a fantasy. Feelings and emotions come into decision making on a regular basis (Artz, 1994), and they have a profound influence upon how people make meaning of facts and information. *Facts* and *information*, in and of themselves, are social constructs, given a sense of weight or reality because of how they, as concepts, are reified as evidence-based sources of enlightenment (Gleick, 2011; Poovey, 1998). These concepts are viewed as value-free and thus impartial—but despite constructions of objectivity, what can be accepted as "fact" or "good information" certainly is influenced by political and social factors (Poovey, 1998). Still, facts and information often feel real in a social world and as such do inform decisions people make, as well as how they feel.

Rather than separating logic and emotion, interpretivist-oriented qualitative research allows for possibilities that in social worlds both are seen as valid ways of knowing (e.g., "Statistics show long-distance relationships can work" can mean as much as "I know in my gut we can make this long-distance thing work") and often in consideration of each other ("I know what the studies say, but I feel like we can survive a long-distance relationship" or "Everything in me says not to trust what my therapist says, but I'm going to give him the benefit of the doubt"). As such, interpretivist-oriented qualitative research is committed to incorporating feeling as a way of knowing. *Feeling as a way of knowing* has profound potential for interpersonal communication. Minimally, it can help to explore (and perhaps expose) the spaces between interpretive and normative research findings (or even between disparate interpretive findings) to reveal how people struggle with a tension between rationality and feeling. Statements that draw from a larger discourse of knowledge ("I know everyone says it is tough to stay friends after breaking up— maybe that's why I feel compelled to tell him I love him still") or that wrestle with competing explanations of what is conceived as a truth ("I know what I said, but it was because I was lonely—or maybe I do really love him?") present a certain emotional-rational messiness in a meaning-making process—and such meaning is dependent upon feelings as one way of knowing.

Not only does embracing feeling allow for a deeper consideration of what constitutes knowledge, but feeling as a way of knowing allows for marginalized voices to become apparent in research situations. This statement certainly has a critical slant to it, but that does not mean it can be enacted only in a critical tradition. A common critique of interpersonal communication scholarship is that it often reduces feelings or emotions to simple variables to be measured (Foster, 2008). Such conceptualizations of emotions certainly hold value, and they have produced a respectable body of theory to this point. Still, many—if not all—of these postpositivist theories belie the notion that even if people do experience affect as an effect, social worlds are loaded with emotional resonance that are not necessarily perceived or experienced as neat and tidy effects (even when articulated that way). Rather, a sense of the unknown or indescribable is likely always accompanying what can be put into words (Sturdy, 2003). By presenting multiple data exemplars that illustrate a concept or theme in qualitative work, the intersection of those data also help to make verbally elusive ideas intelligible through feelings that resonate and circulate throughout the exemplars. As such, things that seem or appear unknown *can* become known through feeling.

Freeing emotion from variables or effect also allows it to be recognized throughout a given social scene as actors in that scene make meaning. Love may well be a psychological mixture of strong emotions and desire to be with another (Hatfield & Rapson, 1993), as it is conceptualized in many interpersonal studies—but it is also a meaning-making construct with potential to resonate in places other than the mind. In that sense, love moves from the cognitive to the interpretive. A man rubbing his wife's back as they stop in at a diner may be read as love because of previous occurrences such as a person's own experience with intimate contact, television representations that show people in love engaging touch, or past discussions with friends about public displays of affection. Back rubbing is infused with meanings of love in an interpretive process—the meaning-making of love is reified, maybe even created. This process may happen in a rational way, where someone sees a couple and logically assumes if the husband is massaging his wife like that, then they are in love. It is also highly likely that this meaning of love comes from a way of feeling—whether it is the person's longing for someone to rub his or her back, how the interaction reminds someone of his or her own love, or a conversation about how it is "adorable." Feeling and emotion resound in social worlds in an interpretive process that allows meaning to be constituted via places, words, objects, bodies, and even spirits.

Presentation Aesthetics Play Into Research Reception

Regardless of whether one is engaging an interpretivist approach nearer to the scientific or artistic end of the qualitative continuum, it is likely that aesthetics play into how research will be received. The aesthetics of a research presentation (be it be a written, oral, or other form of expressive presentation) are also tied to its paradigm. Given many of the aspects of qualitative research, such as inductive approaches to considering data or their embracing of subjectivity, this attention to research presentation must be heightened. For example, if the format of a traditional research report is embraced, it would almost certainly belie interpretive research's inductive and iterative nature (S. J. Tracy, 2010). Additionally, as feelings become evident in considering meaning-making in a social scene, it may belie an interpretivist approach if these emotive interactions are discussed in cold and clinical ways. Beyond the basic writing considerations such as clarity and concision that weigh on the minds of many, an interpretivist writer should—at least on some level—feel artistic license to present a research study in a way that is honest to the data (a tricky notion in and of itself) and embraces an interpretive form of knowledge creation. As Ellingson (2009) and Tracy (2012) note, this is not an easy process. Ideas of what research reports should look like are fairly stable, and defying academic conventions can lead to doubt about the seriousness of a research study as well as a loss of credibility for researchers (see Ellingson, 2009, for an extended discussion of nontraditional research presentation). Thus, interpretivist researchers should be committed to defying—as is necessary—ways of presenting research that hamper or distort meaning and process.

Even if this commitment may be one of the most difficult to navigate, it is still worth the effort. How research is presented does make a difference in how it is received (Ellingson, 2009; Tracy, 2012). Additionally, qualitative research—because it represents a researcher's interpretations of a social scene—is highly personal. In thinking about his personal writing, Pelias (2011b) reflected that, when I write, I am asserting a self, insisting that I matter. In general, I would argue, research is a way of claiming space. It takes an extended turn with the implication that one's writing merits attention. Such a commitment is a call to arrogance and to significance. Research cannot exist without a belief in its seriousness; it cannot prosper in the belief in its singular truth. Research lives in possibility and in promise. (p. 649)

This eloquent statement tempers ideas of vanity in writing while simultaneously celebrating possibilities for research to make a difference in what they present. In qualitative research, Pelias (2011b) notes researchers can make their case for knowledge claims by writing in an evocative way that challenges or even disrupts normative understandings; a reflexive way that always considers a researcher's stance in a social scene; an embodied way that plays into a mind/body split so as to not exclude bodily experiences (and, consequently, privilege cognitive-oriented aspects of a social scene); a partial and partisan way that allows one can never detail everything about a given social scene and that what is featured plays into some ideology; and a way that considers how writing is a material manifestation of one's personal, scholarly, and social expressions.

Writing (or any form of research presentation) can also be considered as a series of choices. Many formats offer constraints for writing that will often whittle away at what one can do with his or her interpretivist expression. For example, one of the few outlets created specifically for qualitative inquiry in the communication discipline is the journal *Qualitative Research Reports in Communication*. The length of manuscripts for that journal—currently 2,500 words or fewer—presents a challenge in stretching aesthetic dimensions too far. The same could also be said for communication journals in general, where 25- to 30-page submissions are the norm. When working with the six research teams that wrote up studies for this book, one of the biggest concerns they articulated was meeting length requirements (we provided the guidelines of *Qualitative Research Reports in Communication* for them to prepare their manuscripts for this book). It becomes key, then, to think about how research can be narrowed in a way that allows a commitment to aesthetic honesty while simultaneously meeting the demands of journal publishing. Throughout this book we present more about this commitment. More considerations about aesthetic possibilities will be explored in the chapter on crystallization (Chapter 8), and Chapter 9 explores, in part, considerations for writing processes.

Interpretive Possibilities for Interpersonal Communication Theory

Reception of writing—at least in the scholarly sense—is also closely related to how theory is integrated into a writing process so as to offer a sense of enduring knowledge. Embracing interpretive reworkings and commitments holds much potential for interpersonal communication theory, both for extending, challenging, or even disrupting assumptions and for the development of new theories. As Baxter and Braithwaite (2008) note, in interpersonal communication an interpretivist approach usually plays out in one of two ways. First, existing theory (or theoretical concepts) may be used as a heuristic tool for understanding within a research process. Use of an existing theory might guide protocol design, allow for considerations about what a study idea could entail, and even point to new areas of focus. Existing theories can also be used as an abductive tool for making sense of data, allowing a researcher to move from a scene and beginning understandings to existing theoretical development or research findings to try to make sense of what is there and back to the scene again—repeating this process until the researcher is ready to make an interpretive claim. This process typically lines up with creation of sensitized knowledge, though it can provide localized knowledge as well.

A second possibility—one that lines up with how most qualitative work is done outside of the interpersonal communication subdiscipline—is that new theories or concepts are developed from data, creating a form of emergent, often localized knowledge. The ultimate goal of theoretical development is to come to deeper understandings of how meaning is negotiated via interpersonal communication and to make those understandings intelligible. This requires not a simple retelling of the data but, rather, deeper explorations and explication that help to make the implicit explicit. Such a process can play out in a variety of ways, and they are explored in the next chapter, as well as throughout this book. Although we may come off as hyperbolic here, we cannot stress enough how important it is to consider (whether one is doing qualitative research or evaluating qualitative research) that for a given study there is no one right way to go, although there may be better or worse choices in a given situation. Moreover, a particular manuscript may focus on one aspect of a study—oftentimes a small portion of data or a specific area of in-depth analysis—of theoretical or conceptual interest. For those doing qualitative work, this suggests that using analytical memos to record ideas about the project and theoretical inclinations is important, as each of them may lead to possibilities for another take on the data that, with care, can be presented through research outlets. It is entirely possible that within one research project all three forms of interpretive knowledge listed in this book (sensitized, emergent, and localized) may be generated. For those reviewing qualitative work, consider that the research project being examined is likely only one take on the data. Rather than telling a researcher what he or she should have done, reviewers should instead consider the study for what it is and whether or not it makes (or can make, with some revision) a valuable contribution to interpersonal communication studies.

The next chapter offers considerations for how a qualitative study can be best designed to meet research goals. After reviewing common research traditions for qualitative researchers, an interactive design model is offered that can be used to develop interpersonal communication studies. The chapter closes with considerations of quality.

Questions for Growth

1. What is interpretivism? How does it function as a research paradigm?

2. Which interpretivist-oriented approach appeals to you most? Why? Be sure to consider the work you wish to do and how a particular approach or tradition might be a good fit.

3. Which of Baxter's (2011) reworkings of interpersonal communication is easiest for you to accept? To reject? Challenge yourself by choosing an assumption for each category even if you have a strong like or dislike for her assertions.

4. How do emotion, intuition, and aesthetics each play into qualitative research? How might that defy traditional ideas about science?

CHAPTER 2

Method and Analysis in Qualitative Relationships Research

Qualitative inquiry demands serious commitments to making sense of data that can often be messy. In this chapter, we explore how interpretivist research is often a delicate mix of careful planning *and* inspired innovation as researchers navigate the possible (and often unique) twists and turns that naturally accompany this work. Early experiences in interview sessions might indicate that a new protocol is needed—or that another protocol might be developed to go deeper into an area that has raised interest but was not originally conceived at the beginning of the study. Time spent observing in the field may indicate a need for focus groups. Then based on those focus groups, a researcher may decide that written statements from participants may offer deeper considerations of a topic. Topics may need to be open to change as well. For example, today's study of pickup lines in bars might become tomorrow's study of how bartenders deal with intoxicated patrons. Qualitative research designs should always be open to the possibility of change.

Once all possibility is explored and data are collected, analytical choices will yield results that either allow some sort of conclusion or indicate a need for further exploration. Sometimes this need stems from data feeling incomplete or missing a particular quality that a researcher experientially sensed in the field, and so a new form of data collection may be in order. In other studies, it may be that the data collected are lending themselves to multiple analyses—some that develop new theory, and others that enhance what is known about existing concepts and ideas. In so many ways, doing qualitative research is like a "Choose Your Own Adventure" book, where one choice opens up many new possibilities until the researcher makes the choices that bring him or her to a satisfying end. Once that end is reached, just like a "Choose Your Own Adventure" book, the researcher can then reenter the story and consider what the data mean from a new perspective. As we mentioned earlier in this book, interpretivist-oriented qualitative research is in so many ways about *possibility*. We now explore some research traditions that help to guide some of these possibilities.

RESEARCH TRADITIONS

Given that interpretivist theory is so possibility oriented, it makes sense that the many different directions qualitative research can take in a given study has also allowed for the development of many different traditions, or ways of knowing, that help to support the work being done by allowing metatheoretical grounding. As many qualitative methodologists assert, qualitative traditions are not necessarily mutually exclusive, and elements from each can be combined to support a given study provided that the parts borrowed are supportive of one another methodologically (Denzin, 1992; Maxwell, 2009). Here we briefly explore three traditions that have come into play frequently in interpersonal communication studies and have largely influenced qualitative studies as a whole.

Narrative

Those embracing a narrative paradigm hold an assumption that stories allow people to make sense of their social worlds. Worlds are messy, and that messiness does not lend itself to an inherent rationality. Rather, people grasp at a sense of rationality through stories (Bochner, 1994). Stories are more than simple accounts of what happened, and unpacking what they mean is a major thrust of a narrative paradigm. As Chase (2008) sums it up, "Narrative researchers treat narrative—whether oral or written—as a distinct form of discourse. Narrative is retrospective meaning making—the shaping or ordering of past experience" (p. 64). Narrative offers insight into a person's point of view; stories contain thoughts, emotions, and interpretations of and about social worlds. Like all communication, stories do not occur in a vacuum. As Bruner (1987) notes, narratives

> must mesh, so to speak, within a community of life stories; tellers and listeners must share some "deep structure" about the nature of a "life" for if the rules of life-telling are altogether arbitrary, tellers and listeners will surely be alienated by a failure to grasp what the other is saying or what he thinks the other is hearing. (p. 21)

In other words, narrative analysis involves analyzing meaning-making for both storytellers and those who can hear and respond to the story presented.

Situation and context also come into play. In that sense, stories are built with the materials of a given social world. Those materials are not necessarily just objects or people but also abstract elements such as thoughts or emotions. Narrative traditions have been highly influenced by feminist studies, especially in consideration of voice (Foss, Domenico, & Foss, 2013).

As Ellingson notes, "The narrative turn followed over a decade of feminist work pointing out how power laden, non-objective, and often overtly sexist our forms of knowledge construction were (and often still are)" (personal communication, September 17, 2012). Narrative as an approach is discussed more in Chapter 8. That chapter includes a research study that embraces a narrative tradition.

Ethnography

Formed from *ethno* (people) and *graphy* (writing), the ethnographic tradition—one of the most prevalent in qualitative studies—tends to examine a particular culture's meaning systems and material existence in order to provide a holistic description. *Holistic* here does not mean totalizing or exhaustive but rather multilayered and widely considered. To do this work, a researcher should be committed to generating data that allows for thick description of what a culture entails and insights into contextual significance (Geertz, 1973). In Chapter 6, we explore a variety of research approaches located in an ethnographic tradition, including participant observation. Included in that chapter is Jennifer C. Dunn's study where she employed an ethnographic approach to consider work relationships and identity. To do that, she had to enter the field. *The field* is a common term used in ethnography that describes the site of where a culture is being observed, and ethnographers must carefully consider how they can enter and exit a field as well as what influence their presence will have (Kaler & Beres, 2010). As one might expect, the ethnographic tradition is also rich with considerations of ethics and how they tie into the work (Van Maanen, 1988).

Grounded Theory

We save grounded theory for last for three reasons. First, even though it is one of the dominant four traditions in qualitative research (the others being phenomenology, narrative, and ethnography), methodologists often warn that trying to learn it at the same time as other research methods can cause erosion of grounded theory's highly scientific elements (Simmons, 2011; Stern, 1994). Second, grounded theory is actually not one tradition with slightly different takes but a tradition where three largely different types of grounded theory come into play (Simmons, 2011). The original conception of grounded theory, offered by Glaser and Strauss (1967), eventually became known as the *Glaserian approach* after Strauss published ideas about grounded theory that Glaser felt went against its principles. Strauss then teamed up with Corbin in 1990 to develop a new approach to grounded theory, and that was quickly (and thoroughly) rebuffed by Glaser in 1992. Both the Glaserian approach and the Strauss and Corbin (1990) approach continue to be embraced by scholars, but because of grounded theory's interaction with other interpretivist methods, many people craved a constructivist version. Charmaz (2006) developed the *constructivist approach*, and it immediately became popular (especially because she so clearly articulates the steps involved; Simmons, 2011; Stern & Porr, 2011). If we were to try to go through the aspects of all of—or even one of—these approaches we would be high-jacking the book and even still be overly abbreviating the complex process of developing a grounded theory.

We fear that in underexplaining grounded theory, we might unintentionally turn people away from its methods. For example, scholars are often shocked to learn that Glaser suggests research interviews not be recorded and that no notes be taken during the actual interview process. Glaser has a solid philosophy underlying this, but if we were to try to explain it in a couple of sentences (something we will not do) it would still leave much unanswered. What we will do is note that grounded theory involves discovering new theories deeply grounded in the research data collected during a study; that it involves several complex but doable steps in order to create that theory; and that the process is so rigid that it is sometimes labeled as a postpositivist approach to theory building (Denzin & Lincoln, 1994). We will also state that developing themes or using constant comparison does not constitute generating grounded theory but rather is a form of methodological fragmentation. If this fragmentation works to answer a research question, that's great. As we have mentioned many times, qualitative research methods are about flexibility. Such fragmentation, as a method, would not be grounded theory, however. It would constitute some form of thematic analysis. To help distinguish between grounded theory and thematic analysis, Chapter 7 will demonstrate how *parts* of grounded theory can assist in the development of themes.

INTERPERSONAL CONSIDERATIONS FOR MAXWELL'S INTERACTIVE DESIGN MODEL

Fully understanding the traditions listed in the last section is not necessarily a prerequisite to putting together a good qualitative research design, but continuing to explore a tradition (both its methodological development and work done within it) can help to indicate palpable choices in design. Designing a study requires several considerations (see Figure 2.1). Those considerations will be explored throughout the rest of this chapter via Maxwell's (2012) interactive design model. The model offers a fluid and largely comprehensive understanding of qualitative research design. In presenting that model here, we draw from other sources to complement Maxwell's (2009, 2012) already thorough guidelines and to help appropriate the design process for interpersonal communication studies. As with most aspects of qualitative research, what is offered here is only a set of guidelines. The key to a good qualitative research process is not necessarily to replicate what others have done (although that is certainly appropriate and fruitful at times), but to instead do what makes sense for a given study. We also caution that just because there are multiple ways to proceed with qualitative research, that does not mean that there are not approaches or tactics considered to be *best* practices. We review some of those practices in later chapters.

As this outline for a research process is considered, we invite you to receive it much as you would the results of a good qualitative study: as *a* way of knowing, but not necessarily the only one. Maxwell (2009), like the overwhelming majority of qualitative researchers, rejects that methods such as interviewing or field observation have but one way to be implemented, and he also rejects the idea that qualitative research can be neatly and completely planned out before data collection begins. This lack of exhaustive preplanning does not mean that researchers should not consider a variety of possibilities and estimate in advance how their research may be useful; rather, it suggests that trying to plan too much of a study at the beginning may be a limitation as it often integrates much assumption and little chance for emergent possibility. To begin the consideration of a possibility, one only needs a topic to study. The rest can be figured out through this process.

Figure 2.1

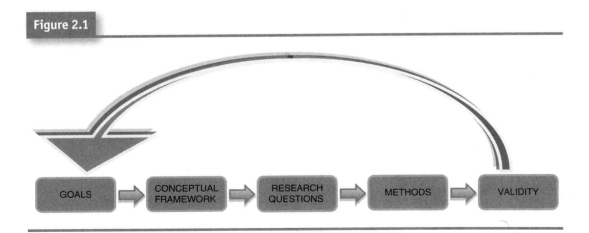

Goals

The first of Maxwell's (2009) five design considerations is goals. Sometimes, most likely for those closer to the realist end of the qualitative continuum, a goal for a research study is evident and a research question can be immediately posed. To illustrate this idea, we turn to the research experiences of Tiffany Emerson, a student who worked with Jimmie on her master's thesis. Tiffany wanted to study how relationships influenced perceptions of sexual harassment cues in the workplace, and because the sexual harassment literature is so rich (including both postpositivist and interpretivist approaches to the topic), she was able to narrow her topic down to a research question she was particularly curious about (i.e., Would the way people recall the same interactive cues be considered flirting in some cases and sexual harassment in others?) and able to articulate a clear goal (i.e., "I want to learn how people construct flirting cues and sexual harassment cues in workplace storytelling"). She then proceeded to develop a clever narrative-oriented interview protocol to tease these ideas out.

Tiffany experienced something that most interpretivist-oriented researchers do not as they begin a study: She knew exactly what she was looking for, and she had a good base to start that exploration. However, most people, especially if they are being honest with themselves, have an idea of what they are looking for but may not be able to pin it down or are reluctant to commit to it because they do not know if there is enough evidence yet (from either prior research or the social scene) to make any kind of fair assessment. Some people are just flat-out interested in an interpersonal communication concept, and although they have no idea where the study will lead, they want to check it out. Such impulses could be topic oriented (e.g., friends with benefits, hooking up, Facebook friends), space oriented (e.g., gay bars, dog parks, physician offices), or even theory driven (e.g., "What might be another good site for examining communication privacy management?"). It is helpful to consider, in addition to a site of exploration, a particular goal for the research. Goals allow researchers to begin a reflexive design that encourages them to consider whether a study is worth doing. It also helps to justify and rationalize a study to grant-funding organizations, department chairs, workplace bosses, or a thesis or dissertation mentor. Considering goals also allows one to consider his or her own sources of bias (Maxwell, 2009). If the answer to why someone wants to study gay bars is "I love gay men! So I'm going to study gay bars and see how they fall in love," it does not necessarily mean that he or she should not study gay bars, but biases ought to be considered and tempered in order to reduce validity threats. The same can be said for less enthusiastic dispositions, such as studying friends-with-benefits relationships but thinking they are "a little gross" or "meaningless." Exploring the three objectives that tend to drive qualitative studies—personal, intellectual, and practical goals (Maxwell, 2009)—not only allows insights into biases but can help to drive a study's design process.

Personal Goals

Personal goals are why someone personally wants to do a given study. Sometimes personal goals are career oriented: A person wants to please an advisor, snag a big grant, or embrace a topic that is publication friendly. Other personal goals are experience oriented, such as the child of an alcoholic who wants to explore alcoholic parent-child relationships. It could also be that someone naturally becomes curious, whether that be from reading a research study (e.g., "If people are lying to their partners about something so small, what happens when something bigger comes into the picture?") or experiencing aspects of their social worlds (e.g., "I never realized so much ritual was involved with Jewish weddings. I wonder if anyone has studied this?"). People sometimes become nervous or anxious about admitting they have a personal interest in their topic and try to minimize talk about such aspects. In many ways, that is dishonest and belies the interpretivist theories undergirding qualitative research. A person's experiences with a topic in many ways shape not only how a study is approached but also how it is articulated. As Maxwell (2009) notes, "Eradicating or submerging your personal goals and concerns is impossible," and instead qualitative researchers should be "*aware* of these concerns and how they may be shaping your research" as well as "how best to deal with their consequences" (p. 219, emphasis in original). The consequences can often be positive. For instance, a man who has been abused by his spouse would likely be able to see insights and nuances in interview data about abusive communication in marital relationships that someone who has not experienced such abuse is unable to recognize. That does not mean that people who have ever had experience with a topic or concept have intellectual authority; rather, it means they might have some hunches or ideas based on their own lives.

Intellectual Goals

Some personal goals blend with intellectual goals, as the paradigms and methods embraced by researchers often play into personal preferences and inclinations. Locke, Spirduso, and Silverman (1993) offer a good question for qualitative researchers that gets at both personal and intellectual goals: "Why do I want to do a qualitative study?" Locke et al. (1993) also suggest that the question must be answered honestly. Part of the answer will get at the personal goals explored in the previous section, but the answer also provides vital clues about what a project can do conceptually or theoretically. At some point, especially if the research is going to be published in an academic journal, theory must be considered. Ideally, theory used or generated will promote some sense of *understanding*. That understanding can play out in many ways.

Meaning. One way understanding can play out is by development of meaning. Meaning is central to interpretive research approaches (Bredo & Feinberg, 1982; Geertz, 1973; Miller, 2004). Interpretivist-oriented qualitative studies demand attention be paid to behaviors or physical events taking place, but central to this focus is almost always how people make meaning of these things (and how such meaning-making may influence behavior). Consider another researcher who worked with Jimmie on her master's thesis, Tracy Songer. She wanted to build a research project that examined the aftermath of Hurricane Katrina for a small community on the Mississippi Gulf Coast. She knew that prior research explored rebuilding processes after crises, but she was curious about *what it meant to those from the community*. She knew this study was a candidate for a good qualitative research project because she was curious about what rebuilding efforts *meant* to the community members involved with them.

Context. As Tracy began to prepare for her stay in the community she was researching, she had to consider context. She started big, examining research about post-Katrina communities in general, as well as learning as much she could about the small town where she would be living. She also began to make contacts with people in the community, and as she did, she noticed many people referred to a church community and some of their extraordinary experiences during the storm. In qualitative research, context is often localized, looking at situations that allow for preservation of individualities among people and their surroundings (Maxwell, 2009). Tracy's attraction to this small church community was yet another indication that she might enact a qualitative approach. Even better, she might be able to provide some localized theory emerging from the church community that could allow understanding in other contexts.

Exploration. While interpretivist-oriented qualitative research is not exclusively exploratory, the exploration that accompanies virtually every qualitative research study can be one of its most exciting qualities. Continuing Tracy's story, after making contact with church members she noticed how people continued to refer to their relationships in consideration of how they responded to the storm. Tracy then considered that a grounded theory about relational meaning as constituted through the storm might be a possibility. Based on these initial interactions, she also wondered if communication privacy management theory and social exchange theory were relevant to the study, and so she carefully reviewed these theories and considered how they might be explored in an interview protocol. That led Tracy to believe that she probably did not want to ground a theory but instead keep her study open to generate new forms of knowledge similar to what a grounded-theory approach would allow.

Understanding Processes. Unlike experimental and survey research, many forms of qualitative research are good at identifying processes by which actions and events occur (Maxwell, 2004, 2009). Qualitative researchers should consider how observing *processes* may play into their studies. Given interpersonal communication's limited use of qualitative methods, it is likely that identifying new processes or aspects of processes already theorized could be a part of a study's exploration. Initially, Tracy did not see process as a part of her study of the church community in Mississippi. However, after she heard many people talk about an attic where they retreated together during the storm, she thought about how process might come into play with her work. Tracy then considered that she might have an opportunity to see negotiated meaning-making in process as she traveled to the attic with group members and observed their interaction there while talking to them about some drawings they had made on the attic's wood when they were in the space together previously. She started to understand their processes of coping and support, and she knew this might be valuable knowledge to advance in a research report.

Developing Causal Explanations. A newer development in qualitative research is the idea that qualitative inquiry can be used to develop causal relationships. For many who have taken a research methods class, this idea may be difficult to accept given the adage that *causation can only be established through experimentation.* This assumption, called *causality*, is no longer limited to quantitative experiments (Maxwell, 2004). Qualitative-derived causal explanations can be generated (see Shadish, Cook, & Campbell, 2002), even though the process of developing them has been labeled as "not an easy or straightforward task" (Maxwell, 2009, p. 221). So, while it may be more difficult to carry out such work, it is no longer perceived as impossible. Finishing Tracy's story, she was new to qualitative research (and research in general), so considering how developing causal explanations come into play seemed a bit intimidating—especially because it was not a natural fit for the project she was enacting.

Practical Goals

In addition to personal and intellectual considerations (and sometimes as a part of them), practical goals also have a deep connection to a study's design. One common practical goal is for the study to yield findings rich with experiential credibility that can be understood both by the people studied and others who engage the research (Bolster, 1983). For example, a qualitative research study may assert that marriage proposals are nerve-racking, but it is the data within the manuscript that allow for that nervousness to be felt, seen, and more deeply appreciated. Reading such research would also most likely allow a sense of what to expect for someone proposing or expecting to be proposed to. This sense of expectation is another common practical goal for qualitative research: it can allow some sort of change in practice or approach (Scriven, 1991) or, at minimum, can give someone an idea of what a particular kind of experience might involve. For example, a study on forgiving family members might be geared toward allowing therapists insights for helping patients engage conversations that promote forgiveness. If the research writing were accessible, it could be shared with patients so they could see some models or even be inspired by how forgiveness is painted through data. Sometimes a practical goal is actually working with a person, group, or community to enact a collaborative research project. Such a goal will likely allow for practical knowledge to be gained by collaborators (Cousins & Earl, 1995; Frey, 2009), and it also presents possibilities of empowerment as research partners begin to consider how they can investigate situations and implement change (Madison, 2012).

Analytic Memos

To help keep track of different personal, intellectual, and practical goals as they develop in the research process (and to consider how they might work in consideration of each other in a given study), analytic memos (Maxwell, 2012; Strauss & Corbin, 1990) can be quite helpful. Analytic memos are notes made (sometimes referred to as a research journal) about particular research moments, whether they are ideas generated during the research process that a researcher does not want to lose, interesting or revealing incidents that happen during a study, particulars of interviews or focus groups not easily reflected in a transcript, or specific ideas about where the current study or a future study might go. Considerations for analytic memos will be discussed throughout this book.

Conceptual Framework

A researcher's conceptual framework is how she or he will frame a given study in consideration of theories, beliefs, and prior research. In many ways, once goals are in place, a conceptual framework is easy to adopt. As Tiffany's and Tracy's stories earlier in this chapter demonstrate, as they developed their research goals, elements of their conceptual framework naturally began to fall in place as they reviewed prior literature, started to make contact with research participants, and considered what they were interested in understanding. For interpersonal communication research, it may be helpful to approach a conceptual framework from four vantage points: the guiding research tradition, literature review findings, experiential impulses, and idea play. The order in which a researcher embraces these vantage points is not important, and they do not represent a checklist that one moves through to get to the end. Like most aspects of qualitative research, they demand reflection, reflexivity, and interplay.

Guiding Research Tradition

In the brief explanation of research paradigms and traditions presented at different sections of this and the preceding chapter, it was noted that while most of the various traditions have more similarities than differences the differences can be important. Sometimes people worry about the differences and fear that they might make a mistake that completely ruins their study as they try to embrace a tradition.

For those who find themselves in those moments of misery, we suggest that they reframe to ask not what they can do for a given research tradition but what that research tradition can do for them. In so many ways, research traditions allow people to move forward with assumptions that have already been worked out via theory. So while it may not be the healthiest approach to ignore the specifics of a given tradition in hope that things will come out in the wash, it is completely okay to blend traditions (Denzin, 1992; Maxwell, 2009) or to appropriate a tradition for use in a study (Maxwell, 2009) as long as it makes some kind of empirical sense and can be explained in terms of how it helped advance knowledge.

Literature Review

As indicated throughout this chapter, consulting existing literature is an excellent way of considering what data mean, even when engaging grounded or thematic approaches. Consider how research findings in one paradigm or tradition may translate into another, especially given interpersonal communication's history of postpositivist studies and realist-oriented qualitative work. Because a lot of qualitative interpersonal communication research tends to be published as book chapters, it is often helpful to examine bibliographies of research studies to find more possibilities for literature that may not easily be discovered in a database.

Experiential Impulses

One's personal experiences may lead to a sense of knowledge about a given topic, and this experiential knowledge base should not be ignored. Sometimes this might be explicitly incorporated into a research manuscript (see Ellis, 2004, for some excellent mixed-method studies blending interviews or other methods with autoethnographic work; or Reason, 1988, for an expanded understanding of how one's consciousness can be a part of qualitative work), but it appears this is not the case with most interpretivist interpersonal work published in communication journals. Still, even if not explicitly listed and explored in a manuscript (it may be an awkward fit), hunches derived from personal experiences should be embraced and considered in light of other evidence. Reason (1988) warns that researchers should not "allow [our]selves to be swept away and overwhelmed by it; rather we raise it to consciousness and use it as part of the inquiry process" (p. 12). In short, personal values or experiences should not replace a critical and reasoned examination of data.

Idea Play

Good, old-fashioned brainstorming can also be beneficial to a study. Lave and March (1975) offer the idea of *thought experiments* where researchers ask *what if* questions to instigate thinking and possible directions for a given study. Sometimes these questions are broad, such as, "What if the only thing making a relationship a relationship is communication?" Other thought experiments might ask questions about a particular theory, and some of the best thought questions explore data that has already been collected for a study. Concept mapping, or creating a visual representation of research ideas and what they may involve, can also allow a new perspective (Maxwell, 2005). Other ideas include trading protocols with colleagues and sharing suggestions, showing protocols to potential participants and getting a sense of their ideas about the research plan, and trying out protocols with participants (as a sort of pilot study) to refine data collection processes.

Research Questions

One of the most important elements of research design is the questions that drive it—even though those questions may change as data are collected. Although qualitative researchers embracing postpositivist paradigms often provide hypotheses and formalized research questions with their work, an interpretivist approach is not focused on testing a preconceived idea. Trying to force a hypothesis on interpretive work is actually a terrible idea because it encourages embedded assumptions for what is supposed to be an iterative process. Interpretivist research instead thrives from exploring research interests and letting a study's interactive and inductive nature shape questions (Maxwell, 2009). As such, research questions will often begin broadly (e.g., "What kinds of stories do people share about terrible first dates?") and become more specific (e.g., "What are common features of 'bad first date' stories?"). It is also completely appropriate for an interpretive researcher to offer a research statement that guides a study rather than a research question (e.g., "This study embraces a narrative approach to understand common features of 'bad first date' stories and what those features suggest about communicating relationships in contemporary culture"). Whether using a question or statement, it should be created in conjunction with researcher goals. Similar to research goals, a lack of predetermined research questions does not mean one starts a study blindly or waits for something to happen. Research questions or statements, even if they continue to evolve, will allow a researcher—and thus his or her study—to maintain focus and provide a sense of guidance for methods and analysis (Maxwell, 2009).

In developing research questions, Maxwell (2009) offers three warnings to qualitative researchers. First, he warns against making a research question general when it is dealing with something specific. One way to avoid this trap is to link the research question to goals about what the researcher wants to understand and accomplish. If a researcher decides to study speed dating there is a big difference between "How do people communicate in speed dating interactions?" and "How do members of the Lucky Lovers speed dating program interact?" One question suggests that knowledge will be less localized and many speed dating sites will be observed, whereas the other makes it clear that localized knowledge is being generated for one group and may later be transferred to other groups via theory. This example also illustrates how method comes into play with research questions. While both of these questions allow multiple possibilities for qualitative approaches, they have different demands in terms of gaining access needed to make a study happen. If access cannot be gained, or a method developed for answering a particular research question does not exist, it may mean some reshaping is in order.

Second, Maxwell (2009) warns against privileging an instrumentalist approach to research questions that belies notions of social reality. Drawing from Norris (1983), Maxwell (2009) characterizes instrumentalist researchers as those who "formulate their questions in terms of observable or measurable data and are suspicious of inferences to things that cannot be defined in terms of such data" (p. 231). An instrumental research question might ask, "What communication behaviors do participants *report* as making a marriage proposal romantic?" instead of "What qualities *help to make* marriage proposals romantic?" In the former question, the qualitative research becomes simple reporting, sharing what a participant said or did—an act that strangles theoretical development and hampers interesting findings. The latter question, however, requires a careful consideration of evidence available from the data to make sense of how meaning is created in a social scene. Validity checks, combined with abductively considering how findings interact with existing research and theory, help to eliminate chances of getting research findings wrong. Even without the power of validity checks, Maxwell (2009) notes, "The risk of trivializing your study by restricting your questions to what can be directly observed is usually more serious than the risk of drawing invalid conclusions" (p. 231). This freedom to theorize is not a license to make claims without evidence—but it is license to make claims by carefully considering the data through a valid analytical process.

A final warning regarding research questions has to do with questions of variance and how they differ from questions of process (Maxwell, 2004; Mohr, 1996). *Variance questions* are research questions that involve difference and correlation, whereas *process questions* examine how and why things happen. A commonly shared fallacy suggests that questions of variance (commonly marked by openings similar to "How much . . ." "Does . . ." or "Is there . . .") cannot be answered through interpretive research (see Maxwell, 2004, for an understanding of how they can). For most interpretivist studies, process questions work best, especially because they allow researchers to draw from what are widely recognized as interpretivism's chief strengths. These questions typically begin with "How do . . ." or "Why . . ." and allow insights into what events and activities mean to people or provide a sense of how social and physical contexts influence such events or activities (Maxwell, 2009). If questions of variance emerge in a study, it will be helpful to begin with process questions (e.g., "How do people who are white see their black-white interracial romantic relationships?" and "How do people who are black see their black-white interracial romantic relationships?") and let that guide the development of a variance question (e.g., "What are differences in how black and white people see their black-white interracial relationships?").

Methods

A research project's methods should always be directly linked to its questions, even if sometimes the methods used for a particular project will precede a question. Again, this notion plays into the reflexivity of a research process. One way to help develop methods and ensure they are linked both to goals and research questions is to develop a *methods matrix* (Maxwell, 2009). To create one, five questions are listed across the top of a piece of paper or writing board, including What do I need to know? Why do I need to know this? What kind of data will answer the questions? Where can I find the data? and Who do I contact for access?

Each of these questions constitutes the top of a column where answers are provided underneath. To the far right of the matrix is a sixth column, "Time line for acquisition," that helps to organize when each research goal will be finished. Then each research question is listed down the left side of the matrix under the first column ("What do I need to know?") followed by the research goal it matches ("Why do I need to know this?"). That allows for the other columns to be completed in a way that forces data sources to be considered and drives method. Revision may be needed for research questions or goals as different elements of methods are considered or learned.

In considering how tight or loose a study's design should be, it is often valuable to consider a study's complexity. New cultures, understudied concepts, or complex social phenomena likely call for a loose design that will be tightened as a researcher iteratively considers what is there; whereas familiar cultures, concepts, or ideas will likely lend themselves to a tighter, more extensively preplanned research process (Miles & Huberman, 1994). Other factors to consider in selecting methods include the kinds of relationships you will have with participants; sampling, or what sources to involve in a study (e.g., people, documents), how they will be engaged (observation, interviews), and even when and where; how those sources will be secured or recruited; and what will need to be done with any data collected to make sense of it.

Common Methods Used in Interpersonal Communication Research

In interpretive interpersonal communication studies, four methods are typically used (Tracy & Muñoz, 2011). The first is taking notes while being involved in a social scene. This method is often affiliated with the ethnographic tradition, and more discussion of this approach is presented in Chapter 6. The second is interviewing, either one on one or in groups. Oftentimes a group interview is referred to as a focus group. Interviews are explored in Chapter 3, and focus groups—which tend to take on different qualities—are examined in Chapter 4. A third method common to interpersonal communication is collecting recordings of natural data and analyzing talk. This practice is part of a larger body of work called *discourse analysis*, and in addition to recorded talk, it can be used with anything involving verbal communication (and, as Albers, 2007, demonstrates, the method is expanding to include visual communication as discourse). Discourse analysis is covered in Chapter 7, and the research study included in that chapter applies a form of discourse analysis to online message board posts made by spouses and partners of soldiers. Finally, Tracy and Muñoz (2011) list analysis of documents and visual texts. As they note, written documents and visual texts require little preparation for analysis because their natural state is what makes them so valuable. But analyzing them, especially in terms of visual qualities, can sometimes be tricky because of the lack of established analytical tools for such documents (Tracy & Muñoz, 2011). These methods can be used as a stand-alone tool (such as in Trix and Psenka's 2003 examination of differences between medical school letters of recommendation for male and female candidates) or combined with other approaches (as in Leeds-Hurwitz's 2002 study of cross-cultural weddings where she asked couples to use their photo albums to help share their stories).

Analysis: An Essential Element of Qualitative Studies

Often one of the most difficult things to explain in a qualitative research manuscript is analysis of data (Tracy, 2012). Analysis often is underused or undervalued, as it is what gives a study its weight (Saldaña, 2009). In many ways, it is a bit artificial to suggest that analysis only happens at one point in a qualitative research study. It more likely happens throughout a given project as goals and research questions are reconsidered and reshaped; as choices are intuitively made during data collection (e.g., follow-up questions, paying attention to a particular aspect of a social scene in observation); as assessments are made about what kinds of data to pursue next (or how to use the data one has); as data are being organized and prepared for coding; and as a manuscript or other form of research presentation is being prepared. In examining the analysis sections of many qualitative interpersonal communication articles, it is apparent that many of them begin the process in the same way: reading and rereading a data set and getting a strong sense of what is there. Because so much of this process is internal and intuitive, it is often difficult to explain to reviewers in a way that sounds scientific and professional (see Tracy, 2012). It might feel a little silly to read or write, "I was trying to figure it out, and then finally BAM! It hit me. For these couples, love was happening through the *monetary value* of the things they own, not the things they own themselves!" That would be honest in many situations, but it probably would not sit well with journal reviewers.

Unfortunately, based on experience, journal reviewers can also be sticklers about statements such as "In line with iterative approaches natural to qualitative research, data were reviewed many times so as to allow a sense of familiarity and to get a good sense of the qualities they contain." In fact, more than one reviewer has made statements such as "How did you read through the data?" or "Ideas don't pop up magically out of thin air. Where did you get them?" Our advice is to do two things. First, ignore reviewers who do not get that, yes, ideas do "pop up" in an interpretive research process as one continues to explore data, and there is value in bringing one's intuitions forward to consider whether or not those ideas have resonance for a social scene. Just as reviewers would not expect a quantitative researcher to explain all the ways he or she played with his or her data in SPSS before writing a report, it is silly to assume that one should try to explain how she or he played with data in his or her mind. Rather, a focus should be placed on whether a researcher was able to locate meaning from his or her data and explain it in a way that is reasonable, appropriately profound, and demonstrates validity.

That brings us to our second suggestion: to build confidence about the exploratory phases, make the explanation of any analytical tools used clear—providing examples, if possible—as well as how any existing theory (if applicable) was incorporated into the study. Statements such as "We used values coding" (Saldaña, 2009) probably won't do because most scholars do not know what values coding is. And even if they did, qualitative research's highly flexible nature includes methods that are difficult to replicate or need adjustment—so it is worth the time and manuscript space to explain exactly how the analysis played out in a particular study. Similarly, "We noticed that the data seemed to match up with social exchange theory" (Thibaut & Kelley, 1978) probably would not cut it either. What about the data matched up with social exchange theory? Instead, an author can pull out data that helped readers to see how the theory tied into analysis. Not only will detailing these processes build credibility for an author and confidence for readers to accept research claims, but this kind of careful writing also helps keep research reflexive and honest.

Coding

To help readers consider coding practices and to explore some new coding methods, we have made analytical tools a big part of each chapter. Coding, quite simply, is a way of drawing out meaning from a datum. A datum is any singular unit from a data set that seems to convey a sense of meaning, and from project to project (or even research question to research question in the same project) what constitutes a datum may differ. We understand that many of our qualitative research peers despise the term *coding* (just as many also love it)—but by using it, we are simply getting at ideas of analysis and coming to a better understanding of data more than we are any kind of required and rigid if/then process. Coding approaches are diverse and offer a lot of ways to consider data. Qualitative researchers should strongly consider investing in a great resource for coding approaches such as Johnny Saldaña's (2009) *The Coding Manual for Qualitative Researchers*. In that manual, Saldaña describes a code as "a word or short phrase that symbolically assigns a summative, salient, essence-capturing, and/or evocative attribute for a portion of language-based or visual data" (p. 3). Based on that definition alone, one may notice elements that feel especially comfortable (e.g., "*Salient*—I like that. It gets at my realist, if still interpretive, leanings," or "Yes! I want to get at emotion and expression! Evocative coding is what I *need*!") or elements one wants to reject ("*Essence-capturing*? Um, no. People can't be essentialized," or "My job is not to evoke; my job is to describe"). Fortunately, any coding process can be adjusted for one's personal inclinations and worldviews while still serving its job of helping to describe what is happening (and how) in research data.

Starting a Coding Process. Coding is one of the most interpretive elements of qualitative research (Saldaña, 2009), even when approached with a realist/postpositivist perspective. Paradoxically, coding both deconstructs data while simultaneously reconstructing it. A researcher is decoding what one means (tearing the data apart to understand what is there) and then re-encoding it in a way that can be meaningful for a study (building the data back up so they fit into the larger picture). At first this may seem awkward, and so coding processes such as *in vivo coding* (Strauss, 1987), where a participant or researcher's actual words are pulled out to form a code, may be used. Similar to this is *descriptive coding* (Wolcott, 1994), where rough codes are assigned in consideration of a research question before being refined and shaped into more firmly grounded codes. These codes are not simple abbreviations of what people said or what a researcher wrote; rather, they consider the topic of a datum. A mixture of *in vivo* and descriptive coding sometimes is helpful for making sense of data where topical codes seem elusive but where the researcher is intent on locking in on them quickly (although *quickly* might be a misleading word, because coding data almost always takes a great amount of time). Depending on the research question, *pattern coding* (descriptive coding with particular patterns) can also come in handy. Hatch (2002, p. 155) offers some patterns to consider: similarity (things happen or are stated in the same way); difference (things happen in different ways but predictably so); frequency (things happen a lot, or they don't happen much at all); sequence (things happen in a particular order); correspondence (things happen in relationship to one another); and causation (one thing leads to another).

In addition to considering pattern, goals and research questions can also allow insights into whether one should try to code in initial stages for cognitive, emotional, or hierarchical aspects (Lofland, Snow, Anderson, & Lofland, 2006). Cognitive aspects are those traced back to how a person thinks and include things such as rules, ideologies, self-concepts, and identities. Emotional aspects are feelings oriented and include things such as showing empathy for another, describing frustration, or expressing contentment in the workplace. Hierarchical aspects are often focused on inequality or power, such as cliques in high schools, women in a male-dominated profession, or disparities in marriage equality. In considering these aspects, it is helpful to think in a larger picture of "the intersection of one or more *actors* engaging in one or more *activities* (behaviors) at a particular *time* in a specific *place*" (Lofland et al., 2006, p. 121, emphases in original). Doing so can allow for these aspects to be organized into social units (Lofland et al., 2006, p. 121) that give a sense of the ingredients of a social scene:

1. Cultural practices (regular, if not always mundane, practices such as work tasks, daily routines, dating behaviors)
2. Episodes (irregular activities or unanticipated events from the perspective of social actors such as weddings, divorces, or the arrival of a baby)
3. Encounters (temporary interaction between people such as checking into a motel, ordering a pizza, or being mugged)
4. Roles (mother, lover, student) and social types (nerd, asshole, hottie)
5. Social and personal relationships (boyfriend and girlfriend, coworkers, partygoers)
6. Groups and cliques (the cool kids, 4-Hers, the New York Feminists)
7. Organizations (corporate offices, universities, prisons)
8. Settlements and habitats (home, Curtis Street, Chicago)
9. Subcultures and lifestyles (anarchists, the homeless, hipsters)

As these categories indicate, simply thinking through them alone, without coding, can assist a researcher in understanding his or her data and what kind or kinds of coding may be helpful next.

Computer-Assisted Analyzing. Many computer programs can be helpful for analyzing qualitative research data—with the key word being *helpful*. Actually, some researchers do not find these programs helpful at all and would rather have their hands in the data, seeing it laid out in front of them and feeling as if they are physically as well as mentally immersed in analysis. Others love the control a data analysis program can give them, and they especially appreciate how easy it makes it to run some of the validity checks that are explored later in this book. One popular data analysis program is QSR International's NVivo. It, like other qualitative data analysis programs, allows transcripts, field notes, or other documents to be imported, as well as audio and visual files—all that can be coded. As data are coded, a particular code can be selected, and all of the data with that code will pop up so that the researcher can work with them. One can also apply different kinds of coding in rounds and then see where codes across rounds overlap. The program even allows for the creation of models and word clouds that can help data be visualized and exported for inclusion in a manuscript or presentation. When completing research as part of a funded project, sometimes a funding agency will ask for statistical data even for qualitative work. Most qualitative data analysis programs (including NVivo) allow for the generation of quasi-statistics (that can also serve as a validity measure—as discussed in the section on validity in this chapter and in the final chapter).

From Initial Coding to Developing Theory. After data have been coded in a first round to make sense of what is there, that may be enough to answer a researcher's questions (or, at least, one or two of them). The codes will still need some refining, reconsideration, and validity checks. Most often, though, researchers will want to engage two (or more) rounds of coding using a more precise coding method that gets at goals and research questions for studies. Some of these second-round coding processes are explored in the research chapters of this book. Regardless of the number of coding rounds, each round of coding should also produce categories. In some cases, the codes turn out to be the category or quite similar to the category, but many times categories will contain many codes. *Categorizing* involves determining which data look and feel alike and putting them into groups (Lincoln & Guba, 1985). For example, codes of *happy*, *sad*, *angry*, and *annoyed* might fit into a category of *emotions*, or codes of *late*, *unkempt*, *unprepared*, and *aloof* might fit into a category of *annoyances*. The process of categorizing should be a clear and helpful step toward answering a research question. If not, that is a sign that recoding and recategorizing may be in order (Rubin & Rubin, 1995). Once codes and categories are derived, it is a good time to develop a concept map where all of the codes and categories are visualized and researchers intuitively ask, "Does this seem to make sense based on my experiences with this study?"

Saldaña (2009) notes that codes and categories are often confused with the idea of developing themes, and it appears this may be happening with interpretive interpersonal communication research at times. Rossman and Rallis (2003) suggest that qualitative researchers "think of a category as a word or phrase describing some form of your data that is explicit, whereas a theme is a phrase or sentence describing more subtle and tacit processes" (p. 282). In other words, developing themes is a step toward theorizing. It is the process of taking the "what is there" in the data—or, at least, one slice of what is there—and offering an understanding of what that means on a deeper, somewhat abstract, and more enduring level. A common question asked by researchers is how much data needs to be coded in order to be able to make theoretical claims. Part of the answer to this question comes with considering validity, the next and final element we explore as part of this qualitative design process. A general answer, though, is difficult to pin down as opinions of qualitative researchers across disciplines tend to differ wildly (Saldaña, 2009), and there does not appear to be consensus even in communication studies. Although Lindlof and Taylor (2011) do not offer an answer, they hint at ways to consider how much data to analyze when they characterize three forms of *process* in data analysis. Their explanation of process also makes a good review for this section on analysis.

First, they consider *data management*, or organizing data in a way that gives the researcher a sense of control. This management includes all aspects of how the data are prepared for coding or analysis: transcribing, preparing Word files for hand coding, entering data into a computer program, setting up a filing system, using color codes to mark data types or to help pull out exemplars for writing, or whatever else may be needed to keep the data in order and help a researcher go through an analysis process. Next, they look at *data reduction*—the step that helps one to consider the "how much" question. Sometimes it becomes apparent quickly that complete sections of an interview protocol may not be relevant to a particular research question (even though it may be used for different studies to answer different questions). Other times, connections are made about how particular pieces of data fit together (accordantly or dissonantly), and so a researcher gains the sense that—at least for a particular research question—only that data needs to be used. To best reduce data, however, one likely needs to at least go through a first-level coding process that looks at it all. Saldaña (2009) especially recommends that novice qualitative researchers (or even researchers with a few projects under their belt) code everything so they can get a sense of their own impulses and how they work. These first two processes should lead to the third, *conceptual development*, where links among data categories become more elaborate and dense. At this point, a validity check is likely in order.

Validity

Most of the considerations of validity offered in this book come in small segments of each chapter, as well as in the final chapter. Validity is not something to be saved until the end of a study, however. Doing so may mean a lot of wasted time and energy as new analytic approaches or even new data collection is needed that could have happened earlier in a study or been prevented with some foresight. For example, the first of Maxwell's (2011) validity concerns for research design deals with *long-term involvement* with research participants. This long-term involvement may not be needed for every research study (just as all of the seven validity concerns listed in this section may or may not be needed for a given study), but long-term involvement (such as repeated interviews, extended participant observation, or other ways of interacting with a study population) can allow a more complete understanding of a social situation than just about any validity check (Becker, 1970; Becker & Geer, 1957). A second consideration is *rich data*. Data may not always need to be articulate or polished (participant voices do not always allow that—and that makes sense if qualitative data, on some level, are to reflect social worlds), but they can be full of variance and details that allow for an expanded understanding of what is going on in a research situation (Becker, 1970). In planning for a study, it is wise to consider whether or not rich data will be allowed by at least one of the methods.

A third validity consideration in design is making sure to plan for respondent validation (Bryman, 1988), more commonly known in interpersonal communication studies as *validity checks* (often called *member checks* in interpersonal work). Validity checks involve going back to a study population and presenting them with data, analysis, or even theorizing to consider how they respond. Even though researchers should take validity checks seriously, they should also keep in mind that, just like the original data they collected, responses to such checks are also an interpretation. As such, these checks are especially useful for making sure that terminology used in a given culture is well understood by researchers, reconsidering assumptions made about data and gaining a sense of how theoretical claims may be received. The fourth validity consideration offered by Maxwell (2009) deals with discrepant evidence and *negative case analysis.* Data that do not fit into dominant themes or even dominant categories or codes should not be ignored. Instead, they should be embraced as clues that tell a different part of the research story and offer a holistic sense of theorizing.

Fifth, *triangulation* should be considered. Triangulation in qualitative research is different from triangulation in quantitative work (Fielding & Fielding, 1986). Triangulation in qualitative research involves collecting data from diverse participants, using diverse methods of data collection, and even trying alternate forms of coding that may help to disrupt simplified understandings. Sixth, *quasi-statistics* may be used to help establish a sense of salience in data. Quasi-statistics are simple statistics that help to demonstrate how readily particular themes can be found in data (Becker, 1970). Instead of claiming how much of something is expected to be found in a social world, however, they offer a sense of how much a particular theme permeates data in a given study (e.g., "Acceptance was identified in 95% of the interview sessions, even though it was not introduced as part of the interview protocol"). As one might imagine, quasi-statistics are somewhat controversial, as many believe they transform interpretivism into a form of inductive postpositivism. Interpersonal communication studies have been generally accepting of quasi-statistics (Suter, 2009), although they may add to the current postpositivist-interpretivist confusion about qualitative methods explored in the last chapter.

Finally, *comparison* may also be planned into a research design to help consider validity (Miles & Huberman, 1994). For example, if someone were studying an afterschool reading club to consider how discussion of books might also allow for relational bonds, even if it were set up as a completely localized study to elucidate how that particular book club worked, the researcher might also plan on attending a couple of book club meetings for other groups to get a sense of how what he or she sees there compares to what is seen at his or her main research site. The researcher might also enact comparison by interviewing people who belong to different book groups, examining advertising documents for other book groups, or even examining other studies done by other researchers about book groups (or similar discussion groups). Following many of these design considerations will also allow for possibilities of generalizing qualitative work, although the type of generalizing found in qualitative studies is *analytic* and not statistical (Yin, 1994). Generalization in qualitative research happens through the development of theory that can be extended to other cases (Becker, 1970; Ragin, 1987)—something Guba and Lincoln (1989) label *transferability.* Understanding how social actors make sense of an idea or concept in one particular space may not perfectly match up to another, but their experiences and navigation of their social worlds will have some qualities that certainly apply to a similar situation—thus, theory developed from their experience has the opportunity to be transferred to another case.

BRINGING IT ALL TOGETHER: CONSIDERING QUALITY

Understanding research traditions and designing a research study within their parameters is the beginning of a qualitative research process. In this final section, we offer two sets of considerations that approach quality through two lenses. We begin with five working paradoxes often present in interpretivist-oriented qualitative research. Generative, thoughtful qualitative research usually takes guts—and those guts often come in the form of navigating salient tensions present in interpretivist theorizing. Exploring these paradoxes here should build confidence for qualitative researchers about how to handle them as they occur. We then move to insights from S. J. Tracy (2010) who offers eight "big tent" criteria for quality in qualitative research (p. 837). We review these criteria in light of interpersonal communication studies here, combining Tracy's observations with experiences of our own and the methodological literature that helped us to navigate them.

Working Paradoxes for Interpretivist-Oriented Interpersonal Communication Researchers

Throughout the last two chapters, many ideas and themes have recurred or recirculated across the different topics explored—but none has been as dominant as the idea that interpretivist-oriented work is driven by reflexively considering situations and the possibilities they entail and then moving forward to make choices. Fortunately, there are no right answers—although when faced with a difficult choice, that *fortunately* might feel like an *unfortunately*. As much advice as we offer throughout this book, we know that it is ultimately the qualitative researcher (or research team) who will have to make a final decision about what to do. Here, to help guide those decisions, we offer some brief sensitization tools that help to make explicit some of the tensions interpretivist-oriented qualitative researchers face as they explore a social scene.

Research Is an Art of Science

In many ways, qualitative research is a form of art. It involves grounded expression, interpretation, and profound understanding. At the same time, qualitative research is also a form of science. It often involves empirical findings generated by systematic (if flexible) approaches to collecting more information about what a social scene entails. Just as artistic innovation comes into play with protocol design, analysis, and presentation of data, scientific rigor comes into play through protocol design, analysis, and presentation of data. Qualitative researchers are allowed to feel and experience as means for generating ideas about a social world, and yet they reflect and revisit to make sure their feelings and experiences are not blindly guiding their understandings. Just as feeling motivates art and allows for deep thought about the world, here feeling motivates science and considers that knowing is not always logical. In a world where meaning circulates throughout a social scene, a full palette of senses must be available to consider the potentially cavernous implications for meaning found in the tiny crevices of a social world. Qualitative research makes the unknown known, the implicit explicit, and the taken-for-granted obvious.

Rigor Comes From Flexibility

Rigor does not come from having everything perfectly preplanned in a qualitative research study. Rather, rigor is allowed by being open to possibility. "Open to possibility," of course, is not code for "anything goes." Qualitative researchers consider a social scene they want to study and what might be entailed to formulate a plan of action. They constantly review their game plan to adjust for emerging interests, theoretical insights, changes in access or availability, and a goal of eventually establishing validity. They conscientiously follow their hunches, fearlessly ask questions about what may be, and try different methods of analyzing to consider other ways of seeing.

Looking In Comes From Looking Out, Just as Looking Out Comes From Looking In

Qualitative researchers examine others, and in the process they also examine themselves. As they get a sense of what is there in a social scene, they look to theory and research outside of the scene to go back into a scene with a richer understanding. That understanding may be that the existing research and theory found do not match up to the current social scene. Other times, it may be that new and exciting things are revealed about theory or past research. Interpersonal qualitative researchers are especially fortunate, as interpersonal communication research has traditionally integrated existing theory as well as developed new forms of knowledge via qualitative studies. Understanding localized knowledge comes from a blend of the etic and the emic; understanding sensitizing knowledge allows deeper considerations of a social scene while simultaneously expanding the scope of an existing theory; and understanding emergent knowledge allows new and potentially revolutionary interpersonal communication theories to develop. All these forms of knowledge depend on looking from a particular scene to larger understandings and from larger understandings back to a particular scene. The resulting research allows people to look inward to understand themselves by looking outward to experience others and their social worlds—in terms of both participant voices and theory. Theories shaped or developed from these social worlds allow transferability to make them meaningful to similar social situations.

Difference Is a Shared Conclusion

In a social world, people can see the exact same thing and yet not see the exact same thing at all. This polysemic notion of meaning-making is often unrecognized by social actors, sometimes because it is subtle and other times because conflicting elements of a social scene do not circulate in a way where such difference is noticed. Qualitative researchers make meaning from these differences. They study a social scene closely, enacting carefully chosen methods that allow them to gain insights into meaning and action. Interpersonal communication scholars can consider how people, as social actors, negotiate their social worlds. They analyze data and take those findings back to the social scene in order to consider whether they fit. If a fit is there, they choose exemplars from data to get at the intersections of meaning—drawing from participant voices or their own observations to demonstrate various ways one social theme plays out. From those voices and observations, the subtle differences that sometimes are muted in a singular, coherent idea are illustrated. Still, qualitative researchers consider other possibilities. Even with conclusions, they consider alternate interpretations and data that do not neatly fit within the themes they have developed. They think deeply about what those things mean.

Making a Conclusion Still Means There Is No Conclusion

Researchers are social actors. Their involvement with a social scene, even as a researcher, means they are a part of that social scene. While methods and analysis can help researchers to consider the possibilities of the impact their being a part of that social world has on their viewpoints, they also have to consider how their conclusion is but one conclusion. Qualitative researchers will review truths *from their perspectives* in a social scene, and as such, they cannot present an exhaustive list of truths. In a research study, then, a researcher doesn't come to *the* conclusion—she or he comes to *a* conclusion. Once a conclusion is made and a study prepared for dissemination—whether that be through writing, performance, or other means of sharing—researchers can return to the data, using different analytic tools to generate other ways of looking at the same data, and disseminate another conclusion. The process can continue as long as there are valid conclusions to be made.

Tracy's Criteria for Quality Qualitative Research

Many qualitative methodologists (e.g., Bochner, 2000; Guba & Lincoln, 2005) have argued against universal criteria for considering quality, mostly because it holds the potential to strangle innovation in qualitative inquiry and reduce its methods to mere cookie cutters stamping out the same old thing. S. J. Tracy (2010) counters these ideas, suggesting that having criteria does not necessarily mean there is only one good way to do qualitative research (or even a set of good, approved ways). Rather, she suggests that any of her eight proposed criteria—developed by reviewing best practices articulated by other qualitative researchers—"may be achieved through a variety of craft skills that are flexible depending on the goals of the study and preferences/skills of the researcher" (p. 839). In other words, S. J. Tracy's criteria for quality, like most elements of qualitative research, depend on the specifics of a given study and how a researcher is able to respond to those specifics.

Exploring the Criteria

Tracy's first criterion is having a *worthy topic*. Many good topics come from personal interests or experiences. Personal interests might even be generated from current events or controversial theories. Topics do not always have to be big or particularly novel, however. Perhaps one of the biggest hallmarks of a good topic is its ability to draw attention to ideas or concepts that may otherwise be taken for granted. In interpersonal communication studies, many topics are considered in conjunction with a hot theoretical or conceptual area (e.g., communication privacy management, relational dialectics theory). Also, given interpersonal communication's close cross-disciplinary relationship with relationship studies, one should consider whether or not a topic contributes deeper understandings of communication in an interpersonal relationship.

Rich rigor is the second criterion Tracy offers. This richness can refer to theoretical constructs (e.g., facework, love styles) as they make a good fit with a given social scene, but it also involves having an appropriately broad set of approaches for collecting and analyzing data in a proper context and with a reasonable sample of people, documents, or experiences. The theories and data for a given study should be "*at least as* complex, flexible, and multifaceted as the phenomena being studied" (S. J. Tracy, 2010, p. 841)—and oftentimes it is through careful consideration of method that rich, multilayered data can be obtained. In interpersonal communication, common questions about data tend to be "How many?" (as in participants), "How much?" (as in writing for field notes), and "How long?" (as in length of interviews or observation).

The answers to these questions are not uniform, and oftentimes it depends on a richness and repetition that allow for theoretical saturation (S. J. Tracy, 2010). Snow (1980) offers two more ideas: heightened confidence and taken-for-grantedness. *Heightened confidence* gets at ideas of credibility. If ideas pulled from data suggest a particular kind of theorizing useful in answering research questions, it suggests that enough data have been collected to offer possible answers. To ensure as many answers as possible, a researcher should then develop a sense of taken-for-grantedness as well. *Taken-for-grantedness* is the idea that a researcher is not surprised by how participants respond or act in a social scene. Even if an event or action occurs that does not usually happen, taken-for-grantedness may be in place if the researcher is able to predict what will happen and articulate why that was his or her prediction.

Considering whether or not enough data have been collected also involves Tracy's third criterion of *sincerity*. Sincerity involves self-reflexivity (reflective and honest thinking about self, research, and audience) and transparency (providing an open and honest account of the research process). Sincerity also involves attitude. As S. J. Tracy (2010) articulates,

> Sincere researchers are approachable rather than self-important and friendly rather than snobbish. They consider not only their own needs but also those of their participants, readers, coauthors, and potential audiences. Sincere researchers are empathetic, kind, self-aware, and self-deprecating. The best qualitative researchers I know are sincere and that is one reason I like them so much. (p. 842)

This sincerity will likely be respected in sites of exploration. Qualitative interpersonal communication studies often involve articulations of feelings and emotions. Sincerity allows participants a sense of caring. Beyond that, it takes a sincere researcher to give qualitative research all of the time it requires.

In that sense, sincerity is similar to credibility. *Credibility*, the fourth criterion Tracy offers, examines how believable and dependable a qualitative research study is. A lot of credibility comes through in writing a manuscript that includes exemplars directly supporting a claim rather than those that simply provide a humorous anecdote or show a participant as profound (although those kinds of exemplars have potentials to demonstrate claims, too). Demonstrating validity allows credibility, as does including numerous voices (such as those of participants or theorists) that can help to develop claims in a way that moves beyond the monologue presented when an author does too much showing and not enough telling. Multiple voices also tie into *resonance*, Tracy's fifth criterion. Qualitative studies should appeal to numerous kinds of readers in different ways, including those who crave theoretical development, those who want to use research to enhance their lives, and even those who are simply curious about human conditions and lived experiences. This ability to extend knowledge speaks to *significant contribution*, Tracy's sixth quality criterion that suggests research should offer something important and relevant to the lives of people.

When a study is completed, it should be presented in a way that holds *meaningful coherence*—the research should do what it set out to do (S. J. Tracy, 2010). As has been asserted in this chapter many times, most elements of a qualitative project grow and evolve as a research process continues. When research presentations are created to represent that work, what is claimed as the research statement or question guiding the study should be satisfied. That is, if a study purports to be about advancing conceptions of dating rituals, then the findings, discussion, and implications should make a contribution to understanding dating rituals beyond what is already known. More than a coverage issue, meaningful coherence also involves using methods that fit a study's goals, employing outside literature to inform process and findings, and tying that study into larger considerations of the world. In many ways, meaningful coherence suggests that everything seems to come together in a nice resolution—even though one should acknowledge what else can be or ought to be explored based on the current findings.

As can be seen by looking across these first seven criteria offered by S. J. Tracy (2010), in many ways they tie multiple ideas together that have been explored throughout this chapter: they are deeply interconnected and often interdependent. And so quality is likely never a matter of going down a checklist to make sure that certain things are done, but rather a process of considering how everything works together in a way that is enlightening, honest, useful, and ethical. The last of those items—*ethics*—is quite important. Qualitative research often deals with highly personal information, and that tends to be especially true with interpersonal communication studies. As participants invite researchers into their lives and share their stories, it is vital that they be treated with care, dignity, and respect. Because *ethical dimensions*, the eighth and final of Tracy's criteria, are so important, we offer an extended discussion of them here.

Ethics

Few actions during a research process are unequivocally right or wrong. Researchers, as the people most involved with a given population and how that population will later be presented, are ultimately responsible for considering how "rightness" and "wrongness" play out in their work in the context of what they know or learn about a social scene. Reviewing writings on ethics (e.g., Christians, 2000; Dowling, 2000) and interacting with institutional review boards can be helpful, but they cannot take into consideration what a researcher will know from being immersed in a scene. That is why ethics is the ultimate responsibility of the researcher. The impacts of ethical decision making can literally mean life and death for participants, as Vanderstaay's (2005) riveting essay "One Hundred Dollars and a Dead Man: Ethical Decision Making in Ethnographic Field Work" helps to demonstrate. Vanderstaay's seemingly harmless involvement with a family he befriends in a research study compels him to loan one of the family members in need $100—and, as he details in his article, it likely led to a man dying. Vanderstaay's story is as frightening as it is intriguing because it demonstrates that even when someone is trying to do something for the right reasons it can lead to a wrong—in his case fatally wrong—outcome. S. J. Tracy (2010) offers four different kinds of ethics one can consider in engaging qualitative work: procedural ethics, situational ethics, relational ethics, and exiting ethics. Reviewing these categories in conjunction with a research design, even if it will not eliminate every ethical quandary that could arise in a study, is a good way to think through research and reduce ethical dilemmas.

Procedural Ethics

As the name implies, procedural ethics are those involved with moving through a research process. An institutional review board (IRB) that asks a researcher to provide documented foresight about what he or she might expect to encounter during a study usually helps to guide an academic researcher. These boards usually involve fellow faculty members, but they may be from departments (or even disciplines) that do not engage interpretivist or even qualitative research methods. Review boards, in general, consider whether a research study's risks are worth its possible benefits. To do that, they ask questions about whether or not a study will likely cause harm to participants, make sure that informed consent procedures are in place and clear, and work to ensure confidentiality or privacy. They also review any claims of fraud, deception, omission, or abuse if reported.

Chances are, if one is reading this book then he or she is familiar with the IRB either from direct experience with submitting a research proposal or from hearing others talk about it. It is not unusual to hear someone mention the IRB at a conference and be met with a collective groan. Review boards are often the butt of jokes (e.g., "I guess they want to make sure I'm not abusing them with my questions about conversations at dinnertime!") or villains in personal horror stories (e.g., "I had to go through 57 revisions—and then they still turned me down!"). These cases of terror are surely out there, but—based on all of the qualitative research being published on a regular basis—obviously many people are getting their proposals through review boards and doing their studies. Between the two authors of this book, IRB proposals have been approved for such sensitive topics as women who have been abused, families negotiating virginity pledges, posthurricane disaster areas, sexual history, sexual fantasies, cyberbullying, sext messaging, relational renegotiation, and grief management. The IRB serves a good function, too. It makes people think about what they are studying, how they are studying, and who (and sometimes what) may be hurt. Some have questioned whether all research should have to go through an IRB process, especially research closer to the artistic end of the qualitative continuum or history-oriented research (Jaschik, 2012). This debate will likely continue for many years to come, with widespread change, if any, taking even longer to implement.

Given that it is essential to gain IRB approval for just about any qualitative research study, a qualitative researcher should think about how to navigate the IRB process. The best advice for doing that will probably come from another trustworthy qualitative researcher at the same university who has submitted many qualitative proposals for review. Insights from actual localized experience are likely better than anything we could write here, although Adrianne has been on an IRB for almost nine years and has drawn from her experiences there to guide ethical approaches in this book. We also have one other piece of direct advice to offer about the IRB, and it deals with quality data as much as it does ethical data: any time an informed consent sheet is written, it should be as transparent as possible. Not only does the informed consent form allow a person taking part in a study to know exactly what he or she is getting into, but it also leads to higher-quality data. "Weak consent," as it is called by Miles and Huberman (1994, p. 291), will leave a participant feeling suspicious or mistrustful of a researcher. This frustration may make it hard for people to share or be open.

Situational Ethics

Because any study has its own distinct and continuously emerging characteristics, it makes sense that it would also have its own set of ethical issues to consider. Thus, situational ethics deal with "the unpredictable, often subtle, yet ethically important moments that come up in the field" (Ellis, 2007, p. 4). Many times these get back to *beneficence*, or the idea that a study should only yield good results for those involved. If a person feels mild sadness at sharing a breakup story, the minimal sadness felt compared to the potential to help others communicate in more respectful or considerate ways when ending their relationships might make the study worth it. Anonymity is another issue to consider with a given situation, especially in interpersonal communication research. If studying how swingers from rural areas find other couples while maintaining their privacy, data probably need to be presented in a way where the rural area is impossible to recognize and where, if anyone involved in the study decided to seek out the article (not as unlikely as one would think in this digitally enhanced information age), other couples who participated in the study could not be identified as swingers. That might result in some of the most interesting or richest data being unusable, but protecting vulnerable participants (swinging generally is not looked upon favorably, even though it usually involves consenting adults) is more important.

One great source for considering situational ethics is exploring other research about a similar population or topic that can allow insights into what one might encounter in a specific site. Another way to consider situational ethics is to talk to someone involved with the topic to get a sense of what they believe might be issues. If someone is atheist and exploring Christian rituals in weddings, it makes sense to talk to someone in advance who is Christian and has been married to consider if any ethical issues might be involved with this seemingly innocuous study. Consulting those who have experience with the topic also is a good way to generate new or more specific research ideas and possibly be introduced or referred to new research participants. If an ethical issue emerges while one is in the field, document it in an analytic memo and reflect upon how it might be avoided in future situations. This documentation may also be helpful later in the research process when trying to decide if data from the ethical quandary should or should not be used in a research report or presentation.

Relational Ethics

Relational ethics are about people respecting each other in their interactions (S. J. Tracy, 2010). People in a research study—and in general—should be treated with dignity and respect. To borrow from Buber (1923), it can be easy to slip into an *I-it* relationship in research interactions where a researcher talks at or makes demands of participants. Sometimes it is not even because a researcher is asserting dominance, superiority, or control but because people naturally might yield to him or her because of title or researcher status. Sometimes it can be helpful to openly address relational ethics with those involved in a study from the beginning. In other situations, there may be a need to address the topic because of particular incidents (such as a participant making a pass at a researcher or a member of a focus group berating another because of an opinion). Other times it is a matter of demonstrating equality—such as offering reciprocal information in interviews or helping people to complete tasks in a field study. Relational ethics are a big part of qualitative research practices, having impact not only on doing the right thing but also on the quality of a study. Rapport building, a dimension of relational ethics, is examined in each of the research chapters.

Exiting Ethics

As researchers exit a social scene and begin to consider how they will interpret and present data they have collected, *exiting ethics*—ethics considering how research will be seen by others—become important. Some of the issues for exiting ethics are similar to situational ethics, such as whether or not people can be recognized based on data exemplars used or specific details provided. Other exiting ethics issues deal with larger representations or understandings of people and groups. Some data may reinforce stereotypes about minoritized groups or may be manipulated for political gain against a group of people or an entity (Fine, Weis, Weseen, & Wong, 2000). Sometimes it may be tempting to use scandalous data to make a manuscript more readable when, in reality, it overstates or overdramatizes what would typically be less drama filled or even mundane. For example, a research report featuring strippers gone wild may draw shock and awe, but if data are cherry-picked to create that image then it is a dishonest representation.

Sometimes ethical situations can be negotiated in advance, and as long as it does not compromise integrity (e.g., removing or abbreviating events that cause data to be distorted; describing falsities or offering misleading statements to create something that is not there), then it can be acceptable. For example, someone may agree to tell a story so that a culture can be understood by a researcher, but he or she could also request that none of the details of the story are used in the write-up of the research or hinted at when the researcher interacts with others. While this kind of "off the record" data can be helpful, researchers should take special care to document the situation and think early about how it can be incorporated into the study without breaking any promises. Overall, the biggest concerns with exiting ethics involve protection and honesty (Fine et al., 2000; S. J. Tracy, 2010). Those particularly concerned about these issues may even include a "Legend of Cautions" in a manuscript that exhaustively lists any ways data may be "misread, misappropriated, or misused" (S. J. Tracy, 2010, p. 848)—although such extreme measures are likely not needed in most studies.

EXAMINING POSSIBILITY

This concludes our overview of general design considerations for interpersonal qualitative research. Each of the next six chapters examines one of the many possibilities for interpretivist-oriented qualitative work in interpersonal communication. As you read each of these chapters, we invite you to continue considering possibility—especially as these ideas apply to your own interpersonal communication studies and your ultimate goals as a researcher.

Questions for Growth

1. Which qualitative research method is most appealing to you? Why? Least appealing? Why?

2. Why are goals so important to a research design? What happens if a researcher sets bad or faulty goals?

3. What does it mean to "code" data? Is it appropriate to code something as personal as interpersonal communication?

4. What are some of the key ethical concerns for conducting qualitative research about relationships?

Interviews, Emotion Coding, and a Family Communication Study

We begin our exploration of individual research methods with interviewing for two reasons. First, interviewing methods share a lot of commonalities with focus groups, open-ended surveys, and ethnographic/participant observation methods. They also, by nature, involve narratives and discourse analysis. So, in many ways, beginning with interviews allows insight into the other methods explored in later chapters. Second, qualitative interviews are an extremely popular method that interpersonal communication scholars have embraced for their research. As this chapter illustrates, interviews have been used to great effect in coming to understand personal relationships and the communication involved as part of them.

INTERVIEWS AND THE STUDY OF RELATIONSHIPS

As Steiner Kvale (1996) so colorfully elaborated, an interviewer is someone who

> wanders through the landscape and enters into conversations with the people encountered. The traveler explores the many domains of the country, as an unknown territory or with maps, roaming freely around the territory. . . . The interviewer wanders along with the local inhabitants, asks questions that lead the subjects to tell their own stories of their lived world. (p. 4–5)

Kvale's (1996) words illustrate the *traveler metaphor* of interviewing, suggesting that a researcher using interviews is traveling into the lives of others and making sense of how they make sense of meaning in their social worlds. The traveler approach is in contrast to a *mining approach* where a scholar is more interested in digging out specific information or details. For qualitative researchers, the choice between the two often comes down to whether the project is closer to the artistic end of the qualitative continuum (traveling) or the realist end (mining). Most interpersonal communication research using interviews seems to fall somewhere in the middle—meaning that interpersonal relationship researchers have a wide range of options when it comes to designing and implementing an interview research protocol.

Flexibility and Probing

When most people think of the term *interview*, what may come to mind is facing a potential employer across a giant desk or a reporter eliciting a celebrity's stories from the set of a blockbuster movie. In the research world, however, interviewing serves a different purpose. As a research tool, interviews offer flexibility and are used to understand and make sense of another person's perspective, with the over-arching goal to tap into his or her rich, varied, and multilayered life experience (Denzin, 1978; Kvale, 1996; Patton, 1990). Given that relationships are loaded with multilayered meaning, interviews are often a particularly dynamic way of examining multiple points of view from a single participant and his or her relationships.

Keyton (2010) suggests that interviewing is a practical research method for discovering how people think and feel about real-world experiences that are not observable and that this methodology enables the researcher to find answers to complicated or sensitive questions about key, pivotal moments. Further, some argue that an interview is a conversation with a specific purpose (Bingham & Moore, 1959; Kahn & Cannell, 1957). It is through this purposeful conversation that the interviewer and interviewee may work together to coauthor (Ellis, Kiesinger, & Tillmann-Healy, 1997) a tale, story, or unfolding drama (Myers & Newman, 2007). As Charmaz (1991) notes,

> To be effective, the interviewer must try to see the issues discussed and the immediate interaction from the respondent's perspective—that is, to adopt the respondent's role and look at the situation from his or her perspective instead of the interviewer's. . . . Hence an interviewer must think continuously about what this conversation seems to mean to the other person. (p. 388)

Frey, Botan, Friedman, and Kreps (1992) explain that an interview typically "involves the presentation of oral questions by one person (an interviewer) to another (the respondent)" (p. 125). The interview can be face to face, over the phone, or mediated through computer software (e.g., Skype or iChat). Regardless of the communication channel for an interview, "qualitative interviewing design is flexible, iterative, and continuous, rather than prepared in advance or locked in stone" (Rubin & Rubin, 1995, p. 46). In other words, even though an interview protocol is often scripted and has particular questions asked of participants, it is also open to flexibility and change as participants (sometimes called informants) help to co-create what happens during an interview. It is helpful to approach interviews as conversations open to multiple possibilities even if the interviewer needs to make sure that the conversation does steer toward the purpose of a given research project.

Many researchers organize interviews around three sections: the background or history of the interviewee and his or her relevant experiences, current experiences of the interviewee, and the meanings of the interviewee's experiences and how those experiences might relate to the future. Rather than those three areas constituting a recipe of what must be included in an interview session, they should be considered as inspirational tracts to help needle and nudge out particular questions or statements geared toward interaction. Based on our own work and the work we have done with students, participants will often naturally share background information and current experiences about a question asked. It is the third section (i.e., the meanings of the interviewee's experiences) where special care is often needed, as many times people being interviewed need encouragement to consider future possibilities and unpack what elements or events in a relationship mean. As interpretivist relationships researchers, it is the meaning-making that is often important and allows for theorizing.

According to Patton (1990), it is sometimes useful to start an interview with noncontroversial topics related to the respondent's knowledge base, behaviors, and activities (where the respondent can talk more generally and descriptively). Beginning an interview with nondirective questions, such as a "grand tour" question for respondents to talk about "how something in their scene or life experience—an activity, an event, a friendship, their career—has transpired" (Lindlof & Taylor, 2011, p. 202) is sometimes a useful tactic to get the interviewee comfortable and talking. For example, in an interview about an online dating relationship it might be helpful to start with a broad question such as, "So how did you two meet online and start your relationship?" That allows the participant to introduce and describe topics and issues in his or her own words, making it more appropriate to ask questions about specific and potentially sensitive feelings, opinions, values, experiences, and interpretations. It also helps to allow the participant agency in co-creating the scene (and allows for the sense that he or she is being listened to in the interaction).

Even though participants should have a sense of agency, Kvale (1996) suggests an interviewer keep the respondent on track with structuring statements (e.g., "I would now like to move to a different part of the interview") and also be willing to accept silence and extended pauses, wherein the respondent has an opportunity to think about and reflect upon his or her experiences. Based on our own experiences, many times it may be helpful to gently probe in a situation where silence looms too long or where a situation seems especially delicate. For instance, if a participant closes a story with "and then he hit me," silence may be a comfortable way of allowing the interviewee to continue or move on. But if that silence lingers too long, there may be a need for follow-up—especially if the interviewer senses there is more to the story that needs to be said. Rather than a command (e.g., "You need to elaborate"), the interviewer might consider repeating the last statement to affirm that the interviewee is being heard and naturally encourage him or her to continue. Voice inflection is particularly important in these cases, both for the interviewer (who should demonstrate empathy) and the interviewee (who should be listened to by the interviewer for signs that maybe it is time to switch to a different line of questions for the sake of his or her comfort).

Other types of interview questions include introducing (e.g., "Can you tell me about yourself?"), follow-up (e.g., "What did you say back?"), probing (e.g., "Can you tell me more about this?"), direct (e.g., "Have *you* ever experienced this?"), indirect (e.g., "How do you think *others* might feel about this?"), and interpreting (e.g., "Can you explain more about what you mean?") (Kvale, 1996). Probing, or asking for additional information, is probably one of the most important interviewer skills in that it can afford the respondent the chance to elaborate, clarify, or offer more detail. Little is more frustrating than revisiting an interview transcript and realizing that a participant introduced a topic or idea where a follow-up was not offered, and, as such, little meaning can be made of the data. Gaining a sense of when (and how) to probe—or when to ask any of the question types just described—can allow for fuller and more fruitful data sets that will lead to stronger theorizing.

As with any methodology, there are different interview types or formats you can employ in research (Frey et al., 1992). The research question or purpose, along with where that question or purpose falls on the qualitative continuum, can help determine the format used. The first interview type is the highly structured (or scheduled) formal interview. In this type, the interviewer carefully constructs a set of standardized questions that he or she intends to ask every respondent in the same sequence.

The highly structured interview is particularly useful when multiple interviewers are involved in a research project and when there is a desire to minimize variation and potential bias across interviews and interviewees (Patton, 1990). The structured interview may have both open-ended or closed-ended questions. The former allows respondents to use their own words and elaborate, while the latter usually leads to an extremely short response such as, but not limited to, yes or no. Other reasons to use the structured format are if the questions need to be approved in advance by a stakeholder or decision maker or if the interview length is limited. Interviews of this type fall on the realist end of the qualitative continuum and, if dominated by "yes or no" questions, would likely be postpositivist (as opposed to interpretivist).

The second interview type is the semi- or moderately structured interview. In the moderately structured interview, the researcher may still follow a list of questions in a predetermined order, but he or she is allowed the freedom and flexibility to probe for extra information when useful. Alternatively, a researcher may conduct a semistructured interview by adopting a general interview guide that merely outlines the issues or topics to be explored. The interview guide serves as a checklist, and the order and wording of the questions may vary as the interviewer adapts to each interviewee and his or her revelations. According to Patton (1990), the guide provides "topics or subject areas within which the interviewer is free to explore, probe, and ask questions that will elucidate and illuminate that particular subject" (p. 283). These interviews likely fall into the middle of the qualitative continuum, although they may end up providing data that can be analyzed through a realist or artistic approach as well.

The final interview type is the unstructured (or informal) qualitative interview where interviewers have goals or purposes for the interview, but they are allowed complete flexibility in terms of how questions are phrased and ordered. Lindlof and Taylor (2011) also group ethnographic, informant, and narrative interviews into the overarching category of the *unstructured interview*. The unstructured, qualitative, "conversational" (Patton, 1990, p. 281) interview relies on continuous and thoughtful probing by the interviewer. Frey et al. (1992) refer to the unstructured interview as a "spontaneous conversation" (p. 127), wherein both parties adjust and respond to the moment. Rubin and Rubin (1995) argue that

> design in qualitative interviewing is iterative. That means that each time you repeat the basic process of gathering information, analyzing it, winnowing it, and testing it, you come closer to a clear and convincing model of the phenomenon you are studying. . . . The continuous nature of qualitative interviewing means that the questioning is redesigned throughout the project. (pp. 46, 47)

Thus, present and future interviews may be shaped by the progress of the current one. Unlike with postpositivist research, where a change in interview protocol or the addition of a question to a survey often means throwing out data already collected, with open interviews such as the ones described here, the changes made based on participant interaction are a part of the data collection. No data have gone bad by making protocol changes—rather, the change in and of itself lends to the meaning-making process and should be considered in analysis. As Patton (1990) argues, the qualitative interview is part of spontaneous questioning within the natural flow of an interaction. This interview type allows for maximum flexibility and is especially appropriate as part of ongoing participant observation fieldwork, as the same respondent may be interviewed multiple times. It is also possible that the interviewees do not feel like they are being interviewed. Indeed, the qualitative interviewer must "go with the flow" (Patton, 1990, p. 282).

Discovery and Elaboration

As the different types suggest, interviews can be conducted with a great deal of flexibility. The key is that interviews provide a researcher with a unique opportunity to discover new and deeper understandings about real people's lived experiences. Indeed, the interview as a research method has many strengths or advantages as compared to other research methods. First, according to Babbie (2010), interviews yield much higher response rates (i.e., 80–85% of those solicited actually participate). Relative to the administration of a survey, the presence of an interviewer tends to decrease the amount of times when a respondent skips a question or says he or she "does not know" the answer to a question. The interviewer also has the ability to clarify questions for the respondent on the spot and, similarly, to ask the respondent to clarify answers or to probe for more detailed information. Also, compared to other research methods such as surveys, an interview setting allows for the researcher to observe both verbal and nonverbal behaviors of respondents and to be flexible in adapting to the interviewee's needs, desires, or idiosyncrasies.

For studying personal relationships, interviews may be especially useful because they provide a context for rapport, trust, and connection to develop between interviewer and interviewee. This makes it more likely that an interviewee will feel comfortable answering questions about highly sensitive or personal, relationship-based topics. Of course, the resulting beneficial relationship between researcher and respondent is definitely facilitated when the researcher uses warm, friendly, compassionate, and attentive listening skills. Ways to enhance effective interpersonal and listening interviewer skills are detailed shortly within the Best Practices section. What follows now are brief descriptions of three relationship-based research studies that use highly structured, semistructured, and unstructured qualitative interview formats, respectively, to illustrate the three.

Highly Structured Interview Format

The *Journal of Personality and Social Psychology* published a study by Dakof and Taylor (1990) that examined the social support provided to cancer patients by spouses, relatives, friends, and health care professionals. The researchers employed a highly structured interview format that began with a scripted statement. Respondents were reminded of the diagnosis of cancer and how the related behaviors of others achieve different levels of helpfulness. They were then asked to consider four specific questions in relation to a person fulfilling one of seven potentially supportive roles or relationships (e.g., spouse, friend, nurse, other cancer patients). For each of the seven targeted potential supporters, the set of scripted questions was repeated to the respondent. Respondents were thus asked to report the most helpful thing done or said, the most annoying or upsetting thing done or said, the most unique supportive behavior or message, and the thing unsaid or undone that was most desired by the patient.

By collecting the data in this uniform manner, Dakof and Taylor (1990) were able to code it with respect to their interest in more and less effective interaction with supporters in various roles. The researchers determined that, overall, examples of esteem or emotional support, as opposed to informational or tangible support, were perceived as "most helpful" in about 70% of responses. Moreover, inadequate esteem or emotional support appeared prominently among references to unhelpful or less helpful efforts. On the other hand, informational support was the type most desired from doctors and other cancer patients. Apparently, the common experiences of cancer patients allowed for particularly efficient communication of support between them, as this quote from a respondent exemplified: "All you gotta do is tell another breast cancer patient, 'my checkup is in 3 days' and we all know what that experience is like" (p. 85).

Semistructured Interview Format

Heino, Ellison, and Gibbs (2010) sought to examine the extent to which a marketplace metaphor represents the evaluative and decision-making processes of online daters who comprise the phenomenon of "relationshopping" (p. 427). For the article they published in the *Journal of Social and Personal Relationships*, the researchers recruited over 30 members of a popular online dating site for interviews that "were semi-structured to ensure that all participants were asked certain questions yet allowed the freedom to raise other relevant issues" (p. 433). While a variety of open-ended questions addressed respondents' online dating histories, considerations for constructing their online profiles, and perceptions of differences with traditional dating, three specific questions targeted the pertinence of the marketplace metaphor. These questions included the following (Heino et al., 2010, p. 433):

1. Has the knowledge that there are thousands of profiles available online changed the way you go about dating? If yes, how?
2. Has it changed the way you view those you might potentially date? If yes, how?
3. Have the responses you've received online changed how you view yourself? If yes, how?

The emphasis on allowing respondents to provide detail only when they have it to offer is evident within these questions in the use of short follow-ups for positive responses. This approach yielded findings for the salience of the marketplace metaphor and for respondents' usage of specific strategies to navigate it. For instance, some respondents described the skepticism they employed in evaluating potential partners who were probably overselling their favorable attributes: "Everyone is so wonderful over the Internet. What the Internet doesn't tell you is that, 'I'm defensive, I talk about my problems all the time, I can't manage my money'" (Heino et al., 2010, p. 435). Other respondents told of changes they had experienced in their own self-image as a result of responses to their profiles. For example, one noted, "I'm much more attractive than I had thought, so that was good. That boosts your morale and punches it up" (p. 436).

Unstructured, Qualitative Interview Format

The family relationships played out in the context of lesbian parenting was the focus of Hequembourg's (2004) study in the *Journal of Social and Personal Relationships*. She considered the differences among these women and their relationships that may result from individual "trajectories to motherhood" (p. 739), the influences of their own families, and the social institutions they face. Forty respondents were questioned within an unstructured format so as to "allow each respondent the opportunity to relate her own experiences in an open-ended manner" (p. 743). In fact, about half of the interviews included the respondent's partner, and about half consisted of interaction with just the respondent. Instead of administering a formalized set of questions that were completely (i.e., highly) or somewhat (i.e., semi-) structured, Hequembourg (2004) mailed respondents a short story about a lesbian mother's experiences and asked them to compare it to their own and to consider how their own stories might be told. In this way, it was only the launching point that was consistent across all the interviews.

Hequembourg (2004) was thus able to detect the similarities and differences of respondents' experiences with those of heterosexual stepfamilies and the problems caused by lesbian mothers' general lack of institutionalized status. The unstructured interview format also allowed for the total discovery of the highly nuanced and specialized situations of particular respondents, such as one renamed Hester for the study. As Hequembourg (2004) noted,

> One of the respondents in this study, Hester, was estranged from her son because she did not have second-parent rights. Hester's partner was pregnant from a previous heterosexual relationship when they began dating. After the birth of her partner's baby, Hester became the stay-at-home mother for the little boy. When the boy was almost two years old, Hester's partner ended their relationship. Although she promised to allow Hester visitation with the little boy, Hester found that her ex-partner became increasingly reluctant to do so as she rekindled her relationship with the boy's biological father. (p. 755)

It might be said that both the widely varying tales of the respondents and the idiosyncratic progression of the unstructured interviews are represented in Hequembourg's employment of the phrase "unscripted motherhood" in the title of her article, "Unscripted Motherhood: Lesbian Mothers Negotiating Incompletely Institutionalized Relationships."

Innovations in Interviewing Practices

Interpersonal relationship researchers should keep in mind that, as useful as the three formats or approaches just illustrated have been and continue to be for gaining insights into interpersonal communication, the potential for advancements in interviewing practices is a possibility. Creative approaches to interviews could yield different kinds of data with different kinds of analytical possibilities. For example, in Manning's (in press-b) study of online dating, he prepared for interviews by first studying each participant's online personal advertisement. He then started the interview session with each participant by asking him or her to describe what they were seeking in a relational partner and what he or she had to offer to someone in a relationship. As participants answered, he took notes about qualities they mentioned that were not included in their personal ads. He then presented a copy of the personal advertisement and asked the interviewee to take him through the choices made in constructing it. Finally, he returned to the list of items mentioned during the interview that were not listed in the ad and asked the participant to discuss why those things were not included. This approach allowed him to gain a deep sense of how, rhetorically, the personal ads were constructed for online dating, but also to ask about what was not included in the advertisement in a way that made it less reflective and more akin to everyday conversation.

Best Practices for Collecting Interviews

As noted in previous chapters, all research methods have strengths and weaknesses. The preceding section noted the benefits of using interviews and offered examples of how they have been used in research involving personal relationships. Here, some of the potential limitations of interviewing are discussed, along with a series of "best practices" for overcoming these drawbacks associated with collecting interview data.

Overall, although interviewing data fosters the collection of in-the-moment, in-depth, personal descriptions of opinions, attitudes, and values, it can potentially become counterproductive if data are viewed as unreliable (e.g., when the same questions are asked of different respondents in very different ways, so as to preclude comparisons). Also, an interview question could inadvertently offend or insult an interviewee, which might make the interviewee reluctant to answer it or other questions. Moreover, when the researcher exerts too much influence over the direction of the interview (e.g., talking too much about himself or herself), this may impact the interview negatively (Babbie, 2010; Fontana & Frey, 2000). Famously, interviews are interpersonal and thus especially subject to a social desirability bias so that interviewees try to answer questions in ways they think will represent them favorably.

As interviews are much more time intensive and involved than handing out surveys, they do not generally produce generalizations about large groups of people. The quality of the data collected may be affected when an interviewer or interviewee feels pressured by time constraints (Myers & Newman, 2007). When a researcher decides it is necessary to interview more people, he or she may need multiple interviewers, which is a threat to consistency across the project.

Indeed, the potential drawbacks of interviews may block the acquisition of valid and meaningful results and conclusions. A theme throughout this book is that research methodology imperfections may be addressed by thoughtful and responsive design practices. Here we offer five guiding principles as best practices to an interview design performance.

Allowing Consideration and Ethics to Guide an Interview

First, given that the interview is basically a conversation between two people, treat the interviewee ethically and with a great deal of respect and care—this will help to set the tone of the interview. Efforts to make sure that the interviewee is at ease and comfortable with the process are crucial. Finding a safe and relatively private space to conduct the interview will help to foster a level of comfort for both parties, as will accessing a "protected time" when outside pressures are low (e.g., time, date, place; Lindlof & Taylor, 2011, p. 188). That place is not always in a laboratory—in fact, for most qualitative research it is not. Consider what the interview is about and how space can facilitate gaining quality information about the topic. If interviewing a couple about their long-term relationship, it may be helpful to conduct the interview in their home. Interviews with people who identify as "casual daters" may be fine to schedule in a coffeehouse or at a restaurant. In addition, at the outset, providing the interviewee with information on the format of the interview—how long it might last, that there are no right or wrong answers, that notes will be taken, and that it will be audio recorded—are useful practices for letting the other person know what to expect. Allowing the interviewee a chance to clarify any doubts or concerns he or she might have about the interview can also enhance participation (although, in most cases, those being interviewed will not have questions). Finally, taking notes during the interview may signal appreciation and worth to the respondent while also highlighting any key features that might not show up in the interview transcription. We have noticed that interviewees tend to elaborate on stories more when we take notes but that, occasionally, they might also ask why something was noteworthy as we wrote it down.

Give research respondents details about the rationale behind the project, why certain questions are being asked (e.g., about private life details), a description of how interview files and transcripts will be handled (i.e., issues of confidentiality), and how respondents can contact the researcher postinterview (Patton, 1990). A consent form detailing this information should be provided to each interviewee, but gentle reminders about why sensitive or difficult information is being requested or reiterating that the interviewer understands he or she is asking for something difficult is seldom a bad thing. The researcher should retain respondent contact information in case something is not clear on the interview tape and needs to be followed up on. Further, compensating the interviewee in any way (e.g., a cup of coffee, a gift card) is a useful tactic. Even a small incentive might let respondents know that they are valued as people and that their interview responses are very important. Depending on the value of such gifts, they may need to be reported on an IRB application. Finally, allowing respondents the freedom to back out of the interview at any time they are not comfortable is a must. Also, if anyone asks, at any point (even months later), that his or her data not be used in a published research report (even with a pseudonym), this request must be respected and honored.

Researching Interview Situations

Second, as an interviewer it is useful to prepare by way of investigation prior to the interview. It is essential to understand, and even anticipate, the social, cultural, and contextual factors that may influence the interviewee's experience and subsequent responses to questions. Preliminary investigative research may also help the researcher to select respondents who will provide the most rich and meaningful data. In addition, consider the "level of entry" in the interview process (Myers & Newman, 2007, p. 4). That is, if a researcher starts his or her interviews with people from the lowest (or highest) levels of an organization or interpersonal network, this may shape interviews with members from the other levels in undesired ways. Try to avoid an "elite bias" (Myers & Newman, 2007, p. 5) by talking only to the high-status or star members of an organization (Miles & Huberman, 1994).

That said, sometimes it is important to consider who might be interviewed and in what sequence in order to gain trust with a community, family, or workplace. For example, when entering a new community it may be that interviewing a trusted community member makes other community members feel comfortable in interviewing as well—especially as the trusted community member vouches for the research project and interview experience. If exploring workplace relationships, it may be helpful to interview the boss first so that a statement such as "Now I've already interviewed your boss, and just as I won't tell you what she said, I won't tell her what you said" can be offered and a more open interviewing climate established. If interviewing multiple members of a family, consider how sometimes they may seek information about each other in a way that is not always straightforward (and may unintentionally reveal confidential information). For instance, a family member might say, "I'm sure my niece told you about our fight." This is a tough situation for an interviewer. If the response is, "Why, yes, she did," then that betrays the promised confidentiality in an interview. If the response is, "No, she did not," then that could reflect upon confidentiality (what is not said is just as important as what is) or honesty. Having a response such as, "Why don't you tell me about that situation?" is good, and if asked directly a response might be, "Just as I won't talk to her about our interview, I won't talk to you about hers." Knowing about the family fight in advance, if possible, can help to create an interviewing sequence that may eliminate such potential discomfort.

Being Mindful About Interview Objectives

Third, the researcher should design his or her interview questions in line with the research objectives and goals. This will help generate the desired kind of data. Clearly, interview questions can be designed so as to produce wonderful interviews; however, if not carefully considered, interview questions can confuse interviewees and lead to interviews not worth including as part of the research. In fact, any question or item that does not either directly elicit desired data or set the context for doing so is essentially a waste of the interviewee's and interviewer's time. Once the interview questions are constructed, they should be pilot tested and asked of a group of people not involved in the research to make sure they are understandable and answerable (Babbie, 2010).

One particular consideration researchers might make about clarity and interviewing is that sometimes, in order to gain a sense of what is happening, it is important to provide information that will allow a participant to do so. For example, suppose a researcher were trying to understand how gossip, rumors, and lies were playing out among coworkers. It is entirely possible that participants do not know the subtle differences between "gossip" and "rumors." Depending on the research question, it may be important to provide the participant with a working definition of each word so that he or she understands how stories solicited about gossip will be different from those about rumors. Explaining a definition is not leading—it is making sure that a participant has the necessary information needed to answer a question and that she or he does not become confused when asked about rumors just moments after being asked about gossip. However, if a research question were seeking to see whether or not people understood the difference between rumors and gossip, then a definition would likely not be offered. As with most qualitative research, the research question or project statement helps to drive what is needed.

Knowing the Interview Protocol Well

Fourth, it is critical that the interviewer is intimately familiar with his or her interview questions and format. If the researcher is using a highly structured interview format, he or she needs to be especially cautious in how the questions get asked in terms of uniformity and consistency. A highly structured format also requires that the interviewer ask every question in the same sequence and exactly as written. An unstructured format, on the other hand, yields more flexibility in terms of how, when, and whether certain questions get asked. Using an unstructured format requires that the researcher is flexible, open, and able to improvise depending on the situation and how the respondent reacts and responds to questions. As noted earlier, using structured or unstructured interview questions is a methodological choice that should be guided and determined by the objectives and goals of the research study. As Dilley (2000) notes, "The questions form a script for us to use, but like every good actor, we should know our lines well before the curtain rises" (p. 133). Researchers should keep in mind that high structure does not necessarily result in high validity. Sometimes too much structure smothers the meaning-making created in an interview. The second and final chapters of this book are helpful in considering just how structured a particular interview (or any other kind of qualitative study) should be.

Being Reflexive

Finally, in the actual interview setting, there is a series of things the interviewer can do to collect high-quality data. Being a focused, attentive, active, and responsive listener is key to an interviewer's interpersonal skills. High-quality interviewers will also pay attention to verbal and nonverbal cues from respondents, especially if any confusion is perceived. Better listening habits tend to generate better interview data (Lindlof & Taylor, 2011). Moreover, the interviewer should ask questions slowly and in a clear and well-modulated tone of voice (Singleton & Straits, 2010). The researcher needs to become comfortable with silence and pausing, allowing a respondent time to answer (sometimes difficult) questions. Thus, it is crucial that the interviewer never assumes answers to questions nor puts answers in a respondent's mouth. It is as important to have the interviewee explain in his or her own words as it is to find out his or her knowledge, perceptions, explanations, and opinions.

To connect the researcher and respondent, take care to avoid an intimidating presence. The interviewer should consider how he or she is dressed and his or her overall demeanor. If interviewing a community of artists, it may not be the best choice to dress in a suit and tie for the interview; although if interviewing a businessman, it may make him at ease and more open if the interviewer is not in jeans and a T-shirt. There is no simple recipe for appearance in interviews, so considering context and adjusting after an initial interview if a bad choice was made can be helpful. Lastly, questions should be asked in a nonthreatening way, and the interviewer should act as an avid and interested learner or student who presents a positive and nonjudgmental stance (Lindlof & Taylor, 2011). Typically an interviewer should not argue, debate, or appear shocked.

Overall, the best practices delineated here will likely enhance the collection of rich, interesting, and meaningful data while demonstrating that research participants are incredibly valuable and important. Interviewing is an art and a skill, one that can be learned. Indeed, "the most effective way to become a better interviewer is to interview, frequently and self-critically" (Dilley, 2000, p. 135).

USING EMOTION CODING IN RELATIONSHIPS RESEARCH

To help guide understanding about how interviewing can be effectively used in interpersonal relationships research, we have included an illustrative research report from two scholars well experienced in using interviews for their work, Laura Ellingson and Patty Sotirin. Before we get to their research study, we want to engage a heightened focus on the analytical tool they used for their study. As we mentioned in the opening chapters of this monograph, much too often analysis is the underused (or even missing) component of qualitative research. Researchers tend to use the same analytical tools repeatedly and oftentimes in a way that does not honor the tool's metatheoretical assumptions. So here—and with the methods chapters that follow—we present a tool that makes a particularly good fit with interpersonal communication research so as to introduce new analytical tools to the discipline and illustrate their use. For this chapter, that tool is emotion coding (Saldaña, 2009). Although here emotion coding is paired with interviewing, this form of coding (as is the case with most qualitative analytical tools) can be used with most kinds of interpretivist data.

An Overview of Emotion Coding

The roots of emotion coding can be found in Prus's (1996) work on symbolic interaction and ethnographic research where he examined how emotional meaning permeates through a social scene. Saldaña (2009) advanced these ideas into a full-blown analytical tool and demonstrated their practicality using interview data from people who went to bars seeking out sexual relationships, demonstrating the anxieties they might face in such a process. As Saldaña notes, emotion coding is "appropriate for virtually all qualitative studies, but particularly for those that explore intrapersonal and interpersonal participant experiences and actions" (p. 86). Even though the connections between emotion and meaning are evident, they largely remain unexplored. As such, using emotion coding allows qualitative researchers an exciting chance to make sense of the sometimes conflicting and often multilayered articulations and demonstrations of emotion within a social scene. In the remainder of this section, we gently reframe emotion coding so as to specifically guide it toward analyzing data about personal relationships. After demonstrating emotion coding through an exemplar, we offer some ways it may be used in interpersonal communication studies.

The job of the interpersonal qualitative researcher often is to consider how emotion plays into (and perhaps even constitutes) meaning. Oftentimes, postpositivist research exclusively places emotion in the mind of a person (Blumer, 1969; Saldaña, 2009), belying the lived notion that emotion circulates throughout a social scene (and ignoring the bodies that perform, respond to, and otherwise display emotion). As Corbin and Strauss (2008) observe, "One can't separate emotion from action; they are part of the same flow of events, one leading into the other" (p. 7). Those using emotion coding, then, will need to consider an entire social scene as part of their analysis and not simply the words used in a research situation. That means that analytic memos may come into play and that emotions observed in a social situation will need to be coded. Coding occurs when emotions are explicitly articulated, made evident through discourse, or observed through action. Here is one example of emotion coding, taken from an interview with a woman whose husband is concerned about his daughter beginning to date:

[Mike], you know, he, [1]uh, he really gets [2]upset	1 *anxiety*
thinking about it. Like when she wants to go to	2 "upset"
a movie in a group date, he really [3]worries and	3 "worries"
thinks she might wanna leave, and [4]you know,	4 *anxiety*
[5]take off with a boy or something instead of stay	5 *ridicule*
and watch the show. He gets [6]that way.	6 worried

As can be seen here, each emotion being coded was assigned a number in the text so as to match the particular code. For three of the items (codes 1, 4, and 5) the emotion coding is based more off of inflection or actions accompanying statements rather than the words in and of themselves. As such, they were labeled using italics (or underlined, if coding by hand) to show that they were observed in the interaction even if they are not necessarily apparent from the transcript. This kind of coding relies on recording good analytical memos or journaling after an interview session about what was witnessed. Notes taken during interviews may be helpful for this kind of coding as well, although researchers should be cautious not to play the naïve psychologist guessing the underlying meaning of every action or word. A researcher may also choose to look exclusively at the verbal elements of emotion, although that should be made clear in presenting the research. Two of the codes (numbers 2 and 3) were placed in quotation marks to demonstrate that they were the participant's direct words (or coded *in vivo*). In later stages of analysis, like words will likely be paired together for broader understanding. Finally, one code (number 6) shows a direct interpretation from the words about the emotion displayed. "That way" is vague in and of itself, but there is enough evidence in the data to indicate "that way" probably means worried.

Alone, the chunk of data as analyzed through emotion coding does not reveal much. It suggests that a father is seen as being nervous or worried about his daughter dating and that his wife might see the worrying as a little much. Because chunks of data will often point to limited, often one-dimensional expressions of emotion, it becomes important to look across the same interview (or other data sources) and data collection as a whole for how emotion varies and what that might mean. Oftentimes magnitude, conflict, or difference in emotional display can lead to a deeper sense of meaning-making about relationships.

For example, if the father mentioned earlier does not exhibit worry about his son dating, then that can lead to one conclusion. Or if the father says it is the mother who worries and then ridicules her worrying, that might lead to a different direction. Looking at emotion across a data set, considering how emotion circulates throughout that data set, and then thinking about how that data speak to the social scene from where they came allow an opportunity for theorizing about meaning-making and relationships.

Because meaning and emotion might vary across a data set, it is almost certain that after the initial coding period (where the *in vivo*, interpreted, and observed emotions are coded), additional rounds of coding will occur where people, things, or ideas are associated with an emotion (e.g., WORRIED—Dad, WORRIED—Mom, WORRIED—Brother, WORRIED—Daughter or WORRIED—Dating, WORRIED—Money, WORRIED—Grades, WORRIED—Happiness). Additional coding rounds might also deal with particular qualities that help to explain the emotion's existence (e.g., WORRIED—Sexual Activity, WORRIED—Illegal Activity, WORRIED—School Performance). Further rounds of coding will depend upon research objectives as well as emerging ideas or hunches that come from reviewing earlier rounds of coding. While the end result of an emotion coding process is open to matching up to a research question or objective, we examine three particularly fruitful possibilities here.

Typology of Emotional Experiences

Emotion coding is ideal for developing a sensitizing typology of emotional experiences. (See Chapter 5 for a description of taxonomic coding, an analytical process that could be used with coded emotions.) For example, a data set about a person's experiences with online dating could be coded in order to provide an understanding of what kinds of emotions one can expect to find in an online dating process. With each of the salient emotions, exemplars could be provided to show how the emotion is being articulated (or how it was observed by the researcher and recorded in memos or field notes) so as to allow a sense of feeling to go along with the analytical description. It may be, depending on the results of the analysis, that different kinds of emotions are associated with different kinds of online daters. Developing an emotional typology would require a clear articulation of who the typology represented, the particular emotions associated with what experiences, and data that undergird and support the categorizing.

Models of Emotional Associations

Oftentimes people make meaning of life experience through the emotions they associate with that life experience. As Albrecht (1980) found when he studied divorce, particular emotions were associated with particular elements that came with the divorce progression. People frequently found themselves faced with emotions of personal failure when coming to the conclusion that divorce was inevitable, hatred when involved with custody hearings, and feelings of revenge when signing divorce papers. As this research demonstrates, particular events in a divorce proceeding are laden with emotions, and understanding these potential emotions can help people as they endure a divorce proceeding. In cases where particular events or activities almost certainly contain particular steps or elements, models of emotional associations can help to unpack meanings associated with such elements and allow theorizing that prepares people for what they might face in such emotional encounters. Unlike other models that are sometimes criticized for trying to make processes linear and rational that probably do not follow a particular emotional trajectory (see Teo, 2005, for a full discussion), the use of emotions is appropriate here because it is not the emotional processes that are necessarily linear; it is the emotional associations to a particular scene that make the models work.

Exploring Emotion in Existing Theoretical Contexts

Emotion coding may allow for understandings of how emotion is laden in social scenes where other theoretical processes have been identified. As explored in the opening chapters of this book, qualitative research can work to extend existing theory (whether it was developed with postpositivist or interpretivist research). Understanding how postpositivist theories materialize or manifest in social scenes, especially as they are lived or experienced by the actors engaged in those social scenes, is one of the greatest unrealized potentials of interpretivist research for interpersonal communication studies. Expressions of emotion are one possible link to extensions of such theories. For example, ethnographic observation of first dates could allow for firsthand experience of uncertainty reduction theory (a postpositivist theory developed by Berger and Calabrese, 1975) as lived experience, and emotions revealed (or concealed) during that process could be coded in order to understand how people come to reduce any anxieties they may have about their potential new romantic paramour. Such an endeavor would first involve the qualitative researcher establishing how the developed theory is at play in the social scene and then applying a coding or analytical mechanism to come to a deeper understanding of the theory.

Another Approach to Emotion Coding

While the aspects of emotion coding listed here hold much promise for interpersonal communication studies, there are other possibilities as well. We now turn to Sotirin and Ellingson's research study on aunting to help illustrate another way emotion coding comes into play. Readers will certainly notice that they do exactly what good qualitative researchers should: they make the coding mechanism their own, using it in a way that is true to their research objectives and metatheoretical stances. Further, they clearly articulate changes they made from the original emotion coding mechanism. Following their research study is an annotated transcript from an interview session where they shared their insights about using emotion coding for the first time as well as their views on interviewing, the future of qualitative research, and working as research partners, among other things.

Aunts and the Emotional Experience of Generativity

An Illustrative Research Study Using Interviews and Emotion Coding

Patricia Sotirin, Michigan Technical University,
and Laura Ellingson, Santa Clara University

One important aspect of many families is extended kinship relationships, yet that topic has been understudied by family researchers who remain more focused on the heterosexual, intact nuclear family (Floyd & Morman, 2006). Aunts and their nieces or nephews are one type of kinship relationship about which too little is understood. Aunts are not nuclear family members, but they also are not distant relations; usually they are a sibling from a parent's immediate family of origin or otherwise closely connected. Evidence of the centrality of aunts in family relations abounds in family stories, everyday conversation, and several popular tributes to aunts (e.g., Christiansen & Brophy,

2007; Sturgis, 2004; Traeder & Bennett, 1998). Family communication researchers typically study women as daughters, sisters, mothers, or grandmothers. Yet many, if not most, women in these roles are also aunts. With few exceptions, the aunt role is glossed over in studies of kinship relationships in favor of framing motherhood as the essential role of women (O'Reilly & Abbey, 2000; Peington, 2004; Rich, 1976).

While some argue that the family is in crisis, we hold that aunting—the communicative practices that collectively enact aunt roles, obligations, expectations, and ideals—is helping to sustain the many forms of contemporary U.S. families that prove resilient under changing demands and conditions (Ellingson & Sotirin, 2006, 2010; Sotirin & Ellingson, 2006). In our research, we have found aunts relate with their nieces and nephews in a wide variety of ways, including as role models, child care providers, godmothers, spiritual advisers, confidantes, intermediaries between parents and children, mentors, and friends. Here we focus on one important aspect of aunting, generativity, or the "concern for and commitment to promoting the well-being of future generations" (McAdams, 2004, p. 236; McAdams & de St. Aubin, 1992). Within aunting relationships, generativity involves the passing on of family heritage, lore, values, and traditions across generations.

Review of Literature

Aunts and Generativity

Not only the content of family stories but also the act of sharing stories connects extended family members across time and place and contributes to the survival and well-being of individual families' past, present, and future (Langellier & Peterson, 2006a, 2006b). Narration is a critical aspect of generativity; both people and families use narratives as a way to create a sense of place in an ongoing story and to nurture or preserve family legacies, traditions, and meanings (Jorgenson & Bochner, 2004; McAdams & de St. Aubin, 1992). Generativity is associated with parenthood and later life, but studies indicate that generativity may develop in the transition into adulthood from adolescence, although young adults may not have the opportunities and resources to realize generative impulses until they are older (Milardo, 2010). Generativity is associated with a wide range of prosocial behaviors and attributes including strong social networks, community and civic voluntarism, and involvement in religious or spiritual communities (Freedman, 1993; Rossi, 2001).

Generativity shifts the focus of research from the nuclear family to multigenerational and extended family relations. Recent research indicates that generativity is expressed among aunts, uncles, nieces, and nephews as well as grandparents, children, and grandchildren (Ellingson & Sotirin, 2010; Milardo, 2010). Not only do uncles and aunts express concern and care for the continuity and well-being of an extended family but also nieces and nephews express their desire to reciprocate these feelings of care and concern.

Emotions in the Family

The expression of emotions within families is extremely complex, with members exerting significant mutual influence. Emotions "can be thought of as the currency of family relationships, imbuing them with meaning and importance" (Fitness & Duffield, 2004, p. 473; for an overview of differing approaches to defining emotion, see de Sousa, 2010). From a functional or pragmatic perspective, expressions of emotions serve to inform others of what matters to us; that is, what we need or desire (Fitness & Duffield, 2004). We tend to communicate our emotions more within intimate relationships as we respond to others' needs and expect them to be responsive to our own

(Clark, Fitness, & Brissette, 2001). People in contemporary Western cultures expect to receive a great deal of love and care within their families, and the family remains the center of emotional experience. Expectations of intense emotional connection within families were not true in the past, often remain unfulfilled today, and do not account for the violence and abuse experienced in some families (Coltrane & Adams, 2008).[1] Most research on emotional expression focuses on spouses and children, although those immediate family relationships and experiences of emotion can be influenced by extended and blended family members, including aunts and uncles (Fitness & Duffield, 2004).

There has been little attention to the emotions that characterize expressions of generativity despite the importance of generativity to family well-being and resilience. In particular, we sought to answer the following research question:

RQ: What emotions do aunts and nieces and nephews report in expressions of generativity?

Method

This analysis forms part of a larger research project on aunts for which we gathered 40 interviews and over 100 written narratives with aunts, nieces, and nephews from across the United States, reflecting a diverse representation across race or ethnicity, age, religion, region, socioeconomic class, and immigrant or citizenship status (see Ellingson & Sotirin, 2010, for complete methodology). For this particular analysis, we used all sections of data that we had previously categorized as reflecting generativity. That is, we scrutinized sections of data in which our participants narrated hopes and concerns regarding both the legacies of their aunts and their own future contributions to their kinship networks as aunts and as nieces or nephews. Because we were interested in emotions, we initially conducted emotion coding, a postpositivist approach labeling emotions expressed by participants' talk with labels that consist of emotions (e.g., *happy, sad, excited*; e.g., Plutchik, 1981; Saldaña, 2009).

After attempting to use this form of emotion coding, we found it inconsistent with our feminist values, priorities, and customary modes of analysis and reflection. While we would not claim that postpositivist emotion coding is ethically objectionable, the practice reflects an epistemology much closer to the realist/postpositivist end of the qualitative continuum than the social constructionist and interpretive (middle and toward the art end) spaces we typically inhabit (see Ellingson, 2009, for a discussion of the art/science continuum in qualitative research). Thus, we developed our own feminist, interpretive approach to emotion coding, which embodies three primary interpretive divergences from the postpositivist version. First, we acknowledge our perspective as communication researchers who study aunts and gendered communication, attentive to narratives, to meaning as relational, and to language as not fixed but fluid. Second, our approach assumes that all categories and themes are researchers' constructions that were not self-evident or preexisting ideas that we simply labeled in our data. Rather, we actively interfaced with the data and constructed our findings intersubjectively (i.e., in dialogue with each other and with continual reflective consideration of participants' voices). And third, we acknowledge our feminist theoretical commitments, particularly our awareness of privileged and marginalized forms of relating and our critique of the idealized heterosexual, intact, nuclear family, which undoubtedly shaped our analysis.

---

[1] Caring remains deeply gendered, with women historically and currently at the center of giving and receiving both physical and emotional nurturing in families (Coltrane & Adams, 2008), despite important changes in men's caregiving activities and expressions (Fitness & Duffield, 2004).

Results

Our participants expressed close associations among multiple emotions as they told stories of aunts that reflected generative impulses. We address each of the primary emotions expressed by participants separately here for clarity of explanation. However, we note that these emotions were deeply intertwined within the data. Participants wove complex narratives with multiple emotional nuances rather than one singular emotion. Research documents that people generally do not experience emotions as discrete but rather in sets (see Plutchik, 2001, for his psychoevolutionary theory of the complexity of emotions). We propose that emotions expressed in relation to generativity include love, grief, gratitude, and hope.

Love

Nieces and nephews who told us of deceased aunts reported feeling deep love for their aunts. Susan, a European American 21-year-old niece, described the close relationship that she had with her aunt:

> My Aunt Phoebe meant the world to me. She was married to my dad's brother and was definitely a loved relative by all. I loved her because she was so real. She was incredibly down to earth and never treated me like I was a little girl. That was my biggest problem growing up the youngest. However my Auntie Phoebe made me feel like the queen of the world. I remember when she gave birth to my cousin Katie. I was only 8 and she let me hold her.

The linkages between love and generativity are evident in the intensity of the language Susan uses to share her story as well as in the story itself about the love her aunt inspired and the love this aunt demonstrated for her niece by including the niece in the celebration of the new baby. The story attests to the importance of generative impulses as kinship-based resources that benefit family members in the face of changing family dynamics, in this case, the birth of a child. Another niece, Leslie, related the lesson of her great aunt's love:

> I learned that everyone needs someone in their life who thinks that they are the greatest thing since electricity and that making investments in the lives of people can change the course of lives.

Framing this as a lesson learned from her great aunt, Leslie clearly takes this wisdom to heart. A loving investment in the lives of younger generations in the family is an enactment of generativity that the niece recognizes as such in this story.

Grief

Many participants shared their profound grief at the loss of aunts whom they have loved. Returning to Susan's story, the news of her aunt's terminal cancer diagnosis evokes tears and an expression of loss:

> I have recently lost an aunt that meant a lot to me. . . . It was six years ago when my mom told me that my Auntie Phoebe had cancer and they did not expect her to live more than five years. I could do nothing but cry.

This story attests to the ongoing significance of a deceased aunt and the grief her passing continues to inspire in the niece. As a story of generativity, the niece's expression of grief links to a larger cultural narrative about the value of deceased and infirm family members and the cultural maxim that love endures beyond the grave (Pratt & Friese, 2004). Grief is intertwined with the experience of love and reflects a sense both of a deep connection between people (aunt and niece) and of a dialectic of familial continuity and loss. The role of a difficult emotion such as grief in generativity attests to the inevitability of loss, change, and adaptation of the family over time as new generations are born and previous ones die off.

Gratitude

Nieces and nephews expressed gratitude for aunts as a source of family context, heritage, and pride. These expressions indicate an impulse to generativity in the commitment of the niece or nephew to carry on, protect, or share with younger generations the family's history and identity. For example, one niece expressed generativity in her appreciation for an aunt's life story and her own subsequent investment in that history:

I admire [my aunt] the more I get to know her and I learn about her life. She grew up in a completely different era, and through her I have learned a new appreciation for my family. . . . Now I really understand what it means to have history. (Jane, a 21-year-old Native American/European American niece)

Another college-aged niece, April, expressed gratitude for her aunt's loving investment in her, a testament to the aunt's generativity:

[My Aunt] Pam's love for me put me on a path I would never have thought possible without her, and I owe much of who I am today to the experiences and encouragement she gave me.

This niece gratefully imagines a path into the future that has been shaped by her aunt and would be unimaginable without her. Projecting into the future and connecting her aunt's encouragement and guidance to her future plans exhibits the deep connection between generations where wisdom and encouragement assist the younger generation in finding their way through life.

Hope

Nieces and nephews who enacted impulses to generativity often did so with expressions of hopefulness. One theme of generativity in our larger study on nieces, nephews, and aunts was "paying forward" or the impulse to pass along to the next generation the care and concern for well-being that an older generation had given to a niece or nephew. Such stories included expressions of gratitude for the aunt's commitment and personal investment in the nephew or niece, along with hope and often an expression of determination to honor and continue the aunt's legacy. Stories of "paying forward" employ narrative as a way to organize the meaning of family experiences "sequentially and consequentially" (Langellier & Peterson, 2004, p. 112). For example, Susan, the niece whose Aunt Phoebe died of cancer, expressed her desire to "pay forward":

My sister had asked me to be Eliza's godmother. I have decided that I am going to be the best aunt to that little girl. I hope that I can be as good of an aunt to her as Auntie Phoebe was to me. Sometimes, kids need that. It can be hard to confide information in your parents. Having an aunt around that you respect can make growing up so much easier. I was very lucky!

One aunt, Elise, expressed an impulse to generativity as a feeling of hope that she might be a source of support to her nieces and nephews, particularly as they approached their teen years:

> I feel like, if I'm not as strict, if [my nieces and nephews] get in trouble, maybe they can, they'll have somebody to come to besides being on their own, you know, that's the kind of relationship I want. I want them to know that they can talk to me, and I'm not going to go tattle to their parents. . . . I like to be there for them, let them know if they need to talk, if they can't talk to your mom and something comes up or whatever, you know, call me—don't get in worse trouble just because they're scared and lonely and don't know what to do. Call me!

In this passage, the emotion of hope is evident in the injunction to "call me!" as the aunt expresses her desire to attend to the well-being of a younger generation and to "pay forward" in kind the care she received from her own aunts, which included an occasional protective haven from parental judgment when trouble arose. As she repeats that she "wants" this type of relationship to develop, she expresses hope that her nieces and nephews will respond to her care and concern for their physical and emotional safety. As an emotion of generativity, hope affirms the commitment and desire to ensure the well-being of future generations, enacted here as a determination to "be there" for nieces and nephews.

Conclusion

The emotions we describe here enrich our understanding both of aunts and the experience of generativity within extended families. The aunt relationship is not always an emotionally significant one, but many people feel rich emotional investments that extend across generations (Ellingson & Sotirin, 2010). In turn, deeply felt emotions underlie cross-generational connections and the desire to pass on the wisdom and nurturance provided by those of a previous generation. A belief in the ongoing history of family life is a central dimension in generativity (McAdams & de St. Aubin, 1992), and our participants' stories demonstrate that those beliefs are intertwined with multiple emotions, including love, grief, gratitude, and hope. Our brief analysis emphasizes that the experience of both aunting and generativity evoked both positive and negative emotions.

Our approach to emotion coding eschews the postpositivist assumption that emotions preexist our interpretive encounters and instead attends to the narrativity of emotional content in expressions of generativity. As researchers, we engaged with the stories of family relationships, generational bonds, and personal connections that our respondents shared with us. These stories were meaningful emotionally as well as sensically. Hence, our emotion coding entailed responsive interpretations, reminding us that research is itself a relational experience.

Future research may expand on the emotional expressions of generativity or explore how such emotions relate to the experience of generativity in other relationships, such as with grandparents and grandchildren. In addition, the possibility that negatively valenced emotions—such as anger associated with family rifts and rivalries—might express generativity should be investigated. Finally, research might explore how emotions that become ritualized in family stories affect impulses to generativity. Altogether, we commend the emotional complexities of generativity as a fertile focus for relational communication researchers.

Reflecting on the Study

Excerpts From an Interview With Laura Ellingson and Patricia Sotirin

Jimmie: Tell me about emotion coding.

Patty: We make this argument that the emotions that we encountered in this data were much more complex than a simple label. . . . We really got that sense. And so in our own responsiveness we recognized the nuances, we recognized the kind of complexities. I mean it's like looking at Laura's cat. So we're looking at Laura's cat. It's a black cat. But it has different colors in his fur. I mean he's got a lot of brown; the color's so rich because there are these different shadings. But if you were to ask me, I'd say he's black, right? And so, for emotions, if you were to ask me, I'd say there's love, there's gratitude, there's grief, there's hope. But there was, there was really more. It was a combination of a lot of these things. There was a very rich, how do you say, a play of these various emotions, that gave it the richness. That gave it the intensity that we responded to. And so I would never want to just pick out one color from the palette.

Jimmie: Right. Right. Which is like a big part of interpretivism and what we're hoping to find through qualitative research. Those shades.

Laura: We have to start saying there's a lot of shades of grey here, or there's a lot of richness in my cat's fur that collectively might be one color but that there's a lot going on in there. And so what I always tell people is to be very, very open to your creative impulses and possibilities and what you can do. And the other side of that is that you have to be honest to the data the best that you can. You have to be a trustworthy reporter of what you did. . . . Sarah Tracy just published a piece in the brand new journal *Qualitative Communication Research*, about the way traditional research forms force qualitative research to make some bad moves in terms of being intelligible because we put the theory up front as if that is the way it came to us, when really we get to the theory much later in qualitative. . . . We don't know how to then fit it back into the box that we have to get it in to publish it. We have to be very open to thinking about the possibilities, and then we have to be skillful in crafting explanations of what we did and grounding those in things that do make sense to editors and other researchers so that we can get them published.

Jimmie: And in that Sarah Tracy piece she talks about making choices and where ideas come from and that we're blocked from honest accounts of what we did with our research. But she still kind of refers back to this idea that there are, as she said in an earlier article, these big-tent concerns we might ought to have about qualitative research. What might be some suggestions, some guideposts or suggestions, that people might consider embracing or avoiding as they are starting this method for the first time?

Laura: That's a good question. I think what I tell my students in my methods classes when they're starting interviewing is that, go in there with an awareness that interviewing is a conversation. It is between two people. It is not you grabbing some data out of the other person's head. And they always nod at me and go, "Yeah, yeah, yeah . . ." But then after they do their first interview, and they're like, "Oh. That was actually pretty hard." And I go, "Yes. There's a lot of skill to it."

Patty: You have to ask good questions. But mostly interviewing is about listening. . . . The whole process is about listening. First you have to listen to yourself. I mean, why am I asking these questions? What is it that I'm really trying to find out? What is it I am trying to know? I find that people ask questions, and they're not really about what they want to know. They're about what they already know. They're trying to elicit something. . . . And then when you go into the interview, I mean the conversation is about listening. It's about listening to myself and how I'm responding. It's about listening to what the person is saying. And not about responding, but responding to what they're saying. What they're really saying. And then how those things are coming together. And then when you get the data it's about listening to the data. It's about looking at the interview and listening to what is going on there and what people are saying. And embracing your data. I always say qualitative data never die. Because you can listen in different ways and embrace your data and how it resonates in a different context. And listening to what my data says in that context. So in many ways it is all about listening. Not only to the other but to yourself and to the data. It's a practice of embrace. Listening is about embracing and being embraced.

Laura: I agree with that. And I also think it's about presence. . . . Sometimes we're not there. Instead, we're worried about what the next question is going to be. . . . Or we're worried about making notes.

Patty: We're trying to tell our own stories. Half of the time I'm listening to the tape and thinking, "Oh my goodness. This is me telling my story and trying to have rapport."

Laura: And so, what I was going to say is that you have to show up, you have to be present. If you're not really listening to your participants, then you're going to have less than ideal engagement with them. You're not going to have a question that follows well from that. And that means you have to be okay with more silence. You have to give them time to think and reflect, and you have to allow yourself to think and reflect instead of immediately jumping into the silence. . . . We're very scared of silence in Western culture. . . . I read once that qualitative researchers must have a much higher tolerance for ambiguity. We have to be okay with things not being clear-cut. We also have to be more tolerant of silence. We want to jump in with another question, the most obvious question or the question we already have written down. And that might mean we don't ask the best question when we follow up, because we weren't listening. It's okay to say, "You know, I wanna think for a second on how to follow up on that."

Patty: And listening is opening. Opening a space for voices. There's no voice without listening. You can open a space, but if you're not listening you're not allowing somebody an opportunity to have voice. If you're not allowing silence, you're also not giving space. I think silence is a part of voice in that sense.

Jimmie: So I want to go back to something you said earlier Patty. You said you were telling your own stories, and then you went back and listened to your tape and had your thoughts. So do you think that worked for the aunting study? I know there are times that you go into a study, and it is completely appropriate—I hate that word—but you go into your studies and sometimes it is an okay time to tell a story and other times maybe it isn't the right time. So any thoughts on that?

Laura: I try to keep my storytelling and sharing until later in the interview. I try to see if I can't get them to articulate as many things on their own ground.... Then I start throwing out my own experiences to get them to respond to. It's what Patty said about space. I don't want to define the space for them using my own views or reactions; I want them to articulate things on their own grounds.... If you are talking about some of your own narrative practices and ideas, then I think it is okay to do that, but I do think it should be written into the methods as part of what you have done. So I tend to save it until late in the interview, but I don't think there is anything wrong with doing it. Quite to the contrary, I often feel like I have a responsibility—most of my research is in health care, even though I do family research as well—but most of my work is in health care, and so I think it would be incredibly unethical for me to ask people to share their own medical experiences and then not share mine. Even in the aunting study when we're talking about trauma, sadness, or anger, or things that weren't so great about aunts. I guess I felt the same kind of ethic. I wanted to be able to share some of my own stories. And I also did that with a pragmatic intent of trying to get as much out of their space as I could. I tried to throw out some of my own stories to maybe give a little more space by offering my stories and seeing where they came from after hearing those.

Patty: We come at this from different places. I never really thought of myself as an aunt. And I know Laura has. So our stories come from different places, too. I had aunts, and so—

Laura: That's why I thought Patty would be great. I knew she had a different viewpoint on aunts going in, and so we had different perspectives that would help offer different ideas.

Patty: And it changed interviewing, too, because Laura had a lot—

Laura: I had a lot of stories, and so it led to some different interview experiences, and that is where the analysis becomes richer, too, because we do have these different perspectives, and so we would come at the data from different points of view and could dig deeper there ...

Patty: Early on we interviewed each other. Because you're immersed in the process yourself. And it's not just about other people. It's also about us. It's not, tell us about your aunt, it's about us, too.

Laura: And this has been a really big process; I mean this goes back to 2002. We've got one book done, a book in press, and a whole bunch of articles. It's been a really good process. We've also been really annoyed at each other.

Jimmie: So tell me about that.

Laura: What?

Jimmie: All the time we hear about how great it is to work together, but we don't hear about the tension.

Laura: It's about being realistic. We work together because we really like each other and respect each other. And we complement each other.

Patty: There's a lot of complement.

Laura: But that leads to the frustration. It's incredibly productive and frustrating. I'm like, "You're not hearing me! I don't care about that! I want to do this!" Or Patty'll be like, "That's not what I wrote!"

Patty: I know. I'm like, "I'm not arguing with her."

Laura: Yes you are!

Patty: No.

Laura: Yes you are! You just do it much more quietly.

Patty: (*Laughs loudly*).

Laura: But really, the development of our friendship for the last ten years, a decade. We've spent that time collecting this data and arguing about aunts and aunting.... I mean, it took a long time to get going. The initial conversations were initially in 2002.... And even now, it's like we're still learning how to do this. We have to do collaboration every day. It never ceases to amaze me how two people who really like and care about each other—

Patty: It's like a stream or a flow. We ebb and flow. Sometimes it goes quickly, and smoothly, and sometimes it gets all bammed up. And it's not like we sit down and just, things come out. We never do that; we have to sit down and think about things and work things out.

Laura:	And this part of the story never makes it into the methods section.
Jimmie:	It doesn't! And that's why we want to talk about it.
Laura:	It's very important. And quite frankly, having a collaborator often takes longer. It certainly doesn't take less long than doing it yourself. But I think the work is so much better. And, quite frankly, I'd say 90% of the time we've had a blast. And then 10% of the time I think Patty's kind of wanted to poke me in the heart with a pen. But I don't blame her for that because I've certainly wanted to do the same thing back. Is that fair?
Patty:	And most of the time when we don't agree, it's so wonderful to have someone invested in the project. Or who you can call and say, "Does this sentence sound right to you?" Laura's the one who's invested. Laura's the one who's there. You know, we tend to write alone and tend to work alone. But we don't do that with a collaborator. It's fantastic! I can call Laura and ask, "What should we do here?" And it is *we*.
Laura:	Yes!
Patty:	It is both of us. And it's so nice to have different viewpoints and someone who is invested …
Laura:	And when I'm mad at her, I know I'll get over it. It's very much like my partnership with my partner.
Patty:	It's generative; it matters to both of us.
Laura:	And that makes it richer.
Patty:	I know Laura has made me think of things differently and do things differently.
Laura:	And Patty makes me do things differently, too.
Patty:	It really isn't just reading about, or even just thinking about, but taking on another perspective.
Laura:	Digging deeper to those connections to theory. Discourses that are already out there about theory and research. I'm drawn to the messy, big pile of data, and I like to play in that. That work needs to happen. Patty is the one who made a lot of the initial connections about what it means, who pointed me in the direction of stuff already written about this or that.
Jimmie:	Let's talk about that writing process a little. Tell me about your feelings and experiences with writing up the research …

Laura: We have to sit at one computer. That's what we're doing right now. You're interviewing us while we're trying to finish up another part of the aunting project. It's inconvenient because we don't always have time to get together when the project cycle is where it is. She's come to San Jose for a few days first.... I've worked with others where we maybe had a phone call or an e-mail and that was it. But Patty and I have to get together and create a productive tension. It's like the work is struggling to be born ...

Patty: We always start with the data. We always start with the stories. That's what we really start with. What's speaking to us? What are the images that are coming to us out of this data?

Laura: I always pick out the parts I like most. I know we're not supposed to say that. But why is that a bad thing to say? Quite frankly, a lot of my job sucks.... I don't see why we should spend a whole lot of time building up this ridiculous myth that we should be so distanced from our work. What do you hope? What do you like? What do you feel connected to? Do your work about that!

Patty: And that's inspiring, that you move toward something that interests you. And that you enjoy.

Laura: And that's how we ended up in here.

Questions for Growth

1. Going back to S. J. Tracy's (2010) big-tent concerns about qualitative research, what might be particularly tricky or fragile about quality interviewing?

2. Think about the things you are interested in researching. What might be some good research questions that would call for an interview study?

3. What does it mean to say interviewers need to establish rapport? How might you go about doing that? Why is rapport so important in interpersonal communication research studies?

4. Taking the metaphor used for Laura's cat into consideration, what metaphor would you put forward to describe qualitative research? Do you believe it would change from project to project?

Focus Groups, Values Coding, and a Romantic Relationships Study

As mentioned at the beginning of the previous chapter, in many ways interviewing is similar to focus groups. As this chapter quickly illustrates, however, the differences between the two methods yield a different set of possibilities that ultimately allow different kinds of data open to different kinds of analysis. Like interviews, focus groups involve a preplanned conversation about a topic or area. But unlike interviews, focus groups allow a sense of audience (in that everyone being interviewed will see each other and hear what others have to say), as well as interaction (in many situations, interviewers will want to take advantage of the idea that those in a focus group will interact with each other). Moreover, focus groups allow insights into relational groups themselves (such as families, coworkers, or civic groups), and so a sense of lived interaction can be observed. As this chapter illustrates, focus groups have been used to great effect in coming to understand personal relationships and the communication involved with them.

FOCUS GROUPS AND THE STUDY OF RELATIONSHIPS

Singleton and Straits (2010) characterize focus groups as "unstructured discussions among a small group of participants led by a skilled interviewer" (p. 325). Similarly, Krueger and Casey (2009) contend that "a focus group study is a carefully planned series of discussions designed to obtain perceptions on a defined area of interest in a permissive, nonthreatening environment" (p. 2). The primary difference between a one-on-one interview and a focus group is that a one-on-one interview only involves the interviewer and the interviewee, while a focus group involves an interviewer or moderator and a small group, ideally six to twelve people (Lindlof & Taylor, 2011). The use of focus groups originated in the field of sociology, but they have also been used extensively in market research (Calder, 1977; Patton, 1990), as a method for probing people's political beliefs (Gamson, 1992), and as a way for health-related industries to understand health and illness behavior (Heary & Hennessy, 2000; Wilkinson, 1998).

With a focus group, the researcher has the ability to observe how people interact or talk about a particular topic or set of topics—to gather a group's "public" accounts (Sim, 1988). Further, people participating in a focus group have the opportunity to "compare, contrast, and critique each other's perspectives on a topic" (Lindlof & Taylor, 2011, p. 184). This observational process or "group interview" (Morgan, 1997) enables the researcher to garner evidence about participants' experiences and opinions efficiently and directly, as opposed to looking at individual statements in interview data "post hoc" to come to research conclusions (Morgan, 1997).

In contrast, individual interviews give the researcher a great deal of control over the situation because of the closer connection between interviewer and interviewee. And the interviewer can gather much more "private" accounts (Sim, 1998) or information about each participant in much greater depth than a focus group might allow. Focus groups "provide less depth and detail about the opinions and experiences of any given participant" (Morgan, 1997, p. 10), and "a 90-minute focus group discussion among eight to 10 participants will, of necessity, generate roughly a tenth of the information that each participant would provide in an equivalently long individual interview" (Morgan, 1997, p. 11).

As an interpersonal communication scholar, it becomes important to consider what, exactly, *public* means to a given study. Who respondents are talking in front of in a given focus group session is that public—and so responses about a similar topic may change based on that public. For example, if someone were studying how parents communicate disappointment to their children, it may be that in a group of parents selected from a community for a focus group, people adjust their answers based on how their neighbors might view them. So admitting to particular forms of punishment may not be as feasible in a focus group session. If the group of parents were all from the same family—say a group of parents were all lined up at a family reunion—it may be that many of the family practices are learned, expected, and understood, and so there may not be as much hesitancy. Still, power issues among various family members may come into play, and minority views may be stifled as people seek to fit into the family. In yet another scenario, it may be that the focus group is performed with two parents and their children, allowing children input on how they see the topic as well. As one might imagine, a completely different type of data would be provided. As such, consider what is being said in front of whom—or the public articulations made in a focus group.

In short, one of the most compelling reasons to use a focus group methodology is the "group effect" (Carey, 1994). According to Lindlof and Taylor (2011), the group effect

> takes advantage of the fact that, in both ordinary conversations and guided discussions, people draw upon a shared fund of experiences. What occurs in this context is a kind of "chaining" or "cascading" effect in which each person's turn of the conversation links to, or tumbles out of, the topics and expressions that came before it. (p. 183)

Thus, group conversation, idea sharing, and storytelling generate more conversation, idea sharing, and storytelling. As our earlier example illustrates, however, a group conversation also leads to particular concerns about validity.

Validity Concerns in Focus Group Studies

In early consumer research, focus groups were often used as an exploratory technique to test hypotheses, develop questionnaires, or generate survey items, but now they are considered a valid and standalone method of data collection. Any seasoned scholar recognizes the fact that "being there" during the research (as opposed to sending out links to online surveys, for example) lends much validity to qualitative approaches and methods (Babbie, 2010). Researchers who use qualitative methods are keenly aware that people make observations in different ways and that the observational process can be highly personal. One of the big validity issues with focus group research is whether people talk similarly about a topic in a group compared to how they would in an individual interview. In a focus group setting, it is conceivable that participants may feel pressure to appear socially appropriate or desirable to the researcher (Byers & Wilcox, 1991), and thus participants may conform or alter their opinions to be consistent with what the rest of the group is saying, a phenomenon called "groupthink" (Janis, 1982, p. 243). Groupthink can threaten the validity of a research study because if people feel they have to work toward a consensus, as opposed to voicing how they truly feel, the data are not accurate or meaningful.

In his classic book on focus groups, *Focus Groups as Qualitative Research*, Morgan (1997) portrays a study of how young men talk about their heterosexual relationships with members of the opposite sex (Wight, 1994). Morgan's (1997) analysis of this study revealed that when the men participated in a *focus group first*, they were much more boisterous and macho in their responses and that these responses carried over to subsequent interviews. In contrast, when the men did the *interviews first*, they had a tendency to present themselves as sensitive and compassionate to the woman's point of view, but that sensitivity tended to fade when the men joined a follow-up focus group. As Morgan (1997) concluded, "If people actually do act differently in groups than they do alone or in dyads, then group and individual interviews will necessarily demonstrate rather different aspects of the overall behavior pattern" (p. 12). Thus, it is important to perform validity checks when conducting focus group research.

Further, Sim (1998) suggests that external validity can be compromised in focus group research. Sim (1998) argues that

> focus group data are firmly contextualized within a specific social situation. They therefore produce "situated" accounts, tied to a particular context of interaction, which may not be a particularly natural one for many participants. Accordingly, it cannot be assumed that what a person says in a focus group is a predictor of what he or she may say in some other social situation. (p. 349)

Another issue to consider regarding the validity of focus groups concerns keeping research questions in mind while conducting focus groups—that is, keeping the entire forest in mind and not getting lost in the tiny trees (or worse, in individual branches). Further, if a researcher is particularly concerned with internal validity, then he or she should ask the same (or similar) questions across the different focus groups involved in a project and have similar (or the same) facilitators conduct the focus groups. Overall, it is possible to conduct focus groups in a manner that enhances validity, particularly if the researcher (or moderator) generates questions and ideas to be discussed in the group that are parsimonious and easy to understand. Moreover, if the researcher stimulates motivation and excitement in the focus group, so that participants really want to talk about the relevant issues, then the results are going to be more authentic, believable, and valid. In addition, researchers should strive to seek out and recruit competent focus group participants so as to improve validity.

Obviously, there are validity issues to consider whenever you are doing any kind of research, including that involving focus groups. Consider the many advantages accrued for the researcher employing focus groups. First, focus group research can serve a heuristic function for other research. For example, focus group data may provide a way to facilitate or pilot test other research methods, such as using focus group questions to discover answers to questions that are then coded as themes that inform eventual survey questions (Keyton, 2010).

Second, because the process of "doing" focus group research is inductive and provides a way to see a real-life, interactive "process" in action (Krueger, 1988, 1998; Morgan, 1997), it is a useful methodology for uncovering feelings and opinions where little is known about a topic (Byers & Wilcox, 1991). Focus groups may also tap into populations that are potentially difficult to access (Keyton, 2010), like people experiencing an illness or members of a sports team. Focus group data can also often be gathered in an economical (Krueger, 1998; Sim, 1998) and efficient (Byers & Wilcox, 1991; Morgan, 1997; Patton, 1990) manner, gaining multiple viewpoints at once.

Finally, research has found that some people really enjoy participating in focus groups (Morgan, 1997; Patton, 1990). Because of this, focus groups may be useful for examining sensitive topics because less inhibited or more outgoing group members may break the ice for more inhibited or shy members (Byers & Wilcox, 1991). Likewise, anxiety-filled people may be more inclined to talk in a group setting as opposed to an individual interview because they feel the power of numbers or bodies. According to Sim (1998), focus group members have reported the experience as a "safe" forum for sharing, and members may "feel supported and empowered by a sense of membership and cohesiveness" (p. 346). Thus, the support that focus group members feel may enable them to agree or disagree, ask questions, and share and compare stories. Morgan (1997) notes that "the comparisons that participants make among each other's experiences and opinions are a valuable source of insights into complex behaviors and motivations" (p. 15). Extreme positions are usually remarked on so people "provide checks and balances on each other that weed out false or extreme views" (Patton, 1990, p. 336). Further, focus groups can be empowering in the sense that participants feel like they are contributing to the process of research.

Employing Focus Groups in Interpersonal Relationship Research

Two published studies illustrate particularly well the strength of focus groups for eliciting *why* relational phenomena occur as they do. Both studies motivated discussion among participants, who were relatively homogeneous in age and sex, to determine the factors that foster or constrain their feelings and social behaviors.

In *Archives of Sexual Behavior*, Graham, Sanders, Milhausen, and McBride (2004) presented their findings about women's sexual arousal based on the interaction of 80 women across nine separate focus groups. The researchers were interested in developing a questionnaire about sexual excitation and inhibition and used the focus group format to inductively inform their efforts. They included English-speaking participants who, though all women at least 18 years old, represented diversity among demographic variables including age, ethnicity, education level, and relationship status. To do so, a variety of tactics were employed for recruiting such as advertisements in newsletters and newspapers and fliers posted in churches, community centers, and campus buildings. When potential participants indicated willingness during a screening interview on the telephone, a demographic survey was mailed to them.

Six mixed groups were organized for age-related homogeneity so that each incorporated only women of ages 18–24, 25–45, or 46 and older. Graham et al. (2004) were quite purposeful with regard to other important variables. By way of overestimation to allow for cancelations and no-shows, a dozen women were assigned to each group. The six mixed groups, that each included no more than six white women or six students, featured two each of the three age ranges. There were also two focus groups comprised of lesbians and/or bisexuals, one of which was for those under 25 years of age, and an 18-years-old-and-above group of African American women.

A discussion guide was constructed to direct moderators. It included a description of the study's purpose as helping to develop "a better understanding of women's sexual arousal . . . and the factors or types of situations that promote or interfere" (Graham et al., 2004, p. 529). Guidelines for participation encouraged respect, privacy, and the sharing of experiences. The guide also included questions representing the three featured topics of sexual arousal and awareness, sexual interest and its relationship to arousal, and factors that enhance or inhibit arousal. Strict adherence to the schedule was not a requirement of the researchers, as ideas for prompting elaboration and allowing participants to generate directions of discussion were included. However, there was expectation that the topic of arousal factors, as a critical objective of the project, would be thoroughly explored.

Though some factors were portrayed at times as either promoting or discouraging arousal, eight categories of arousal-enhancing or arousal-inhibiting factors were identified among the nine focus groups' transcripts. Facilitating arousal were positive feelings about one's body, feeling accepted by potential partners, and feeling desired rather than used. Restricting arousal were factors such as reputation implications, reasons for "putting on the brakes" (e.g., involvement in another relationship), pregnancy and contraception concerns, and negative mood. Sexual approach and initiation was also identified as either enhancing or inhibiting depending on its style and timing. Women described outcomes as being dependent on a man's "game," whether they appreciated being "surprised" or even "overpowered," and whether they responded to polite requests for certain sexual activities. Clearly, Graham et al. (2004) illustrated the ability of the focus group to explore sensitive subjects in great detail and to empower women to literally have a voice in studies about their own sexuality.

Tokic and Pecnik (2010), in the *Journal of Social and Personal Relationships*, examined the perceptions of adolescents regarding the impact of their parents' behaviors on their disclosure to their parents. The researchers acknowledged that self-disclosure by adolescents is critical as a chief source of parental knowledge about their children that, in turn, predicts adolescents' positive adjustment. Identification of factors such as aspects of parental behavior that facilitate or discourage adolescent disclosure is thus an important research objective in family communication and child development studies.

In their native Croatia, Tokic and Pecnik (2010) targeted youth 13–14 years old, as that age has been shown to be one of declining disclosure to parents and increased orientation instead to peers. As members of single-sex adolescent groups have been shown to be more comfortable, four focus groups of four boys and four focus groups of four girls were randomly chosen from a school in Zagreb.

One author moderated the female groups and one moderated the male groups with the direction of a semistructured guide that previewed the purpose and procedures of the meetings, planned questions, and offered a closing commentary. The preview described the participants as the "experts" in parent-adolescent communication to stress the value of their full input. Focus group members were prompted to recall situations in which they disclosed to their parents and parental behaviors that encouraged them, as well as situations in which they instead withheld information and reasons why they decided not to disclose. Questions were framed as generally as possible before being further specified to avoid leading too much.

Transcripts of recorded meetings were content analyzed so as to code "participants' open-ended talk into closed categories that summarized and systematized the data" (Tokic & Pecnik, 2010, p. 206). Five themes of disclosure-enhancing and disclosure-inhibiting factors were identified among prior parental states and behaviors as well as their reactions to disclosures. Facilitators of disclosure included interpersonal involvement (e.g., positive affect, having fun), autonomy supportive involvement (e.g., unobtrusive questioning, inviting unconditional disclosure), autonomy support (e.g., empathic understanding, attentive listening), autonomy supportive structure (e.g., constructive feedback, instrumental support), and structure (e.g., approving adolescents' requests). Inhibitors were lack of interpersonal involvement (e.g., negative affect, distraction), autonomy unsupportive involvement (e.g., intrusive questioning, teasing and frivolousness), lack of autonomy support (e.g., interrupting, not trusting, breaking confidentiality), autonomy unsupportive structure (e.g., nagging, anger, punishment and yelling), and structure (e.g., expressing disapproval in advance, disapproving requests).

This focus group study promoted discussion to the extent that the researchers also reported "serendipitous findings" (Tokic & Pecnik, 2010, p. 216), including that parental gender and personality and context/situational aspects, such as content of the disclosure and history of offenses, were also significant factors.

Best Practices for Conducting Focus Groups

As with all research methods, there are more or less effective ways to conduct them. To this point, we have highlighted the strengths of focus groups, with an emphasis on how they have been used to study personal relationships (e.g., Graham et al., 2004; Tokic & Pecnik, 2010). As with any method, it is important to consider the potential shortcomings as a means to overcoming them. So, in addition to noting a potential weakness of focus groups that can be reframed for use in the best way possible (our first suggestion that follows), this section also includes a discussion of best practices that are not as complex and fragile (the last four items). So while everything here is a best practice, the first item on our list is almost a "must practice" given how it is often the greatest source of weakness in a focus group study.

Carefully Consider Group Dynamics

Consider that, when six or more people are recruited and joined together to talk about an issue they care about, they may have intense emotions or disagreements (and some people are just naturally more outgoing and comfortable voicing their opinions in a group setting). Thus, it is possible that one member of a group can feel so passionately about a given topic that he or she starts to dominate the conversation (Sim, 1998), which can lead others to experience negative emotions or feel silenced. According to Lindlof and Taylor (2011), "The trick is to empower people to speak more candidly than they normally might in 'mixed company,' without raising emotional temperatures or pitting one against another and without the participants taking offense at others' viewpoints or retreating into a defensive crouch" (p. 184). And while the goal is to get people feeling comfortable enough to share their opinions, there is really no way to guarantee confidentiality (Patton, 1990). This is why the researcher must try to ensure confidentiality as much as possible, both in consent forms and by strongly encouraging participants to "keep the discussion within these four walls."

Moreover, Krueger (1988) argues that, as compared to individual interviews, the researcher has a lot less control over the focus group conversation. Usually the group determines where the conversation might lead, and it takes an especially skilled and practiced moderator or facilitator to bring the conversation back around to the issue at hand. In addition, instead of one person asking a question and one person responding (like in an individual interview), with a focus group, a moderator may ask a question and five people might respond, and so untangling the responses from one another during the transcription process can be difficult. Such piggybacking of comments can also lead to the conversation straying further off track from the intended topic.

Finally, the kind of interaction found in a focus group is less natural than that found in everyday life. The interaction in a focus group is not totally natural because it is stimulated by a moderator who has the capability to overinfluence the group or stop the group when immersed in an issue that does not conform 100% to the moderator's list of questions (and sometimes this deviation is where the most compelling or interesting data gets produced!). Keep in mind, too, that not everyone has to talk within a group for the data to be meaningful and valid. Just as some folks never talk in everyday conversations, some folks will also be silent in focus groups. That is a part of everyday interaction, and in that silence meaning can also be found.

Consider Research Objectives When Considering Who Will Be in a Focus Group

Determine the objectives of the research and the kind of data that would be most useful for meeting those objectives (Axelrod, 1975). Consider whether more "natural" (or unstructured) or more formatted (or structured) focus group interaction is more useful for answering a particular study's research questions. Clearly, the level of formality in a focus group is going to vary greatly depending on who is participating and the nature of the subject matter. As an interesting example, Morgan (1989) studied "widowhood" and asked *only one question* across six focus groups—"What kinds of things have made being widowed either easier or harder for you?" (Morgan, 1997, p. 18). The study was very unstructured and informal, but the participants were very committed to the topic and wanted to talk about it. Obviously, the one question that Morgan (1989) asked generated the type and kind of data that he wanted to examine for his study.

Think About Recruitment as a Focus Group Session Is Being Designed

Consider how the focus group study participants will be recruited. One rule of thumb is to always overrecruit, as many of your participants will fail to show up. As noted earlier, the ideal focus group has between six and twelve participants (Lindlof & Taylor, 2011). If you wanted to ensure a six-person group, it might be wise to recruit eight to ten people for that group. Even after you have a participant's word that he or she will be there for the study, be sure to call them and remind them in advance. Further, if there is any way to offer some type of incentive for participating (e.g., a gift card, a small amount of cash, a free lunch), then do it! Tell participants in advance that they will be at the focus group meeting area for two hours. While most focus groups do not last beyond 90 minutes, you definitely do not want people getting antsy at the 90-minute mark. Further, assemble the group in an environment that feels safe and where people feel comfortable sharing (a living room or an office space set up with comfortable chairs and low lighting).

In addition to general recruitment issues, it is probably wise to design your focus group study so that you have three to five focus groups. Having more groups affords a way to enhance reliability, while more than five groups probably will not lead to new insights (the goal, of course, is saturation; Keyton, 2010). Consider the type of people you want participating in your group—do you want them to be similar to or different from one another? According to Lindlof and Taylor (2011), groups of strangers are better for exploring more public issues, tend to be more responsive to the moderator, and tend not to get distracted by one another. However, Lindlof and Taylor (2011) contend that preexisting, or more homogeneous, groups with a shared history (and possibly similar social backgrounds, education, knowledge, and experiences) have the advantage of being able to engage in and maintain a healthy flow of conversation without a lot of prompting.

Find a Neutral and Skilled Facilitator for Focus Group Sessions

A skilled yet seemingly "neutral" (Krueger & Casey, 2009) facilitator or moderator should conduct the focus group. A moderator's interpersonal or conversational skills, personal characteristics, personality, and social identity can influence data collection (Keyton, 2010). Often a moderator opens the session by introducing the topic in an honest yet general way. Another effective practice is to start with an icebreaker question to get participants comfortable with one another and the group setting. In addition, informing participants that there are no right or wrong answers may lead to more interaction and less self-censoring. According to Lindlof and Taylor (2011),

> Moderating the focus group is a challenging job. There are fine lines to walk between encouraging each person to speak and promoting a positive group feeling; between promoting a robust, uninhibited discussion and gently tamping down a domineering group member; between ensuring that all key questions are asked and not inserting oneself too forcefully in the discussion. (p. 185)

Moderators have to be well prepared and consistently balance a comfortable talking space while keeping the discussion focused and on task.

Moderators also have to balance the roles of passive observer or listener and active participant (Axelrod, 1975; Sim, 1998). With the help of a skilled moderator, "a sense of supportive intimacy can flourish" (Lindlof & Taylor, 2011, p. 183) such that people feel open to discussing potentially sensitive or controversial topics. An effective moderator knows how to deal with domineering participants and extremely shy participants (Patton, 1990). One effective practice may be for a moderator to watch a tape of himself or herself moderating a focus group. We all learn from our mistakes and achievements, and seeing them live can contribute to this learning process. In addition, it may be useful to have two people "moderating" the focus group—one person asking the questions or facilitating the conversation and the other person taking notes. So, even if the focus group is audio or video recorded, the note taker may catch fine nuances or changes in the interaction that the other moderator or recording devices miss. Also, having two moderators gives them a chance to discuss the strengths and weaknesses of how the focus group went so that errors can be avoided in the future.

Link Analysis Back to Who Is Saying What in Front of Whom

Pay a great deal of attention to the analysis of the focus group data (Axelrod, 1975). Consider the actual words, the meaning of those words, and the context in which those words were shared (Krueger & Casey, 2009). Pay close attention to changes in people and in the overall group interaction as the focus group progresses, as these changes can provide valuable insights (Krueger & Casey, 2009). One key to strong analysis of focus group data is noting how interaction is occurring. While it should not be obvious, it is not a bad idea to have helpers in a focus group (maybe even a confederate, depending on design) who do not interact with other members but take notes about how interaction is occurring, including nonverbal behaviors. Oftentimes focus groups are filmed, rather than simply audio recorded, in order to notice nonverbal communication (although this can be tricky, too, because one camera usually cannot capture all of the people involved in focus group interaction).

The best practices just discussed are likely to maximize the benefits of focus group data collection by researchers hoping to obtain meaningful data while also respecting and caring for their research participants. Given the similarities between focus groups and interviews, keep in mind the advice presented in the previous chapter regarding question construction and creating open questions that avoid leading or embedding assumption. Finally, those interested in reviewing a well-theorized, clearly articulated research example should locate Koenig Kellas and Suter's (2012) write-up of a study involving focus group interviews with mothers who identify as lesbian. That article does an especially nice job of clearly identifying where data exemplars come from across focus groups.

USING VALUES CODING IN RELATIONSHIPS RESEARCH

The illustrative research report included in this chapter comes from Laura Stafford, an interpersonal communication scholar who is well known and respected for her quantitative work but new to interpretivist-oriented qualitative research. We asked her to consider trying on this form of research and analysis to allow readers insights from someone who typically uses (and was largely trained in) postpositivist analysis. Laura agreed to use focus group data about friends-with-benefits relationships after we requested she contribute to this book. She teamed with Rachel Price and Molly Reynolds, two graduate student colleagues, to conduct the study, analyze the data, and write up the research report. At our request, she agreed to analyze her data using values coding (Saldaña, 2009). In this study values coding is paired with focus groups, but just as with emotion coding in the previous chapter, this form of coding can be used with most kinds of interpretivist data.

An Overview of Values Coding

Values coding is a method of analysis that examines how attitudes, values, and beliefs are articulated or otherwise performed in order to understand how a values system interplays with meaning in a social scene. The roots of values coding trace to work from Gable and Wolf (1993) and LeCompte and Preissle (1993), all of whom explored how values played into their analysis. In a study of why people found theater important, Saldaña (1998) drew from those sources to begin considering how values are weaved into social constructions. His observations of values eventually led to the development of values coding (Saldaña, 2009) as a general analytical tool for interpretivist researchers. Here, we modify values coding so that it can be used in research exploring interpersonal relationships. Given its focus on understanding how elements of social worlds interweave to form complex and multifaceted systems of meaning, values coding is an excellent tool for coming to deeper understandings of what people believe about relationships as well as how they feel about them. Values coding is also an attractive tool for interpersonal communication researchers who align with critical theory, as it allows for insights as to why marginalized relationships (or marginalized people in relationships) may be discriminated against or otherwise oppressed by people or cultures.

The key to understanding and using values coding is to examine the three elements coded within a set of transcripts, field notes, or memos: beliefs, attitudes, and values. *Beliefs* are anything that a person holds as true or factual (Saldaña, 2009). It is not the researcher's job to determine whether or not something is true in values coding; rather, it is the researcher's job to determine whether or not something is being presented as true. Many times multiple truths are presented by different people in a given social scene, and considering what these truths mean allows insights into the relationships within that scene. The second coded element is *attitudes*. An attitude, as defined by Saldaña (2009), is "the way we think and feel about oneself, another person, thing, or idea" (p. 89). In short, attitudes are the dispositions people hold toward others, objects, and ideas. Beliefs and attitudes often reflect upon people's *values*, the third coded element in values coding (and one of the trickier elements to define). Saldaña (2009) characterizes a value as "the importance we attribute to oneself, another person, thing or idea" (p. 89), but in many ways values move beyond simple importance and more into the philosophies or principles that undergird people's beliefs and dispositions.

Values coding is particularly helpful at pointing to how people make sense of relationships within their cultural or societal system; how what people hold as true plays into how they assign meaning to relationships and issues surrounding relationships; and where conflict may exist about how people should or should not "do" their relationships. Values coding allows for deep insights into participant motives, ideological systems, and agency. As Saldaña (2009) notes based on his observations of LeCompte and Preissle (1993), combining interviewing and field observation (see Chapter 6) with values coding can provide a particularly interesting point of view for the researcher, as the researcher can compare what members of a social scene say in interviewing sessions with what they do as members of a social scene. As this observation suggests, "Beliefs may not always be truthful or harmonize with [participants'] observed actions and interactions" (Saldaña, 2009, p. 90).

Because determining beliefs, attitudes, and values can be difficult at times, making careful analysis is a must when using this coding mechanism. Keep in mind that this particular coding scheme is not mutually exclusive. Articulated beliefs or attitudes may also indicate a particular value, and so the same piece of data may be coded more than once. The point of the analysis is not to simply code for the three elements to determine a simple list of which beliefs, attitudes, and values are there but rather to examine how the three interact together to indicate a complex sense of values and how those values play into relational meaning. For example, consider the coding of the following data from a father talking about his choice to teach his daughter about sex directly and not to allow it to happen in school:

F: Because I [1]don't like liberals.	1 A: Liberals bad
I: Can you tell me more about that?	
F: I [2]don't like what they stand for.	2 A: Liberal values bad
Pretty much [3]every liberal wants to legalize	3 B: Liberals want to legalize abortion
abortion, for one thing. I [4]don't like that. I	4 A: Code 3B bad
[5]don't like people trying to, to tell us	5 A: Competing moral perspective bad
something's okay when it isn't.	
I: Mmm-hmmm.	
F: It's just [6]wrong.	6 V: Pressure for legal abortion wrong

I: Mmm-hmmm.

F: So the liberals [7]need to quit trying to

[8]take over sex education. And until they do,

[9]there's going to be a need for what we're

doing.

7 A: Code 8B bad

8 B: Liberals trying to take over sex education

9 A: Home talks needed

In examining this coding, there would likely be little of interest from simply listing the attitudes, values, and beliefs as parsed out here. By examining how these elements play into each other as well as how they play against alternate values invoked in a social scene (in this case, the pro-life values presented by someone who is pro-life as they play out against what he believes to be the view of someone who is a liberal), a richer understanding of how the father is making meaning about the conversations he has with his daughter about sex education can be ascertained.

The coded example also allows insights into how values coding can play out in practice. As shown here, data are numbered as they indicate to the researcher that a belief, attitude, or value is in play. Then each numbered piece is assigned either a B (belief), A (attitude), or V (value) as appropriate along with a brief description of what that belief, attitude, or value is. The coding presented here is the rough first-round coding. As such, it has few values (V) codes included, but the researcher will likely return to the data for a second round of coding to include values (as after going through and coding values and beliefs for an entire data set, he has a better idea of how values might materialize through attitudes or beliefs). The researcher has also started to try to connect attitudes, values, and beliefs through some of his coding—see code number 7 where an attitude (A) suggests that the belief (B) listed in code number 8 is bad. That also implies that he is reading larger chunks of data before trying to code the pieces, something that will likely help with context and making larger sense about what all of the coding means. None of the interviewer data is coded in this case, but if an interviewer were to present attitudes, values, or beliefs in a conversation then that should be coded and considered as part of the analysis—especially if an interviewee responds to dispositions or facts presented by the interviewer.

Researchers should keep in mind that when enacting values coding, it is highly likely that their own values will come into play. Because values coding is a form of interpretive analysis, this subjective viewpoint is somewhat to be expected, but as with all interpretive research, these viewpoints should also be reflexively considered. For example, if a researcher were to label a person's statement that interracial marriage is "gross" because "we white people should stick to our own," the attitude might be labeled as "interracial marriage is bad" with the value labeled as "racist." That "racist" label might not be the best one for a value, however, even though the discourse would fit what most people tend to agree is racist. The person probably does not value racism but instead things that would be *characterized as racist.* Finding a label that looks at those specific values (e.g., white supremacy) would likely offer more insights into how the attitudes and beliefs work into a system that undergirds those specific values. Moreover, it allows the code assigned to be a direct reflection of the evidence at hand ("I can find 17 statements that tie into the idea that this person values white supremacy") rather than the researcher's personal attitude toward a value ("This person is racist").

The tension between a person's own values and what is present in a social scene gets at a larger tension between a person's articulated values and the values he or she invokes within a discourse or through actions in a social scene. One possible outcome from values coding is what Manning (2010c) has labeled in his research a *values structure*, or a model that emerges from values coding analysis to demonstrate the architecture of values embedded within a particular social scene (or type of social scene). To build a values structure, one would first categorize (see Chapter 7 for ways to simply categorize data, sometimes called thematic analysis) all of the beliefs that could be identified in the data; then the same would be done for attitudes and finally values. After all data are coded, connections with each category would be examined (e.g., all of the beliefs would be compared, contrasted, and considered) and connections across categories considered (e.g., how do beliefs tie into attitudes?). Finally, after immersing himself or herself into the attitudes, values, and beliefs, the researcher determines what seems to be the structure for allowing these three elements to come together into an intelligible whole. For example, in a study it might be that two beliefs—that crime is higher than ever before and that police are letting petty crimes slide—are driving an attitude that police officers are too nice (an attitude because it is a disposition about how officers interact with people). That particular attitude, in turn, might indicate why people are not seeing interpersonal interaction as a value in law enforcement.

Through coding individual elements and examining how those codes come together to form a structured whole, a values structure offers insights into how meaning is made. Each of the elements of the structure can then be supported with data exemplars to offer ideas of scope and dimension. Finally, one can theorize about what the values structure means to understanding relationships. Regardless of whether or not a values structure approach is used to using values coding, researchers should be careful to provide evidence that demonstrates how beliefs, attitudes, and values are working together. Evidence demonstrating careful theorizing about the coding results as they pertain to the local situation or a more generalized understanding of social worlds will also increase a study's validity. For a full-length example of a research study that uses values coding, see Manning's (in press-b) exploration of the rhetorical dimensions of online and offline dating discourses. In that study, he matches logos, pathos, and ethos to beliefs, attitudes, and values in to explicate how discourses suasively function both in online personal advertisements and in offline social presentations of dating qualities. Ultimately he uses the data and analysis to theorize about what he calls articulated and presentational rhetorics.

Now we turn to Stafford and colleagues for a research report that examines values associated with friends-with-benefits relationships and does some theorizing of its own. As one might imagine, this topic is a good fit with values coding because sexual relationships are often privileged in committed romantic relationships and not in casual domains. As such, the study is labeled as one that explores romantic relationships because its examination of the overlapping domains of romantic relationships and friendships allows more insight about what we expect in the former even though participants explicitly label the relationships they describe as the latter.

Also, as a warm-up for the next chapter exploring open-ended surveys, we make one exception to including an interview with the researcher and instead follow this illustrative study with the written responses Laura Stafford made to an open-ended survey about the work she did with her colleagues here. It is our hope that as readers examine the responses to our open-ended questions they consider how the data look and feel differently than in the other chapters where interviews are presented.

Adults' Meanings of Friends-With-Benefits Relationships

A Romantic Relationships–Oriented Study
Using Focus Groups and Values Coding

Laura Stafford, Rachel Price, and Molly Reynolds, University of Kentucky

Formal dating has existed for several decades (Stafford, 2008), and research on dating relationships abounds (for a review, see Surra, Boettcher-Burke, Cottle, West, & Gray, 2007). Beyond traditionally construed dating relationships are numerous other nonmarital relationship forms, many involving casual sex. Though it is unlikely that casual sexual relationships are new, research on such relationships is at a comparatively nascent stage. Labels for casual sexual involvements include *hookups*, *booty calls*, *one-night stands*, and *friends-with-benefits*. Friends-with-benefits relationships (FWBRs) are beginning to receive research attention, most of which has focused on young adults. However, researchers have noted the importance of considering the possibility of FWBRs beyond a college population (Bisson & Levine, 2007; Owen & Fincham, 2011). Thus, the purpose of this investigation is to explore the meanings of FWBRs from adults' perspectives.

Mongeau, Shaw, and Knight (2009) defined FWBRs as platonic friendships where partners engage in some form of sexual behavior, ranging from kissing to sexual intercourse. Hughes, Morrison, and Asada (2005) described the unique nature of FWBRs as they combine "the benefits of friendship with the benefits of a sexual relationship, yet avoid the responsibilities and commitment that romantic relationships typically entail" (p. 50). Succinctly put, "Friends with benefits (FWB) refers to 'friends who have sex'" (Bisson & Levin, 2007, p. 66).

Though these definitions seem straightforward, FWBRs can be quite ambiguous. Mongeau et al. (2009) explored this ambiguous nature of FWB, which they argued could be considered a potential benefit or disadvantage because

> the term communicates enough (i.e., two people are having sex but aren't dating or in a romantic relationship), without saying too much (i.e., doesn't communicate how close partners are, the frequency and nature of the sexual interaction, or the potential for a romantic relationship). (p. 741)

Various expectations or reasons for involvement and advantages and disadvantages of these relationships have been explored. People involved in FWBRs may vary in their expectations of receiving positive social and/or emotional consequences (e.g., Levinson, Jaccard, & Beamer, 1995; Paul, McManus, & Hayes, 2000). Overall, Owen and Fincham (2011) noted that FWBRs are reported to have more positive than negative relational consequences. In their examination of the attitudes of college students, Bisson and Levine (2007) found the most prevalent attitude about FWB among people who had experienced a FWBR is that they are relationships that can remain friendships without sexual activity damaging the friendship. Some people did express concern that a sexual relationship might harm their friendships, and a few found the idea of FWB as morally wrong.

The majority of research on FWBRs has focused on young adults (i.e., college students). Research on casual relationships among adults may be lacking due to a perception that such relationships are more common among college students. Indeed, Bisson and Levine (2007) reported that 60% of their college sample had been involved in a FWBR. Therefore, this exploratory study examines adults' meanings of FWB through a consideration of their values, attitudes, and beliefs about FWBRs.

Method

Recruitment and Participants

A recruitment e-mail was sent to a network sample and to leaders of local social groups. Criteria for inclusion were that participants must have been over the age of 24 and currently unmarried. Participants received $20 for their participation. The research team conducted eight focus groups with 44 participants. Groups varied from 2 to 9 adults. The age of the participants ranged from 25 to 70 (M = 45.89, Mdn = 49, SD = 13.93). Of the participants, 84% were female (n = 37). The majority of participants were Caucasian (95%; n = 42).

Data Collection Procedures

The focus groups were conducted on campus. Groups were audiotaped and participants were given a code number to ensure anonymity. Following informed consent, participants were asked to reflect upon the types and characteristics of romantic and/or sexual involvements that they experienced as unmarried people. The focus group leader acted as a guide, paraphrasing participants' responses and probing for further description or to clarify responses.

Each focus group lasted about one hour. Participants then completed a demographic questionnaire and address form to receive compensation. Sessions were transcribed and reviewed for content related to FWBRs.

Data Analysis

Affective coding mechanisms are used to help understand meanings through the identification of subjective qualities of the topic of interest (Saldaña, 2009). Transcripts were analyzed through a form of affective coding—values coding. Values coding seeks to aid in the understanding of participants' inner cognitive systems as comprised of values, attitudes, and beliefs. These are three interconnected but differing constructs that can represent people's meanings based on their experience and actions within a given context. According to Saldaña, a *value* is "the importance we attribute to oneself, another person, thing, or idea" (p. 89). Values of FWBR were determined by identifying responses that indicated how important a FWBR is or what an important characteristic of FWBR is. An *attitude* is "the way we think and feel about oneself, another person, thing, or idea" (Saldaña, 2009, p. 89). Attitudes were identified by considering evaluative and affective responses. Last, a *belief* is "part of a system that includes our values and attitudes, plus our personal knowledge, experiences, opinions, prejudices, morals, and other interpretive perceptions of the social world" (Saldaña, 2009, pp. 89–90). FWB beliefs were identified as responses that were structured within a system.

Saldaña (2009) suggested that coding values, attitudes, and beliefs is a difficult task as the three categories are similar (and potentially overlapping). Researchers must code with regard to their perspective—statements can be coded "any number of ways depending on the *researcher's own* systems of values, attitudes, and beliefs" (Saldaña, 2009, p. 93, emphasis in original); in other words, "Values Coding is values-laden" (Saldaña, 2009, p. 93).

The research team participated in training sessions to determine what constituted units of analysis and how to categorize values, attitudes, and beliefs. Two transcripts served as training for coding. Once the researchers reached agreement on the constituent elements of values, attitudes, and beliefs, the researchers created a codebook to categorize attitudes, values, and beliefs and find examples of the three categories from the training transcripts. All of the transcripts were unitized and coded by two members of the research team. Saldaña (2009) argues that researchers must not adhere to rigorous formulas. Because of this, the research team met periodically throughout the coding process to discuss categories and concerns with coding. The third member of the research team was present at these meetings and reviewed parts of the transcripts to solve any discrepancies between what qualified as a value, an attitude, and a belief. In addition, the researchers were able to resolve discrepancies by looking beyond the labeling of units to consider how participant responses could be linked to make connections (Saldaña, 2009).

Analysis and Discussion

Values

Friendship as Priority

Participants suggested several values indicating what is important in a FWBR. As suggested by several definitions of FWBRs (e.g., Hughes et al., 2005; Mongeau et al., 2009), participants noted that the friendship is at the forefront of the relationship. For example, "We have stayed friends through it all. He said I am a friend first." The importance of friendship was also highlighted by discussion of how liking and caring for the other person plays a role in the relationship. Participants also indicated that FWBRs can occur as the partners move through similar life circumstances, as in other friendships. One participant noted, "We just kind of bonded together because we were in the same situation with recent divorces. Dealt with sadness, difficulties, all the stages of that, so we just became [FWB]." Participants also cited an emotional connection in FWBRs, suggesting that the connection is indicative of the level of friendship: "With the booty call, there is no emotional connection where with the FWBR, there is an emotional connection." The friendship was the priority.

Nonsexual Activity

Another value that seemed to exemplify friendship was the importance of investing time and interacting in ways other than sexual activity. Otherwise, the friendship aspect of the FWBR would not exist. Participants implied that without this companionship, the relationship might be characterized as a hookup, booty call, or one-night stand. One participant said, "It's not like a one-night stand where I am going to a bar. . . . You enjoy hanging out with them and you go out to dinner and have drinks with them." Participants noted how FWBs participate in group socializing, "and so we did stuff in groups and we met on campus a time or two" and engage in fun activities: "I will call someone and we will go out to lunch or for drinks. Heck, we have gone and played tennis."

Minimization of Shared Values

Another value that emerged was the awareness of the lack of shared values and beliefs. Whereas in a dating relationship, there is an emphasis on shared values and beliefs (Larson & Holmes, 1994), participants suggested that shared values and beliefs are not important to the FWBR. As one participant stated, "We started dating and didn't have the same values on certain things, so it's a friends with benefits on the side." Another participant stated, "We dated for three months, and it was one of those things where we wanted different things and ended it."

Nonexclusivity

Some participants indicated that FWBRs are not characterized by commitment and exclusivity. Commitment is not desired; the freedom to be involved romantically with others is. For example, "[FWBs] are free to date other people." One participant noted the presence of a desire to date others: "I think a true FWBR is just friends first, and you start doing that, but you want to start seeing other people."

Emphasis on Sexual Compatibility

Finally, also related to the definition of FWBRs, sex and sexual compatibility were emphasized: "For a lot of people, it is purely sexual with a friendship below all of it." Participants also noted the importance of physical attraction between partners. "You can please each other there, and it's a physical attraction." From the analysis of values expressed about FWBRs, it is clear that friendship is the vital facet in the relationship and sexual activity is an important but secondary component.

Attitudes

Trust

Participants revealed several attitudes in regard to FWBRs. Participants suggested FWBRs are safe arrangements, characterized by comfort and trust. As one participant stated, "It is nice to know that comfort is there if I want it and if I need it." The attitude of appreciation for FWBRs was conveyed as participants discussed how the relationship occurs when you are "not ready emotionally to invest in a dating relationship" and when you "don't want the emotional connection" in a relationship.

Affect

Participants also expressed a positive attitude when discussing how FWB care about and like each other. Though it is possible some people find such relationships to be immoral, as indicated by Bisson and Levine's (2007) results, such attitudes did not emerge in our data. Rather, the attitudes of these participants implied only positive evaluations of FWBRs and the characteristics and circumstances that define these relationships. For example, one participant contrasted FWBRs with the negative connotation of a one-night stand: "If I have a one-night stand, it is done and over. You were drinking, and this has a negative connotation. [For a FWBR] there is more time invested, and I care about them in a friends and physical sense."

Beliefs

FWBRs Is Not Dating

Participants reported attitudes and values that seemed to fit within a social structure. Many beliefs focused on how FWBRs compare to other nonmarital relationships. Participants indicated that a FWBR is not a dating relationship as there is no romantic interest. One participant noted, "Let me be clear. It [a FWB] is someone you enjoy hanging out with . . . and you go out to dinner and have drinks with them. You know that it is not going to be a date or a relationship." Likewise, FWBRs were believed to be distinct from hookups, one-night stands, and booty calls. Participants also noted that a romantic emotional connection is hard to achieve, indicating that while an emotional connection at a friendship level is important, a more intimate connection is not common: "You're not necessarily emotionally connected as in that you care deeply about this person, but you get along and are having sexual relations."

Potential Future Interaction

A second belief that emerged was related to the potential future of the relationship. Participants suggested that FWBRs could become a dating relationship but that such progression is not common. Though participants acknowledged that such a progression is possible ("I've seen [FWBRs] turn into marriage"), the belief that such relationships do not become more serious romantic involvement seemed more prevalent (e.g., "It's almost as if there is a fatal flaw as to why that relationship doesn't go on further"). Or as another stated, "That doesn't necessarily mean that it's going to continue on; it could just be something until you're with someone else."

In brief, FWBRs fit into a larger belief system, encompassing attitudes and values, about the nature or types of romantic relationships. FWBRs are a distinct, unique, real part of the social world of adults' nonmarital relationships.

Concerns

Although this study provides insights into the meaning of FWB among adults, there are several concerns. First is the homogeneity of the participants. The participants were predominately heterosexual females from the same geographic area. Additionally, numerous people in the study were members of organizations such as singles' meet-up groups and religious organizations. Such inclusion provided insightful discussion yet could have potentially represented a different view than nonmembers of such organizations. Additionally, the nature of focus groups may have silenced those who had negative feelings about FWBRs.

At times participants discussed FWBRs in conjunction with other relational involvements (e.g., booty calls, one-night stands, hookups, dating). Therefore, the researcher(s) had to differentiate between these terms, inferring meanings, both explicitly and implicitly. However, the need for such interpretations on the part of the researchers was minimal as focus group leaders specifically attempted to discuss one type of relationship at a time and asked participants to indicate characteristics or differing features among relationship types.

Conclusion

Rather than continuing to exclusively explore the perspectives of college students and emerging adults, the study provided insight into single adults' meanings of FWBRs through an examination of the values, attitudes, and beliefs regarding them. Overall, FWBRs are seen in a positive light. A high priority is placed on the friendship, which is sustained through activities outside of the sexual involvement, though sexual attraction or compatibility is also important. FWBRs are characterized by a lack of long-term commitment or exclusivity. Finally, though they are typically not expected to progress to future or long-term romantic involvement, such a possibility exists. Future research should continue to include single heterosexual adults, as well as explore additional populations (e.g., homosexuals and high school students) in order to further understand the nature of FWBRs and the relational functions they serve. This research suggests that FWBRs are a distinct and well-known type of relationship that occurs beyond the college population.

In addition to gaining a better understanding of FWBRs, Saldaña (2009) argues that values coding is particularly appropriate for interpersonal qualitative studies that explore participant experiences and actions. In this study, values coding was a valuable tool used to explore participants' experiences and actions with FWBRs. The results of this study not only provide insights into FWBRs but also indicate how focus groups and values coding can be used to gain a deeper understanding into participants' "lived experiences."

Reflecting on the Study

Excerpts From an Open-Ended Survey Completed by Laura Stafford

Open-Ended Survey Question 1: *What were some of the challenges/constraints/frustrations associated with using focus groups?*

Laura's Written Response: As in any group, some individuals didn't talk much while others talked a lot. Since our topic dealt with taboo topics of sex and casual relationships, some individuals were reluctant at times to share their experiences. We also had the experience of having one or two participants dominate a group. We had individuals who loved to share and disclose, sometimes to the extent of overshadowing other focus group participants. Therefore, balancing both extremes was challenging at times. In addition, the nature of the topic led many participants to speak of tangentially related experiences . . .

Open-Ended Survey Question 2: *What were some of the strengths associated with using focus groups?*

Laura's Written Response: Some individuals were probably more open than they might have been in one-on-one interviews since other participants were also sharing. Also, using focus groups allowed for us to extend questions or take the discussion in new directions based on feedback from participants. There were times that participants brought up topics that we had not, and we may have missed these opportunities for learning and engaging with participants if we used interviews or quantitative methods.

Open-Ended Survey Question 3: *Did you learn new things about yourself as a scholar by using this method?*

Laura's Written Response: One of our team members (Molly) realized that she is very comfortable with facilitating focus groups. The part of research she tended to enjoy the most was the interaction with participants. She was worried initially that she might be embarrassed discussing some of the topics face to face with the participants, but after running the initial focus group she realized that the conversations were natural and seemingly cathartic for most of the participants who were involved in the study . . .

Open-Ended Survey Question 4: *People often say the writing is a big part of the process when doing qualitative research. Tell me about your feelings and experiences with writing up this research.*

Laura's Written Response: It is important to write and be reflexive throughout the whole life of the study, rather than start writing at the end, when considering results. I noticed that during this study in particular, I had so many notes while I was leading the focus groups, and it allowed me to keep coming back to the goals and purpose of this study to make sure I was truly being representative of both the participants' voices and my own voice and role in the study. These notes also were helpful as we worked together with our coauthors, striving to ensure that the understanding and identification of attitudes, values, and beliefs were consistent.

Open-Ended Survey Question 5: *Did the word limit or page count for this project count as a constraint in your reporting of results?*

Laura's Written Response: It was difficult at times because we wanted to make sure we were highlighting the use of values coding and still having the space to let the participants' experiences be represented and stay at the forefront of the study. There were many times that we would cut out a quotation to save words, only to realize that the quotation was imperative to understand the participant's perspective. Then, we would need to cut information from other parts of the paper. So it was an exercise in writing concisely. The ability to include more quotations from the participants might have been helpful.

Open-Ended Survey Question 6: *What advice would you give to someone who was doing a study similar to yours?*

Laura's Written Response: Engage in training with members of the research team on conducting focus groups and coding, even if you have utilized the method and type of analyses previously. Through each training activity, your comfort level increases and you can help members of the research team also find their comfort level and role(s) in the project.

Questions for Growth

1. Returning to the commitments for qualitative researchers presented in the first chapter, what might be the toughest to maintain in focus groups? Why?

2. What are the key differences between focus groups and interviews? How might those especially play out in the interpersonal communication research you want to do?

3. What interpersonal communication topics that you want to study would be especially good fits for focus group research?

4. How did the answers provided by Laura Stafford in her survey differ from the answers provided by Laura Ellingson and Patty Sotirin in their interview? What do you believe caused these answers to be different? What were the similarities between the two? How might you consider these similarities and differences in your own research design?

Open-Ended Surveys, Taxonomic Coding, and a Friendship Study

A NEED FOR SURVEY RESEARCH

Many qualitative researchers find that they crave structure in their research, especially those at the realist end of the qualitative continuum. Although many variations of surveys exist, here we dive into a particularly structured version of surveys that retains the open nature of qualitative data while guiding participants in a certain (but not entirely predetermined) direction. Paired with an analytical tool that also leans toward the realist end of the continuum (as we do here with taxonomic coding), surveys can offer a structured view of a social topic. This chapter, in comparison to the two that came before it, may feel a bit more certain. For those interested in the middle and artistic portions of the qualitative continuum, the look at data offered in Chapter 8 (where we explore narrative research) may be a more comfortable fit. Still, open-ended surveys can be adopted for most qualitative orientations and traditions, especially when a researcher wants to allow participants more time to consider answers and the space and flexibility to reconsider and revise what they offer.

Allowing Space and Time Through Surveys

Open-ended (or free-response) surveys are data collection tools wherein respondents are asked to answer questions using their own words, thoughts, and feelings (Babbie, 2010; Keyton, 2010). In contrast, closed-ended (or fixed-response) surveys are data collection devices wherein respondents are asked to select predefined answers from among a list provided by a researcher (Babbie, 2010; Keyton, 2010). Although each may be used for various purposes in qualitative research, for interpretivist analysis of surveys open-ended answers are essential. Once again, the reason for this returns to differences between certainty and possibility. Closed-ended survey questions are typically used for contextualizing data or for postpositivist research studies. For example, a researcher examining how a person might inform his or her romantic partner that he or she has been unfaithful, a researcher who already has a strong idea of how this may be happening (and who, consequently, might be looking toward hypothesis testing), could ask a question similar to this one:

1. You have recently cheated on your romantic partner and the guilt is overwhelming. How might you break the news to him or her?

   a. By phone
   b. Through Facebook
   c. Via a text message
   d. Face to face
   e. Other (please list) _____

Including the blank with option 5, "Other," ensures that the survey possibilities are exhaustive. Many would not consider the open line as a qualitative element of the survey, however. Some researchers may also engage a mixed-methods approach when presenting this question, asking "Why?" after the question. That would be an open-ended option, but the analysis would almost certainly be postpositivist-oriented given that it is paired with closed-ended choices.

Providing a completely open-ended opportunity for research participants, as this chapter illustrates, definitely changes the nature of the research and creates a data set that allows for interpretive analysis. An open-ended survey is typically used when exploration is in order (Babbie, 2010), but it may be used for a variety of reasons where participant-directed answers might be more beneficial (as is discussed in this chapter). Consider this example:

1. You have recently cheated on your romantic partner and the guilt is overwhelming. How might you break the news to him or her?

As is evident, the wording for this particular question did not change when moving from a closed-ended to an open-ended prompt. Many times, however, careful wording must be considered so that a question that allows for an open response is constructed in a way in which people feel like they want to give such a response. By not providing a list of choices, however, the psychology of completing the survey changes. Clearly, the open-ended version of this question allows a respondent to elaborate on his or her thoughts and feelings regarding the infidelity, while the closed-ended version only allows the respondent to pick the option (i.e., the communication medium) he or she identifies with the most, thus not allowing for any additional comments related to the topic. The open-ended question also enables the respondent the opportunity to provide a much more nuanced, detailed, and semantically rich answer than the closed-ended version. Some might even argue that an open-ended response could be more honest, in this particular case, because if actually faced with the situation of disclosing infidelity, he or she would not have a list of choices on a piece of paper to choose from. Thus, the open-ended response makes a person turn to the resources he or she can think up (and encourages the respondent to share how he or she might seek out those resources if unable to think of any).

Still, open-ended surveys are not right for all research. Kahn and Cannell (1957) suggest five important factors to consider when determining whether open-ended or closed-ended questions are most appropriate for a survey: the goals of the study, the amount of information respondents have about the research issue, the extent to which respondents have considered or thought about the research issue, the motivation level of respondents to engage or participate, and how much the researcher knows about the psychological, emotional, or physical characteristics of potential respondents. If a goal of the researcher is to tap into relatively unstudied or exploratory phenomena, then an open-ended question format is likely desirable. In addition, open-ended questions may be preferable to closed-ended questions when respondents are likely to possess greater knowledge and passion about a given phenomenon and be willing to share their thoughts and feelings on it. So, returning to the earlier example regarding how a person might reveal infidelity to a romantic partner, the open-ended version would be preferable when the researcher assumes that the respondent actually knows, cares about, and is willing to talk about, in detail, his or her approach to disclosing romantic infidelity. By contrast, the closed-ended version is preferable when the researcher assumes that the respondent knows, or cares to share, only the communication medium that he or she would employ.

A useful metaphor for thinking about survey design as a creative process comes from Singleton and Straits (2010), who contend that,

> like an artist, the survey designer selects "raw materials" and combines them creatively within certain principles of design. . . . The survey designer's raw materials are such things as free response and fixed choice questions. . . . However, the survey designer is unlike the artist in at least one important way: An artist is mainly concerned with expressing his or her own personal ideas, emotions, or other subjective experience, whereas the designer of a survey instrument must be concerned ultimately with getting reliable and valid reports about other people. . . . The reports may be of subjective experiences, such as values, opinions, fears, and beliefs; or they may be of overt experiences, such as job history, salary, political behavior, place of residence, consumer behavior, or leisure activities. (p. 309)

Thus, designing a survey must be a thoughtful, careful, and deliberative process. Accordingly, open-ended surveys may be chosen to study research phenomena when the goal is to collect original, text-based, qualitative data from a population too large to observe directly.

Encouraging Openness and Detail

Because open-ended surveys allow for the open, elaborated, and detailed expression of thoughts and feelings about particular people, relationships, or situations, they present many strengths and advantages. First, if it is possible to obtain a random sample, then the open-ended survey method may allow the researcher to make generalizations about the overall population (Babbie, 2010; Frey et al., 1992; Keyton, 2010). In addition, an open-ended response format encourages respondents to get involved with, and feel interested in, the research, as opposed to the mundane experience of just filling in circles or checking boxes on closed-ended format lists. Also, compared to other research methods (e.g., interviews, focus groups), open-ended surveys are relatively inexpensive, efficient and convenient (in the sense that they can be broadly distributed either in person, by phone, by mail, or via e-mail), fairly reliable to measure (standardized questions are asked in the same way of all respondents), and valid in that respondents are anticipated to share "true" experiences in detail. In addition, the open-ended survey method (especially when self-administered via mail or e-mail/online) allows respondents to take their time, revisit, and possibly even change their answers, which would be at least unwieldy in an interview setting.

For studying personal relationships in particular, open-ended surveys are useful when investigating potentially sensitive or controversial phenomena (e.g., how people talk about sexual preferences, past sexual experiences, or sexual fantasies). The details of such information might be withheld in an interview-based format, for example. An open-ended survey allows a participant the freedom to be open and share his or her true thoughts, feelings, attitudes, or beliefs about a given relationship-based topic without the potential of feeling judged or scrutinized, particularly if the researcher guarantees anonymity and confidentiality of responses. According to Singleton and Straits (2010),

> The greatest advantage of the open question is the freedom the respondent has in answering. The resulting material may be a veritable gold mine of information, revealing respondents' logic or thought processes, the amount of information they possess, and the strength of their opinions or feelings. Frequently, the researcher's understanding of the topic is clarified and even completely changed by unexpected responses to open questions. (p. 313)

By encouraging freedom of expression in response, the open-ended survey is quite desirable for examining relationship-based phenomena.

A relationship-based study recently published in *The Journal of Sex Research*, "'Let's (Not) Talk About That': Bridging the Past Sexual Experiences Taboo to Build Healthy Romantic Relationships" (Anderson, Kunkel, & Dennis, 2011), is a grand exemplar of the utility of the open-ended response format. In this study, the researchers were interested in understanding why people are often uncomfortable discussing past sexual relationships and past sexual experiences with their romantic partners. Respondents were not asked to provide any identifying information on the survey, thus making the participation experience, and the data they provided, anonymous and confidential. The open-ended format used in this study allowed respondents the opportunity to discuss, in detail, the main reasons for, or concerns they had about, discussing these emotionally charged topics with their partners. Specifically, the study asked the following:

> In your own words, if your, or your current partner's, past sexual experiences are something you would rather avoid discussing in your current relationship, *what concerns cause you to avoid* the topic?

Next, respondents were given a full-page white box wherein they could write their answers. Some interesting quotes or examples reported by respondents included the following: "What is done is in the past, and it doesn't change the way we feel about each other," "I do not want to know details of what she did with anyone else," "It's not really my responsibility to have to share what my sexual history has been," and "I don't want to be thinking about anything but her when we are making love."

After carefully analyzing and coding the open-ended data, the researchers found that respondents were uncomfortable discussing these sensitive topics (i.e., past sexual experiences) with partners due to the belief that the past should be kept in the past, identity issues, perceived threats to their relationship or relationship partner, and emotionally upsetting feelings (Anderson et al., 2011). A closed-ended survey format would have been unable to garner such precise information about people's fears and concerns in discussing such topics. Instead, the open-ended format enhanced discovery about the relatively new and uncharted research territory of relationship taboos.

Another relationship-based study published in the *Western Journal of Communication*, "Identity Implications of Influence Goals: Initiating, Intensifying, and Ending Romantic Relationships" (Kunkel, Wilson, Olufowote, & Robson, 2003), examined the concerns people have, and construct messages regarding, when they begin, deepen, and end romances. The researchers used open-ended questions to determine the potential face threats that young adults encounter when attempting to initiate, intensify, or terminate romantic relationships. Kunkel et al. (2003) had college students read and respond to three hypothetical situations in which they might define or redefine a romantic relationship. As with the previous study, respondents had a full-page white box in which to write their answers. After indicating what they would say (i.e., the exact message) in response to each of the three situations, respondents were asked to answer additional open-ended questions about the concerns that both parties might have in each situation (e.g., "What kinds of *concerns* would you have about seeking to *initiate* this relationship?" "How would it make *you feel* to attempt to *intensify* this relationship?" "How do you think the *other person* would *feel* about your *terminating* this relationship?").

After examining and coding the open-ended responses for each type of relational goal (i.e., initiating, intensifying, and terminating), the researchers classified responses into several interpretive themes that included some of the following concerns: appearing unattractive, coming on too strong, or appearing desperate (initiation situation); appearing needy or moving too quickly (intensification situation); and appearing heartless or uncaring or being perceived as a "jerk" (termination situation; Kunkel et al., 2003). The open-ended format was especially appropriate in this study because the researchers did not want to anticipate or prejudice the types of concerns that people have when they negotiate romantic relationships.

The themes Kunkel et al. (2003) derived from the open-ended responses were used to generate a 40-item closed-ended survey of specific face threats that people experience when initiating, intensifying, or terminating romantic relationships. This new survey was administered in a later, related research project (i.e., Wilson, Kunkel, Robson, Olufowote, & Soliz, 2009). In fact, using an open-ended survey to develop a close-ended survey is quite common in communication-based research (Frey et al., 1992).

As with any research method, an open-ended survey can be designed in a manner more or less advantageous to the collection of reliable and valid data. The earlier sections highlighted several of the strengths of open-ended surveys, with a specific emphasis on, and examples of, how they can be used to study personal relationships. It is vital, of course, to also consider the possible drawbacks or limitations of the method, as well as means for alleviating the likelihood and severity of such shortcomings. Thus, in addition to noting the weaknesses of open-ended surveys, this section includes a discussion of the best practices in collecting open-ended survey data.

Overall, while open-ended survey data foster the collection of detailed and elaborated accounts of experiences and opinions, survey data (whether it is open ended or closed ended) can be said to compare unfavorably to other research methods (e.g., ethnography, discourse analysis) with regard to external validity. Relatively speaking, open-ended surveys do not witness actual interactions and may be considered somewhat artificial, removed, and lacking contextual cues (Babbie, 2010). Open-ended survey data also rely on respondents' self-report capabilities (i.e., what they remember doing or thinking) and, sometimes, responses to hypothetical situations (i.e., what they think they might do; Babbie, 2010; Frey et al., 1992). In addition, people have a tendency to respond to open-ended questions on surveys differently (e.g., some people will write a lot while others will be more reticent; some will be articulate and clear while others will be vague and difficult to interpret; Singleton & Straits, 2010). Moreover, the issue of bias arises potentially for all researchers inquiring of human subjects. Some people will respond to items in a way they think researchers would like them to so as to appear socially desirable, as opposed to responding in a way that indicates how they actually feel or think. Still others may overreport phenomena if they believe it is what researchers are most interested in (Babbie, 2010; Keyton, 2010).

In addition, if a respondent fails to understand an item, he or she may decide to skip it or answer it in a way the researcher was not anticipating.

Certainly, all the limitations of the open-ended survey format threaten the validity of research results, findings, and conclusions. However, given the well-evidenced premise that no research method is perfect, it is also clear that open-ended surveys may be structured to best foster the collection of valid, interpretable, and interesting data. There are at least six guiding principles underlying such a best-practices approach to open-ended survey design.

Best Practices for Collecting Open-Ended Survey Data

Some survey practices are more beneficial than others for a particular research study. Here we examine some key considerations for survey research, especially as it applies to qualitative inquiry about interpersonal relationships.

Ensure That All Questions Tie Back to Research Questions or Objectives

A tight connection between the research topic and the survey is essential. As such, every item on an open-ended survey should be relevant to the research purpose(s) and objectives. Do not overwhelm or burn out potential research respondents by including every question imaginable—each item should count. Keyton (2010) suggests that theoretical and practical considerations should be heavily researched and considered in advance. That does not mean the qualitative researcher is hypothesizing what she or he will find, but it does mean the researcher is considering what might be particularly rich areas of exploration. Questions should also be considered in terms of required mental or emotional energy. It may be wise to place demographic questions (e.g., sex, ethnicity, education) at the end of a survey when respondents may be worn out or drained from completing earlier sections, as these questions require very little thought or effort.

Make Survey Items Direct

Open-ended survey questions (and accompanying instructions) should be clearly stated, unambiguous, and straightforward. Jargon, slang, abbreviations, and highly biased or technical terms should be avoided. In addition, leading (i.e., questions that make people feel like they "should" answer in a particular way) and double-barreled (i.e., complex questions with multiple parts wherein only a single answer is desired) items should not be used on an open-ended survey (Babbie, 2010). Moreover, instructions for each item (or each subsection) of the open-ended survey should be carefully worded and precise. If the survey extends across several pages, then the instructions need to be repeated and highlighted. Assume that survey respondents will not remember instructions once they are out of view. Further, if there are multiple sections to a survey, it may be useful to introduce each section with a short statement about the content and purpose—this will give potential survey respondents a rationale for why they are being asked certain questions. Of course, care must be taken in this case to again not lead participants to respond with content they would not otherwise have considered. A focus on clarity does not have to mean a diminishment of creativity, either. A survey can request, for instance, that a picture be provided. In such a case, the researcher should make it clear exactly what is being sought from the participant so that useable data can be obtained.

Testing Surveys Can Help Refine Them

To help ensure that survey items are understood and request feasible responses, researchers may engage in pilot testing or pretesting. In fact, one great idea for any researcher is to literally take his or her own survey (this is even better than proofreading because it will enable the researcher to really experience and identify any potential problems). It is also useful to have colleagues and uncommitted, random people review or respond to your open-ended survey to make sure they understand it. After a small sample of people take the survey, the most important practice for the researchers is the revision or adaptation of questions based on feedback. Sometimes, when doing research with a unique or difficult-to-recruit population, piloting a survey can be risky because it lessens a participant pool. Consider a participant pool in advance, as it may mean using alternate methods that do not involve testing the survey out on an actual participant.

Another tried and true approach in the pilot phase is to include an item at the end of the survey that asks respondents to comment on problems or difficulties they experienced. This decreases the odds that they will forget them, or be too reluctant to disclose them, in conversation with the researcher. Even the detection of a single respondent's objection to a vague, offensive, or poorly worded item may be worth its weight in data gold. Because it is generally understood and accepted that qualitative protocols or approaches will continue to grow and evolve, changes can be made in the survey based on that feedback (although researchers will likely need to approve such changes through an IRB), and data collected prior to the change will probably still be useable for analysis. A trusted colleague (who is experienced with survey methods or the topic) can be asked to perform a *tautology check*, or a close examination of the questions asked, to consider whether they tend to lead participants to one or more particular answers rather than an answer that may be truer to their social worlds.

A Survey Should Be Attractive

Open-ended surveys should be aesthetically pleasing, attractive, uncluttered, and easy to complete, rather than overwhelming. Saving paper should not be a goal when constructing a solid and meaningful open-ended survey. It is advisable to have open or white space on the page, particularly so as to encourage respondents to write in as much detail about their experiences, thoughts, or feelings. If respondents are provided insufficient space to write their answers, they will in turn provide less detail than otherwise desired. Further, if the open-ended survey is offered online through a variety of formats or providers (e.g., SurveyMonkey or Qualtrics), set the survey parameters so that respondents cannot move ahead in the survey if they leave a question or section blank. When conducting online surveys, try to be clever or to find incentives that keep people involved (Markham & Baym, 2009). Online surveys are not a magical force that ensures people will find them and fill them out completely. Luring participants to the surveys is a first challenge; keeping them there is another. Facebook advertisements can be aimed at particular demographic or psychographic groups and are relatively inexpensive. Cards or certificates promising gifts for completion can get people excited, especially if the gift is something useful and substantial. Even recruitment often involves pleasing and attractive (but always honest!) persuasive appeal. Aesthetics can help in gaining a respectable participant pool.

Participants Should Feel Comfortable About the Information They Provide

Many populations are nervous about the information they provide online (Markham & Baym, 2009). Even with paper surveys, nerves can still be in play. Anonymity or confidentiality should be assured for participants by not collecting any identifying information. If respondents feel that a researcher cannot associate answers with his or her identity, the respondent may be more likely to be honest and forth-right in his or her answers, particularly if the survey includes potentially sensitive or controversial items. Thus, the likelihood of social desirability issues arising is minimized. On the other hand, there may be situations wherein a researcher would prefer to have the ability to contact respondents after they have completed the survey (e.g., possibly screening them for another study or simply a desire to probe further on a particular item). If having respondents' contact information is desirable, the best thing to do is to include a final item at the end of the survey asking for it. If respondents are comfortable, they will provide this information, though there certainly will be many who leave the item blank.

Participants Should Know Exactly Why They Are Providing Information

One of the most important practices with any research methodology (including open-ended surveys) is for researchers to always remember that research respondents are irreplaceable and incredibly valu-able. So, providing a rationale for why particular questions are being asked (e.g., personal information), a description for how responses will be handled (e.g., entered into a database of answers or password protected on a computer), information about whether responses will be shared (e.g., in a publication), and how respondents can contact the researcher is crucial. Most researchers will include this type of information on a consent or information statement about the research. Respondents should have an opportunity to obtain their own copies of this information for their records. In addition, when possible, participation may be compensated or incentivized (e.g., extra credit in a college course, cash, gift cards, coupons). This may encourage respondents to realize that they are cared about and valued, as are the data they provide. Another key is to be respectful of respondents by displaying politeness and gratitude for their efforts.

The best practices just discussed are likely to maximize the benefits of open-ended survey adminis-tration accrued by researchers hoping to obtain meaningful data while treating their respondents ethi-cally and with care and respect.

DEVELOPING TAXONOMIES (OR TYPOLOGIES) THROUGH INTERPERSONAL COMMUNICATION RESEARCH

As this chapter probably implies, open-ended survey research may be an appealing fit for those who tend to lean toward the realist end of the qualitative continuum. The same can be said for taxo-nomic analysis (Spradley, 1979, 1980), sometimes referred to as *typology development* (although the two are actually different things, as is soon explained), which tends to point to ontological concerns of *what is there*. This sense of what is there remains an interpretively derived effort, as the data will not point to a "truth" about what is found in any given social scene that fits the param-eters of the data set. Rather, taxonomic analysis allows for identifying elements likely present in a particular situation, context, or even culture. As that description implies, taxonomic analysis is ideal for research situations where the question or objective relates to substance (e.g., "What are common concerns articulated in safe-sex talks between fathers and sons?") or particular behaviors (e.g., "What behaviors do people find desirable during a first date?"). Data exemplars become key to taxonomic work, as they provide a deeper understanding of the labels derived during analysis.

Common Results of Taxonomic Analysis

Taxonomic coding can yield both specific and more esoteric (but still clearly defined and illustrated through data) labels. One of the more specific outcomes of taxonomic analysis is a typology. When taxonomic analysis is used for typology development, the result is a list of *how things are done* or *what kind of things may occur*, among other possibilities. Taxonomic analysis can be helpful, too, in pointing to broader elements of a social scene that are still being analyzed in terms of *what one might expect to find there* (as this chapter's illustrative study demonstrates). In interpersonal communication studies, taxonomic analysis is often used in conjunction with interview data (see Baxter & Braithwaite, 2002, for example), and this could be because the analytical method originated when Spradley (1980) sought to dialogue with members of cultures in ways that helped organize their experiences in intelligible categories of meaning. As Spradley (1980) notes, "Every culture creates hundreds of thousands of categories by taking unique things and classifying them together" (p. 89). Even though these categories of meaning circulate through a social scene, they often remain tacit. The interpretivist-oriented researcher, by way of taxonomic analysis, can help to make these implicit qualities explicit. Though developed in the ethnographic tradition and through interview data, taxonomic analysis can easily be adapted to most interpretivist-oriented traditions and data derived from other qualitative methods.

Key to this analytical method are *folk terms* and *analytic terms* (McCurdy, Spradley, & Shandy, 2005, pp. 35–36). Folk terms are those introduced by members of the social scene, whereas analytic terms are those derived and labeled by the researcher. Spradley (1979), who is largely credited with developing taxonomic analysis, never provided specific directions on how one should develop a taxonomy—as is noted by Saldaña (2009), who in turn provides a more structured approach to enacting this work. Spradley (1979), however, did set up a rich guideline for considering what kinds of taxonomies or typologies may be developed, and he presented those in terms of the *forms* they may take and explained how such forms are defined by particular *semantic relationships* (Spradley, 1970, p. 111). Spradley's (1970) conceptions of form (how a quality materializes in a social scene) and semantic relationships (how the researcher places that quality into an explanation) are particularly useful for interpersonal communication scholars, as the limited amount of interpretivist research exploring interpersonal relationships means interpretivist researchers have little to use in sensitizing themselves to social scenes. New developments of taxonomic understandings of interpersonal phenomena are welcome and significant.

To promote such research, we present Spradley's (1979) nine forms and their related semantic relationships in Table 5.1 so that interpersonal relationship scholars can use them to develop taxonomies or typologies that may be useful in developing explicit understandings of tacit knowledge that permeates situations, contexts, scenes, or cultures. To put the various forms into context, possible applications are provided using a qualitative data set where participants shared their views regarding flirting in the workplace.

Taxonomic coding can be used as a researcher sees fit for a given study, but two ways may prove especially fruitful to interpersonal communication studies. First, some researchers—especially those studying a new area or one where the elements of a social scene may not be apparent from past research—may wish to read the data using each of the nine taxonomies presented in Table 5.1 as they fit with a given topic

Table 5.1	Taxonomic Possibilities for Interpersonal Relationships Researchers	
Form	**Semantic Relationship**	**Possible Application**
1. Strict inclusion	X is a kind of Y.	*Teasing* is a type of *flirting.*
2. Spatial	X is a place in/part of Y.	*The neck* is a part of the *no-touch zone.*
3. Cause-effect	X is a result of/cause of Y.	*Discomfort* is a result of *unwanted flirting.*
4. Rationale	X is a reason for doing Y.	*Favor seeking* is a reason for *flirting.*
5. Location for action	X is a place for doing Y.	*After-work functions* are a place for *flirting.*
6. Function	X is used for Y.	*Flirting* is used for *control.*
7. Means-end	X is a way to do Y.	*Attacking* is a way to stop *flirting.*
8. Sequence	X is a step/stage in Y.	*Forgetting* is a *final* stage of *office romance.*
9. Attribution	X is an attribute/characteristic of Y.	*Charisma* is a characteristic of the *attractive office flirt.*

or research question. For an example of this approach, see the research study included in this chapter from Erin Sahlstein. In her study, Sahlstein uses four of the semantic relationships she found particularly useful for understanding long-distance friendships as the core of her research report. That approach—using all of Spradley's (1979) taxonomic categories and then determining which ones are clearly at play and best answer the research question—is excellent for making sense of qualitative interpersonal data and determining possibilities for future research on the topic. This *broad taxonomic approach*, as we call it, also is ideal for generating a general research report like the one presented in this chapter.

Another method is a *specific taxonomic approach*, or one where a specific typology is developed. Usually a clear research question or direct objective is required for such an approach. For example, Manning (in press-a) wanted to know the positive and negative communicative behaviors associated with "coming out" conversations. The research goal he presents is quite specific and can be easily identified in the data. Had his goal been something broader, such as "What is the nature of 'coming out' conversations?" then another approach may have been warranted (such as thematic analysis or a broad taxonomic approach) before moving into a specific taxonomic approach. Even with his specific goal in approaching his study, Manning still had to consider what semantic relationships might be the strongest fit for taxonomically sorting his data. For example, if participants tended to convey their coming out narratives in terms of cause and effect, that might be a good indicator that the cause-effect semantic relationship would be a good one for sorting the data into a taxonomy. In examining his data, that was not the case. Instead, he noticed that participants tended to present their data using a semantic relationship of strict inclusion.

Using that semantic of strict inclusion allowed Manning (in press-a) to set up the guiding coding principles of "x is a bad coming-out conversation behavior" and "y is a good coming-out conversation behavior." He could then move through his data and pull out instances where participants implicitly or explicitly articulated behaviors in that manner, consider those instances across each other, and report the most salient instances as part of a taxonomy. For example, in developing a taxonomy (or typology) of positive behaviors, he found that these were salient:

1. Open communication channels
2. Affirming direct relational statements
3. Laughter and joking
4. Nonverbal immediacy

As can be surmised from looking at the labels for the taxonomy, it may not be entirely clear what each means. It is up to the researcher, then, to provide a brief description of each item in the taxonomy (especially what would and would not be included) as well as exemplars that help to demonstrate the range of the taxonomy. For example, in Manning's taxonomy, he noted in the "laughter and joking" category that not all kinds of jokes were welcomed in conversation and that some might even be considered a negative communicative behavior.

Those developing or using qualitative taxonomies should consider that even though qualitative taxonomies do lean toward the realist end of the qualitative continuum, they typically cannot predict what will happen in a particular social scene with any kind of certainty. They also should not be used to determine how often something occurs or what percentage of a particular type of communication may dominate a social scene. Rather, the purpose of a taxonomy is to offer a strong sense of what may be part of a social scene, including how participants make sense of it and what one might experience. Those limitations and strengths stated, a taxonomic approach is one where quasi-statistics (see Chapter 2) might make a particularly strong validity check, as they can allow those examining the research a sense of how dominant a particular taxonomic item might be. They can also help researchers to notice items not elaborated upon by research participants but still frequently present across interviews, surveys, or observations.

Taxonomic Trees

One final consideration for taxonomic coding is the development of a taxonomic tree. We were unable to identify any interpersonal communication studies that make use of this approach, but a *taxonomic tree* is a complex diagram that serves as both a model of how taxonomies circulate within a social scene as well as a form of localized theory grounded in the qualitative data (not to be confused with grounded theory, although the two have some similarities). Such an approach to analyzing qualitative data is time consuming and difficult, but it also appears to be especially rewarding—especially in how it serves as a form of model making that is both sophisticated and illuminating. The approach has been used to build a sense of hierarchical organization (see Saldaña, 2009, for more details). Such a structured approach to understanding relationships may not be appealing for those who embrace qualitative research "not to generalize across cases but to generalize within them" (Geertz, 1973, p. 165). But for those who do gravitate toward the realist end of the continuum (and for those who want to use interpretivist findings to inform their postpositivist studies), the possibilities are rich.

Now that we have examined open-ended surveys and taxonomic analysis, we turn to an illustrative research study that employs both to explore interpersonal communication in friendships. As you read the study, consider how the author modifies taxonomic coding in a way that makes it a best fit for her data set. Consider, too, how the data exemplars reflect upon the nature of the data collection and its implications for the research report. The tone change you probably noticed in going from the interview presented at the end of Chapter 3 to the completed survey presented at the end of Chapter 4 is still present, but it is a lot more subtle when exemplars come into play. An interview with the author follows her research report.

Domain and Taxonomic Analysis Is a Way to Analyze Qualitative Data

Using Semantic Relationships as a Means for Studying Long-Distance Friendship

Erin Sahlstein, University of Nevada, Las Vegas

Over 15 years ago, Rohlfing (1995) deemed long-distance relationships (LDRs) an understudied relationship type. Since then, studies examining LDRs have increased (see Stafford, 2005, for a review of the research). Interpersonal communication scholars lead this work, and a special issue of the *Journal of Applied Communication Research* dedicated to the topic of distance and communication appeared in 2010 (Sahlstein & Stafford, 2010). LDRs of all types (e.g., dating, marital, family, coworker, and friendship) are seemingly more acceptable and available due to advances made in communicative technology and decreases in long-distance communication costs. Arguably long-distance friendships (LDFs) have seen the largest increase given the invention and proliferation of Facebook and other social networking tools facilitating the maintenance of LDFs from close friends to weak ties from the past and present (Johnson, Haigh, Becker, Craigh, & Wigley, 2008); therefore, these relationships are the focus of this analysis.

The research conducted on LDFs, as well as LDRs in general, is almost exclusively based on self-reported behavioral patterns of individual relationship partners. Scholars have recently examined relational maintenance (Johnson, 2001; Ledbetter, 2010), commitment (Johnson, Becker, Craig, Gilchrist, & Haigh, 2009), turning points (Becker et al., 2009), and media use (Utz, 2007) within LDFs. While this research is undeniably informative and practical, Sahlstein (2010) characterized it as *distance-as-context* research—or research that examines what occurs within long-distance relationships, usually from the perspective of one partner. This type of research treats distance as the state of relating and then examines the communicative and/or relational activity between partners within that context (e.g., Dainton & Aylor, 2009). A potentially useful line of research is the solicitation and examination of how people construct LDFs. The latter is what Sahlstein (2010) termed a *distance-as-discourse* approach where scholars seek out how people make sense of LDRs through their talk. Stafford (2005, p. 9) usefully points out four primary cultural assumptions concerning "close" personal relationships in the United States that likely situate how people construct and understand LDRs. The three most relevant to LDFs are the following: frequent face-to-face communication is necessary for close personal relationships; geographic proximity is necessary for close personal relationships; and shared meaning is necessary for close personal relationships (Stafford, 2005). If these assumptions are as prevalent in American culture as Stafford argues, then constructions of LDRs, and especially LDFs, should reflect them. Previous research has not examined how people perceive and make sense of LDFs; therefore, the current study asked the following research question:

RQ: How do college students construct long-distance friendships?

Method

Procedures

With the help of 24 student researchers enrolled in a communication methods course, potential participants accepted questionnaires after volunteering in undergraduate courses or through network sampling. Three hundred and ten participants with an average age of 20.01 years ($SD = 1.08$) returned completed questionnaires (47.1 % males, $n = 146$; 52.9% females, $n = 164$).

Student researchers provided the potential participants with a questionnaire and a stamped envelope addressed to the author. Participants took the materials home, read and signed the informed consent form, and completed the questionnaire. Participants either returned the materials to the researchers sealed in the envelope provided or submitted them via the mail. Participants spent approximately 30 minutes completing the questionnaire.

Questionnaire content

The questionnaire consisted of four parts. Part one of the questionnaire solicited demographic information from participants (e.g., age, sex). Parts two through four addressed the participant's experience with three types of LDRs (i.e., long-distance dating relationships, LDFs, and long-distance kinships, respectively). Along with several questions regarding their current and past experiences with each LDR type, each part of the questionnaire included an open-ended question soliciting the participants' opinions (both positive and negative) of these relationships. The researcher analyzed participants' constructions of their LDFs for the current discussion.

Data analysis

For the purposes of this study, the author performed a taxonomic analysis (Spradley, 1979). This process involves analyzing information collected from people who have firsthand knowledge of a subject. Researchers using taxonomic analysis seek to maintain participants' language use and perspective throughout the process while simultaneously differentiating the information into a useful set or system of categories that elevates one's understanding of the data. The categories are what Spradley (1979) termed "semantic relationships." For example, data collected might best reflect a strict inclusion relationship (e.g., X is a type of Y) if participants report different forms of a given relationship (e.g., a long-distance friendship is a type of long-distance relationship).

The process of identifying semantic relationships in the current data set proceeded in several steps. First, the researcher chunked (Lindlof & Taylor, 2011) the constructions of LDFs reported into distinct units or opinions. Given that participants primarily listed their constructions, this was a relatively easy task. A research assistant checked the author's work using a random sample of the data (25%), and only a few disagreements emerged (98% agreement). The author resolved discrepancies by assessing the differences between delineations and making final chunking decisions before her analysis. Second, the author constructed an initial coding scheme for the data set using an iterative process of constant comparison (Strauss & Corbin, 1990). After establishing preliminary content categories, the author then identified semantic relationships within the data (X is an attribute of LDFs). The author did not look for a specified set of semantic relationships; rather she used Spradley's (1979) existing semantic relationships templates (e.g., X is a type of Y) as a guide and let the data drive the analysis.

Results and Discussion

At the time of the study, approximately 83% (n = 257) of the participants reported currently maintaining LDFs. These participants reported maintaining on average ten LDFs. They cited several reasons for their current LDFs such as their friends working full time, attending high school in another city, serving in the military, or attending another university.

Four semantic relationships reflected participants' constructions of LDFs: attribute (X is an attribute of LDFs), necessary maintenance (X is necessary for successful or satisfying LDFs), rationale (X is a reason for maintaining a LDF), and cause-effect (X is the result of being in a LDF).

While all of the data were categorized into these four types, given space limitations I discuss only the specific manifestations that repeated with frequency in the data [i.e., where at least 5% of the participants reported them (13 or more)].

Attribute

The first semantic relationship identified in these data was attribute (X is an attribute or characteristic of an LDF). While participants reported several attributes of LDFs, I report only the three attributes meeting the frequency criterion noted earlier. First, *LDFs are characterized by picking up where you left off*. Due to gaps in interaction, LDFs are perceived akin to a movie one must stop and start because of interruptions. These relationships will be there when partners return, and they can be reignited when partners are able to do so. A second LDF attribute is that *they are easier to maintain than other LDR forms* (i.e., long-distance dating relationships and long-distance kinships). Given participants reported their constructions for all three relationship types within the same questionnaire, it is not surprising that they mentally compared them and some would report the results of their comparison as one of their constructions. For example, several participants expressed that "LDFs are much easier than LDRs." The attribution that they are easier might come from the often-associated voluntary nature of friendships along with their (perceived) less rigid rule structure as they are "voluntarily undertaken and self-managed" (Wiseman, 1986, p. 192). Given that romantic and familial relationships may be seen as more labor intensive in their maintenance, the attribution that LDFs are easier to maintain than other LDRs makes sense. Participants also reported a third related attribute that *LDFs are difficult to maintain*; therefore, while LDFs are easier than other LDRs to maintain, they still present challenges, such as their expense (e.g., costs of face-to-face visits) and conscious maintenance (e.g., LDFs must make efforts to contact otherwise risk fading away). Thus, they may be perceived as more labor intensive than proximal friendships.

Necessary Maintenance

The second semantic relationship noted in these data was in the form of necessary maintenance (X is necessary for Y), most notably that *using technology is necessary for maintaining a successful/satisfying LDF*. Participants reported that, in order to keep the relationship going, partners must use available technologies or the relationships would likely end. For example, participants viewed using e-mail, mobile phones, and social networking sites as

necessary for maintaining these relationships, and without them their LDFs would fade or cease to exist. One participant wrote, "If you don't talk on the phone or e-mail enough then your LDFs will fade away."

Rationale

Participant constructions also reflected the third semantic relationship of rationale (*X* is a reason for maintaining
a LDF): Traveling is a reason for having an LDF. Participants cited that *LDFs make them travel more*, which they
reported as justification for maintaining long-distance ties ("I like having LDFs because I get to visit different
places"). Those reporting this perception viewed LDFs as positive because of the travel involved, but implied in this
set of constructions is that face-to-face communication is necessary for the successful maintenance of relationships. Therefore, if a person wants to maintain a friendship, then he or she must take the time to see the person in
the flesh. Stafford (2005) argued two cultural assumptions about close relationships: they should be maintained
through face-to-face communication, and geographic proximity is necessary. These assumptions seem to under-
write participants' constructions of LDFs as they view traveling as necessary for maintaining these relationships.

Cause-Effect

The last semantic relationship was a cause-effect relationship (*X* is the result of being in a LDF): *Spending time
at a distance from a friend will help improve the relationship*. Participants' constructions falling into this category
reflected the sense that if friends can survive a period of distance (e.g., one friend studies abroad while the other
stays back home) then they will become better or good friends as a result of living through separation. This construction integrates a negative and positive view of LDFs; distance is an obstacle for maintaining friendships (negative),
but if endured then LDFs either reflect that a good relationship was in place to begin with or the distance strength-
ened the bond between partners (positive). Again, we can see the cultural assumptions that relationships are best
maintained through face-to-face communication and in geographic proximity in these constructions. If partners
can maintain their relationships across a separation, or at least significantly decreased frequency of face-to-face
communication given the lack of geographic proximity, then the relationship must be a strong one.

Future Research Considerations

Future research should seek to contextualize constructions of LDFs. Lists of positive and negative constructions
do not capture the lived experiences of their content. LDF scholars should move to longitudinal analyses of how
these "pros" and "cons" are experienced and how the "lists" may change across the course of the relationship. Sahlstein's (2004) discussion of the dynamics of moving between moments of togetherness and separation propel LDR
scholarship in a useful direction but could be expanded.

LDR researchers should also examine how *distance, relationship*, and related terms are used in everyday and
public discourse. Talk frequently functions to manage distance or separations in personal relationships (see Sigman's [1991] prospective continuity construction units, for example; "I will see you later"). Metaphors of distance
are also employed in constructions of relationships (e.g., "I don't feel close to you anymore"; see Hess, 2002, for a
discussion of distance regulation in personal relationships). Baxter's (2011) recent iteration of relational dialectics
theory is a promising approach for looking at discourses of distance given her attention to competing constructions
of relational life. If we treat "[distance] as a complicated and shifting terrain of bodily and public discourses that
situate, reproduce, and disrupt communicative and cultural activities as well as identities" (Malin, 2001, p. 217),
then we can move into new areas of LDR research. As reflected in the current study of participants' constructions,

distance is not only a roadblock to relationships or a state of relating. Distance is also a concept participating in how relating is viewed and likely discussed in everyday talk. Qualitative data collection and analysis will facilitate a rich understanding of such issues, and specifically Spradley's (1979) taxonomic analysis can provide ways of seeing patterns in form underlying content-related themes.

Reflecting on the Study

Excerpts From an Interview With Erin Sahlstein

Adrianne: I wanted to start out by thanking you for your contribution to our book.

Erin: Sure.

Adrianne: It's just a perfect interpersonal contribution.... So, I will get started and ask you, what were some of the challenges or constraints or frustrations that you experienced using the method that you were asked to use?

Erin: That's a hard question to answer because I actually really appreciate this particular method but just sort of the general form of doing this kind of work where you're inductively looking for these themes and so forth and then you try to put them into something that helps someone else makes sense without it . . . being too reduced or just too much in its raw form. So I guess the challenge is . . . to present something in such a way that goes beyond common sense or goes beyond what might be sort of easily identified even if you weren't doing the research. [So you have to ask yourself,] "Is what I've done going to be helpful for someone else, either a researcher or somebody who's in these relationships?"

Adrianne: Absolutely.

Erin: But again . . . what I feel like I struggle with most is trying to make sure that I'm . . . presenting something that's new to someone else, or at least it gives them a new way of looking at it. And maybe through the semantic relationships, that's a way that I have done that for someone else.

Adrianne: Yeah. . . . What do you think some of the strengths are with using the method that you used for your contribution?

Erin: Well, what I really like about it is that it . . . gives you a form for what you're looking at . . . that's where the meaning comes from. . . . It gives me a way of thinking, a framework, that is quite flexible, you know, but allows me to go into depth on something with this frame. So I feel like that's really its strength: it isn't dictating what I should see; it isn't prescribing a certain relationship between concepts or variables. It's giving me a skeleton that then I can take and utilize from the ground up with my data.

Adrianne: Yeah. . . . It's such a learning process . . . .

Erin: I know, exactly. I was just thinking that last week when I was working on something. I had several, like, little epiphanies, like, "Oh my gosh, I could've done this in another study," or "I wish I'd thought about this earlier." I'm constantly learning when I do this kind of research.

Adrianne: Yeah. People often say that writing is a really big part of the process when you're doing qualitative research. So tell me about your feelings and experiences that you had while you were writing this up.

Erin: Hmm. . . . Writing up the report itself was quite easy, and I always enjoy writing up qualitative reports . . . just because I'm really persuaded by qualitative data. To me it's more persuasive, at times, than quantitative data. . . . And I guess for me most of the time it is [more persuasive] because that's why I decide to do that kind of research. So in terms of writing it, it's a wonderful experience because it's like, OK, finally; I've done all this work in terms of gathering the data and the hard work putting in analyzing it, and now I can put it into a form that someone else can digest and consume—or consume and digest. So, I really enjoy it. I don't find it that much of a struggle, you know, in terms of writing it. It takes a lot of time, it takes a lot of care, to make sure that, for example, you're not overstating your interpretation of something . . . .

Adrianne: Yeah.

Erin: So to me that's a challenge in trying to write it up and make sure that it's . . . credible. You know, one of the hallmarks of a good qualitative—and quantitative—report is being credible with what you do; the evidence that you provide is convincing in terms of what you're trying to present. So, I really enjoy it, but I think I enjoy it because I know that the outcome, if done well, can be such a wonderful thing for a reader, you know, to actually come across. I mean, again, I love quantitative research, and I've done it myself, and I advise students to do quantitative studies, and I teach a quantitative methods course at the undergraduate level . . . because I completely see the value in it. But I have, in my experience, had more gratification in conducting a qualitative study, analyzing qualitative data, and writing a qualitative report, far beyond the kind of, I guess, benefits or feelings of when you're patting yourself on the back or something at the end of a quantitative report.

Adrianne: Right, right.

Erin: Again, for people who do quantitative, I'm sure they get that same kind of jolt or, you know, kind of excitement, around finishing that kind of project, and I used to have that same feeling, but now I'm much more interested in doing this kind of work.

Adrianne: OK... so what advice would you give to someone who is like new to this kind of process? Are there best practices that you could recommend or... if somebody said, "I have a question that seems to warrant using this kind of qualitative method," what would you advise them of, like either the best things that could happen or things they should definitely avoid?

Erin: Hmm... I would avoid relying far too much on participants just to know what you want, to leave things too open-ended. I think some people like qualitative work—and I do, too—because it gives voice to the participants, it honors their perspective, and you try to maintain their language and their meaning system in what you're doing with it, so that's great. But you can rely far too much on them, or give them too much leeway when you're collecting the data, and then you come back with just far too much to filter through and make sense, I think.... [So] one of my cautionary notes to [graduate students as they design their] projects is to make sure that they take a lot of time thinking about their interview protocol.... So being very clear about what you want, but at the same time balancing that with giving the participants freedom to present their perspective or their experience. That's a hard thing, I think, to negotiate as you're gathering qualitative data: make sure you're getting useful information and you're not just sort of sifting through the haystack trying to find that needle.

Adrianne: Yeah, I totally agree with you.

Erin: So that's one big thing I do. You know... you should really be careful with how you design the study in the first place. Because again, I think too many, at least new, qualitative scholars just say, "I'm going to do an interview and I'm going to ask them a set of questions, and then I'll just kind of worry about finding the patterns or finding these interesting themes later."

Adrianne: Yeah.

Erin: I don't know if they're specifically thinking that in their heads, but they're a little bit too open in the data collection phase, and then that leads them to trouble in the data analysis phase; and then during data analysis, again, not having at least some kind of frame, you know, that you're working from to try to come up with some findings, relying far too much—to me, relying far too much on the content will not lead you necessarily to useful findings about communication as a process or as an idea. So, again, I would caution them, any kind of qualitative researcher, to have more of a plan of how you're going to analyze that data once it comes in.

Adrianne: Yeah, I agree with you. I'm wondering, since you and I were both trained quantitatively, do you think that your answers could be—I'm just thinking out loud, but do you think maybe your answers are kind of reflective of your initial training, too?

Erin: Oh yeah, I'm sure.... Because ... when I was at Iowa when I was getting my doctorate, I took courses from Kristine Fitch, an ethnographer.... And there still is quite a difference between my qualitative scholarship and what I would say she's doing. And she's full on qualitative because she trained with Gerry Phillipsen ... and others. I think her complete training was solely qualitative. I feel like I'm more of a mixture, and like you said, even my qualitative sort of thinking is informed by quantitative scholarship.

Adrianne: Yeah.

Erin: Because I can't ever imagine just using one relationship and going into depth on that. I'm not sure if that would be—like a one-case approach, I couldn't do that. I'm not sure I even still have some of the ways of seeing that some, you know, *real* on-the-far-end-of-the-spectrum qualitative scholars have.

Adrianne: Yeah.

Erin: And I wish I had, you know? Like I said, I tried to take courses that would help me get in that direction, but I still think I have some quantitative leanings or something.... And my advisors were Leslie Baxter and Steve Duck ... [and] they're not, you know, some of the scholars you might think of that are absolutely ... you know, end-of-spectrum qualitative scholars like Carolyn Ellis or Sandra Faulkner.

Adrianne: Right.

Erin: When you think of full-on qualitative people, those are the ones I think of that are at that end of things.

Adrianne: Yeah, definitely.

Erin: We didn't do that kind of work.

Adrianne: There's definitely a spectrum, absolutely. Well, you kind of answered already my last question, which was ... what are the things you have to consider as you work between the quantitative and qualitative paradigms?

Erin: Right ...

Adrianne: Do you ever feel that people question you and ask, you know, like, "Are you on the fence with methodology?" because you can work in both types of methods. I know some people get leery of that, like purely qualitative people and then purely quantitative people are like, "How could you possibly do both?"

Erin: I would say recently I haven't had those kinds of questions necessarily come up; but, you know, over my career, absolutely, especially when I went from my master's program into my PhD program and then those first few years out, because I was doing, for example, meta-analytic work, you know, with Mike Allen and . . . that's really quantitative.

Adrianne: Yeah.

Erin: And he was one of my professors at Milwaukee, and I still write with him and do things with him. So kind of more early on, I think people could see sort of those things directly, like see me publishing kind of both kinds of work; and now, most of the things that I've done are qualitative. I guess really from my own perspective I see that. I don't feel like I get those questions as much, but, you know, people do wonder, "Why don't you just stick with both?" And then there are people who want you to kind of advocate only one or the other, which I absolutely can't do. I can't say, "Well, there should never be any more quantitative work."

Adrianne: Right.

Erin: I don't believe that, and I can't imagine when people—when I have come across folks who I think *do* honestly believe that, that communication research should be qualitative, or folks who are quantitative who think, "Oh, I can see some value in qualitative design and data, but I eventually want to take that, move from that, and be quantitative," and so really they're advocating quantitative as what it is most useful, ultimately, to the questions they're asking or to test their hypotheses. But to me, it's better to think about method as a tool. You know, I don't think that someone has to stay consistent in what they do, because depending on a question, I certainly will turn to a quantitative design and analyze my data quantitatively versus a qualitative design.

Adrianne: Good for you. Hurray, there's more of us on the planet.

Erin: And I think there are a number of us out there.

Adrianne: Oh, I do too.

Erin: Yeah. . . . And it seems to have changed in interpersonal so much just even within the last 10–15 years in terms of what's getting published and the books that are coming out. You know, people are starting to recognize more of the value of qualitative and they're being public about it. . . . It's in the written record . . . that there's value in it. So it's really changed . . . .

Adrianne: Right.

Erin: I think just because personally my career track, but also just the discipline as a whole in terms of interpersonal, that particular area, people are much more accepting of qualitative work.

Adrianne: Yeah.... I hope it's really starting to change, and that's obviously one of the reasons we're writing this book ... because we want it to change more.

Erin: Right.

Adrianne: And you know, our comrades in organizational communication have learned this long ago, so we have much to learn from them, I think, too.

Erin: Right, yes, yes.

Adrianne: Well, Erin, that's all the questions I have for you.... I really appreciate you taking the time to talk to me. I know you're teaching and you've been dealing with other things, so thank you.

Erin: Thank you.

Questions for Growth

1. What advantages might open-ended surveys offer your research? What limitations might they present for your studies?

2. How can survey participants be recruited? How might you maintain their interest in completing the survey once recruited?

3. What possible taxonomies or typologies might be helpful tools in your area of interpersonal communication inquiry? How might you go about developing them?

4. Do you believe research findings about taxonomies or typologies are generalizable to a wider audience than the participants studied? Why or why not? If you conducted taxonomic analysis, how would you defend your results?

Ethnography, Dramaturgical Coding, and a Sexuality Study

ETHNOGRAPHY, PARTICIPANT OBSERVATION, AND THE STUDY OF RELATIONSHIPS

The nature of ethnography requires that our approach to writing this chapter be different in some ways. Perhaps more than any other method covered in this book, ethnography requires the spirit of embracing possibility and being prepared for the twists and turns such studies tend to offer researchers. Whereas interviews, focus groups, and open-ended surveys embrace a sense of structure and allow for easier approaches to planning and adjustment, many times ethnographers will find that they must adjust in the field and make quick—and often unplanned—decisions about how to proceed or what path to follow. As we indicated in the first two chapters of this book, ethnography is also more than a method of inquiry. It is also a tradition or approach to doing research that carries with it its own sense of values, assumptions, and even aesthetics. It may be this embracing of language and feeling that has made ethnography such an unpopular choice for interpersonal communication scholars. In seeking out exemplars for other methods chapters in this book, it was quite easy for us to locate many essays in communication journals that provided solid research examples. That was not the case with ethnography.

This lack of ethnographic essays may be in part because many ethnographic projects tend to manifest as books or are presented in nontraditional formats such as performances. It also appears that many ethnographic projects on relationships and communication may not be labeled as interpersonal communication projects. To be fair, interpersonal communication studies (and personal relationships) are not the easiest subjects for outsiders to observe in a natural environment. To see how people "do" romantic relationships, friendships, or family may require an ethnographer to be in highly private spaces and to be witness to deeply intimate interactions. Such exigencies or limitations entrenched in traditional ethnography help to explain the value of autoethnography, as the lived experience that accompanies that form of research writing allows the researcher access into space and place—that is, highly personal situations not otherwise accessible. Still, it is a worthy endeavor for interpersonal communication scholars to consider how they might ethically and nonintrusively observe interpersonal relationships in a natural environment.

We offer this chapter, then, in hopes of encouraging and inspiring interpersonal communication scholars to consider how ethnographic field studies may be of benefit to their research. We particularly examine three areas of ethnographic research that interpersonal communication scholars (and scholars in general) struggle with as they begin to embrace ethnographic field studies: entry and acceptance in the field, writing good field notes, and ethical decision making in the field. As experienced ethnographers, we can tell you that diving into the messiness of this methodological approach can be particularly frustrating and, at times, humbling. But we can also tell you that making sense of this messiness and coming to understand communication as it is lived, breathed, and enacted in a natural context is both intellectually rewarding and personally gratifying. We offer our own struggles here in hope that you might be able to use them to minimize or eliminate struggles you might face in your own studies.

ETHNOGRAPHY: THE BASICS

Many ethnographic studies are enacted as *participant observation*, or a method where researchers "become active and involved members of an existing group, adopting roles that other members recognize as appropriate and nonthreatening" (Lindlof & Taylor, 2011, p. 3). It is a method that especially allows insights into "the obligations, constraints, motivations, and emotions" that people experience within a social scene (Lindlof & Taylor, 2011, p. 3). Less common are simple *ethnographic field studies*, where participants observe from a distance and are not actively engaged in the scene as a participant (Emerson, 2001). Even though an active role in the scene may not be performed or enacted, the very fact that an observer is on the side and observing the social scene means that a sense of presence is established. As such, it is difficult to argue that any observer in an ethnographic study is observing as if she or he were not there (Gubrium & Holstein, 1998). As this suggests, ethnography can happen along a continuum that includes detached observation at one end and full-fledged active participation on the other (Emerson, 2001; Gubrium & Holstein, 1998). The researcher's presence, however, will likely introduce change or awareness, and as such ethics become an important part of the ethnographic experience (Emerson, 2001).

Ethnography was not developed in the field of communication studies, but after it gained traction in anthropology and sociology, it was quickly adapted by communication researchers. It was an anthropologist, Dell Hymes, who started a type of inquiry he called *The Ethnography of Speaking* (1962). As he posited, "The ethnography of speaking is concerned with all the situations and uses, the patterns and functions, of speaking as an activity in its own right" (Hymes, 1962, p. 16). The ethnography of speaking soon came to be known as the *ethnography of communication* so as to expand the focus beyond speech and into mediated discourse and nonverbal codes (Lindlof & Taylor, 2011). The ethnography of communication (EOC) approach came into full focus with Philipsen's (1975) "Speaking 'Like a Man' in Teamsterville" study that examined connections among language, masculinity, and role enactment in an urban, working-class neighborhood. Philipsen (1992) would later detail three key premises or assumptions related to an EOC approach. The first, that "speaking is structured" (Philipsen, 1992, p. 9), suggested that rules guide interaction about who can talk to whom and about what (and in what particular place). This idea also embraced social constructionist theories that were continuing to emerge in social science studies. The second assumption is that "speaking is distinctive" (Philipsen, 1992, p.10). Different speech communities adopt different codes of interaction, and as such, language and other forms of interaction can only be recognized as being deeply entrenched within a particular culture. Finally, Philipsen (1992) surmised that "speaking is social" (p. 13). That third assumption not only embraces the idea that communication serves as a way of interacting in a social scene but that it in and of itself is what creates a social scene.

Philipsen's (1992) assumptions are helpful in drawing out how an ethnographic approach can be beneficial to communication research, but EOC is one of many ways ethnography can be considered in interpersonal communication studies. As we continue to unpack the potential for ethnographic methods in studying interpersonal relationships by examining other approaches, it quickly becomes evident that in addition to observing and participating in social action, recording careful notes about what is experienced, and using some sort of analytic approach to generate research reports or presentations, other methods besides observation-oriented ones will come into play. Oftentimes, an ethnographer will conduct interviews with people—sometimes individually and sometimes in groups—after they have observed a social scene and will ask questions that offer a sense of validity to what is observed or that can help to offer sharper insights into future observations (Baxter & Babbie, 2004; Lindlof & Taylor, 2011). Many times, the mixture of methods can be creative, such as creating space for members of a social scene to interview each other (Ellis, 2003) or inviting participants to collaborate on a creative project (Ellingson, 2009) in order to gain different insights. In planning an ethnographic study, however, one should remember that the centerpiece for success is the ability to observe interaction in a somewhat natural setting.

THE SPIRIT OF ETHNOGRAPHY

We turn to three scholars in the communication discipline who help to illuminate the spirit of ethnography and its many possibilities for understanding lived experience. None of these scholars is an interpersonal communication scholar per se, but all of them offer keen insights or awareness into various aspects of ethnography, especially as it relates to respecting the privilege ethnographic researchers are allowed by a community or household in sharing life. The claim that ethnographers "share life" with those they observe is not stilted or overstated. As the work from these scholars helps to make clear—and as the rest of this chapter extends—when one chooses to engage ethnography, he or she is making a decision to have a palpable and potentially interventive influence upon a group of people.

Dwight Conquergood and Exploring Dialogue

One of the best-known ethnographers in the communication discipline, Dwight Conquergood generated a body of ethnographic work (e.g., 1992, 1998) that helped to establish the value of what he would frame as *dialogical performance*. For Conquergood, ethnography was not as much about reaching conclusions about individuals or groups as much as it was about reaching openness with them (Conquergood, 1991, 1992). In other words, understanding in a social scene is especially likely to happen when viewpoints can be honestly offered and even challenged or debated. This interplay, Conquergood believed, offered a true sense of engagement and understanding. For interpersonal communication scholars, embracing Conquergood's sense of dialogic performance in the field means dropping any pretenses of being an expert about the people in that space and even suspending judgment about observed relationships based on disciplinary expertise. Rather, it encourages understanding through the negotiation of a space where both the researcher and those who regularly live in the space are comfortable with questioning what is happening. This idea applies both to the logistics of the study as well as to questions members of the social scene (which includes the ethnographer) may have about why people believe what they believe or why they are perceiving what it is they perceive. Embracing a lived social scene means dialoguing *within* that social scene, not from above it (either as an expert or a scientific, objective observer) or below it (as someone who is waiting to be taught or filled with knowledge by those being observed).

D. Soyini Madison and Positionality

Another ethnographer particularly concerned with viewpoint is D. Soyini Madison, who openly embraces one that is critical (Madison, 2011). Those who do not typically embrace a critical stance with their scholarship (or even scholars who reject critical theory and approaches) still have much to learn from her commitment to understanding *positionality* in ethnographic fieldwork. Drawing from Fine's (1994) work exploring positions of qualitative researchers and Davis's (1999) considerations of reflexivity in ethnography, Madison (2005) asks compelling questions about how the position of ethnographer is a privileged one and suggests that in critical ethnography it may be possible for a researcher's voice to dominate or oppress those that she or he is trying to empower. In response, Madison (2005) calls for greater commitments to reflexivity regarding an ethnographer's position or positions in the field. Specifically, she suggests ethnographers "examine our methods, our intentions, and our possible effects" (Madison, 2005, p. 14) and hold themselves accountable "for our research paradigms, our authority, and our moral responsibility relative to representation and interpretation" (Madison, 2005, p. 14).

As interpersonal communication scholars, one's own positionality should be considered both in terms of assumptions held about what makes good relationships and good relational communication as well as how one's personal experiences with relationships may play into participation and observation of a social scene. For example, if a researcher were observing divorce mediation processes in a courtroom, his or her own experiences with divorce (or lack of experiences, even) may influence what he or she sees. Opinions about divorce or values about marriage in general might also shape the ethnographic experience. Questioning those positions, and thus the researcher's positionality, will not eliminate bias or expectations, but it can help the researcher understand how to deal with them as research is being analyzed and disseminated. It might also be that certain situations or topics raise "what if" questions for an ethnographer. The researcher observing divorce mediation might find his or her mind wandering from time to time about how to handle such a situation if he or she were ever to divorce. Paying attention to these mind wanderings might also help to reveal one's own positionality in a particular research situation. That could come into play with writing and other forms of analysis.

H. L. Goodall and Writing the New Ethnography

H. L. Goodall (2000) advocates that good ethnography comes from good writing but that writing well is a challenge. As Goodall (2000) so eloquently states,

> Writing ethnography is difficult to learn because no matter how many exemplars you locate, no matter how many hours you devote to editing and rewriting, and no matter how much you love language, are skilled with metaphor, and are aware of representational limitations, what

may be truest about writing is this: The tensions that guide the ethnographic writer's hand lie between the felt improbability of what you have lived and the known impossibility of expressing it, which is to say between desire and its unresolvable, often ineffable end. (p. 7)

As Goodall (2000) also notes, writing is inextricably connected to all other aspects of ethnographic fieldwork. It involves observation because that observation must be recorded in writing, and as those observations are being entered as writing, the self certainly comes into play through past experience and present tensions (Goodall, 2000). Fieldwork itself is tough because as much as someone teaching it might try to share all there is to know with his or her students, "it is what is left unsaid that will be likely to prove the character and creativity of the fieldworker" (Goodall, 2000, p. 7). So, in ethnographic fieldwork one should master a sense of the field, master a sense of writing, realize how self comes into play with both, and then consider how all are meaningfully connected. The rest of this chapter attempts to help interpersonal scholars consider how they might do those things.

MOVING INTERPERSONAL COMMUNICATION INTO ETHNOGRAPHIC REALMS

Entering the Ethnographic Field

Entering the field, or engaging and observing a lived social scene, begins far before a researcher starts that observation in earnest. Janesick (1994) offers eight considerations researchers should make as they begin an ethnographic study. This "'warm-up' period," as she calls it (Janesick, 1994, p. 211), starts with considering what questions or premises will guide the study. This step may seem obvious, but it is often neglected. Many an ethnographer enters the field with absolutely no idea about what it is she or he is supposed to be observing, and as a result, field notes are difficult to write because there is a lack of focus. As Chapter 2 detailed, even though qualitative research is inductive, it is still guided by informed questions or interests. It may be that inspiration strikes for many at the site of research exploration, but with some deep consideration about what one might find in the field, valuable time can be preserved for focused observation. It can also help with determining time needed, how one will position himself or herself in the field, and what can be answered by that observation. Think about questions in terms of the level of communication that can be observed. For most cases, "I want to examine interpersonal communication within restaurants" will be too broad, even for a starting research statement. "I want to examine interpersonal communication as people eat dinner" is better. "I want to examine dating communication over dinner in upscale restaurants" is still appropriately broad, but it gives a sense of where the field might be and what kind of communication will be examined. It also points to bodies of literature that can help the ethnographer to think about what might be happening in the field.

That second step of preparation, the literature review, is often neglected as well. Some ethnographers proclaim they want to be a blank slate as they enter the field and, consequently, that no research needs to be done in advance. This, they believe, will allow for a completely objective and open mind. With ethnography being an interpretivist-oriented endeavor, however, there is no need to pretend that objectivity can be achieved. In fact, conducting a literature review can lead a researcher away from his or her naïve assumptions or biases and toward what Strauss and Corbin (1990) call "theoretical sensitivity" (p. 41).

Theoretical sensitivity is a researcher's ability to develop insights about theories and concepts related to the phenomenon being observed. In the case of conversations during restaurant dates, that could mean exploring dating communication, communication at dinnertime, or public conversations. As research about those topics is reviewed to enter the field, this also allows an opportunity for the third preparation activity suggested by Janesick: serious self-reflection. An ethnographic researcher is constantly writing, observing, and analyzing, and that should be happening even during the period of preparing for the field. During preparation for entering the field, a series of questions should be asked and considered through reflective writing. What biases are present? What about existing research seems to make sense, and what does not? What specific interests or ideas are more alluring? What is less appealing? What would be the ideal finding? Or the ideal scenario in the field? What would be terrible to find in the field? The written answers to these questions—and others—may be considered later during the study and should especially be considered as research reports or other forms of research presentation are generated. These answers are part of the ethnographer's written record.

Fourth, Janesick (1994) encourages thoughtful selection of a research site. For interpersonal communication research, the selection of a research site is particularly important because it will ultimately determine the context and situations that tie into what can be observed in a given relationship. A husband and wife interacting in a grocery store will likely be different from a husband and wife interacting in their kitchen. Space, place, and audience will all play into the social scene, and ethnographers must consider how they do so. These considerations get back to the first consideration offered in this section, the research question or statement. What is it that the researcher wants to know about interpersonal communication? Then questions must be asked about where that might most naturally be observed and whether or not access is possible. Interpersonal ethnographers should keep in mind that their very presence within the social scene will likely alter that social scene in some way (Emerson, Fretz, & Shaw, 1995). This has profound implications for both what is being observed as well as for ethical situations such as those we discuss later in this chapter. After much consideration, it is highly likely that an interpersonal ethnographer will not find *the* best possible space but instead *a* best possible space where observation can be made and ideas about what it means to transfer knowledge gained from that observation into a larger theoretical or conceptual domain. For example, an ethnographer observing a toy aisle in a department store to make sense of how parents tell their children "no" has the potential to develop a rich data set derived from observation of natural interaction. In addition to localized observations about that space, the ethnographer can also consider how that might transfer to other similar spaces (such as other toy stores or even other sections of a department store) as well as to other contexts or situations. Again, qualitative research allows for localized theoretical development as well as the transferability needed to develop broader theory and concepts.

As mentioned, the role of the researcher plays into what can be claimed about what is observed. As such, it should also be considered before entering the field (Janesick, 1994). The methodological discourse generated about the "crisis of representation" (see Chapter 1) has heightened consideration of what an ethnographer can know and from what vantage point. Gold (1958) points out four vantage points from whence an ethnographer may work: the complete-participant role, the participant-as-observer role, the observer as participant, and the complete observer. The complete participant interacts in a group or scene as a full member, not revealing his or her stance as a researcher. In interpersonal communication research, one might seriously consider the ethical implications of such a role. If entering a scene and befriending people to learn more about their relationships, questions about whether it is right or just to take information given as a friend and use it as an ethnographer are certainly relevant. Still, this role has a place in interpersonal ethnography. It is likely not harmful to enact the role of shopper in a toy aisle in order to watch parents interact with their children. Similar to the complete-participant role is the participant-as-observer role where an ethnographer reveals his or her status as a researcher but still actively participates in a scene. This disclosure can alleviate many (but not all) ethical concerns, and oftentimes people become comfortable and open with an ethnographer and tend to see him or her as part of the group.

For some studies, full participation may not seem as important, and an emphasis should be placed on observation, with occasional participation in group activities or the social scene in order to get a sense of what those in the field are experiencing. Gold (1958) labels this as the *observer as participant*, and while it has been critiqued as superficial for many communication studies (see Lindlof, 1995), it may be a good fit for interpersonal communication studies because of the nature of relationships. If one is observing married couples in their homes each evening, the best he or she could hope for is to observe their interaction and maybe, from time to time, join in on some of their activities such as helping to prepare dinner, watching a television program, or making a house repair. Again, situation and context are important to consider. It can change a dynamic completely to have three people (instead of two) working in a kitchen to finish dinner. If one of the partners is running late, however, it may be the perfect opportunity for a highly observational ethnographer to try out a bit of participation by offering to pitch in and help the other partner cook for the night. It certainly would not mean that the ethnographer would have a full understanding of what it is like for the couple to cook together, but the experience might allow for some insights not fully gleaned while observing from the sidelines. In many cases, however, even partial participation may not be possible. That is when the complete-observer role is enacted, or one where it is understood by those in the social scene that the ethnographer is present and observing and that he or she will not be participating in any activities or sustained interaction with the group (beyond, perhaps, research interviews or surveys).

As Gold's (1958) taxonomy of observational roles suggests, different viewpoints may be possible for different studies, and ethnographers knowing their role as they enter the field can help in understanding what kinds of data will ultimately be collected. These roles play into a sixth consideration for entering the field, informed consent. In many situations, ethnographers do not enact any sort of informed consent procedures because they are observing publicly accessible spaces and are not recording what is happening in that space via audio or video (Lindlof & Taylor, 2011). Because understanding communication in interpersonal relationships potentially involves spaces that might be private and intimate, informed consent will likely need to be a part of entering and observing some spaces. Observing children in the toy section of a department store would probably not need any kind of informed consent procedure because department stores are open to the public and the behaviors observed are quite public, too. Field notes could be generated in a way that would not directly link back to people observed in the situation. Alternately, observing a couple as they interact in their home at night would certainly need informed consent. Obviously, their home and interaction within that home is all typically private. They would need to know what kinds of information would be included in field notes and would probably appreciate knowing the character of the project, as it could best be described at that point, too. Ethical considerations may drive decisions about gaining informed consent as well. Perhaps the hardest situations to gauge in terms of consent as interpersonal ethnographers are spaces that fluctuate within a personal-private tension. A weekly support group for widowers may be open to the general public, but is it necessarily right for an ethnographer to attend those meetings and not disclose that research is being conducted? The answer to that question may vary from situation to situation, and so in many cases it is helpful to consult with (and maybe even get informed consent from) a gatekeeper familiar with the dynamics of the group who can assist with field entry.

That gets at Janesick's (1994) seventh consideration for entering the field, sustaining access. Finding someone willing to sponsor the researcher can allow for members of a social scene to trust that person even more and can relieve tensions. In snowball sampling, a sponsor can also share his or her experiences with the researcher and convince other individuals, couples, families, or groups to join a study. Of course, some sponsors are better than others, and from time to time they may overstate their authority or lead a researcher in a bad direction. An ethnographer should consider how she or he is being welcomed into a complete social scene as the study continues and check perceptions with others to make sure that the scene remains a productive and ethical space for research. One element allowing comfort for those in a social scene as well as for the ethnographer is the development of a strong time line, Janesick's (1994) final consideration for entering the field. The time line is essentially a plan that ensures the researcher will have enough field access to make a valid and credible claim; that those being observed, in the cases they are aware they are being observed, have an idea about how long a researcher will be in their space; and that the researcher has a reasonable idea about where the study is headed. It is almost certain that an IRB is going to want to see a time line for the study. Further, it is also almost guaranteed that this time line will have a deep impact upon how field notes are written and what those field notes contain.

Writing Good Field Notes

Once an ethnographer has prepared for entry into the field, it is time to step into the field and to carefully construct field notes about what is observed and experienced there. Let us begin this section by telling readers up front: we cannot even pretend that in the space of this chapter we can teach anyone how to write perfect field notes. Ethnographers have written entire books about it (e.g., Emerson et al., 1995), and even they admit that they cannot cover every aspect that accompanies this complex and often insightful form of writing. Beyond space limitations, teaching how to write good field notes is also difficult because it is so personal. What works well for one person may not work at all for another, and, by the nature of ethnography, the focus the researcher embraces as she or he continues work in the field will determine what is recorded and why. That said, we have looked across multiple resources—some centered in communication, some not—to examine some of the most salient themes and advice regarding field note writing in communication studies. Our findings, similar to those of others who have tried to tie together common understandings about field note writing (such as Jackson, 1990), resulted in little overall agreement about how field notes should be done. So the overview we offer here is based not only on reoccurring ideas or themes about what makes good field notes, but also on what might be especially helpful for interpersonal ethnographers.

An Overview

Lindlof and Taylor (2011) offer seven principles of good field note writing for communication researchers. First, they suggest that field notes be written as quickly as possible after a field session. One way to ensure this is to schedule time for writing field notes immediately following field observation time. If that is not possible, then time should be scheduled within the next 24 hours and certainly before the next field observation. If interpretivist qualitative research is a meaning-making endeavor, then it is helpful to remember as many details or as much about the context as possible so that meaning can be as fully constructed on the page as possible. Writing field notes quickly while notes and memories are fresh helps to ensure that happens.

Second, the amount of notes written should correspond with the amount of time spent in the field. Lindlof and Taylor (2011) suggest ten pages of notes for every hour in the field. While that number is not necessarily going to work for everyone, the idea underlying that number is important: shortcuts should not be taken simply because a lot of time was spent in the field. Rich and thickly descriptive field notes should be provided across all time a researcher spends in a social scene.

Third, Lindlof and Taylor (2011) highlight the importance of a chronological record of involvement in the scene. That begins with the preparation for the field mentioned earlier in this chapter: notes should be taken about how members of a setting respond to outsiders and how welcoming they are of a researcher (if, indeed, the researcher is identified) within the space. Ultimately, an ethnographer should be able to look at field notes over time and develop a sense of how relationships and openness, among other constructs, developed throughout the study.

Fourth, engaging a social scene and writing about it involves preserving the situated characteristics of that social scene (Lindlof & Taylor, 2011). Rather than jumping right on top of the phenomenon or phenomena being observed in early field observations, a researcher should embrace the inductive nature of qualitative research to consider how activities are organized, who the key participants are in the social scene, and how knowledge or feeling circulates within the social scene. Doing so allows for a record of how the members of a social scene communicate, and it allows the researcher to consider how she or he might communicate within that social scene as an engaged participant.

Fifth, ethnographers should be careful to list early in their observation all possible questions that might be answered from their observation or what findings might be generated in the future. It may be that the original reason a researcher entered the field is eclipsed by other more pressing (or, frankly, more interesting) findings. Considering what these might be early allows for expediency in reconsidering research questions or statements and in keeping track of more comprehensive observations that may turn out to be important later even if they were not important to the original reason the researcher entered the field.

Sixth, throughout the process field note writers should engage extensive description of appearance and activities by asking good priming questions (Lindlof & Taylor, 2011). The questions of who, what, where, when, and how can be used to unpack the particulars of what is happening in a social scene and will ideally and ultimately allow for understandings of *why*. Though it may be exhausting at first, this recording of rich detail will eventually become second nature and, if the researcher is ethnographically inclined, perhaps even enjoyable. As Lindlof and Taylor (2011) emphasize,

> We cannot repeat it enough: the goal here is to provide *rich, specific detail* about the communication you observe. . . . You should pay special attention to its sensuous textures: urgent voices, pungent odors, garish colors, bitter flavors, delicate touches, and so on. (p. 158, emphasis in original)

Finally, Lindlof and Taylor (2011) suggest that the actual form and style of field note writing have implications for research. We review their suggestions—and the suggestions of others—later in this chapter.

Resocialization

Over time spent in the field, it is entirely possible that an ethnographer will begin to be a part of the group or scene under study in more ways than simply as a researcher. That is, it is not unheard of for a researcher to "enter into the matrix of meanings of the researched, to participate in their system of organized activities, and to feel subject to their code of moral regulation" (Wax, 1980, p. 272). Whether or not this is appropriate depends on the situation and context, and it could mean that the researcher might need to leave the field as a researcher. Assuming that no ethical obstacles stand in the way of continued research, resocialization can be both a strength and a weakness for ethnographic work. Strengths include the ability to interact with those in a scene on their terms and with a common sense of understanding. Limitations include being subject to the same worldviews or blind spots as those within a social scene. Thinking about this in light of writing field notes may be helpful, but reviewing differences in language across field notes allows for insights into how socialization may be occurring between the ethnographer and the social group she or he is studying. Journaling about feelings toward those being observed can also help to alert the ethnographer to his or her enamoredness or disgust by members of a social group (or the social group as a whole) and, consequently, adjusting his or her observations unintentionally or even intentionally about what is being observed.

Writing as Method

As this discussion about affect implies, the data that materialize through field note writing is simultaneously an emerging form of analysis. This chapter has already made it clear that field notes can never be an objective recording of the facts as they happened. Instead, writing field notes involves "active processes of interpretation and sensemaking: noting and writing down some things as 'significant,' noting but ignoring others as 'not significant,' and even missing other possibly significant things altogether" (Emerson et al., 1995, p. 8). Writing, then, becomes the conduit for the reflection of a social world and the record of what was selected as important and deflected as not important. As one continues to write field notes, it is beneficial to start playing with that writing, then, so as to best take advantage of how that social world can be reconstructed given these inevitable limitations. One way to expand possibilities of representation is to experiment with language choices or writing styles (Lindlof & Taylor, 2011). It may be that the same adjectives are being used and reused to describe situations or people. While that can point to theoretical saturation, it may also point toward deflection of other, perhaps more nuanced emotions or other qualities circulating through the social scene that are lost through the ethnographer's limited vocabulary. Field notes do not have to be comprised exclusively of words, either. A diagram or picture can sometimes capture elements of a social scene that no turn of phrase can.

Many experienced ethnographers (e.g., Emerson et al., 1995; Lindlof & Taylor, 2011; Saldaña, 2005) also encourage playing with viewpoint. After writing up one's own account of what he or she observed in a social scene, try imagining and writing up what a particular member of that social scene might have observed. Would that person have the same vocabulary? The same perspective of events? The same assumptions about what was happening and how? It may also be helpful to write a set of field notes with a particular audience in mind (even if the notes will not be given to that audience). For example, if a researcher is writing in his or her typical writing voice (that, most likely, will be aimed at an academic audience), then a switch may be made or a set of field notes rewritten as if they were going to be read by a nonacademic friend or family member or a member of the community from which the participants come. These exercises in intersubjectivity can allow one to break a field note writing rut as new writing patterns and language choices are explored, and they can allow for new discoveries about the social scene and the potentials for data to be extracted from it.

Ethnography and Ethics

As any experienced ethnographer knows (or should know), ethical issues often emerge in the field and in writing about what is observed or experienced in the field. Although just about any form of communication research probably makes some kind of change in an involved person's life (see Manning, 2010b), with ethnography the idea of "consequential presence" (Clarke, 1975, p. 99) is often of concern. That is, the very presence of an ethnographer in the field can lead to reactive effects. People being watched tend to act differently than they do when they do not believe they are being observed. What is learned from an ethnographic research process can also have a big impact on people or a community as they read that research after it is published. Jimmie, after submitting several ethnographic research protocols to observe and work with communities in post-Katrina Mississippi, was asked by his IRB to delay writing about any of the data collected for five years. Given that so many aspects of community life and personal relationships were shaky after the storm, it makes sense to prevent any ethnographic field notes and interview data from being released—even if it were difficult or even impossible to identify specific people in the study. In the spirit of ethics, he was happy to comply.

As all of this suggests, ethics must always be considered and reconsidered throughout ethnographic research processes, starting with conceptual decision making and continuing through the dissemination of the research findings. Sometimes this is felt as a private-public tension, where an ethnographer is privy to seeing or hearing something not meant for the public but then has to consider how that is disseminated as public scholarship. At other times, there may be questions about exploiting an observed group of people as opposed to exploring their lives. Something exciting or controversial may be gleaned within a social situation, but if reporting that means exploiting participants then it may not be worth reporting. Ethical considerations may also mean that ethnographic work is delayed. Ethnographic work, in general, is time consuming. Those who are engaging ethnography for thesis or dissertation projects or in pursuit of tenure or promotion may wish to consult with their chairs or mentors to ensure that enacting quality, ethical ethnographic work does not delay or destroy chances of academic and professional progression.

ETHNOGRAPHIC INSPIRATIONS

In order to inspire those considering ethnographic research, we offer two exemplary research studies that have embraced ethnographic research as well as some nuggets of caution about doing fieldwork in an interpersonal context. The first of our two exemplars is Fitch's (2003) essay, "Cultural Persuadables." Drawing from ethnographic work exploring interpersonal connections and possibilities for persuasion in middle-class Columbian culture (Fitch, 1998), she develops a theoretical construct as well as a cultural model of persuasion. The concept and model answer two questions posed in the article: Of what may people be persuaded? And with what? Through careful iterative analysis of her own observations about cultural persuasion—itself rooted in her earlier work on cultural premises, or "the 'common sense' of what is possible and impossible, desirable and undesirable in the (interpersonal) world" (Fitch, 2003, p. 112)—as well as the ethnographic work of others, she answers the first question by suggesting that people in a given culture are limited in what they may be persuaded about because of the constitutive nature of what their social world represents and the second question by suggesting that cultural codes and relationships (particularly friendship, romance, and families) allow for fluctuation within particular latitudes of persuasive possibilities. In short, the very constitution of a culture determines what, exactly, is up for negotiation (or persuasion) within that culture. These cultural constructions happen not only through speech codes but also through the relationships enacted within that culture.

Fitch's (2003) essay serves as a model for interpersonal ethnography for a variety of reasons. First, it examines findings across many localized levels to generate larger theoretical understandings that can cross many domains. Or, to paraphrase how Goodall (2000) might put it, by exploring the mysteries or questions that emerge from one group's stories, larger life mysteries can be considered, explored, and—to a degree—answered for a variety of people. Beyond that, it serves as inspiration for how long-term ethnographic research can pay off with strong theoretical models; serves as an example of a clearly written essay that does not fall prey to artificial deductive writing when the theorizing was inductive; and uses an interpretivist background to examine how theories and concepts across multiple communication contexts can be combined for understandings that carry across subdisciplinary silos. Fitch's (2003) essay also features extensive discussion on how ethnographic data contributed to the theorizing, and it suggests that future studies exploring persuasion and interpersonal communication may benefit from ethnographic approaches that allow for deeper understandings of cultural specifics related to persuasion.

For those interested in examining how an ethnographic research project becomes a written document, Laura Ellingson's (2005) *Communicating in the Clinic: Negotiating Frontstage and Backstage Teamwork* offers an excellent view. Much like Fitch's (2003) work, Ellingson's draws from and offers explanations across multiple contextual areas of the communication discipline, including group communication, health communication, and (most relevant to this book) interpersonal relationships. Specifically, the book shares a long-term ethnography of interdisciplinary geriatric oncology team members as they work in a regional cancer center. Ellingson explores how behind-the-scenes communication about patients—what she calls "backstage communication"—plays into the care of patients (or "frontstage communication"). The book is engaging for many reasons, but one of the most fascinating aspects is how candid and open Ellingson is about her experiences negotiating place and space as an ethnographer in the clinic. Interpersonal communication scholars will also find interest in explorations of relationship building, interpersonal elements of student training, physician-patient interaction, and even topics such as how interruptions are handled. Ellingson also takes her localized findings and helps make sense of them in context of existing theories or constructs, clearly advocating all advancements in context of her data.

Exercising Caution

In addition to these two exemplars and the advice this chapter has offered about engaging ethnographic projects, we offer three more nuggets regarding caution in the field and in approaching ethnographic studies in general. The first caution we offer is the limitation of ethnography as it is presented in this chapter. We have tried to make it perfectly clear that this chapter is only a sampling of ideas. We believe them to be salient and practical, but the ethnographic tradition is a frequently feisty and sometimes wildly contested one. We would be irresponsible if we did not warn readers to be prepared to defend all practices based on their own inclinations and experiences. Readers should also keep in mind that our presentation of ethnography leans closer to the realist end of the qualitative continuum than most. That is not to suggest we are advocating that interpersonal ethnography *should be* there, but given the current state of interpersonal communication studies and that we knew we could not cover the totality of ethnographic principles and ideas, we thought our approach prudent. In addition to our own cautions, we also turn to Lindlof and Taylor (2011) for two more caveats. First, they warn that researchers may be tempted to label research as ethnographic that may not necessarily fit what most people see as the tradition. For example, simply engaging interviews with members of a culture is not necessarily ethnography if a genuine attempt to understand communicative life as it is situated within that culture is not made. One way to ensure that a genuine attempt is there is to spend some time within the culture—not just interviewing others but spending time interacting and observing natural interaction.

Second, Lindlof and Taylor (2011) draw from Punch (1986) to caution about ethical temptations researchers might face in the field. These include claiming to observe something they did not; claiming to have participated in an event that did not happen; claiming direct knowledge when it was actually gained indirectly; characterizing contrived instances as spontaneous; and misrepresenting more calculated acts as authentic. In reviewing this list, it may seem that many of these items are contrived lies, but when lived in the field, sometimes it is easy for an ethnographer to use strategic ambiguity to imply something not stated outright. Sometimes an ethical bind is in play as a researcher tries to decide how to protect all participants in a situation where it seems as if only one participant can be protected. Dishonesty is also used as a way to avoid conflict in the field. While many who write about ethics in ethnographic fieldwork suggest that being dishonest is probably inevitable due to the nature of such work (see Brooks, 2006; Fine, 1993; Punch, 1986), an ethnographer should always seek the high road. Brooks (2006) suggests handling these temptations toward dishonesty by engaging a model of field ethics that mirrors the ethics people often carry toward their interaction with friends: reasonable inclusion, displays of affection, engagement of dialogue, willingness to collaborate, and accountability for actions. Lindlof and Taylor (2011) suggest that fieldworkers continuously reflect upon their actions and words so that when faced with similar situations they may handle them with greater ease and ethical certainty.

Dramaturgical Analysis

The illustrative research study included in this chapter uses both ethnographic research methods and dramaturgical analysis to generate its findings. Dramaturgical analysis (or dramaturgical coding) draws from theoretical concepts brought to the forefront by Goffman (1959) and developed further by Feldman (1995) to offer a method of qualitative analysis that frames social reality as a form of drama (Saldaña, 2005). Through a lens of dramaturgical analysis, the qualitative researcher (whether an ethnographer or a qualitative researcher from any other tradition) approaches the actors in a social scene as performers, and thus, anything enacted in the field or as a part of the research process is a performance (Saldaña, 2009). Key to this conceptualization of data is conflict, and so situations where conflict is especially noticeable or central to a research question are especially strong fits for dramaturgic analysis. As Saldaña (2009, p. 102) writes about dramaturgical analysis,

Life is perceived as "performance," with humans interacting as a cast of characters in conflict. Interview transcripts become monologue, soliloquy, and dialogue. Field notes and video of naturalistic social action represent improvised scenarios with stage directions. Environments, participant dress, and artifacts are viewed as scenery, costumes, and hand properties.

Saldaña (2009) organizes this approach by using *strategy codes* (Bogdan & Biklen, 2007). Table 6.1, derived from Saldaña (2009), outlines the commonly used codes.

Although dramaturgical coding is probably best used in analyzing "self-standing, inclusive episodes, or stories in the data record" (Saldaña, 2009, p. 103), it is applicable to any data that can be storied—especially data that paint a clear picture of a scene of interaction. It is also a good pairing with motive-oriented research questions (Saldaña, 2009) or those that might eventually be disseminated in artistic or presentational ways (Cahnmann-Taylor & Siegesmund, 2008; Knowles & Cole, 2008). While dramaturgical analysis "is generally used to explicate very public performances such as organizational rituals" (Feldman, 1995, p. 41), it "can also be used to understand relatively private performances such as the execution of parental roles" (Feldman, 1995, p. 41). Saldaña (2009) agrees that interpersonal interactions are rife for dramaturgical analysis, especially those that explore intrapersonal or identity issues (such as the illustrative research study featured at the end of this chapter). Lindlof and Taylor (2002) seem to concur, noting that *motive* is central to many communication studies and that "the drama frame is well suited for studies concerned with communication as performance" (p. 236). Lincoln and Denzin (2003) also elaborate upon a dramaturgical metaphor for data analysis, positing that "culture is an unfolding production, thereby placing performances and their representations at the center of lived experience" (p. 328).

Table 6.1	Common Dramaturgical Codes	
Strategy	**Definition**	**Code Mark**
Participant-actor *objectives*	Motives in the form of action verbs	OBJ
Conflicts or *obstacles*	That confronted by the participant-actor that prevents him or her from achieving objectives	CON
Participant-actor *tactics* or *strategies*	How one deals with conflicts or obstacles and achieves objectives	TAC
Participant-actor *attitudes*	Dispositions toward setting, others, and conflict	ATT
Participant-actor *emotions*	Feelings toward setting, others, and conflict	EMO
Participant-actor *subtexts*	Unspoken thoughts or impression management, in the form of gerunds	SUB

Drawing from an ethnographic interview data set involving families in post-Katrina Mississippi, we code some data here to illustrate how strategy codes can be combined with a frame of drama to enact analysis. As the data illustrate, a story is being told during an interview process. Conflict and motive are also clearly at play in the interview snippet. And though not immediately noticeable to those who did not collect the interviews or observe the families and community, the coding makes it clearer how performance is also at play as Rose, a survivor of Hurricane Katrina, tells her story:

So I said, I said, "Are you going to fill out[1] the paper?"

[1]OBJ: Complete form.

And, and he goes, "I'm tired.[2] I just want to rest my

[2]CON: Exhaustion.

eyes." And I said, "I know that, sugar, I know that.

But, but that form needs to be filled out. That form is

our future.[3]" And he just, he just laid back and rubbed

[3]TAC: Highlight importance.

his eyes again. And he kind of sighed.[4] And I said,

[4]SUB: Doesn't want to discuss.

"Sugar, could you please fill out your part of the form.[5]

[5]TAC: Repetition.

I have done all I can.[6] And I'm tired, too.[7] But that form

[6]TAC: Highlight lack of agency.

is our future." And he just said, "I promise you I'll get to

[7]TAC: Shared understanding.

it when I wake up.[8]" And he took him a nap. And he did

[8]CON: Delay until later.

not fill out the form.[9] And then I got angry.[10]

[9]CON: Inactivity.

[10]EMO: Anger.

As can be seen, the data represent a dramatic moment of conflict. In this case, that dramatic scene is provided via the monologic voice of an interview participant, but similar data can be constituted from focus groups, ethnographic field notes, or even surveys. The data were considered and labeled based on dramatic elements, and from that coding an understanding of the multiple tactics used by the narrator (highlighting importance, demonstrating lack of agency, establishing identification or shared understanding, and repetition) becomes more obvious than it probably would have been just from listening to the account being shared. Similarly, the multiple conflicts become more evident, as does subtext and emotion. Coding this simple vignette shows how it is laced with complex meaning—and the coding of additional vignettes from the same interviewing session or the complete data set would likely reveal more and allow for a researcher to get a sense of the multiple and competing dramas that are a part of the research situation.

As noted earlier, dramaturgical analysis allows a researcher to dig deeper into how conflict circulates through a social scene and the motives people have for being involved with that conflict. This endeavor can be quite valuable, as "we often cannot explain why we act as we do. People act out motives and interests that they may or may not be able to articulate" (Dey, 1999, p. 191). Dramaturgical analysis' power to draw these seemingly unintelligible motives to the surface also presents it with one of its toughest challenges—establishing validity. Coming at these motives from multiple angles may allow the best opportunity to theorize about them. Pairing methods—such as interviews with field observation—would likely allow an interpersonal researcher greater insight into the dramatic elements at play.

Drawing from multiple methods may also allow for a stronger sense of what Saldaña (2009) calls the superobjective, or the "ultimate goal of the participant in the social drama" (p. 104). It makes sense that the more ways of observing and analyzing the public faces put forth by a given participant—what Goffman (1963) refers to as ways of establishing social identity—the better opportunity a researcher has of understanding common threads or ideas (if they exist) that come together to form a superobjective. It may even be that two superobjectives are at conflict in a given situation. In fact, one can imagine that would be the case in many interpersonal communication situations. For example, one's superobjective to have the perfect marriage may be at conflict with one's superobjective to have the perfect career. Dramaturgical analysis could unpack the superobjectives of each to examine how motives may be playing against each other, how one set of motives is outweighing the other, or how those competing motives are presented in order to present a best possible public face within a given context.

In this chapter's illustrative research study, "face" takes forefront as author Jennifer C. Dunn explores how personal identities—ones highly entangled in public perceptions of sex and sexuality—are enacted by sex workers at the famous Moonlite Bunny Ranch in Nevada. As the illustrative study makes clear, Dunn puts her own unique spin on dramaturgical analysis while staying true to its aims and goals. She also offers a lot of reflexivity in her writing, as is the tradition for ethnographic research. Following the study is an interview that allows for additional insights into Dunn's research and writing process.

Prostitutes as "Sex Workers"

A Dramaturgical Analysis of Identity at a Legal Brothel

Jennifer C. Dunn, Dominican University

When I first set out to research life at the Moonlite Bunny Ranch, I was motivated by the desire to find out if the positive portrayal of the legal Nevada brothel on HBO's *Cathouse* was all it was cracked up to be. Can prostitutes really enjoy getting paid for sex? Can they really make a lot of money? How can they live with themselves? These questions are not surprising since, for most of us, media portrayals of prostitutes are the only exposure we have to their lives, and most of these depictions conclude that what prostitutes do is wrong (Hallgrimsdottir, Phillips, & Benoit, 2006). However, what I found in my research was that the women in my study define themselves as "sex workers." That is, they see what they do at the Ranch as legitimate work. Even so, they are highly aware of how they are judged. In order to examine how these women define their identities in relation to the social judgments they feel placed on them, I first discuss how identity is performed. Second, I explicate how dramaturgical methods can be employed to explore performances of identity. I then analyze what I observed while visiting the Moonlite Bunny Ranch using that dramaturgical frame before discussing the implications of this analysis.

Theory—Identity, Performance, and Work

This study employs a communicative concept of identity. First, I do not view identity as an individual, static, one-dimensional construct as early theories have conceived it (Erikson, 1968; Marcia, 1980). Rather, I see identity as multidimensional, constructed through interaction, and involving change (e.g., Cheney, 1983; Cooley, 1902;

Goffman, 1959; Mead, 1934). Second, because identity is performed through communication, it is as much a process as it is a construct (Côte, 1996; Jung & Hecht, 2004; Mokros, 2003). The processes through which identity is constructed and performed are context specific. Finally, although I intend to explore the characteristics of identity of legal commercial sex workers, I do not believe there is *an* identity of *the* legal commercial sex worker. For this reason, this research focuses on the interactionally constructed identity/ies[1] of the women of this legal brothel.

More often than not, adults in American society use their jobs to define who they are. As O'Hair (2006) contends,

> One of the most consistent and predictable conversational turns in early acquaintanceship is the inquiry focusing on our jobs or careers. *What do you do?* or *what is your line of work?* crop up early in relational talk, serving as relationship building devices and points of departure for further conversation. For most of us, work is a primary focus of our lives and occupies a substantial portion of what we talk about. It constitutes a large part of our identity. (p. 5)

For legal sex workers, one considers not only how they define themselves but, because of how American society usually considers prostitution as illegal and illegitimate, also what identity/ies they contrast through interpersonal interactions to necessarily define themselves.

Methods of Inquiry

Given the performed nature of identity, analysis of this concept in practice requires use of investigative practices able to assess the concept as process and performance via interpersonal interactions. One such method is dramaturgical analysis. Taken from the work of Erving Goffman, dramaturgical analysis approaches communication as performance. Thus, the communicators are performers whose motives and attitudes are revealed in the words and actions in which they engage (Goffman, 1959).

Goffman (1959) claims there are two kinds of communication: *expressions given* and *expressions given off,* where the former is what we say and intend and the latter is primarily nonverbal, often unintended messages that others perceive of us. My role as the researcher, then, requires that I make inferences of others' actions and motives. To ensure that my interpretations are consistent with what the participants' intended, as well as what they "give off," I used 27 typed, single-spaced pages of field notes gathered from 12 visits over five weeks during November and December 2007 as my primary focus. In addition, I drew on 113 typed, single-spaced pages of interview transcripts from nine women who worked at the Moonlite Bunny Ranch during this period as a check on the validity of my interpretations.

I coded the observations and quoted materials using categories suggested for dramaturgical analysis according to Saldaña (2009), including the objectives of the speakers; conflicts or obstacles faced by the participants; tactics or strategies used to achieve objectives in light of conflicts; attitudes toward the objectives and conflicts; emotions about the objectives and conflicts; and subtext, or my interpretations of what they meant by particular ways of talking about themselves and their work. I included a table that includes examples to demonstrate how I went about coding observations and quotes from two participants (see Table 6.2). I found evidence to support interpretations in each category but also that some evidence interacted with that in other categories, such as when participants'

---

[1]Unfortunately, I cannot come up with a single term to refer to this multidimensional process of identity. As such, I use the term *identity/ies* and refer to its construction/performance through use of the terms *construction* and *performance* together and separately throughout this paper. All uses are intended to represent this multidimensional process as described at the outset.

statements suggested both their attitudes and emotions. So, while I used these categories for heuristic purposes, it should be clear that they interact with one another to support the conclusions I have drawn. In other words, I was able to identify what we said to one another into these distinct categories, but in drawing conclusions about what they meant I had to see how they interacted with one another.

Results

The women employed at the Moonlite Bunny Ranch perform identity/ies of *legal sex workers*. Although I heard these women refer to themselves as many things, including "working girls" and "prostitutes," they did not use the term *sex worker* to refer to themselves. As an observer, I chose this term to refer to the identity/ies these women performed because *this* legal context[2] in which they work heavily influences their identity/ies, the sexual nature of their work features prominently, and they do explicitly refer to what they do as work. This insight was gleaned from the *strategies* they used to define their identity/ies. The primary tactics they used were to emphasize the activities they do for their jobs and distinguish their work as legitimate in opposition to how others judge it.

In my application of the other dramaturgical concepts, the *primary objective* I identified was the desire to define what the women in my study do as *work*. This objective was framed by the *central conflict* the women working at the Ranch seem to experience. I identified their central conflict as trying to define what they do as legitimate work in

Table 6.2	Dramaturgical Analysis Categories With Sample Quotes and Interpretations	
Dramaturgical Analysis Categories	**Participant #1**	**Participant #2**
Objectives	Defines prostitution as "work"	Defines prostitution as "work"
Conflicts	Ex-boyfriend says what she does is not a "real job"	"Others" say she doesn't work hard and it's not work
Strategies	Equivocation: it is a real job Defiance: stop dating him	Justification: works 12 hours a day, gets paid well Equivocation: "just like any job"
Attitudes	Confrontational	Defiance
Emotions	Frustration, annoyance	Righteousness
Researcher interpretations	Needs to define identity in relation to others' judgments	Needs to define identity in relation to others' judgments

[2] When writing about *this* legal context, I am referring not to working in legal brothels in Nevada in general but to working at the Moonlite Bunny Ranch specifically. In this context, the laws requiring each woman to work as an independent contractor are enforced. This allows the women to set their own prices and choose who they will work with and what they will and will not do with their customers. Although these practices should be followed at all Nevada brothels, research indicates that this is not always the case. Other brothels, which do not appear on television, often require minimum pricing and require the women who work there to take any customer and do anything the customer wants them to (Albert, 2001; Farley, 2005; Herbert, 2007).

contrast to perceptions of prostitution as illegal and illegitimate. This *identity in relation to what they are NOT* was important in defining who they are and how they go about their jobs and everyday life at the Ranch. I observed their interpersonal interactions with each other, their customers, other employees, and even with me to discover how they define themselves.

These objectives and central conflict emerged from analysis of my field notes from a dramaturgical perspective and were confirmed by what the sex workers I interviewed had to say. The conflict these women experience daily is the stigma society holds for the work they do. As research focused on media depictions of prostitution by Hallgrims-dottir et al. (2006) and McLaughlin (1991) concludes, representations of prostitution are locked in reform/punish-ment discourses. That is, when prostitutes are featured in the news, on talk shows (such as *The Tyra Banks Show* and *The Bill Cunningham Show*), in fictional television (e.g., *Law and Order* and *CSI*), and movies (from *Taxi Driver* to *Pretty Woman*), their stories suggest that prostitutes need to be either reformed—such as when a woman starts tak-ing drugs and turns to prostitution to support her habit—or punished—such as when a woman unabashedly works the streets and is murdered by a pimp or john. These refrains are familiar because they reflect mainstream beliefs about prostitution. So, when discussing their work, the women of the Moonlite Bunny Ranch feel the need to explic-itly say their work is legal and/or to focus on aspects that distinguish their work from that of illegal street workers.

The *strategies* these women employed to construct their identity/ies as legal sex workers reflected ambivalent *attitudes* and *emotions*. Every interview and every day of observation I conducted included these women talking about how what they do *is work*, how great it is, *and* how hard it can be. Because they were trying to distinguish their experiences working at the Moonlite Bunny Ranch from cultural characterizations of prostitution, many of these sex workers used the strategies of justification and equivocation in interpersonal interactions to explain what they do as work. Kandi[3] explains,

> I don't really consider myself any different than any human working because it's a job. Does anybody else put a roof over my head or food on my table? You know . . . to criticize what I do? No. I'm not out on the streets. I'm not a homewrecker.

Despite seeing what she does as a real job, she still feels the need to distinguish herself from street workers and clarify that she is not a "homewrecker." Additionally, the way she justifies what she does as work suggests an atti-tude of defiance. She suggests that others may see her or street prostitutes as homewreckers but states that she is not. She also defies criticism by suggesting that her critics would not support her.

Kandi's defiance became clear to me when we first met. She introduced herself after the first "tea party" (weekly staff meeting between the management and the sex workers) I attended and told me she was from Portsmouth, Ohio. As she knew I was living in a nearby Ohio town, she told me she did not care who I told about her because "if they don't know already, too bad. . . . My family knows and they don't judge me." She went on to explain that she did not want to kill herself to make good money but that being a "working girl" was a relatively easy way to make good money and provide for herself and her daughter in a way that most jobs would not allow. Perhaps, as Clair (1996) suggests, characterizing the job as "easy" devalues it as legitimate work. Kandi's defiant attitude in the way she talked with me about herself, however, suggests she feels righteous about what she does and why she does it.

When another worker, Kitten, heard what I was doing at the Ranch, she immediately volunteered to do an inter-view with me. She told me to be prepared and write everything down as she would "tell (me) the truth," tell me

---

[3] Per their preference, all sex workers' names used in this chapter are the pseudonyms they chose as their work names. Some use first and last names and others just a first name.

"everything" I ever wanted to know. As such, Kitten's perspective reflects similar strategies, attitudes, and emotions to Kandi's. She made it clear that if anyone wanted to criticize her for what she does, she "doesn't give a fuck." She explained that she did care whether or not her mother supported her choice (she does), but "Anybody else? I don't care. . . . They can go pay my bills. So, I don't care what they say." She works hard for her money, pays her own bills, and as long as no one else is going to step up and take care of her, she will do what pays the best. Just like Kandi, she did not explicitly say that anyone did criticize her or that she actually wanted to be taken care of, but because of her knowledge of the criticisms sex workers face, she still felt the need when speaking to me about herself to respond to such assumptions—once again defining her work and its worth in relation to how she thinks others see her in interpersonal interactions.

Summer Verona also pointed out how hard she works for her money and explained that the issue came up for her when friends or family members wanted to borrow money. She said,

> I work hard for this money. Believe it or not. You think it's easy money 'cause I make it in 30 minutes, what you make in two weeks, but I'm not gonna give it to you. I work hard for it, and it's not being selfish.

Summer recognized that she may have made more money in less time than others, but she said that it was not her fault if these people who asked her for money had crappy jobs or did not manage their money. She was the one who had to do the work, pay her doctors' bills, had to have a needle stuck in her arm once a week for medical testing, and not them. So, she spoke to their assumptions (that she is a prostitute and that prostitution is not really work) by resisting them, justifying why she should not have to give them money, and reflected similar emotions of righteousness when talking about herself when invoking the phrase, "work hard for this money."

As Vivian West puts it,

> I'm a firm believer that this is a real job because there are certain people out there, like my ex . . . who doesn't think this is a real job, and I was like, oh, that's great. So, for the last eight years then, since I started stripping I've been making monopoly money. That's amazing! . . . No, this is a real job, man.

What Vivian suggests with this comment and other stories she told is that what makes it a "real job" is that you are paid for your labor. Additionally, Vivian told me that she did not "escort" (prostitute illegally with stripclub customers) prior to working at the Bunny Ranch because it would jeopardize her work in porn. If she were to get arrested, even once, she would be banned, unable to make movies. Given the amount of money she makes in porn, she said it wasn't worth it. But she also said that this was why she jumped at the chance to work at the Moonlite Bunny Ranch when Dennis (Hof, owner/proprietor of the Ranch) offered it. She saw this as yet another legitimate way to make money, along with featured dancing and porn.

Beyond justification, and defiance, Vivian added her work at the Bunny Ranch to her résumé, which includes her porn movies, appearances on Spice TV, and work as a featured dancer. Vivian told me that when she travels she carries an entire suitcase with just her videos (for sale) in it. When a man helped her put this luggage in the overhead compartment, he commented on how heavy it was and asked what was in it. When she told him "porn," he responded by attempting to lecture her for an entire two-hour flight. She vehemently explained to him that this is how she supports her family and that he had no right to judge her. This further supports the idea that Vivian's objective in interpersonal interactions is to define what she does as work, "a real job." Additionally, it shows her attitude of defiance against her ex-boyfriend and the male stranger on the plane who negatively evaluated what she did by suggesting it was not legitimate work. Additionally, it shows that Vivian also feels proud of what she does.

Although sex is considered primary in their work, to further their characterization of prostitution as a "real job," another strategy the sex workers at the Bunny Ranch employed was to explain that their work involves more than just sex in an attempt to equivocate it with other legitimate jobs. When I asked what "work" meant to her, Bunny Love defended her work against the assumptions of outsiders:

> I'm at work right now.... Most people ... when they hear that we work 12-hour days, they're like, "Oh my God! How do you do that?" And they think we're like havin' sex all day, with 500 people, and it's really not like that. ... My 12-hour day consists of waking up, getting ready, watching TV, doing lineups, doing bills, answering e-mails, goin' on the message board, posting comments, ... givin' a live chat, and ... pretty much just bein' here. And, people come in, even if they don't come in to party, they come in. They've seen me on radio shows. They've seen me on TV shows. They want me to sign somethin' or take a picture or show 'em around. So, I mean, it's kinda like tour guide, and like bein' on-call pretty much, but you get to lay in bed.

Bunny's description of the typical day for her was repeated in my observations on a daily basis. There were often women on their laptops in the parlor, doing each other's hair, attending lineups, giving tours, doing photo shoots, and more. Even so, Bunny's strategies in our interpersonal interactions reflect those of the other women when she replies to a fictional critic and righteously conveys how what she does is work.

Despite Bunny's characterization of her work as "like other jobs," unlike most jobs, Kitten notes that her job also includes more than just sex *and* is fun. Kitten said,

> To me, seriously, havin' a good time and making money having sex. Or not even sex. Some people think it's all about sex. We get guys who just want a massage. You get guys that ... just want to spend some time with you alone and talk. You get guys who just wanna get in the hot tub.... And it's all work. So, I would say sex with fun.... Partyin', just partyin' is work for me.

Unlike dominant discourses that discuss the horrific working conditions that prostitutes are forced to endure, Kitten focused on the fun she has entertaining customers and making money doing it. Yet she still characterizes what she does as fun. Her positive attitude about her work is reflected in characterizing it as "partying" and explicit use of the word *fun*. Along with Vivian, Kitten feels a sense of pride that her work is fun. She also feels proud of what she does because it is easier than a "real job" and allows her to spend more time at home with her family than working.

At the same time, their strategies included venting, which revealed more negative attitudes about other aspects of their work, such as when some spoke about men they did not enjoy servicing or those who talked trash to them. Kandi explained that when she gets bored with a customer "pounding away" she will think of the "Coach purse she's gonna buy" with what she makes from the "party." Kitten described the advantages of having orgasms at work yet in one case having to escort a customer out for shouting racial epithets at her. Each of these examples revealed how these women expressed their ambivalent feelings in interpersonal interactions, as Kandi did not enjoy all of the aspects of her work but did enjoy the rewards while Kitten usually enjoys her work but revealed it has its dark side as well.

Trying to define their identity/ies as "sex workers" and what they do as legitimate work in opposition to cultural concepts of prostitutes involves strategies of justification, equivocation, and defiance. Even so, the women in my study also felt the need to vent about some of the more negative aspects of their work. Despite such attempts to distance themselves from women working in other contexts, such ambivalence closely resembled the perspectives of sex workers working elsewhere (Delacoste & Alexander, 1998; Nagle, 1997). More importantly, it demonstrates that the redemption/punishment dichotomy in dominant discourses is too limited to explain the lived experiences of sex workers in this specific context as well as that such ambivalence is revealed in studies of work in general.

Discussion

The primary objective I identified in my field notes that was supported by what I found in the interview transcripts was an attempt by the women at the Moonlite Bunny Ranch to define their identity/ies as "sex workers" (i.e., women who were paid for sex and other services). Because of the central conflict involved, that is, societal judgment of what they do, they felt the need to define themselves in contrast to such negative evaluations. *Strategies* they employed to do this were to justify and equivocate what they did as legitimate work and defy such judgments by explaining what they were achieving from the work, be it support of themselves and others or fame and fortune. Their *attitudes* and *emotions* reflected feelings of irritation and pride, sometimes at the same time. Taken together, the subtext of the ways these women spoke about themselves was that they were ambivalent about their work experiences and how they had to explain themselves to others.

Interestingly, the ways the sex workers at the Moonlite Bunny Ranch define their identity/ies in interpersonal interactions in contrast to how they believe society sees them may in fact act to create space in society for how they see themselves. As Goffman (1959) explains,

> When an individual projects a definition of the situation and thereby makes an implicit or explicit claim to be a person of a particular kind, he automatically exerts a moral demand upon the others, obliging them to value and treat him in the manner that persons of his kind have a right to expect. (p. 13)

Without such a moral demand, prostitutes have always been negatively evaluated in society. Perhaps if both their ambivalence about their work and justification of it as legitimate were recognized they could create the possibility of society seeing them not just as they are represented in the media but as they see themselves. Society might consider what they do as work as well.

Dramaturgical methods of analysis proved useful in discovering the strategies my participants used to define themselves in interpersonal interactions in two important ways. First, embedded in the ways these sex workers communicated were tactics of defining themselves in relation to what they believed others thought about them. Only by attending to both their "expressions given" and "expressions given off" (Goffman, 1959), which dramaturgical analysis necessitates, was I able to examine their motives and therefore, the strategies they employed in defining their selves and their work. Second, dramaturgical methods aided my analysis by directing my attention to these women's performances of identity/ies in interpersonal interactions. Assuming identity is a multidimensional communication process necessitates studying it *in process*. Using dramaturgical analysis allowed me to examine their identity/ies during interpersonal interactions with others; therefore, seeing them define themselves as it happened.

Reflecting on the Study

Excerpts From an Interview With Jennifer C. Dunn

Jimmie: So, my first question: what were some of the challenges or constraints or frustrations associated with using ethnography as an interpersonal method?

Jennifer: I thought access was going to be the big issue. And it did take me six months to get access. Actually, it took me six months to get the guy I needed on the phone. Once I had him on the phone, it took all of three minutes to get access. What I did not think about was that gaining access did not guarantee getting time there. So when I first actually met them face to face, the owner and manager sat down and talked to me, and I overviewed the project, and they just kept saying, "Yeah, uh huh, okay. Uh huh. Yeah. Okay." And they're used to media wanting to do interviews but not research. So I don't think they were listening when I told them I had to be there for multiple days and for hours at a time. But they were, "Okay. We'll just see how it goes." And so I arranged for days to come, and I started by spending three hours watching. And I felt like, okay. That's good for today. And then I went back. And then I went for my third visit, and what we said was that I was going to come on Saturday. And we didn't say a time. And I had planned on coming during the evening. Because I wanted to see a busy night. But I knew I wanted to be there when it was busy and I could really observe some of the interaction. And the minute I came in the manager said to me in a sharp voice, "What are you doing here? I thought you were going to be here earlier today!"

Jimmie: Wow.

Jennifer: And she was sitting there with the girls, playing a board game. And so I said, "Oh, I'm sorry. I didn't know if we set a time. Is it okay that I'm here?" And she just ignored me. And so I sat down; it was an uncomfortable position. Because the girls all defer to her, right? So I kind of sat down. Everything was uncomfortable, and I sat off to the side while they were playing their game. And I thought, "Okay. I need to go, and, go and smooth things out with her." Make sure everything is okay. But before I did that, the girls came over to me. Like, that was the first time they came to me. And before I left that night, I had four interviews set up for the next four days. Before I left, I did go check on things and try to make things okay with her. . . . And so trying to build that relationship with her was really important for me so I can have the time I needed there. But I also made plans to be there when she wasn't. So I made friends with the cashiers, because they were kind of in charge when she wasn't there. And they welcomed me with open arms. We really got along, and would sit and chat, and they were easy to work with. So the biggest thing was access. I needed time.

Jimmie: So what were some of the strengths with using participant observation—okay, so I'm (starts laughing). Sorry. I guess for this study you definitely wouldn't be using participant observation.

Jennifer: (*laughing*) No.

Jimmie: So this is definitely a space where traditional ethnographic observation or a traditional ethnographic approach would be needed.

Jennifer: Yes (*laughs*). Yes.

Jimmie: So how did you know what to watch for?

Jennifer: Well, the thing that instantly stood out to me is that there was so much down time the women have. And during that time, some of them are trying to drum up business. They're talking online and talking to regulars or doing interviews and publicizing the work there. But others are doing other things: watching TV, taking naps, doing each other's hair, changing outfits. I mean, they work 12-hour shifts. And during those shifts, they might have one or up to nine customers. And some, some customers want to spend the whole day. But it can be from 15 minutes to a whole day. And so I started to understand a lot of that was spent interacting and waiting together. And that's different from the TV show, where it makes it look like they are partying all the time. But it is a lot of napping and TV watching and drinking and just chilling out in between parties. . . .

Jimmie: So you were interested in this space because you saw the show.

Jennifer: Yes. And it was different. A thing they show on the show, that they participate in on a regular basis, is the lineup. And so if a customer rings the bell, someone lets the customer in and the women all come to do a lineup. And so the way that is portrayed is that the women all stand in a line there and then the men walk by and check them all out as they pick one for a party. But that is not at all how that happened. Like, most of the time the men would not be able to walk by them and look them over. They'd look down, and they'd feel nervous. Or they'd ask if they could go have a drink because they didn't feel comfortable. So this regular practice, that on TV looks as if it is this objectifying moment, is different on the Ranch. You can see more how the workers are in control, and the men can be nervous or not in control. You don't get that sense on the show. They make it look like the guy is driving the party.

Waitress: More hot water for you?

Jennifer: No, I'm good.

Jimmie: So one of the things . . .

Waitress: You doing okay?

Jimmie: I'll take a warm-up. And some Splenda if you have it.

Waitress: Okay. Yeah. I'll get that for you.

Jimmie: Thanks.

Jennifer: They're so good here.

Jimmie: The food looks good. So, I was going to say. I notice you are using the term *party*. One of the things about ethnography is that it is a method where people can see language being performed or people living words. Did you get that sense?

Jennifer: Absolutely. The term *party* became a part of my vocabulary, and soon it became natural for me to use that word.... This project, it pushed my boundaries. I needed to be in the space, to see the interaction happen, or else I wouldn't have understood the interviews as fully as I did, I don't think. Even my earlier interviews, they didn't feel as comfortable. And even after I was comfortable, it was still sometimes hard for me to feel comfortable. I mean, they do this all of the time. And so they are talking to me as they would to someone from the media, and I am learning through all of this and I'm trying to be comfortable. So it's not a real conversation at the beginning.

Jimmie: Tell me about that.

Jennifer: I feel so uncomfortable in that position. Part of the reason I did this was because it took me outside of my comfort zone.... And so it takes me as a researcher more emotion to do this work. Because it's not a way I do interpersonal relationships, to try to build relationships to learn what you want to learn. So I had to do that....

Jimmie: And so this was actually your first qualitative study, right?

Jennifer: Yes.

Jimmie: And this was your first interpersonal communication study, too, right?

Jennifer: Yes.

Jimmie: So tell me about that.

Jennifer: It was really about me making sense of the environment, because I was interested in how the show was portraying these women. I didn't really think of this as an interpersonal study at first; I thought of it as a media study. I feel like the knowledge that I use to do textual analysis and rhetoric guided me. But at the same time, most of the interviews took place in the rooms where these women live and work, and so we're sitting on the bed where they do a lot of that work and talking. And at a point I realized I was in their lives. And I saw how they related to each other and how they related with their clients. It was very interesting.

Jimmie: So it sounds like this study touches on a lot of communication contexts: interpersonal, media, even organizational.

Jennifer: Yes! I'm gonna give you one example to demonstrate this. As I began writing, especially the methods section of my work on the original project, I started to refer to *my* work at the Bunny Ranch, and of course the project was about *their* work at the Bunny Ranch. And yet I was doing my own work. And so it became an issue of not only how do *they* define work— but also how do *I* define work? It became complicated, about how I worked in that place. There was something there . . . .

Jimmie: A tension?

Jennifer: I don't even want to call it a tension. It's something that can't be easily defined, but it's something I can feel. I tried to draw it out during the writing process. That's what we do in ethnography, right?

Jimmie: Yeah. Or that we try to draw out in an interview. So it isn't a tension. What *was* there?

Jennifer: I think it was more an issue of how do they define work, and how do I define work. I mean, earlier we joked about how it wasn't participant observation, but in a way it was. I was doing my work there, and they were doing their work there. It's something about how the structure of what was going on and the structure of the environment. I mean, the place is set up to be filmed and part of a media show. And so you have people living there, living their lives. And they are doing their work there. And then they are on television.

Jimmie: What a great space to study.

Jennifer: Yes, it was. When I initially saw the show *Cathouse*, it demonstrated something I didn't usually see on television. And that disconnect made me want to look at the narrative of the show.

Jimmie: What do you mean by *disconnect*?

Jennifer: This show is so different in that the women on this show, they have sex for money, and they are not punished for it. They seem to be having a good time, and they are taking matters into their own hands to make a lot of money.

Jimmie: And some are critical of that.

Jennifer: Yes, and people want me to take a critical stance, but I wasn't interested in that.

Waitress: All right.

Jennifer: Oh, here we go. Thank you.

Jimmie: Thanks.

Waitress: Ketchup or Tabasco?

Jimmie: Both, please.

Jennifer: This looks great!

Jimmie: I only have a couple more questions, so let's just finish up while we eat. Is that okay?

Jennifer: Yeah. Definitely. So, uh, they want me to take a critical stance. But I don't. I do critical work as well. But in this case, what struck me from the beginning is that this story really goes against, what, what we as a society think.

Jimmie: And in this case, that can be critical.

Jennifer: But people want me to jump on what they do and be critical of that. And why should we? I have a couple of good quotes in my dissertation, and they ask why should we jump on it immediately? Do we always have to be critical up front? Why is that the assumption? I get that many women have to go into something like this, and they don't have a choice. But the women I talked to were making a lot of money through this and looked at this as a life choice, and I don't think there is anything that has to be wrong with that. It doesn't have to be critical.

Jimmie: Right. I hear you.

Jennifer: Yeah, people want me to make judgment. And when I don't, they accuse me of being naïve. But I wanted to create a space where they can tell their stories. And what I saw during my time there didn't conflict with that.

Jimmie: I mean, I'm actually glad you said that. It was the same thing with me interviewing the families about purity rings. People wanted me to be critical. Or, I've even presented studies on how gay men negotiate sex, and people want me to bring a critical perspective to that. And, while I do like critical studies and believe they can be important, sometimes you have to say, "Well, can't we also be interested in understanding how people make sense of their lives?" I don't know why there are some individuals whose lives always have to be trapped in a critical space, at least in the scholarly world. In some ways, that's just as oppressive.

Jennifer: Exactly. I know ethnographic work assumes there's bias, but why does the bias always have to be negative? That something like this is all bad?

Jimmie: I think we have an essay here.

Jennifer: I can still be a feminist and understand how some people are oppressed without judging other people's lives. And so it has been a struggle. But hearing their stories, and understanding the women's lives, that has been helpful. . . .

Jimmie: So what would be something you could share, or that you could write about, that helps to move the focus on their relational lives?

Jennifer: One of the things that really stood out, and you don't see this on the show, is the relationship between the women and their families. You might assume that their families don't know, or that they're not involved, but the families do know, and they communicate with their families, and their families are usually supportive. That became a focus, the relationships the women have with their families.

Jimmie: So are you going to write about that?

Jennifer: I want to . . . that's one of the hard things. I have my notes, and I have the interviews, and this data is so rich. And space is so limited.

Jimmie: Especially for what you had to do for this book.

Jennifer: Yes. You and Adrianne were good editors, and you really helped me to think about where things could be cut out. That was helpful. . . . But after you get it to the page, it can be tough. It can be tough to pull back and take something out that you feel is so important for explaining what you see. . . . Or to take away from where they are telling their stories. . . . For what I wrote for your book, I think I used three or four women involved with the study, and I talked with over 30 and observed more. So the space limitation is a limitation, because it limits what I can tell. There's much richer data that can be used. So getting all of that into an article is tough.

Jimmie: Sounds like you've got the makings of a good book.

Jennifer: We'll see. There's a lot there. We'll see.

Questions for Growth

1. What ethical considerations might be important to the ethnographic work you want to do? How can you continuously keep your ethics "in check" when doing interpersonal ethnography projects?

2. As the chapter mentions, few interpersonal communication researchers engage ethnography. Why do you believe this is? What might make some good projects for an interpersonal ethnographer?

3. Do you see Dunn's work as participant observation? Why or why not? Based on her interview answers, what might be her opinion? How might this play into any ethnographic work you might do?

4. What might be the best methods to use with an ethnographic approach when studying families? How about romantic relationships? Computer-mediated communication?

Discourse Analysis, Thematic Analysis, and a Study of Computer-Mediated Communication

DISCOURSE ANALYSIS AND THE STUDY OF RELATIONSHIPS

Like ethnography and narrative inquiry (which will be covered in Chapter 8), *discourse analysis* is a collective term that refers to a variety of analytical possibilities for drawing out implicit or explicit meanings from words and even images. In the opening chapter of the book, we caution that those using qualitative methods have to be especially aware of what particular strand of a method a researcher is drawing from in his or her studies. Given that 20 distinct approaches to discourse analysis have been identified (van Dijk, 1997a, 1997b), that is especially true for discourse analysis. In addition to considering what brand of discourse analysis is being used in a given study, consumers of discourse analysis research, or those who explore discourse analysis beyond this chapter, should be aware that many times the term is mislabeled or conflated with *conversational analysis*. Conversation analysis is a form of discourse analysis, but whereas practice-oriented discourse analysis largely focuses on construction of meaning and how discourse constitutes a situation or social scene (Holstein & Gubrium, 2011), conversation analysis tends to focus on naturally occurring elements of interaction such as paralinguistic features or other nonverbal cues (Baxter & Babbie, 2004).

Discourse analysis has a rich, vibrant, and vast history across several academic disciplines. It has been used well in interpersonal communication studies, with two scholars—Karen Tracy and Leslie Baxter—developing new forms of discourse analysis as they engaged their studies. We spend much of this chapter focusing on Tracy and Baxter's developments because each scholar looks at discourse in different ways and tends to draw from two forms of data. We also consider many approaches to using discourses to understand interpersonal relationships, including their functions. As a final consideration, we offer an overview of the Critical Discourse Analysis movement that has received strong support as a methodological approach. This is followed by an examination of another form of discourse analysis that might allow for an interesting turn in interpersonal communication studies, *discourses-in-practice*.

The illustrative research study for this chapter uses a specific kind of natural discourse, computer-mediated communication via message boards, making it a fit for this chapter—but rather than a traditional discourse analytic approach, it draws from thematic analysis to make its conclusions (demonstrating that natural discourse does not always have to pair with a discourse analytic method). To begin all this, explanation about how discourse plays into interpersonal communication studies is offered.

CONNECTING EVERYDAY TALK AND OTHER TEXTS TO INTERPERSONAL RELATIONSHIPS

The basic assumption that seems to guide most discourse analysis in interpersonal communication studies is that discursive practices, made up of discourse, play into individual and relational identity (Tracy, 2002). As Tracy (2002) posits,

> The relationship between discursive practices and identities is a reciprocal one. The identities a person brings to an interaction influence how that person communicates. At the same time, the specific discursive practices a person chooses will shape who he or she is taken to be, and who the partner is taken to be. (p. 21)

This explanation stops short of considering outside discourses, or the discourses about a person, his or her identity, and his or her relationships. We contend that these distal discourses can play just as much into the reciprocal nature of identity as well.

The reciprocal nature of discourse and identity illustrates the power of communication in relational constitution. Not only are the discourses *within* a relationship of concern, but so are the discourses *about* a relationship. Combined, the two make the relationship. Although that premise may seem simple, understanding the various types of relational discourses and how they work together is anything but. In fact, van Dijk (1997a, 1997b) contends that all of his 700+ page, two-volume collection on discourse is an elaborate answer to what the word *discourse* means. So, while some will refer to discourse as practices of talking and writing in a general sense (Woodilla, 1998) and others will examine macro or micro elements of discourse (Cooren, 2010), all of those studies will buy into ideas of how the world is made meaningful through discourse processes and how that world itself is constructed through those discourses (Phillips & Brown, 1993).

Discursive Practice

The majority of this chapter focuses on discursive practice (Holstein & Gubrium, 2011; Tracy, 2002), or elements of discourse analysis that focus on social interaction. This interaction can be approached from a *structural perspective*, or how words, sentences, or collections of utterances constitute a social scene (Schiffrin, 1994). As the name implies, this approach places emphasis on understanding how the structure or grammar of language and interaction form a coherent (or sometimes incoherent) system of meaning. That differs from a *functional perspective*, or how people use discourse to achieve means

(Schiffrin, 1994). That use is not completely removed from its structural elements, and so those are considered in conjunction with how discourse is used, but the primary focus when using this approach is what a discourse does.

Discursive Practices in Everyday Talk

Probably the most popular approach to discourse analysis in interpersonal communication studies is the analysis of everyday talk. Everyday talk is "the ordinary kinds of communicating people do in schools, workplaces, in shops, and at public meetings, as well as when they are at home or with their friends" (Tracy, 2002, p. 5). Understanding how everyday talk is structured and how it functions in relationships can be valuable for interpersonal communication researchers and relationships scholars in general. Tracy (2002) identified eight common discursive practices in everyday talk. We present them here, divided into more structural practices—what Tracy (2002) describes as "talk's building blocks" (p. 43)—and those that extend beyond a structural focus and into more multifaceted territory, what Tracy describes as "complex discourse practices" (p. 111).

Talk's Building Blocks

These discursive practices help to illuminate how discourse is structured. By understanding these practices, interpersonal communication researchers can understand some of the building blocks of a social scene.

Person-Referencing Practices. These are words or phrases used to address other people or to refer to them in conversation. Person-referencing practices include discursive building blocks such as names, identity categories (including ethnic labels), titles, or roles. As Tracy (2002) notes, the ways people address other people can indicate closeness ("Mr. Wilson" versus "George" versus "My Georgie") and formality ("Dr. Wilson" vs. "Dr. Kim" vs. "Kimmy"). Person-referencing practices can also indicate context and what social identities are being drawn from in conversation (Sacks, 1992). For example, if a man notices a woman playing with her child he might refer to her as a "mother" rather than as a "human," "lawyer," or "Madonna fan"—even if those other identities are valid. In that case, he would be drawing from the social scene to determine a membership categorization (Sacks, 1992) entrenched in larger cultural ideas about women's roles in families.

Speech Acts. One of the biggest advancements in thinking was crystallized by Austin (1962), who observed that people used language as more than a simple descriptive tool. Words were also used to do things. Speech acts, then, are acts that are performed through talk. Austin (1962) suggests there are as many speech acts as there are verbs. Even though speech acts may be unlimited, Searle (1979) developed five categories that serve to describe speech acts. *Directives* attempt to get a person to take action ("Please hand me my purse"), *representatives* establish a situation or condition ("It is raining outside" or "This room is tense"), *commissives* illustrate some sort of commitment or intent ("I will buy you the toy" or "Do it and I'll slap you!"), *expressives* display, reveal, or establish feeling ("I'm just shocked!" or "You know what I'm in the mood for?"), and *declaratives* transform social understandings ("I now pronounce you man and wife" or "You are fired"). As Tracy (2002) notes, speech acts can be multifunctional and fall into multiple categories.

Speech acts are referenced in the next chapter on narrative inquiry where it is noted that sometimes narratives can serve as speech acts. That should not be confused with narrative analysis as a form of discourse analysis (Riessman, 2007), even though discourse analysis can be enacted using narratives.

Sounds of Speech. This category refers to paralinguistic features. The in-depth analysis of such features is typically studied through conversation analysis, as opposed to the form of discourse analysis covered in this chapter. All discourse analysts should consider, however, how the sound of talk can provide context for a discourse.

Language Selection. Tracy (2002) notes that there are discourse implications for those who choose to speak one language over another. Language selection here, then, is different from general word or phrase choice. Instead, it examines how someone who speaks multiple languages may choose which language to speak in a given context. Some may also mix languages within the same utterance, and there are likely implications there, too. For example, a young boy may know that his mother is really upset when she yells at him in Spanish instead of English. That same mother may throw in some Spanish words in her primarily English utterances as she tells her friend what she misses about living in Mexico, and in that case the code switching would not indicate anger but instead fondness. Of course, many people may not have the ability to draw from more than one language in their utterances. That may have relational implications in and of itself.

Complex Discourse Practices

The four previous categories move beyond simple structural issues and into rhetorical and cultural elements of talk. The practices that Tracy (2002) labels as complex do the same but in much more sophisticated and multifaceted ways.

Interaction Structures. Much of the research exploring interaction structures focuses on two primary ideas: turn taking (Sacks, 1992) and adjacency pairs (Schegloff & Sacks, 1973). Turn taking examines how people tend to know when it is their turn to speak in a conversation and is often the work of conversation analysts. Adjacency pairs also explore ideas about order in conversations but on a more discursive level. Examining adjacency pairs means looking at the words or phrases expected to follow a particular utterance in conversation. Some of these are phatic, such as "How's it going?" paired with a response such as "Pretty good." Others seek answers, such as "Want to see a movie?" paired with "I really have a lot of homework." If the question about seeing a movie were answered with "Ice cream is delicious," then there would likely be confusion because the rules implied by the adjacency pair are not being followed. In terms of relationships, the refusal of an expected adjacency pair can indicate problems. A wife might ask her husband, "Who's my big bear?" and get the response, "Why don't you ask Tim?" instead of the mock growl that he usually offers. That could indicate that things are not so great between her and her husband, and he may be jealous of the time she is spending with Tim. Relational partners can also play with adjacency pairs in fun ways to add excitement or novelty to a relationship. The response of "The big bear wants to take his hot momma to the cave!" would indicate something completely different.

Directness Styles. Directness in interpersonal communication offers insights into both relational form and situation. Norton (1983) argues that people have conversational styles, or a general and consistent way of speaking. Differences in conversational style can be distinct across people, and they may vary based on whom the conversation is with and under what circumstances. Directness is one of these styles, and how directly a person uses language both in general and in a particular situation can allow understandings of how a relationship is constituted through conversation. Tracy (2002) notes many ways this can play out in interpersonal communication, including information seeking ("I didn't want to ask him, so I kind of hinted at it"), expression of opinion ("Yeah, uh, I think the president is doing an okay job"), making an argument ("The dress is too expensive. Period"), or emotional expression ("I like you. I really do. I like you so much. I just don't know if I'm ready for that yet"). For each of the discursive examples listed, the directness of the language used probably indicates something about that relationship. Interpersonal communication scholars would do well to consider how other conversational styles play into the constitution of relationships.

Narratives. Tracy (2002) identifies narratives as a form of everyday talk as well. As explored in the next chapter, narrative inquiry focuses on the narratives as a whole, but discourse analysts may want to focus on parts of the narrative or more on the content of stories as separate from the stories themselves. The concepts, approaches, and tools used throughout this chapter can assist in doing such work.

Stance Indicators. The "linguistic, vocal, and gestural means of conveying an attitude toward a topic or the conversational partner" are what Tracy (2002, p. 173) terms *stance indicators*. Drawing from the work of Ochs (1993), Tracy (2002) suggests that stances often serve as what one person presumes to be the internal, perhaps enduring, state of another. As the definition for stance indicators implies, much of the work surrounding them falls into the domain of conversational analysis. Still, considering stance indicators in discourse can be a fruitful exercise for interpersonal communication scholars. For example, Tracy (2002) notes one linguistic choice that people use, marked and unmarked forms that can discursively indicate stance. An unmarked form indicates what a person sees as normal, whereas a marked form notes what a person sees as unusual, atypical, or unique. For example, a parent may indicate that his daughter is a "female basketball player" where he simply calls his son a "basketball player." That marked form probably indicates he buys into a larger social understanding that men are typically thought of as basketball players.

From Talk to Analysis

The ideas explored here are but a beginning to the possibilities of understanding how talk can be studied in order to better understand relationships. As is probably evident from reviewing these concepts, the line between method and concept is blurred. It could be that stance indicators, for example, are used as a method for uncovering the answer to a research question. Or it might be that they are used in conjunction with another method in order to allow for greater or more nuanced insights. We now turn to deeper considerations about how discourse may be analyzed.

ANALYZING DISCOURSE

In communication studies, discourse is often analyzed with either some sort of rhetorical question or purpose in mind or, more often the case in interpersonal communication studies, some sort of cultural question. A rhetorical approach to studying interpersonal communication (Duck, 2011; Manning, in press-a; Tracy, 2002) assumes that people are often strategic and purposeful in using discourse and that much of their discourse is goal related. That does not necessarily mean that people are fully mindful or that they tend to be manipulative; rather, it embraces Burke's (1966) notion that language and discourse reflect, select, and deflect particular ideas or realities. Much more common in interpersonal communication studies is the embracing of a cultural perspective that examines *interpersonal ideologies*, or "communities' beliefs about interpersonal issues" (Tracy, 2002, p. 35). As that definition illustrates, a cultural approach examines how a relational discourse is embedded in a larger community of discourse, and that larger community of discourse certainly plays into proximal relational discourses, too. Qualitative researchers do not have to choose between rhetorical and cultural approaches. In fact, for a given research question, both approaches may be used with the same data set to understand multiple aspects of a discourse. Understanding whether a question will likely involve a rhetorical or cultural approach (or both) can be useful in allowing for the selection of a discourse for a given study.

Selecting a Discourse

Selecting a discourse often depends on what kind of discourses can be captured and to what extent. For most situations relational discourses—especially natural talk in an everyday environment—will be difficult to capture. That probably helps to explain why interview methods are so popular in interpersonal communication studies. Even if interviewing is a productive method that generates solid interpersonal communication theory about interaction social scientists may not ever be able to witness, it does not mean that other discourses cannot help to expand understandings of a given phenomenon or be used as another source of data in a given research study. Discourses are enacted and embodied in many kinds of texts, and the discourses found within a given text are all connected to other discourses that allow them to be intelligible (Phillips & Hardy, 2002). Chalaby (1996) offers the idea that in many ways a text is where a discourse materializes, but that materiality is indicative of something more than the text alone. Common texts include spoken words, writing, artifacts, media productions, or any unit contained and defined for the purposes of a study (Grant, Kenoy, & Oswick, 1998). Tracy and Muñoz (2011) note that two common sources of discourse for analysis in interpersonal communication studies are captured talk and documents with written or visual text.

Captured Talk

When possible, audio recordings of talk in natural environments can allow for rich exploration of discourse. Interpersonal communication scholars have located tapes from institutions where recording is a regular occurrence—such as Tracy and Agne's (2002) study of 911 calls—as well as in situations where recordings could be captured as a part of daily work (Mirivel, 2007) or at public meetings (S. J. Tracy, 2010). Semipublic meetings also make a good place to capture interaction, but just as with ethnographic observation, consider the ethics involved. Dennis, Kunkel, and Keyton (2008), for example, captured discussions in a breast cancer support group with the group knowing in advance that they were going to be analyzing the discourse. Interpersonal communication scholars should continue to consider how they can access naturally occurring interaction in private settings without being overly intrusive. It may be that, as interpersonal communication becomes more digitally mediated through platforms such as Skype, this kind of data is easier to capture than ever before, but all advances must be made with careful ethical considerations about what it means to ask participants to give up their privacy.

In recording public, semiprivate, or private meetings or interaction, test recording conditions in advance so that there are no surprises. As technology prices continue to go down, it is not difficult to find a professional-grade recorder through online sales outlets that will allow for crisp, clear audio. These recordings do constitute identifiable data, and so researchers will want to handle any recordings with appropriate sensitivity. Tracy and Muñoz (2011) reviewed best practices for capturing discourses, and they suggest researchers ask many key questions:

> Should they video- or audiotape, and what kind of equipment should they use? How important is it to be unobtrusive, and how important is it to capture facial expressions, gestures, and the use of objects in the environment? Will it be difficult to tell who is talking without a video? If videotaping, how many cameras should there be and where should they be positioned? Which actors should the cameras foreground if not everyone can be easily seen? (p. 68)

In offering these questions, Tracy and Muñoz (2011) note there are no correct answers. Instead, researchers have to assess what makes sense for their particular studies knowing that competing concerns may require tough choices.

Qualitative analysis programs such as NVivo now allow for coding of recordings, both audio and visual, but in most cases any captured recordings are going to have to be transcribed. Transcription is as frustrating as it is rewarding. Good transcription takes time, and as Tracy and Muñoz (2011) note, it is one of the few areas of qualitative research where reliability is of great concern. Also of concern in the textualization process is how the transcription will appear once the words are captured (Ochs, 1979). Will it look like a play script? How will overlapping dialogue be handled? How will things such as laughter or deep sighs or gestures that accompany particular words or phrases be noted? How will emphasis on words be recorded? Once again, these are concerns that must be handled on a study-by-study basis as the researcher iteratively makes decisions that best work for the data at hand. As those questions suggest, farming recordings out to a transcriptionist for recording may be problematic because the transcriptionist did not capture the data and, as such, may not be able to record it on the page in a way that honors or preserves the interactive situation. That is not to say that in some cases hiring someone else to do transcription is a bad practice—but it may be a bad practice for a particular study. We are often careful to try to transcribe at least some—if not all—of our data for a given study. This choice is not only a matter of representation on the transcript page but immersing ourselves in the data and what it means. As most qualitative scholars will probably tell you, as frustrating as transcribing is, it is where a lot of ideas come into focus.

Written Documents and Visual Text

Whereas preparation is often a concern for recorded discourse, discourse via written documents, visual texts, and other artifacts is often minimal. Sometimes capturing and transcription issues can come into play with media texts. For example, a researcher may come up with a great idea for an interpersonal communication study that involves analyzing a group of television programs. Once those episodes are secured—whether it is through recording them, purchasing them, or negotiating access from the producers—a researcher has to consider how to handle the text. Considerations for how to best navigate these waters can come from our disciplinary colleagues in media studies or rhetorical theory. Relationships scholars might also look to the innovation these areas are demonstrating. For instance, the continued study of public memorials (e.g., Dickinson, Blair, & Ott, 2010) and other forms of material rhetoric should serve as inspiration for interpersonal communication studies of personal memorials in and out of the home.

In some cases, preparation of documents is needed, but in most cases documents and other artifacts will be ready to analyze and need no special preparation. The bigger concern will likely be *how* the materials are analyzed, as document and material analysis are newer to interpersonal communication studies (Tracy & Muñoz, 2011). Because this kind of research is different for the subdiscipline, it does not mean that it has to be far removed from the kinds of work interpersonal scholars do. Textual analysis can be highly personal. For example, research has used wedding photo albums in order to understand cross-cultural relationships (Leeds-Hurwitz, 2002), and studies of personal ads (e.g., Coupland, 1996; Manning, in press-a) involve texts that are or were actively being used to initiate relationships. In considering studies that might involve texts or artifacts, researchers should not feel limited to those already in existence. The work of Harter, Leeman, Norander, Young, and Rawlins (2008) should serve as inspiration in this area. In this study, the researchers employ a conceptual framework that explores aesthetic practices and imagination to understand how members of an art organization that works with people with developmental disabilities relate with their clients through art. Through iterative analysis, the study generated three themes: "art as creation and vocation, art as ephemeral integration, and art as survival and social change" (Harter et al., 2008, p. 423).

As part of the total research process with the organization, art was created by clients and served as an artifact for analysis. As Harter (2009) later reflected about the experience,

> For individuals with limited language skills, the arts offer a range of media for self-discovery and expression. For several years, I've been involved with Passion Works, an art studio for individuals with developmental disabilities (see Harter et al., 2008; Harter, Scott, Novak, Leeman, & Morris, 2006). A majority of the artists have difficulty communicating using speech because of congenital disabilities or illnesses and injuries that substantially limit their language abilities. The studio offers artists opportunities to engage their imagination and storytelling sensibilities using genres such as painting, drawing, and sculpting. I've developed a richer understanding of cerebral palsy and cerebellar spinal degeneration by painting with Passion Works artists, and I've been reminded of the centrality and significance of *imagining* in everyday life. (p. 148, emphasis in original)

The use of art and other nonverbal-oriented expression can allow for new possibilities in discourse analysis.

Manning's Multiadic Approach

While analysis of documents and other nontraditional texts offers room for innovation in discourse analysis, novel approaches to a *variety* of discourses collected for a given study can allow for fresh perspective as well. Manning (2010a, in press-a, in press-b) offers a multiadic approach to discourse analysis (or qualitative research in general) that calls for a variety of discourses to be collected so that they can be compared and contrasted to allow for multiple ways of knowing within a given study. For example, in a study that explored relational turning points (Manning, 2010a) each member of a couple engaged a retrospective interviewing technique (see Huston, Surra, Fitzgerald, & Cate, 1981) in a separate room in their home. Then, after they were interviewed apart from each other, the couple was brought back together and asked to examine both of their turning points charts generated during their interview sessions. As they were comparing their charts, their interaction was recorded to capture a discourse that allowed a different kind of insight into how relational memory materializes. In that study, the researcher encouraged both discourses, even if only one was structured.

In another study (Manning, in press-a), the discourses of personal ads were analyzed and compared to discourses generated in interviews with the same people who posted them. As part of the interviewing procedure, participants were first asked to tell what they had to offer in a dating relationship and what they were looking for in a dating partner. That allowed for two types of discourses for comparison—an articulated discourse as delivered to the interviewer and a presentational discourse as delivered through the personal advertisement. In the second half of the interview, the interviewee's personal advertisement was presented to the person who posted it and questions were asked about choices made in the advertisement. This line of questioning allowed yet another type of discourse to be generated in the study. The unprovoked discourse—the personal advertisement—now has two provoked discourses as companions for analysis that allows for comparison and validity. Again, multiple discourses allow for multiple understandings.

Tools for Analysis

As this chapter illustrates, discourse analysis serves as both method and methodology (Phillips & Hardy, 2002). It is a form of interpretive analysis just as much as it is an approach to how social worlds are constructed (Parker & Burman, 1993). Wood and Kroger (2000) elaborate upon this duality, noting that discourse analysis

> is not only about method; it is also a perspective on the nature of language and its relationship to the central issues of the social sciences. More specifically, we see discourse analysis as a related collection of approaches to discourse, approaches that entail not only practices of data collection and analysis, but also a set of metatheoretical and theoretical assumptions and a body of research claims and studies. (p. x)

Interpersonal communication studies certainly adhere to this connection between method and methodology—or a direct connection between theory as analytical tool.

Here we offer two such cases. The first, Baxter's (2011) contrapuntal analysis, demonstrates a structural approach. The second, Tracy's (2005) action-implicative discourse analysis, demonstrates a functional approach. We offer these overviews as an introduction to the analytical tools and the theories that undergird them. Those interested in enacting them should seek out the resources associated with each method so as to best put them into research practice.

Baxter's Contrapuntal Analysis

Contrapuntal analysis (Baxter, 2011) was developed in conjunction with relational dialectics theory (Baxter, 2011; Baxter & Montgomery, 1996), an interpersonal communication theory that examines how meanings circulating around individual and relational identities are constructed via language (Baxter, 2011). In particular, relational dialectics theory (RDT), in its most current iteration, examines how "meanings are wrought from the struggle of competing, often contradictory discourses" (Baxter, 2011, p. 2). Understanding RDT is essential for understanding contrapuntal analysis. Baxter and Braithwaite (2008) provide three propositions to illustrate the primary features of the theory. The first is what is often identified as the key proposition for the theory, the idea that meaning comes from contradictory discourses. The second proposition is that "the interpenetration of discourses is both synchronic and diachronic" (Baxter & Braithwaite, 2008, p. 353). That is, a discourse involves ongoing communicative work over time (diachronic) but also materializes in the moment (synchronic) as part of an utterance chain. Finally, Baxter and Braithwaite (2008) posit that "the interpenetration of competing discourses constitutes social reality" (p. 355). This idea is both different from and the same as the constitutive principle mentioned throughout this book. It is similar in that it assumes discourse constitutes social reality (in the case of RDT, that is often relationships), but it is different in that meaning is located in the interpenetration of different, even opposing discourses.

For the beginner interested in contributing to the development of RDT and using contrapuntal analysis as a discourse analytic method, Baxter (2011) recommends texts of analysis where competitive discourses are bold. She also suggests that contrapuntal analysis can be used well for critical endeavors where some voices are marginalized and others are dismissed. The general guiding question for contrapuntal analysis is, "What are the competing discourses in the text and how is meaning constructed through their interplay?" (Baxter, 2011, p. 152). The first step to performing the analysis is to complete a thematic analysis of the text to identify its discourses (see the Thematic Analysis section that follows for details). Next, the researcher analyzes where discourses compete. Baxter (2011) stresses that these discourses should compete from the participants' (or what she calls *natives*) point of view. Competing discourses might negate, counter, or entertain (Baxter, 2011). *Negating* claims another discourse is irrelevant or rejects it. *Countering* offers a particular discursive position in place of another. *Entertaining* does not completely reject or dismiss a discourse but does counter that it is but one possible discursive position.

Next, the researcher is ready to identify where and how competing discourses interpenetrate (Baxter, 2011). This interplay can indicate *dialogically contractive discursive practices* or *dialogically expansive discursive practices*. As those category names imply, interplay can lead to some discourses being muffled or silenced (dialogically contractive) and others being encouraged or amplified (dialogically expansive; Baxter, 2011). The completed analysis allows for a stronger sense of how meaning is located within a text and how the structure of a text supports or constitutes such meaning.

Those wishing to enact contrapuntal analysis are strongly encouraged to explore Baxter's book *Voicing Relationships: A Dialogic Perspective* (2011), as the entire text is dedicated to elaborating upon RDT, with the sixth and final chapter providing a thorough primer for engaging analysis. For an excellent research study that uses contrapuntal analysis, see Norwood's (2012) study of family discourses constituting transgender coming out experiences.

Tracy's Action-Implicative Discourse Analysis

Action-implicative discourse analysis (AIDA) is the analytical manifestation of grounded practical theory (Craig & Tracy, 1995; Tracy & Craig, 2010). Grounded practical theory is a metatheoretical reconceptualization of the communication discipline as a practical-oriented endeavor. That is, grounded practical theory positions research as a tool for understanding a social scene and how communication theory can be a tool for understanding and attending to its particulars (Tracy & Craig, 2010). Grounded practical theory and, consequently, AIDA focus on practices within institutions (e.g., patient-client interaction) as well as more generalized contexts (e.g., negotiation). Through AIDA, tacit situations can be made explicit so as problems can be addressed, ideas for best practices or ideal conduct can be ascertained, and action—especially communicative action—can be adjusted (Tracy, 2008).

Karen Tracy's (2010) recent book, *Challenges of Ordinary Democracy: A Case Study in Deliberation and Dissent*, offers a strong example of how AIDA can be applied in qualitative research. Using a multiadic approach that includes captured interaction from public meetings, accounts from newspapers, and interview data, the practices of discourse analysis are applied in light of grounded practical theory to offer palpable considerations for action. The research demonstrates all three of the ways AIDA can reconstruct communicative practices. First, it addresses many of the problems diverse participants face in their roles (Tracy, 2008). Situated understanding on the individual level is a key consideration for AIDA. Second, it addresses the technical aspects of AIDA (Tracy, 2008). That is, constructions of interactional behaviors are considered in terms of their problems, and communicative strategies for solving them are developed. Finally, the third and most abstract level, the philosophical, is engaged as overarching ideas about democracy and its principles are normatively considered as they are facilitated through communication. In short, the approach uses discourse analysis to seek out and resolve interactional dilemmas (Tracy, 2008).

The Critical Discourse Analysis Movement

For those interested in engaging critical studies of interpersonal communication, both AIDA and especially contrapuntal analysis are good analytical fits. Another brand of discourse analysis, made popular by European discourse analysts such as Fairclough (2009), van Dijk (2009), and Wodak and Chilton (2007), is specially designed for critical-scholarly purposes. As Fairclough (1996) narrates, critical discourse analysis (CDA) "developed in a particular location within a particular political situation—out of a tendency of the political left and within the new social movements (feminism, ecology, etc.) toward cultural and ideological forms of political struggle from the 1960s onward" (p. 52). Generally defined, CDA examines how discursive practices (both verbal and visual) lead to or constitute social injustice or inequalities (Fairclough & Wodak, 1997). Like discourse analysis itself, it is not a single approach but rather a school of thought that uses multiple methodological approaches (ethnographic observation is often a favorite tool) toward exposing oppressive or unjust discourses as they circulate in a culture. So in many ways CDA is like other forms of discourse analysis, only the axiological motives are centered upon emancipation for minoritized or oppressed people. Important studies exploring racism in everyday talk (van Dijk, 1987) demonstrate the peripheral value CDA may offer to the development of interpersonal communication theory, but studies such as Bartesaghi's (2009) that explored family conversations surrounding first clinic meetings in a therapy center show how CDA can be at the heart of relationships studies. CDA is especially beneficial as a micro-level practice, but we close our discussion on discourse by examining a critical approach that tends to work with macro-level discourses but has received little to no attention in interpersonal communication studies.

Discourses-in-Practice

As promised near the beginning of this chapter, most of it has dealt with discursive practice or the constitutive power of discourses in everyday life. We close with a brief—but we hope important—mention of an alternate approach to understanding discourse. As Foucault (1972) explains, discourses cannot be characterized as "a mere intersection of things and words: an obscure web of things, and a manifest, visible, colored chain of words" (p. 344). Instead, discourses are "practices that systematically form the objects [and subjects] of which they speak" (Foucault, 1972, p. 49). That notion is not dissimilar to the ideas undergirding discursive practice explored in this chapter. For Foucault, however, "the accent is as much on the constructive *whats* that discourse constitutes as it is on the *hows* of discursive technology" (Holstein & Gubrium, 2011, p. 344). In other words, rather than seeking to understand a situated discourse in the current moment, Foucault's work seeks to understand how these discursive understandings have formulated as privileged or powered over time. If scholars examining discursive practice seek to understand how people use discourse in their social activities (broadly defined) and how discourse creates their social worlds, then discourses-in-practice seek to unpack historical understandings that help to illustrate what the outcome of discourse is likely to be.

Much of Foucault's research dealt with institutional sites such as prisons or asylums. These systems were of interest to him because they allowed for inquiry into discourses of power and knowledge (Foucault, 1980). In examining how discourses operated on a practical level, Foucault was able to link constructions of lived experiences with discourses of particular subjectivities (Foucault, 1988). Or as Holstein and Gubrium (2011) explain, "It is an orientation to practice that views lived experience and subjectivities as always already embedded and embodied in their discursive conventions" (p. 344). That is, broad discursive understandings constitute regimes of historical and institutional power that govern and discipline members of a social world (Foucault, 1979). As Holstein and Gubrium so vividly illustrate in their example,

> [I]n a Western postindustrial society, to seriously think of medicine and voodoo as equally viable paradigms for understanding sickness and healing would seem idiosyncratic, if not preposterous, in most conventional situations. The power of medical discourse partially lies in its ability to be "seen but unnoticed," in its ability to appear as *the* only possibility while other possibilities are outside of the plausible realm. (2011, p. 344, emphasis in original)

Interpersonal communication scholars might ask, then, what goes "seen but unnoticed" in our studies? How are the discourses we study historically situated?

The dominant mode of discourse studies in interpersonal communication interrogates localized and situated understandings of discourse as it constitutes a social scene. Such studies of meaning-making in relationships are no doubt important and a worthy endeavor—especially given that they make up so little of interpersonal communication scholarship. Those who study interpersonal communication and relationships in general might also consider how Foucault-driven *discourse-in-practice* may also be studied to allow a fuller understanding of relational discourses across institutions and across times. As we engage these endeavors, we should be particularly mindful of avoiding the parallel nature most discourse studies have already taken (see Holstein & Gubrium, 2011)—that is, rather than exploring discursive practice and discourse-in-practice alongside each other, we might also set a superordinate goal of working toward ways these two bodies of discourse studies might overlap.

THEMATIC ANALYSIS

As noted in an earlier section of this chapter, thematic analysis may be a form of discourse analysis when that analysis is carried out in search of discourses. Thematic analysis can be used as a sorting mechanism for data in just about any way conceivable, however. It is often used as a first-cycle coding or sorting method, with deeper analysis usually following based upon these findings. Thematic analysis is not the only first-cycle method (see Saldaña, 2009, for an idea of others available), but it is one of the most common in interpersonal communication studies and the communication discipline as a whole. It often serves as an appealing option because it helps a researcher to have a keener sense of what is there, in terms of the data, and what possibilities lie ahead for interpretation. Earlier we cautioned that many studies carry out thematic analysis and leave it at that and that such practices were likely not giving full attention to the data and drawing out sophisticated or nuanced answers to research questions. In some cases, however, thematic analysis is appropriate as a stand-alone analytical approach, and so we explore it here.

Two situations in particular are choice for thematic analysis. First, topics or concepts that are largely unexplored or that have been explored in another domain or context other than interpersonal communication may rely upon thematic analysis to contextualize or recontextualize the topic as one that is interpersonal, communicative, or both. For example, grocery stores may not be a topic many think of as interpersonal. A study examining interpersonal communication in grocery stores may begin with thematic analysis of what interpersonal elements tend to circulate within grocery stores. Moving to a second ideal situation for thematic analysis, it also makes for excellent shorter research reports. Such reports would likely offer a primary focus on the data and its nature rather than the elaborate theoretical or conceptual elements derived from such data. As most of the research reports included in this book demonstrate, however, it is entirely possible to write up research studies using coding methods or forms of analysis other than thematic analysis.

As mentioned earlier, many times thematic analysis is given the misnomer of *grounded theory*. Grounded theory is something else entirely, and unless a researcher is following an established grounded theory tradition (such as Charmaz, 2006; Corbin & Strauss, 1990; or Glaser & Strauss, 1967) then that label should be avoided. That said, some methods of "theming" the data, such as Strauss and Corbin's (1998) framework for coding, draw from a grounded theoretical background without fully enacting grounded theory. Thematic analysis can play out in several other ways (see Auerbach & Silverstein, 2003;

Boyatzis, 1998; Rubin & Rubin, 1995; and van Manen, 1990, among others), and although the details vary from scholar to scholar, all of the forms focus on dividing data into "an implicit topic that organizes a group of repeating ideas" (Auerbach & Silverstein, 2003, p. 38). That foundation, in turn, can allow for larger or smaller categories to be formed that cluster together similar themes or divide some themes into even more intricate ones. Themes should be essential and derived across data and not incidentally formed from one or two instances, although those one or two instances may highlight possibilities for negative case analysis. Van Manen (1990) offers one consideration for whether or not a particular element of data should be themed, noting that a theme should represent "what it is and without which the phenomenon could not be what it is" (p. 107).

The process itself helps to illustrate the principles that undergird it and how it might be useful to qualitative scholars. Here we outline Braun and Clarke's (2006) approach to thematic analysis, one that involves six steps. The first step is to become familiar with the data set. That often means reading through transcripts or field notes many times, but it could also mean repeatedly listening to interviews or other recorded data. Second, the researcher moves through the data and creates initial codes. How these codes are generated depends on the research purpose. For a research question asking, "How do people communicate in supermarkets?" one code may be "to get meat" (or simply "get meat" or even "meat" or "at the meat counter"—at this point, the important thing is for the researcher to find a way of coding that works for his or her style). Another code could be "to maneuver around people." Yet a third could be "to greet friends." All of the data continue to be coded, with new codes created for each additional and unique datum (an individual datum could be one word up to many sentences or whatever makes best sense with a visual text) and with created codes used as many times as is necessary and appropriate.

Third, themes are generated from the codes. Just as with the development of codes, the development of themes is an iterative process. Continuing with the previous example, the codes of "to get meat" and "to get deli items" might be combined with other similar codes to create a theme of "customer-counter communication." Similarly, "to maneuver around people" could be combined with "to get help reaching an item" and other such codes to create a theme of "customer-customer communication." The two themes could then iteratively be placed into one larger theme of "practical communication." The theme then serves to answer the research question: one way people communicate in grocery stores is for practical reasons; this plays out in their role as a customer as they communicate with the various supermarket counters as well as other customers. Within each of those categories are particular ways of communication salient to supermarket experiences. Of course, other themes will also come into play that elaborate upon the research question. All of these themes are reviewed in the fourth step of analysis. One way of doing this is to reapproach the data and consider whether it can all be represented by the generated themes. At this point, it may also be helpful to run a member check to see if the themes make sense to those who are directly or indirectly involved with the social scene or one similar. Adjustments should be made to themes and codes as necessary.

Once that is complete, the fifth step of determining final theme names and defining them occurs. Names should be clear and appropriate and indicative of the social scene. Sometimes they are taken from names or slang terms used in the social scene, but the researcher might apply a name that is more clinical but still honest to the data as it reflects a social world. Definitions explain each theme and clearly indicate what would and would not be included. During the fifth step, more validity checks may also come into play (the final chapter of this book reviews some of these later-stage validity concerns).

Finally, data exemplars are selected that best illustrate the theme. When the data lend themselves to it, the exemplar choices help to give color to the category names and definitions, illustrating what the researcher may not be able to concisely or eloquently put into words. Sometimes a researcher may be tempted to include data exemplars that are particularly polished or colorful, or that avoid the messiness often found in interactive social worlds. Resisting that impulse may be important, as the exemplars help to characterize the social world that the researcher is claiming to represent. However, that does not mean such data need to be buried. Instead, elucidate explanations of the data's character (e.g., "One participant was more direct than the others in presenting her take, stating that . . ."). Once these steps are followed, the results should illustrate not only a data set but also the social world from which it was culled.

We now turn to a research report that employs a different form of thematic analysis to explore a computer-mediated discourse. As you read the study, consider how the research report offers a sense of what the discourses look like as well as clear understandings of how the discourses are themed. Additionally, this study is a strong example of sensitized theorizing. It uses the relational turbulence model (Solomon & Knobloch, 2004) as a heuristic for understanding the iteratively generated themes found in the data set. An interview with one of the authors follows.

The Online Discourse of Wounded Warrior Wives

A Study of Online Discourses Using Thematic Analysis

Victoria Jennings-Kelsall and Denise Haunani Solomon, Pennsylvania State University

As the War on Terror enters into its second decade, the number of wounded, injured, and ill (WII) veterans continues to grow. The WII veterans, commonly referred to as "wounded warriors," include servicemembers diagnosed with, among other conditions, posttraumatic stress disorder (PTSD), traumatic brain injury (TBI), and trauma from burn injuries and amputations. Responsibility for caring for the WII often falls to military spouses, who must manage the complications of living with and caring for a wounded warrior alongside the other stressors that confront military families (e.g., child care, education, and career issues [Drummet, Coleman, & Cable, 2003]; military relocation [Black, 1993; Kelley, 1994]; loss of network support [Drummet et al., 2003]). For these couples, the consequences of combat can extend beyond personal injuries and impose a transformation of the marital relationship. Our goal, therefore, is to understand relationship issues that may emerge in the experiences of WII spousal caregivers.

Our perspective is informed by the relational turbulence model (RTM), which highlights tensions that characterize relationships in transition (Solomon & Knobloch, 2004). The theory posits that transitions within romantic associations create uncertainty about involvement in the relationship and increase goal interference; in turn, relational uncertainty and goal interference promote reactivity to irritations, suspicions, and hurtful comments. *Relational uncertainty* encompasses doubts about one's own commitment to the relationship, a partner's involvement in the association, and the nature of the relationship as a whole (Knobloch & Solomon, 1999). *Interference from a partner* reflects the extent to which one person impedes the goals of the other partner (Solomon & Knobloch, 2004). RTM was developed through studies focused on transitions that occur in dating relationships (Solomon & Theiss, 2011), and it has been extended to married couples dealing with the stresses of breast cancer or infertility (Solomon, Weber, & Steuber, 2010); however, the extent the theory applies to traumatic marital transitions, such as those imposed by serious combat injuries, remains untested. By considering RTM in conjunction with the experiences of spousal caregivers of the WII, we hope to provide insight into both the theory and the relationships between spousal caregivers and their wounded warriors. Thus, although this study employs grounded theory, we are sensitized by prior research to especially consider how relational turbulence may inform our findings.

Description of Data

We examined discussion boards and blogs dedicated to women caring for WII servicemembers. Specifically, we focused on discussion forums and blogs that offered personal accounts from spousal caregivers who were new to the experience of caregiving for a wounded warrior. In contrast to surveys or interviews, these venues allowed the examination of actual discourse that was motivated and facilitated by servicemembers' wives, girlfriends, and fiancées. Consequently, this discourse reveals issues especially important to women experiencing the stress of military life (e.g., dealing with deployments, coping with frequent moves, social isolation, and child-rearing concerns) and the experience of caregiving for wounded warriors.

Sample

We conducted a Google search using the phrases "wounded warrior spouse (or wife) and discussion boards" and "wounded warrior spouse (or wife) and blogs." Discussion boards are asynchronous online venues in which people can post a message or comment on an existing post. The compilation of messages in response to the original message is called a string, made up of individual posts, and for the current study, each post on a string was considered one unit of analysis. In contrast, blogs are conceptualized as online diaries created and posted by one person with the knowledge that others will read the entries. Blogs in this study were treated as one unit.

Discussion board strings or blogs that met the following requirements were included in the analysis: they were written by the spouse of a wounded warrior, and they referenced either a personal relationship or partner issues. Posts that were purely informational or task focused were excluded; however, we adopted a decision rule favoring the retention of ambiguous posts within the data set. A reliability check was conducted by the research assistant who reviewed approximately one-third of the final sample to identify relationship or partner issues, thus ensuring the inclusion of the sample's content was acceptable. Each unit was printed, and the final sample comprised three blogs in their entirety and 819 discussion board strings ($N = 822$ units).

Method

Open Coding

Following Strauss and Corbin's (1998) framework for coding, open coding was performed to identify the central concepts and their dimensions with the data. The first author and one research assistant reviewed the entire data set three times with an eye toward identifying recurrent themes discussed by the contributors to the blogs and the discussion forums. After the readers had acknowledged a saturated sense of familiarity and a holistic view of the discourse, the readers conducted a fourth review of the data. On the fourth review, the readers employed the constant comparative method to make sense of the data by identifying themes that permeated the discourse (Glaser & Strauss, 1967). In particular, the identification of the themes was based on the frequency, extensiveness, and intensity (i.e., powerful emotional discussion) of related discourse (Krueger, 1998). Then, the readers independently reread the transcripts to identify points of departure from the framework of the themes that had been developed thus far. This reading allowed refinement of the identified themes to capture the issues in the discourse more completely. Last, through discussion between the readers, we collapsed common themes and identified those that were unique. The analysis yielded eight topical categories: waiting for administrative decisions, dealing with logistics of treatment, experiencing effects of WII issues, coping with a new identity, missing the "past," social isolation, financial issues, and dealing with the outside world.

Axial Coding

Following the open coding process, the first author read the discourse again using axial coding techniques to investigate the existence of relational uncertainty and partner interference within the topical themes. Whereas in the open coding process two readers were necessary to ensure the framework of themes emerged in an organic and inductive manner without individual bias, the axial coding process was employed to relate categories at the level of properties and dimensions in accordance with the first author's knowledge of the relational turbulence model (Strauss & Corbin, 1998). Accordingly, the first author indicated the commonalities and discord in how relational uncertainty and partner interference surfaced within the eight stressors identified through the open coding procedures. In practice, this step of the analysis involved attention to the ways in which commitment ambiguity and discussions of goal obstruction surfaced in the discourse surrounding the stressors confronted by WII spouses.

Results

Permeating the eight stressors identified through the open coding analysis were two themes related primarily to goal interference (i.e., protection of the wounded warrior and lack of effort by the wounded warrior) and two themes related primarily to relational uncertainty (i.e., adjustment to a new sense of normal and anxiety related to the unknown).

Partner Interference Themes

Protection of WII

Wives of the WII expressed an overwhelming desire to protect their husband from anything that would cause him discomfort, anxiety, or harm. One woman characterized this responsibility by stating, "My sole purpose in life is to be his advocate." Additionally, many women explained that protecting their husband from the public was in essence protecting him from "triggers," things that would cause flashbacks, anxiety, stress, or other ill effects of PTSD. One woman wrote,

> Every aspect of our lives both inside and outside the home has been affected by the startle response, and my protective actions are so ingrained that they have become habit. When we're out in the truck I announce when I'm going to drop down the tailgate. When we're seated in a restaurant I warn him when someone is about to come into his field of vision from behind. Our daughter even announces when she is going to pop the top of a soda can in such a casual manner you would think it's something all teenagers do.

Another woman shared,

> Here's a shout out to all the ladies like me that constantly work to avoid the stressors or "triggers." I was so mad one day (he said I don't ever do anything around the house) that I made a list of 63 items I have to do each and every single day to avoid the meltdowns.

These quotes illustrate how the spousal caregiver's efforts to protect her husband from the side effects of his wounds required her to alter daily routines, goals, and expectations. These quotes also highlight the struggle that wives face: they must choose between reintegrating with their spouse into society or withdrawal to protect their husbands from the angst that interfacing with society can create. Protecting their wounded warrior was a priority for women, one intertwined with the conduct of their daily lives and marital relationship.

Lack of Effort

Spousal caregivers expressed frustration with their husband's failure to accomplish tasks related to both his own treatment and involvement in the intimate portions of their relationship. These disclosures were fraught with guilt, distress, sadness, and dissatisfaction with how the responsibility of caregiver morphed the role of wife into that of a parent. One woman wrote,

> I want my marriage to work but I feel like I am the one doing all the work. I feel very alone in this. I don't know how much more I can give of myself.

Similar sentiments were expressed more emphatically by another woman:

> I am going to explode. I CAN NOT take this crap ANYMORE. I am SO sick of being the only responsible one. I am SOOOOOOOO TIRED of having to pick up the slack. I am NOT a mother. I don't know what the hell I am doing! I don't care what the situation is NOBODY can do this forever. . . . There is just too much going on and nobody to help me. There isn't even a way for someone to help me other than my husband and he won't. He can't, he won't, whatever the reason is . . . .

Another woman's comments exemplify how the lack of engagement in the marital relationship included a lack of intimacy or emotional availability:

> For the last 6 months we have not even shared a bed, for the last year we have not gone out together, I practically had to force him to touch my hand, kiss me or hug me. . . . In these last few months I have felt very lonely for my husband that I used to know.

These quotes underscore how WII servicemembers' conditions disrupted their spouse's fundamental goal of participating in a mutual partnership, while also hindering the caregiver's daily activities and goals.

Relational Uncertainty Themes

Adjustment to a New Sense of Normal

Spouses of the WII must quickly adapt to their new role as caregiver, which is consumed by managing treatment appointments, administrative paperwork, finances, and other needs of their husband. These changes in circumstances created turmoil within the spousal relationships. One woman characterized a general sentiment of the stress created by this adjustment as she wrote, "I'll just be glad when things are back to normal. Whatever that is." Other women emphasized the pressure and even disdain they felt when attempting to understand their husband's transformation. One woman exclaimed,

> I am at my last rope also. I know it's not my husband's fault, but at the same time. This isn't what I signed up for. This isn't the person I married. It sounds horrible to say . . . but that's how I feel sometimes. The pressure and stress is overwhelming . . . .

Others expressed similar sentiments by yearning for their "old relationship" or for the man their husband used to be. For some spousal caregivers, life involved a cycle of fighting and making up, which often left women feeling guilty that they were not holding the relationship together. One woman wrote about succumbing to defeat:

> Mike was going back and forth between being nice and mean last night. One second he threatened to take my car and wanted the money in the account. The next he said he was going to wash the clothes he threw in the front yard. In the end, he snapped again, because I wasn't playing his games. I am still at my friend's and am in the process of planning my way out. I failed to make this work. I can honestly say I have never tried so hard at something in my life. I wish this wasn't happening.

Meanwhile, women who stayed with their husband struggled with whether they had the right to feel as though they were drowning in their role of caregiver. One woman captured this sentiment:

> There is a stigma attached to admitting you are unable to cope, overwhelmed and uncertain what to do. . . . It is easy to become angry about being the one that makes sure everything keeps functioning as it should. . . . It can leave you feeling swamped almost to the point of breaking. But how do you say I'm hurting too, when your loved one has just returned from combat?

Running through the discourse were women's feelings of uncertainty about the validity of their own feelings, their spouse's engagement in the marriage, the viability of the relationship, and the perceptions of others.

Anxiety Related to the Unknown

A prominent theme permeating the stressors expressed by wives was uncertainty about the future. Women stated they felt stressed, anxious, overwhelmed, fearful, unsure, and yet sometimes hopeful when it came to issues such as financial security, their husband's health, and the future of their relationship. Even when women held out hope, the uncertainty and stress they experienced eroded trust and intimacy within the marriage. Often, the wounded warrior was implicated in unjustly blaming the caregiver for transgressions, which coincided with intense expressions of tension, frustration, and anxiety about the future. In one woman's words,

> He blows up over the smallest thing. Everything I do it seems wrong. I don't know how to relate to my husband anymore and I don't like living here.

Women also indicated their distress about when or how they would be sexually intimate again. Women struggled with understanding if their husband's injuries prevented him from performing intimate acts or if their husband just preferred to remain emotionally and physically distant. One woman revealed,

I wonder how this will ever happen or when. I know this is probably too much information but I have been deprived for most of the year so it is something I want with my husband of barely a year. I am trying to be patient.

As these quotes illustrate, problematic communication, feelings of being blamed, and the absence of physical intimacy undermined women's interactions with their husband and raised doubts about the nature and future of the relationship.

Compounding their uncertainty was what wives referred to as the "teeter totter" or "roller coaster" in their relationships. As a case in point, one woman stated,

Some days he wants me to go, some he says please help me. Then when I try to help, it's back to leave me alone. I also teeter. There are days when I want to chuck the whole thing, then other days where a long for him so badly that I sit in the bathtub and just stare, unable to feel . . . .

Similarly, another woman explained, "One minute I am the world's worst wife, a whore, the next minute he loves me, always will love me." As illustrated by the following quote, wives acknowledged that the only certainty in their future was uncertainty:

Life can be such a roller coaster never knowing what kind of ride it will be. There are times when you think you are about to get off the ride and it keeps going and going. When will it stop? No one really knows.

These quotes underscore the long-term burden of caregiving for a wounded warrior. With negative experiences so prevalent and positive intimate moments so rare, women experienced a loss of closeness coupled with turmoil and unpredictability within their marriage. Although women expressed understanding that the roller-coaster effect within their relationship could be attributed to their husband's injury or illness, their husband's actions and words and women's reactions to them fed into an experience of relational uncertainty.

Discussion

The goal of this work is to illuminate how the experience of spousal caregiving of wounded warriors transforms the marital relationship. An analysis of discussion boards and blogs revealed eight themes significant to the experience of WII spousal caregivers. Partner interference permeated these categories through themes focused on protecting the WII and lack of effort by the WII. In addition, we found that relational uncertainty emerged when women steered a new life course as a caregiver and established a new sense of normal, as well as when they experienced anxiety related to the unknown.

Although the relational turbulence model (RTM) treats the phenomena of relational uncertainty and partner interference as separate and distinct, we discovered in our findings that these two mechanisms were often interwoven (Solomon & Knobloch, 2004). For instance, the "lack of effort" theme highlights how the husband's failure to act both interferes with his wife's goals and calls into question the nature of the marital relationship. And, as women experienced interference from their husbands in their efforts to enact their role of caregiver, wife, and intimate partner, feelings of relational uncertainty surfaced. For many of these women, then, partner interference functioned as a gateway to relational uncertainty.

This project highlights the strengths and limitations of using online discussion boards and blogs to access naturally occurring discourse. By examining computer-mediated communication resources, we were able to capture personal accounts from spousal caregivers representing all branches of the military. Further, these discussion blogs and forums allowed the examination of discourse motivated and facilitated by spousal caregivers, thereby revealing issues especially salient to the women experiencing the stressors. Walther (1996) argued that online communication can be "hyperpersonal" because the absence of distracting and irrelevant cues present in face-to-face interaction allows people to communicate with greater intimacy and depth. Thus, our focus on online blogs and discussion forums allowed us to gather particularly candid and rich discourse among wives of the WII.

Our research methods, however, also had limitations. For example, our methods did not allow us to guide discussions or investigate topics in the same way that is possible through interviews. Furthermore, we did not have power over the size or the representativeness of the sample. In particular, people who do not have Internet access, generally those who are of a lower socioeconomic status, were excluded from this sample (Calvert, Rideout, Woolard, Barr, & Strouse, 2005). Collecting data through discussion boards may also limit our ability to identify the demographic information from participants.

The interpretive methods applied in our analysis allowed us to employ naturally occurring data to examine the constructs highlighted by the RTM. The first step of our procedure revealed the frequent, intense, and extensive stressors experienced by the wives that emerged from the data. The second step of the analysis, notably, was driven by theory as we elucidated themes related to relational uncertainty and partner interference. Certainly, alternative insights could be gained from applying a different theoretical framework. Our results allow us to draw conclusions about both the relevance of relational uncertainty and interference from partners to the expressed experiences of spousal caregivers of WII and the integration of relational uncertainty and partner interference within complex life transitions that married partners must sometimes navigate.

Reflecting on the Study

Excerpts From an Interview With Denise Haunani Solomon

Adrianne: I wanted to start out by thanking you for your contribution to our book.

Denise: We were delighted.... So, let's have a conversation....

Adrianne: Did you experience any challenges or constraints or frustrations when you were using the methodology that you used?

Denise: I think that the key issue for us was trying to sort through the ... there's a lot of overlap in the themes, and there's a lot of complexity in people's accounts, especially because people were describing such ... oftentimes very poignant situations.... A lot of things co-occurred....

Adrianne: Uh-huh.

Denise: An issue might be a loved one's health issues, but that overlapped with concerns about kids, and that overlapped with concerns about self. And so, I think for us it was trying to see and untangle the nuances that were often so woven together within the discourse that we examined.

Adrianne: OK. Yeah, that's definitely a challenge of doing this kind of work.... Did you feel like you learned new things about yourself as a scholar using this method? Was it new territory?

Denise: I've used this method a few times as formative research when I'm entering new subject domain, so I've used it in looking at the experiences of breast cancer survivors and of people coping with infertility. And so ... I kind of grappled with the difficulty I mentioned before in other contexts, but I think at a personal level I think I came to such a deeper appreciation for the challenges that the families of the wounded, ill, and injured are experiencing. I mean, it's just such a ... when somebody has cancer or when somebody has an experience of infertility, these are sort of ... well, seemingly random, even though there's some contributing factors on both accounts.... But random events that can strike anybody. But when somebody is injured in the line of duty ... that's an occupational hazard, and so ... I had a different emotional reaction to the discourse that we were reading, just because the experiences that the servicemembers were going through and their wives were going through had come at the cost of them serving in the military.

Adrianne: Right, right. So what was that emotional reaction like?

Denise: Yeah.... I can't really describe it just as—it would be incorrect to just say it was something as simple as sadness. I was in some ways awed, and I felt a really deep sense of respect for these families....

Adrianne: OK. I know you've mentioned some of the constraints and some of the challenges of using this kind of methodology. What are some of the strengths that you see?

Denise: Well, I think certainly the ways in which you're able to come to terms with and reveal the richness in the discourse....

Adrianne: How did you feel about using this method to understand and develop interpersonal communication theory? I mean, obviously, your work is hooked to a theory.

Denise: Right. I mean ... I think this is a nice marriage. We tried not to be too top-down in using the theory, because it is a grounded approach.... But we ... can't change the fact that ... as scholars, we're attentive to questions of uncertainty and interdependence and how those unfold within a variety of different kinds of experiences. So part of my research program that's looked at different kinds of difficult situations for families, such as a diagnosis of breast cancer or a discovery of infertility, have been about trying to understand ... by examining the natural occurring discourse of people going through this, do we hear echoes or loud screams that are related to uncertainty and interference? And so ... I feel like we've learned so much more about those constructs by doing these kinds of applications and ... really understanding the ways in which they weave together.

Adrianne: Mmm-hmm.

Denise: Because I think when we developed the relational turbulence model, we really did so thinking about, well, here are these two mechanisms: one is intrapersonal, and one is interpersonal.

Adrianne: Mmm-hmm.

Denise: And so, in our research, that was a survey and experimental, it was always, what's uncertainty doing and what's interference doing? But when we let the voices of the people experiencing difficult situations in their relationships describe and discuss what's going on, it becomes much more clear now that uncertainty and interdependence issues are really intertwined with each other. ... That people have relational uncertainty because they can't seem to facilitate each other's goals or because they're interfering in each other's goals. Or, because people aren't sure where they're going or where they are in their relationship, they experience interference. So, what has been really helpful through all of the series of qualitative studies we've done of this sort is that we've learned more about how the experience of uncertainty and interference kind of go hand in hand a little differently depending on the specific context. But it's really helped us think at a theoretical level about the relationship of that intrapersonal and interpersonal process, both processes together.

Adrianne: OK, great. ... People often say that writing is a big part of the process when doing qualitative research. How did you feel about writing up the research?

Denise: I think that's when ... I go back to research from the late '60s that talks about the transmission ... that when we're receiving information, we tend to allow it to exist in sometimes contradictory and incompatible and nuanced ways. But when we communicate or articulate information—I guess Pennebaker's perspective says the same thing—we have to kind of resolve those ambiguities and that we often become more polarized as we articulate a position, for example, because we have to clean it up so that it can make sense to somebody else.

Adrianne: Right.

Denise: And to me that's always the big shift when you do this kind of research, is between this very open immersion ... reading the discourse over and over again, to just try to get to where—I mean, Victoria can recite passages—to where you know all that detail, and then you shift and you have to explain it to somebody else.... That writing process forces you just like any articulation of a thought forces us to round things off a little.... And sharpen distinctions ... just as we select the words we use to describe this theme versus that theme. So, there's a sense in which that—I mean, it's a natural cognitive process, but it's a critical one in this kind of research because you're shifting from ... that sort of murky way in which you internally remember the dream you had last night ... to that more narrative, organized, and concrete way in which you describe that dream to somebody else.

Adrianne: Yeah.

Denise: So we spent a lot of time between the two of us.... Victoria is one of the readers in the process, and me trying to say, "Well, that sounds like this" or "That sounds like that." And having her [say], "Well ..., no," and kind of getting to the place where she's comfortable that the representation we've crafted jives with all of these sort of, for lack of a better word, feelings and impressions that she has.... So I don't think you could do this work alone, frankly, because ... the partnership was ... she was the one who had all of these nuanced impressions, and then we would talk about them, and I would almost kind of extract from her a sense of what these themes were, and she would let me know, "Well, yeah, but it's not like that. That's not quite right."

Adrianne: Sure.

Denise: In ways that it might be hard for the person who had those impressions firsthand to—by virtue of her articulating them, she might run the risk of losing some of that complexity.

Adrianne: Yeah, I feel the same way, too. OK. What advice would you give to someone who is new to using this kind of method? Do you have some best practices?

Denise: Well, I would say that the one thing that has been both part of the burden but I think is a strength of a practice has been that we have always had sort of large discourse sets to work with.

Adrianne: Mmm-hmm.

Denise: We're downloading from discussion boards lots of material. We sweep up a lot, and it makes the reading process arduous, but there's also ... I think your pool has to be that deep for you to get surrounded enough by it that you start to see specific things.

Adrianne: Yeah.

Denise: So sometimes I worry about small sample.... The sample always has to be relevant to what your research goals are. But if I were doing this with a small sample of, say, 30 interviews or something like that, that wouldn't feel like enough for the kinds of things we've been doing, because I don't know that it would be noisy enough. . . . So, for the way we've done it and the questions we've asked, I think that you actually want an overwhelming volume of data.

Adrianne: Yeah . . . that makes sense.

Denise: Because you need to be overwhelmed by it. If you're not overwhelmed, then there's something wrong. . . . I guess my first tip is to have an overwhelming data set.

Adrianne: Mmm-hmm.

Denise: It takes . . . I mean, seven, eight, nine reads through it for you to really be immersed within it.

Adrianne: Yeah.

Denise: So, for us, that's really always been critical. . . . So we read it three or four times, kind of to the point where the person . . . isn't surprised by anything that comes out. . . . And *then* we have the conversation between our other reader, and *then* they start to form these impressions, and *then* they go back and read it a few times again to . . . see whether or not these impressions . . . for us, that keeps it from being top-down.

Adrianne: Right, right.

Denise: I think those two issues are really important. I guess my third point—I don't know how much this reflects . . . my training is not in qualitative research, so I don't know if this is—and sometimes we get critiqued for this, but my own bias is that I couldn't go into these kinds of projects unless I had a conceptual framework in mind.

Adrianne: Mmm-hmm.

Denise: I think somebody could look at this discourse and have an eye toward looking at something very different, and they would be able to organize this discourse in a way that made sense for that. . . . And so we always try to be upfront about the fact that we do have constructs that come to us from a theoretical domain, and we're trying to engage in a method that would allow us to . . . that . . . prevents us from finding those constructs even if they don't exist. . . .

Adrianne: So I completely understand what you're saying.

Denise: But I don't think I could just go in blindfolded. . . . I just don't think I could do it.

Adrianne: OK, yeah, that makes a lot of sense. Are there things that you should avoid when using this method?

Denise: Well, I'll say this is something that's been helpful in our methods, and that is, it's been really helpful for us to distinguish the two sort of levels of conceptualization about what's going on: the first one where we sort of identify the, for lack of a better word, sort of more concrete and somewhat more distinct categories of phenomena.... And then where we start to think about the themes that run through it. I always think the really interesting insights come at the second layer, when we think about what are the dimensions or the poles or the tensions. I at least find that—again, it could be because I'm quantitatively trained—but I find that the first layer helps us ... almost create the ... terms or the concepts, and then we can talk about how they relate to each other....

Adrianne: That makes a lot of sense.

Denise: So I think trying to ... maybe to list this as a pitfall.... I think if you jump too quickly to thinking about the dimensions of overlap and opposition, until you've got kind of a clear understanding of what the key concepts or ideas are, for me would be conceptually challenging....

Adrianne: Yeah, that makes a lot of sense. Well, you kind of already answered this question, but maybe there's something else you want to say regarding your thoughts here. So your work is predominantly quantitative in nature, although you've done some of these more qualitative studies, too, but what are some things that you've had to consider as you've worked within an interpretivist paradigm as a quantitative person? ... Is there anything else that you've had to do or that's been challenging?

Denise: I think there might be things, as I suggested, that I bring to this methodology because my background is more primarily in survey and experimental design research.... That might be a little bit hard for me to see and articulate. But ... as I said, some of that is ... I tend to do more hypothesis-driven research, and so letting go of those expectations is something I work to do.

Adrianne: Yeah.

Denise: And it's helpful for me when things are distinct rather than messy. So, I think those are the two things that I have to be self-aware about when I enter into this process. But, on the other hand, I think that, for me, I'm not doing qualitative research on the same kinds of ideas that I would evaluate in a quantitative mode.... I really have turned to qualitative methods when I need to understand a new population and a new context and I need to understand experiences that I've never had.

Adrianne: Right.

Denise: And so I can't begin to make assumptions about what it's like to be a woman, or a spouse of a woman, diagnosed with breast cancer. I haven't lived that experience. I have lived college-dating relationships, so I felt pretty—even though we started that with some qualitative research as well. . . . But when I go into these situations that are really defined by the phenomenology of some extreme experience, I couldn't even begin to approach that . . . from a quantitative point of view until I have learned about the population, the community that I was specifically interested in studying. So there's lots of ways to do that. . . . I could read about a subject area, or I could read other accounts of this. What I have really enjoyed about the methods we've used—and . . . this is a tool only born of the Internet—is that by going to the discussion boards, we get to see what people are talking about to people *like* them.

Adrianne: Right, right.

Denise: And that's so different to me than what an interviewer has gleaned or what an expert might have written in a magazine or a newspaper or a news account or a book account of . . . the life of the military family or something like that. So that has been, to me, we have this way of getting direct insight into what's on the minds of people who are going through things. . . . And I can't enter into these domains without this kind of research, because I don't have any firsthand experience with these populations. In that sense, it's not hard to leave my quantitative roots behind at all, because it's an entirely different goal and enterprise.

Adrianne: That's great. And actually, that relates to my final question, and that is how did you decide what message boards or blogs to focus on?

Denise: Well, we really wanted to look specifically at message boards and blogs that were devoted to the wounded, ill, and injured. . . . We only ever went to discussion boards that there was public access to. . . . If you had to be a member, or develop a password account or any kind of identity to get to it—even though . . . in a sense, those are still public—we felt like that was posing as a member to get insight to data.

Adrianne: Exactly.

Denise: So for us it was always publically accessible discussion boards and discussion blogs. In that sense, it's akin to studying letters to the editor. And we thought that was important because people who are posting on those sites . . . don't perceive that they have member boundaries, and so, even though they're not identifiable, that to us felt like we're not violating somebody's experience. So, generally, our search has been pretty broad for finding message boards or blogs. . . . And, as in previous studies, we always contacted the person hosting the site to let them know we were doing this, and if they had a concern, they would let us know.

Adrianne: OK.

Denise: But typically . . . people know we're working for good, not evil. . . .

Adrianne: OK, great . . . thank you so much for your responses.

Questions for Growth

1. What interpersonal communication topics or concepts of interest to you might benefit from discourse analysis? What types of discourses would you pursue to help you understand each topic?

2. Because just about any relationship involves words, does that mean that all relationships could be considered through discourse analysis? Why or why not?

3. As Chapter 1 articulates, few interpersonal communication studies involve a critical approach. What might be some good ideas for critical discourse analysis research about interpersonal communication or close relationships?

4. It is helpful for many to practice discourse analysis prior to collecting discourses. Transcribe one minute of your favorite television show. What do you notice about the discourse? Try identifying some of the building blocks of discourse presented throughout the chapter as you come to your conclusions.

Narrative Inquiry, Crystallization, and a Study of Workplace Relationships

NARRATIVE AND THE STUDY OF RELATIONSHIPS

Much like ethnography and discourse analysis, narrative is more a tradition or approach to qualitative research as opposed to a particular method of inquiry (Andrews, Squire, & Tamboukou, 2008). Although *narrative inquiry* is, in many ways, a portmanteau term covering a variety of methods and analyses, as this chapter quickly details, it is typically reserved for research with a direct focus on analyzing narratives—not research that happens to have narratives in it (Chase, 2008; Riessman, 2007). That distinction is important, because as this chapter also quickly explains, most of what can be conceived in this world is made intelligible through narratives (Bochner, 2002; Fisher, 1989). In conceiving this book, we felt that some of the unique elements of narrative research—as well as its popularity in interpersonal communication studies—made it an important addition. We also see narrative inquiry as a much-needed space where those who lean toward the artistic/expressionist end of the qualitative continuum can do their work, even if a narrative approach does not mean one has to gravitate to that end. In fact, many narrative studies are realist in nature, too.

We offer this chapter in hopes of extending other methods presented in this book into the narrative inquiry domain. To do that, we first examine the metatheoretical elements of narrative studies in interpersonal communication studies so as to demonstrate the complexities of narrative inquiry and consider how narratives can be texts for study, a methodological choice, and even the product of a research project. We then move more directly into how narrative inquiry can be used to understand interpersonal communication and personal relationships. As with other chapters, we offer some exemplary studies that researchers may want to explore before they do their own narrative work, as well as some best practices. We also offer a short postscript that asks important questions about the potential for narrative inquiry to help balance the lack of critical scholarship emanating from interpersonal communication studies. That segues nicely into this chapter's analytical tool, crystallization, as it also has critical (particularly feminist) leanings and is ideal for those who gravitate toward the artistic end of the qualitative continuum. That leads to a study from Rebeccah Dohrman and colleagues that uses narrative inquiry to understand workplace relationships and presents those findings in the form of a reader's theater piece.

THE IMPORTANCE OF NARRATIVE AND STORIES IN RELATIONSHIPS

When examining narrative-oriented studies, understand that scholars generally treat the terms *narrative* and *story* differently, even if the two share many similar qualities and functions. Scholars generally use the term *narrative* more broadly, whereas *story* tends to refer to specific situations or events as recounted or created (Koenig Kellas, 2008). However, stories are sometimes viewed the same as narratives, too, with scholars not distinguishing between the two. For example, Ochs (1997) explains, "The term 'narrative' is used either in a narrow sense to specify the genre of story or in a broad sense to cover a vast range of genres, including not only stories but also reports, sports and news broadcasts, plans, and agendas among others" (p. 189). Ochs's (1997) explanation is but one of many, and the fluidity of the narrative tradition means scholars are probably approaching narrative inquiry with their own sets of unique metatheoretical assumptions. One should unpack how ontology, epistemology, and axiology play into a given research study, both when consuming narrative research and creating it.

Narrative Studies of Interpersonal Communication

To assist in these considerations of metatheory, we draw from Koenig Kellas (2008), who offers an impressive overview of how narrative theories are used in interpersonal communication studies. Beginning with a foundational framework provided by David Maines (1993), she points to narrative as a "communicative phenomenon, and one that deserves more focus, attention, and expertise from those who ground themselves in the study of symbolic meaning-making" (Koenig Kellas, 2008, p. 244). She notes that despite this clear and direct link to interpersonal communication studies, narrative research tends to happen in other disciplines more than it does in communication studies and that oftentimes such research focuses on master narratives or the details of personal stories rather than the communicative features of telling stories or sharing narratives (Koenig Kellas, 2008). To illustrate where communication scholars have been and where they might go, she articulates narrative metatheory in terms of ontology, epistemology, individual construction, and relational process.

Narrative Ontology

Narrative has especially gained traction in communication studies when constructed as a paradigm. Fisher's (1989) narrative paradigm is probably the best known of these ontological approaches. Frequently used as a tool for rhetorical criticism, the paradigm suggests that narratives are not mere stories but rather a way of making sense of the social world. This sensemaking is then articulated coherently and with a sense of fidelity toward others' lived experiences (Fisher, 1989). The focus of this approach is not on interaction or the particular story but rather the construction of the narrative itself. As Koenig Kellas (2008) so eloquently explains,

> By viewing humans as storytellers and human communication as narrative, interpretable, and assessed against a larger historical context, scholars like Fisher . . . established narrative as the way that humans exist within, and make sense of, the world. (p. 245)

That approach is different from the one that seems to dominate most interpersonal communication research, an approach that centers narrative inquiry in stories (Koenig Kellas, 2008). Bochner (2002) looked at the *what* of narrative in a slightly different way, instead characterizing personal relationships as narratives in and of themselves. Not only are personal relationships narratives, but research about them is a narrative, too (Bochner, Ellis, & Tillman-Healy, 1997). As that suggests, ontological agreement across both perspectives indicates that in the world of communication studies narratives are "inseparable from the ways in which we exist within, interpret, and understand personal relationships" (Koenig Kellas, 2008, p. 246).

Narrative Epistemology

If a person's way of interpreting his or her social world can be looked at as an object of inquiry, it stands to reason that there may be different ways of observing or considering a text and that a given way of seeing will play into the nature of that text. So, as is the case in many communication studies, narrative ontology and epistemology are closely linked. That may help to explain why so often in narrative inquiry lines are blurred (sometimes carelessly) between narrative as object of analysis and narrative as method of analysis. To borrow from Orbuch (1997), narrative can be a *means* of inquiry as well as a *product* of inquiry—and that differs from it being the *object* of inquiry. As Koenig Kellas (2008) notes, communication scholars will sometimes contend they are using narrative theory when they are actually using narrative methods. Theory describes how narratives are being used in social worlds, whereas method intentionally draws out narratives from research participants in order to make sense of a social phenomenon. In turn, researchers then provide a narrative about their research process as that research is disseminated (Bochner, 2002). In the face of such epistemological confusion about object, means, and product, some narrative scholars—such as Reissman (1993)—advocate that narrative inquiry and theorizing can only occur when stories or narratives are the primary focus of such research. In terms of interpersonal communication, that means a study examining how romantic infidelity is communicated to a partner by collecting narratives of how such conversations occurred would not be seen as narrative inquiry by Riessman (2007) because the study is looking at disclosure, not the narratives themselves. However, if a researcher were to examine how people share narratives about romantic infidelity, then that constitutes narrative inquiry because the narratives themselves are the object of focus, and theorizing about narrative qualities is possible.

Narrative as Individual Construction

If one buys into the idea that narrative inquiry happens when narratives themselves are analyzed, then that epistemological understanding is still open to different approaches. One of the approaches identified by Koenig Kellas (2008) as common in interpersonal communication studies is *narrative as individual construction*. Such an approach examines how researchers "collect and describe stories from individuals about themselves, their families, or their personal relationships" (Koenig Kellas, 2008, p. 246). As that implies, the focus is on the structure and content of personal relationship stories, something that interpretive analysis is ideal for revealing. A common approach to this kind of theorizing is Labov and Waletsky's (1967) structural perspective. This perspective involves a taxonomy of narratives that includes an abstract or summary of the story, an orientation that introduces characters and setting, key actions that characterize what the story is about, a resolution that draws events to some kind of end, and a coda that frequently offers a moral. Examining narrative as individual construction allows for insights other than how stories are structured, however. In the context of personal relationships, narratives reveal how people construct their relational identities (as well as their personal identities). They also allow insights into how a story's structure in and of itself is a constitutive element of a relationship. A story's structure and content, then, may be a strong indicator of a relationship's status or health (Koenig Kellas, 2008).

Narrative as Relational Process

Because storytelling is not only an individual effort, it can be important for interpersonal communication scholars to consider how those in relationships work together to tell stories and how such stories play into relationships. This form of narrative inquiry constitutes theorizing about narrative as a relational process (Koenig Kellas, 2008). In these studies, the focus "is on how audience members or relational partners negotiate the story itself or the history and 'reality' of their relationship together" (Koenig Kellas, 2008, p. 247). This form of theorizing considers both how storytelling is a joint and performative relational act and how relationships are revealed not only through story content but also through collaboration as stories are jointly negotiated and performed. In other words, stories are another way of "doing" relationships, and examining those stories allows for an intricate sense of how meaning is made between people as well as how that meaning is indicative of the relationship as a whole (Koenig Kellas, 2008).

Autoethnography

In addition to the two theoretical approaches presented by Koenig Kellas (2008), we also offer up a brief reminder about autoethnography, an increasingly popular form of narrative inquiry that serves as both narrative process and product. The method itself—in autoethnography a researcher writes about his or her life—allows deeper understanding of the self through narrative (Bochner & Ellis, 2006). Evocative narratives are especially suited for this form of research (Anderson, 2006). Chapter 1 goes into greater detail about this inherently narrative-oriented qualitative research method.

Uses of Narratives in Interpersonal Communication

As this chapter indicates, many times narratives are used to understand how a relationship is storied (Bochner, 2002) and what stories might indicate about aspects of a relationship as well as the relationship as a whole (Duck, 2011). Narratives function in other ways, too, and understanding those functions may inspire research questions that can be answered by narrative inquiry or assist in the actual analysis of narratives. Here we briefly examine some of the functions of narratives offered by Sunwolf and Frey (2001) through an interpersonal communication lens to prompt thinking about how narratives can be considered in interpersonal qualitative research. These functions especially draw upon how narratives function as a form of everyday talk (Tracy, 2002).

Argument Making

Rhetorical scholars often use Fisher's narrative paradigm (1989) to understand the suasive dimensions of narrative. Interpersonal communication scholars might consider narratives in a similar light, determining both their implicit and explicit suasive qualities. A father may not have facts and statistics on hand when he catches his son using drugs, but he might be able to tell a personal story about his own mistakes with drug use in order to help his son understand why drug use may be bad. Researchers should also consider that arguments do not always equal fight or conflict. For example, a boyfriend who sees that his girlfriend is down in the dumps because she is afraid she does not qualify for a job she was hoping to receive. The boyfriend shares a narrative that indicates just how much she has grown as a person in the time he has known her and that lists all that she has accomplished. He closes by saying, "So you have to know you are qualified." In this case, the story serves as an argument, and that argument is more inspirational than debate oriented.

Performing Speech Acts

Similar to how narratives may form an argument, they can stand in for other speech acts as well. For instance, a woman may not feel brave enough to tell her girlfriend that she loves her, and so instead she might tell a story that details how she has been looking for love her whole life. That story, followed by a hug, may indicate "I love you," without the actual words ever being stated. When narratives serve as a speech act, there is always the possibility that they may be challenged if the audience for the story questions why the story is being shared or what it means (Tracy, 2002). Continuing with this example, while being hugged, the girlfriend listening to the personal narrative might ask, "So are you saying you love me?"

Positioning the Narrator (Especially in Ongoing Conflict)

As earlier discussion in this chapter illustrates, many times narratives serve to build individual or relational identity. An individual narrative or story can also play into a larger or overarching narrative or story. Slightly different from both of those ideas, and drawing from both, is the idea that narratives will sometimes place (or construct) the person telling the story in a particular place, space, or time. As Tracy (2002) and Sunwolf and Frey (2001) note, this is especially true in cases of conflict. A man may have trouble dealing with a new boss who continues to insult and abuse him in the workplace. In his weekly phone call to his mother, he may share a story or two about the latest offenses. Some of those stories ("Can you believe she called me a stallion? And implied that I needed to be castrated?") might indicate that outrageous behavior continues to escalate, giving one kind of sense about how space and place have changed over time (and, likely, will continue to change). Others ("I filed a sexual harassment complaint today. I know I was warned against doing it by my boss, but it is the right thing to do") could indicate progress toward resolve and reveal future plans—another play on the construction of space and place and time. Such narratives could examine, among other things, the construction of workplace relationships and the tactics used to establish the setting.

USING METHOD TO ENCOURAGE NARRATIVE

The functions just presented, along with the discussion of metatheory, help to illustrate the many ways narrative can come into play with qualitative research. Taking these ideas back to the research-planning considerations presented in Chapter 2 will likely allow for productive interpersonal communication studies using narrative inquiry. Here we offer additional ideas and sources of inspiration for engaging narrative inquiry.

Narrative Interviews

Unlike other interviews, narrative interviews have two unique considerations (Lindlof & Taylor, 2011). First, they are as interested in the performance of the narrative they seek to capture as in the narrative itself. Second, they are interested in the total narrative—not simple phrases or facts or ideas or vignettes. In other words, they are not simply about capturing information but are interested in looking at narrative as a performed, embodied, and symbol-using storytelling act (Chase, 2008; Lindlof & Taylor, 2011; Riessman, 2007). Lindlof and Taylor (2011) identify two types of narrative interviews that tend to be used in communication research: personal narratives and organizational narratives. Personal narratives create "a dynamic interplay between self and others" (Corey, 1996, p. 57) and often are solicited through interpersonal interaction between the interviewer and the interviewee(s). While not always explicitly labeled as such, they embrace feminist ideas of dialogue (Graham, 1984) to avoid dominant and totalizing options for narrative.

Organizational narratives are quite similar to personal narratives, with the key difference being that the stories collected from organizational members "make up a web of collective reality" (Lindlof & Taylor, 2011, p. 182). Organizations, like relationships, can be viewed as storied (Ashcraft & Pacanowsky, 1996; Boje, 1995). While that may seem like an idea more relevant to organizational communication scholars, interpersonal communication scholars should consider that close relationships still occur in those narrative environments and that the stories of those close relationships are likely interweaved with the stories of the organization. We turn to Gubrium and Holstein (2009) to explore these ideas more fully.

Narrative Environments and Close Relationships

Gubrium and Holstein (2009) offer up the idea of *narrative environments*, or "contexts within which the work of story construction and storytelling get done" (p. xvii). They advocate that these environments are "critical for understanding what is at stake for storytellers and listeners in presenting accounts or responding to them in distinctive ways" (pp. xvii–xviii). Gubrium and Holstein (2009) contend that the interaction in close relationships constitutes a narrative environment, and we agree. Further, we believe from our own work and from reviewing the work of others that these narrative environments can be particularly tricky, as the narratives shared in these environments can be brief or fleeting. Catching these brief and fleeting moments—sometimes presented as narratives within narratives—can be helpful to understanding an overarching (sometimes referred to as the "grand") relational narrative that will, in turn, point to rich and enduring findings when data are analyzed.

Gubrium and Holstein (2009) offer suggestions for analyzing narrative data in a close-relationships environment. First, they suggest that researchers not fall into the trap of limiting themselves to thinking of narratives only as indicative of identity but to also consider how narratives explain or even direct action. That advice might be particularly helpful for ethnographers who are trying to make sense of the behavior they observe. Second, in observing narratives of close relationships consider how narratives not only allow a sense of relational identity to others but also function to reinforce or even create the proximal identity for those in the relationship. In other words, a story establishing a family as hardworking serves to construct that family as hardworking to others as well as reinforce that hardworking status for members of the family. Third, in analyzing narratives, consider their intertextual nature. Gubrium and Holstein (2009) do not actually use the term *intertextual* but instead borrow *interpretively reproductive* from Corsaro (1997, p. 18) to illustrate how a story frequently contains elements experienced firsthand as well as accounts from other people. We agree and suggest that many times stories will use other stories—and not just accounts—to make their point or otherwise establish the story. For example, someone frustrated with the inappropriate way she was dumped may use the "Post-It Note" episode of *Sex and the City* to illustrate parts of her breakup narrative. In that case, she depends upon the story of the episode to advance or allow meaning for her own story. This sense of conversational intertextuality certainly plays out in contexts other than narratives as well. Whether *interpretively reproductive* or *conversationally intertextual*, considering how stories are interweaved with and constructed from other stories allows for deeper insights about narrative meaning or function as well as new analytical connections between the narrative of focus and other relational elements or qualities.

Additional Narrative Exemplars

Those excited to engage narrative inquiry about relationships have a wide variety of research exemplars from which to choose and learn. We highlight two here, especially focusing on the strengths of their approaches. The first of these is the book *Storytelling in Daily Life: Performing Narrative* where authors Langellier and Peterson (2004) develop narrative performance theory. As its name implies, that theory examines how narratives are performed and the implications of such performances. The data exemplars are rich, especially in the portion of the book that examines how Franco American family members join together to "do" their relationship through storytelling. The in-depth qualitative analysis considers what stories families share, how they share them, and how that storytelling creates family identity. Though the book is not only for those who do critical research, those who find themselves leaning in critical research directions will especially appreciate how the text unpacks material constraints of storytelling and affords power to those who are speaking. The book also moves beyond positive aspects of narratives, examining how sharing narratives can allow for the possibility of individual or family critique or even denied relational legitimacy.

For an exemplar that moves closer to the realist end of the qualitative continuum, Wildermuth and Vogl-Bauer (2007) offer a clearly written study that analyzes 202 written narratives about online romantic relationships to answer the research question, "How do participants describe online romances when they tell the story of their relationships?" The essay demonstrates how narratives are elicited with open-ended surveys, offering transparency by presenting the actual narrative prompt used for the survey:

> Please tell me the story of your online romantic relationship. How did you meet? How did you develop your relationship? If your relationship is over, how did it end? If it is ongoing, how are you maintaining your relationship? From your perspective, what is being in an online romance like? What do you think are the issues of concern and sources of joy in such relationships? (Wildermuth & Vogl-Bauer, pp. 213–214)

The study also demonstrates how a large data set can be reduced for wieldy analysis, something that may be necessary for a collection of narrative data. The study also uses quasi-statistics well to establish validity and clearly organizes exemplars, sometimes through tables, so as to allow the reader a sense of the narratives. These segments from narratives are still placed into a larger context, however, staying true to the spirit of narrative inquiry.

As a final note, many great narrative studies overlap interpersonal and health communication contexts. For example, in a study from Walker and Dickson (2004) narrative analysis was used to demonstrate how couples' illness narratives were indicative of their identity and relationship culture. That is, the five couple identities revealed from interactive analysis—sympathetic, independent, mixed, nonreciprocal, and rejecting couples—all matched up to the narratives jointly offered by the couples. In another study, Arrington (2005) examined how prostate cancer survivors told their stories in consideration of family, especially how they constructed their wives in their stories. His findings allowed understandings about how narratives can both constitute a relationship and allow for insights about the construction of illness in context.

Feminist Inspiration and Critical Potential: Narrative as Dialogic Liberation

We close our overview of narrative inquiry by acknowledging its feminist inspirations and by noting some of its critical potentials for interpersonal communication research. Feminism can be defined as "the belief that men and women are equal and should have equal respect and opportunities in all spheres of life—personal, social, work, and public" (Wood, 2008, p. 324). This body of theorizing does not necessarily advocate that men deliberately create systems to oppress women, but it does recognize that women's voices (or feminine discourses in general) can be muted by masculine dominance (see Wood, 2008, for a full explanation in an interpersonal communication context). Narrative inquiry, then, allows for some form of voice for the traditionally marginalized or ignored. In a review of interpretivist paradigms, the feminist paradigm is described as embracing lived experience, accountability, reflexivity, emotion, and embodied, lived experience (Denzin & Lincoln, 2011). It is a form of theory based in the standpoints of diverse people, and it embraces the stories they have to offer (Denzin & Lincoln, 2011). Although feminist approaches to scholarship initially were partial to white, Western viewpoints, the feminist paradigm continues to expand to include people of different sexes, races, ethnicities, national origins, and a variety of other identity markers (Foss, Domenico, & Foss, 2013).

Those same feminist qualities that undergird a narrative paradigm—as well as the research from other disciplines that embrace narrative inquiry—indicate that narrative inquiry is an ideal method for incorporating critical viewpoints into interpersonal communication research. Not only can narrative research methods allow minoritized people a sense of voice (see Bochner, 2008, or Ellingson, 2009, for further discussion), but they can also hope to expose how relational stories serve to oppress some while liberating others. That does not always have to happen in a critical domain. As Duck (2011) notes, narratives are a way that social control is asserted over relationships. Narratives can also function as mechanisms for promoting stereotypes or stigma toward diverse others (Tracy, 2002). Critical analysis of when race is and is not mentioned in stories, for instance, might reveal the sensitivities people have about race relations while simultaneously providing awareness about how race fits into interpersonally shared narratives. Exploring diverse narratives may also reveal hegemonic dimensions of relationships yet to be unearthed in communication subdisciplines such as intercultural communication, media studies, or organizational communication that tend to do the heavy lifting in critical approaches to social science.

QUALITATIVE CRYSTALLIZATION: REPRESENTATION ACROSS MULTIPLE GENRES

The analytical tool presented in this chapter is not a tool in the traditional sense. It is also much more than a way to disseminate research findings. When used to its full advantage, crystallization (Ellingson, 2009) is a form of postmodern triangulation that involves multiple ways of knowing. Crystallization can use multiple methods for the same project, multiple analytical processes to examine that data, and—perhaps most unique to the approach—multiple ways of disseminating those findings (Ellingson, 2009, 2011). Ellingson grounds her framework for crystallization in the work of Richardson (1994, 2000), who developed the foundational ideas; her own work with Ellis (Ellis & Ellingson, 2000) that examines how qualitative research happens along a continuum; and her own frustrations with having to choose a camp or methodological allegiance for her work, as well as the inability of the general public to read her work (Ellingson, 2009). She also acknowledges that qualitative crystallization is inspired by feminist understandings of openness and respecting multiple voices (Ellingson, 2009).

Crystallization was introduced Chapter 1, and Ellingson's (2009) qualitative continuum has been used throughout to refer to the methods and approaches and their capacities for enacting artistic- or realist-oriented research (or research that falls somewhere in between). In many ways, it dismisses the idea that a researcher has to belong to one specific paradigmatic camp, thus rejecting that any kind of singular truth can be found for a given phenomenon. An interpersonal scholar can embrace realist, interpretivist, or critical approaches for his or her research as fits the project—or all three for the same project. As Ellingson (2009) explains it,

> Crystallization combines multiple forms of analysis and multiple genres of representation into a coherent text or series of related texts, building a rich and openly partial account of a phenomenon that problematizes its own construction, highlights researchers' vulnerabilities and positionality, makes claims about socially constructed meanings, and reveals the indeterminacy of knowledge claims even as it makes them. (p. 4)

Crystallization, then, follows a constitutive research model, where findings can be considered in light of each other for fuller understanding.

Five guiding principles are used to guide a crystallized project (Ellingson, 2011). First, as with all qualitative methods and approaches covered in this book, crystallization seeks knowledge through deep and revealing interpretation about a particular phenomenon. Second, and also covered throughout this book, crystallization encourages an awareness of the qualitative continuum and designing a project to include at least one middle-ground or middle-to-right (realist leaning) approach as well as one creative or artistic approach. That ties into the third principle, that crystallized research should include more than one genre of representation. The most common is the research report (Ellingson, 2009), but scholars continue to find new and exciting ways to distribute their research. Interpersonal communication scholars can disseminate their work as a theatrical play that demonstrates research findings about romantic relationships through a narrated story, a documentary film that examines communication in workplace relationships, poetry that articulates dimensions of friendship discovered through interviews, or any other creative endeavor the researcher can imagine and execute.

Fourth, crystallization should reflect "*a significant degree of reflexive consideration of the researcher's self*" in the process of research design, collection of empirical materials, and representation" (Ellingson, 2011, p. 605, emphasis in original). That principle may be tough for researchers in general, but it could especially be daunting for interpersonal communication scholars dealing with highly personal and sensitive topics. Ellingson (2011) notes that this reflection, reflexivity, and demonstration may be subtly demonstrated or creatively manifested—and so there is a level of freedom as well as encouraged creativity in adhering to this principle. Finally, as reflected in the other principles, crystallization rejects singular ways of knowing. Instead, it "celebrates knowledge as inevitably situated, partial, constructed, multiple, and embodied" (Ellingson, 2011, p. 605). These five principles are enacted through two primary crystallization types: integrated and dendritic. Integrated crystallization features multiple genres in a single representation (e.g., a book, performance, or film) whereas dendritic crystallization engages multiple genres across multiple texts (Ellingson, 2009, 2011). Integrated crystallization can be woven (where two genres are layered together in an intricate blend) or patchwork (where multiple genres are clearer and demarcated and possibly even labeled; Ellingson, 2009, 2011).

The illustrative study included here is an example of dendritic crystallization—meaning it embraces one genre, but the larger research project it is developed from will yield research in other genres. The genre is a reader's theater, or play, meant to be read rather than traditionally performed (although it could be presented in a traditional way). It presents the results of a narrative inquiry into workplace relationships in a way that a traditional research report certainly could not. An interview with coauthor Patrice M. Buzzanell follows.

Crystallization

Performing and Analyzing Women Engineers' Workplace Stories and Interpersonal Communication

Rebecca Dohrman, Maryville University; Colleen Arendt, Fairfield University;
Patrice M. Buzzanell, Purdue University; and Natalie Litera, KSM Consulting

Over the years, many research reports and funded projects have been conducted by researchers across the globe in an effort to understand the careers of women engineers and to locate ways of encouraging women to stay within majors and jobs in STEM (science, technology, engineering, and math). Many efforts have focused on the interpersonal interaction that young women experience during their early years of socialization or messages that can have long-term impact (e.g., Buzzanell, Berkelaar, & Kisselburgh, 2011, 2012; National Academy of Engineering, 2008; Stohl, 1986). Other studies have noted that strong math backgrounds are necessary for success and that women who leave engineering are not simply moving into easier college majors or occupational fields but rather are locating work that is multifaceted and congruent with their values, competency beliefs, and interests in helping others (Eccles, 2007). Furthermore, research has noted that masculine occupational narratives in STEM—as well as their inconsistency with women membership and (perhaps) relational goals—can prompt reconsiderations of STEM membership. Expanding gendered and occupational identities may allow women to find a place for themselves in STEM (e.g., Diekman, Brown, Johnston, & Clark, 2011; W. Faulkner, 2009; Kisselburgh, Buzzanell, & Berkelaar, 2009; Park, Young, Troisi, & Pinkus, 2011).

We maintain that a topic as complex as women in STEM requires a methodology that enables us to draw upon the sensemaking processes (Weick, 1993, 1995) inherent in narrative, the performance of gender and occupation, and the foundations for—as well as outcomes of— interpersonal interactions in the workplace. These foundations might be childhood experiences that produced STEM career self-efficacy, that is, women's beliefs that they can do a particular career in STEM or interactions with family members and teachers when the women model behaviors indicative of success in a STEM field, such as high math aptitude. In our case study, these foundations become the (re)collected memories, material data (i.e., tools, locales, embodiment of doing engineering work), and discourses (i.e., talk-in-interaction through narratives, conversation, and other texts), as well as the overarching language frames such as gender, economics, and technology whereby our everyday talk becomes sensible and potentially changeable.

The concept of qualitative *crystallization* (Buzzanell & D'Enbeau, 2009; Ellingson, 2008; Richardson, 2000; Richardson & St. Pierre, 2005) enables us to explore our topic by encouraging us to draw upon these diverse data and analytic lenses to understand a complex communication phenomenon in the workplace. As Richardson (2000) explains, crystallization occurs when

> the scholar draws freely on his or her productions from literary, artistic, and scientific genres, often breaking the boundaries of each of those as well. In these productions, the scholar might have different "takes" on the same topic, what I think of as a postmodernist deconstruction of triangulation. (p. 934)

Ellingson (2009) adds that crystallization, a methodology that "depends upon including, interweaving, blending, or otherwise drawing upon more than one genre of expressing data" (p. 11), has taken hold among researchers who embrace narrative representations in their varied forms and who resist conventional writing and analysis. Moreover, crystallization highlights scholars' own vulnerabilities, positionalities vis-à-vis their subject matters, and embodied engagement with their work.

To perform and analyze women engineers' workplace stories, we draw upon 45 interviews that we conducted with women engineering undergraduate and graduate students aged 18 to 35 years who studied in all of the engineering majors offered at a large Midwestern university. We note that as soon as men and women enter their engineering majors, they receive interpersonal messages whereby they are called "engineer," with their classrooms and related activities becoming their workplace experiences. All engage in engineering design work. Some create solutions in engineering classes to real-world problems.

To gather our data, we designed an interview protocol that asked some specific questions but also encouraged our research participants to tell their own stories (e.g., "Tell me the story of how you became an engineer"). Through an iterative process that was simultaneously inductive and deductive, we derived some patterns in participants' individual and collective explorations, and sensemaking, of their experiences. After inductively generating emerging patterns and themes from our data, we then disassembled our findings by going through our data again, looking for supporting and disconfirming evidence within our data, as well as from studies in social scientific, creative, qualitative, and other research genres. In addition to our disassembling deductive process, we move from patterns in results to explanations and theoretical development. We also immersed ourselves in our findings as we noted our personal experiences of teaching and working with engineering design teams, high-tech entrepreneurs, and science communicators.

Findings

In keeping with the assumptions and postmodern dialectics of fragmented and unifying accounts that underlie crystallization and our own purposes, our presentation of results is not traditional. Rather, we weave together a performance of our interviewees' stories in their own words (but using pseudonyms) to create a broader narrative of women in STEM. We framed their stories within their self-described key career experiences: nurturing early talents and confidence, developing skills, engaging and (re)creating professional caregiving networks, and (re)framing gender. Crystallization and performance make visible the lived and recalled interpersonal experiences these women associate with their choices to study and work in male-dominated workplaces and professions (see W. Faulkner, 2009). Throughout this section, a narrator provides context for the quotes. We use our narrator in this fashion to aid our readers in understanding this written performance script.

Nurturing Early Talents and Confidence

Narrator: For many students, early interpersonal experiences with family members or friends remain very important experiences that shape the narrative of why the individual chose engineering for a major.

Shelly: A couple months after my third birthday, I had gotten a tricycle for a gift. And my dad was enjoying the holiday, so I wanted to put it together. So I put it together and took it to the neighbors to tighten the bolts. So I effectively assembled my tricycle correctly shortly after my third birthday. There was a natural aptitude in me for engineering from an early age. One of the really influential characters was my grandfather. He had a penchant for education for women, and from a very early age he told me, "You're going to be a great engineer." So he started when I was just three years old.

Grace: My dad was a big influence. I have a brother and a sister and he raised us so gender was not an issue in our house. If he was building a cement wall in the backyard on a Saturday morning, all of us were out there helping. It wasn't boys' and girls' jobs, and he never said things like "boys do this and girls do that." It was just, we're all gonna do this.

Hillary: My mom has constantly said since I was born that engineering would be really good for me because there's not very many women in engineering, and she said that I'm very strong willed and so I'd be able to make it.

Narrator: As this section illuminates, several of the women talked about alternative messages they did or did not receive (i.e., present or absent messages) or explicit interpersonal interactions that often involved "doing" activities consistent with technical, engineering, and related work. Most interpersonal exchanges were with close family members who encouraged the students toward, or away from, the field of engineering.

Engaging and (Re)Creating Professional Caregiving Networks

Narrator: Other interviewees reported receiving interpersonal support through professional caregiving networks that the student engineer self-selected. Doing so opened up the possibility of richly detailed positive messages for the student engineers.

Suzy: Going to the Society of Women Engineers (SWE) national conference was amazing. Seeing all of those other women in engineering just made me really believe that becoming an engineer was possible. It was an amazing feeling.

Kim: The Women in Engineering director was just exactly what a girl in engineering needs. You walk into the office and she goes, "Keep going! You're doing great." She also led the seminar for women in engineering where she would bring in different women from industry to come in and talk to us about what they do.

Michelle: I went to this luncheon one day and the keynote said, "Engineers make a difference," and I never put those two together. Even though now that I've done it and I am an engineer, it's a very obvious thought. You know we do make a difference. We affect everything. But you don't see it.

Suzy: My advisor wasn't really very helpful, and he didn't seem to be supportive of my involvement with the Society of Women Engineers. He just didn't want me to waste time with anything. He kind of pissed me off. He wasn't the kind of advisor I wanted, but I sacrificed that because I think he is very smart. But he yelled at me several times, and he said things like, "Well maybe we just shouldn't work together," and all this other crazy stuff. I'm not submissive, and I think he wanted me to be, so the way I got around it was to just do things. Like, I went to the SWE conference, and I just took days off and just was done with it. I actually ran and got a position on SWE, and he didn't know about it. He didn't have a clue. I don't tell him, and he doesn't ask. He's very good in the field, and he's probably a very nice person. In my opinion, he's probably the least evil of all the professors.

Elizabeth: My roommate helped me so much my freshmen year. She was actually a sophomore in engineering. So it was nice because she had taken a lot of the same classes that I was getting ready to take. And so having her there to sort of tutor me in some of the classes was nice, and also just—it was kind of stressful being a female in the engineering class because of course you're surrounded by male engineers. There were only five of us in our graduating class. Five females in our graduating class. Out of about 75 to 100. So it was really nice to have someone to talk to because you feel like a minority. (Beat.) Which I guess you are.

Shelly: Most of the classes, I was one of the few women in the class, if not the only. Where I saw [hardship] more is with the minority students, and what ended up happening is that the misfits form their own group. That's what I saw. What they did was to create a community themselves in order to get the work done. Not for a social community, but I've seen it happen for the actual classroom experience. I've seen the likes get together and then the "others," which includes women and minority students and international students all having to hook up together. It's usual that the minority hasn't gotten the strength of education that the majority has, so there's an additional handicap, which tends to form within the group that I noticed. There were more roadblocks and more stuff you've got to do and put up with.

Narrator: As these messages show, the experience of feeling alone or lonely is often counteracted by interpersonal messages or experiences with members of professional and caregiving networks that exist expressly to support young women interested in these areas. Many of the women mentioned these messages as central to the reasons why they stayed in the field. They also note the hardships that happen when they and others feel alone because of perceptions about their lack of competence or training and because they are categorized in social identity groups different from the majority, male engineers.

(Re)Framing Gender

Narrator: Another key experience frequently mentioned by the women engineers was the idea of (re)framing gender and gender practices through messages they exchanged with close friends and family members as well as members of their work environment at school [see Jorgenson, 2002].

Kim: When I initially decided to go into engineering, it threw a lot of my friends off. "You want to go into engineering?" It didn't really fit my mold or my personality. In high school I was more of the girl who was really chatty, and a girl who really liked to shop and dress nice and flirt with boys a lot. And I wouldn't say I was a ditz, but you wouldn't think I'd like to study a lot and really thought it was cool to learn some chemistry in class. I just think people would have never pictured me going into chemical engineering—something so intense. People had no idea I liked math and science so much.

Greta: My family was really supportive, but some of my friends thought that it's weird that a girl is in engineering. There are some girls that think it's weird for a girl to be in a science program at all, and then there's some guys that think girls shouldn't be engineers just because they're girls. (*Pause*) I don't really respond. Most of the time with the girls they just think it's weird, and they really don't say anything about it. But with the boys a lot of times they'll give me a hard time or whatever.

Megan: There are some people out there that don't think that females should be engineers, which is what I've come across. That and it's an earth-shattering experience to have people actually tell you, "No, I don't think females should be engineers." Actually, this past summer I had a supervisor that, right before I got there, had been in a group of people, and they were all males. But he just happened to talk about how he didn't think females should be engineers, and he was my supervisor all summer.

Suzy: It was hard for me to work with guys, because if you try to be their friend or partner, they would always in the end take it as you want them. And I told quite a few of my friends, "I'm not interested in you like that," but this one guy just didn't get it. And there were these little sexual innuendos, like the one time one guy—an older man who was in the military and came back to school—he actually smacked my ass one time. I knew they [the guys] were working together, but I never felt a part of it. Whenever I went to talk to them, they just decided I was stupid or I didn't know what was going on enough to help out.

Jessica: Certain professors, for example, one is older and he's very traditional, very conservative. I mean, he'll make comments in class about women and minorities. He definitely made some comments about women in the workforce, women in upper-level senior management positions, and things of that nature, and how he didn't feel like it was right.

Narrator: For these women, the ability to reframe themselves as engineers despite messages of incredulity (engineers were not girly girls in high school), not belonging (women should not be in engineering), and stereotypical reactions (women were sex objects and not worth helping) presented ongoing interpersonal struggles and gendered performances for legitimation in a male-dominated career. Through such reframing and everyday performance, women engineers articulated their resistance to the status quo.

Discussion

Although we have not documented fully the many investigations that have created opportunities and removed obstacles in the career paths of women in STEM, our use of crystallization, narrative, and performance both invokes and attaches human faces and lived episodes to this research. Our study enables us to see *women's everyday interactional labor* from their earliest to current experiences in STEM careers. They do interactional labor through conversations and ongoing sensemaking processes about who they are and what they can do to achieve their dreams in environments where some people exert power to maintain the status quo and others affirm these women's choices. Their tales of workplace interactions speak about the ways they maneuver to gain legitimacy and voice in their occupations.

We rendered their stories into a performance so that our readers could envision these women doing their interactional labors. To create this performance, we did not simply devise a script with a narrative plot but worked inductively and deductively to form patterns of meanings that could be personalized and theorized by layering in women's voices, research reports, and other details. We remind our readers that this performance consists of contemporary women's stories. Although many things have changed for women in STEM over the last few decades, much has remained the same.

Note: We thank the Purdue University College of Liberal Arts for a grant that funded most of our transcription costs.

Reflecting on the Study

Excerpts From an Interview With Patrice M. Buzzanell

Adrianne: I wanted to start by saying thank you so much for contributing to this book. Your piece is—it's a unique piece and obviously a unique method that you used, so it adds a lot to the book.

Patrice: Well, thank you, and thank you for asking us. I mean, I was just thrilled to be invited to do this, and so were my colleagues, and we were happy with the feedback that you gave us and everything....

Adrianne: So I was wondering if there were some challenges or constraints or frustrations that you found when you used the method.

Patrice: Well ... that's a really good question. I wouldn't say that there were frustrations necessarily, but there are challenges with using this method. One of the big challenges is trying to figure out exactly how to present the research.

Adrianne: Yeah.

Patrice: Because when I've done this work in the past, you know, with Suzy D'Enbeau, and I've done other work in the past that has utilized this method, when it's done, it looks like it just emerged seamlessly. It looks like, "Oh, of course this conversation would lead to you examining this body of research, and of course you would write these kinds of stories and this would enable you to investigate or study something in particular." So, for example, in our case, you know, you'd look at it and you'd say, "Well, you know, of course you'd want to organize this so that it fits a certain pattern and you're getting certain results." But it's just—it's a lot harder than it looks.

Adrianne: Yeah.

Patrice: And so you don't really have the format. I mean, the advantage of APA style and some of the other styles is you've got a format, you know where to put things. You may not know exactly what your findings are—with qualitative research, that's always the big uncertainty all the way through is, you know, what are you going to find? It's not like you set it all in motion in the quantitative research and, you know, you know what your contribution *should be*, you know what your findings are.

Adrianne: Right.

Patrice: You kinda know what your contribution *might be* in qualitative research, but you never really know what the data are going to tell you.

Adrianne: Yeah.

Patrice: And so you *think* that this is what you're studying, you set it all up, and then you find out there's this whole idea or kinds of experiences for a particular group that just aren't anywhere in the literature.

Adrianne: Yeah.

Patrice: And so a lot of times with this research, it's not only that kind of uncertainty, but it's the presentational uncertainties … and opportunities.

Adrianne: Right.

Patrice: And really the need to go through and to figure out what is it that your readers are going to pick up. You know, it's not whether something is significant or substantive or not, or heuristic or not, but it's really, are they going to enter into this questioning and this iterative process with you? Are they going to see the value of the different kinds of research? Are they going to respect the particular traditions that they come from and see how it's woven together and whether or not that makes sense? Because really, this is kind of a sensemaking analytic tool as you go through and look at it, not only in terms of the subject matter and the methodology, but the kind of . . . the ways of knowing and being and valuing and practicing. So it's a pretty interesting process.

Adrianne: Yeah, definitely. . . . And I like how you framed it as presentational uncertainty, yet it's also an opportunity, because it seems like it's an opportunity to be creative, too, in the format.

Patrice: Yes, very much so. *Very*, very much so. And with creativity, you know what *you* intend, but again, you don't know exactly what your audience is going to pick up from it.

Adrianne: Right, right.

Patrice: So, you know, for all of the . . . the whole . . . obviously, I'm talking about dialectics . . . and dialogic processes, because it really is a dialogic method. So it's just kind of interesting to work through a lot of that.

Adrianne: Definitely, definitely. So, do you have . . . some strengths that you see in using the method? I mean, you've mentioned a few, but any others that you want to highlight?

Patrice: Well . . . when you use this method, you're tapping into a wide range of possibilities for readers to engage with the content—and the context. I mean, because they are drawn into the context in different ways. And so that's a *huge* opportunity. And for me it's kind of interesting because you may discount, or a reader may discount, a particular way of knowing. So perhaps they don't value necessarily the autoethnographic quality or maybe the narrative or the social scientific parts. You know, it doesn't matter which parts it is. But perhaps they don't, but then they'll pick up on something else, and maybe then they'll question a little bit differently what's going on.

Adrianne: Yeah, definitely. . . . When you use the method, do you feel like you learn new things about yourself as a scholar?

Patrice: You know what? It's interesting when I see it on paper. Because we talk through our research a lot. I mean, it is this ongoing sensemaking and everything. And then when you see it on paper, you go, "Oh, that's an interesting spot that got captured here." And maybe it's just one line that's transitioning from one thing to another, but that one line sticks with you. So it's just a fascinating process. You do learn about yourself as a person, and you learn about yourself in terms of relationships, both in doing this kind of research as well as engaging with readers, engaging with the materials, and so on. So you learn a lot. You learn a lot about the subject matter, too. The thing is, you just really—they were at a . . . a pre- or a nonverbal or . . . you know, I mean, like an unconscious or mindless kind of level that you begin to realize you've got this captured in a phrase or a statement or an image that you just hadn't really put together before, and there it is.

Adrianne: Yeah.

Patrice: Yeah. So it's fun.

Adrianne: Do you feel like there are advantages to having collaborators when you do use this kind of method?

Patrice: Oh absolutely, absolutely. . . . Most of my qualitative research is collaborative. And it's not that I wouldn't be capable of going through and doing analyses, but it's just that working with other people just brings so much insight, different kinds of insight, into a piece.

Adrianne: Yeah, that's what I've found.

Patrice: I think it makes it much richer and stronger.

Adrianne: Yeah, definitely. OK, yeah. The study examines a facet of interpersonal communication. Do you think that using this method provided any insights into understanding and developing interpersonal communication theory?

Patrice: Hmm. Well, as you know, I'm not an expert in interpersonal communication. . . . And so there's probably a lot I would miss with regard to that question . . . [but] I think that you could take it in a variety of different directions. I think that some of what people express in the piece is interesting to me because they feel safe in the environment, and obviously in this interview they had felt safe. And knowing people who are in these programs—and I don't even teach that much over there; you know [I have a courtesy appointment in the School of Engineering Education at Purdue]—I recognize people. And so looking at that, it was interesting to me to see how vulnerable people made themselves.

Adrianne: Yeah.

Patrice: And so, you know, what kind of space is created in an interview where somebody feels this free to be able to express oneself and to engage really in dialogue. Because a lot of these people weren't simply recounting their lives, but as you run through all of the interviews, you see that they've been grappling with a lot of these issues, so they've been engaging with other people *and* with the interviewer *and* with the subject matter. You know, as I mentioned before, certainly their dialectics are in operation, you know, throughout this— certainly the little snippets of narrative that come across, weaving together into a broader narrative, you know—and tracing the discourse and the themes throughout the different excerpts and the different sections and so on. I mean all of this certainly is amenable to different types of interpersonal theory. But I was also taken aback—and this is where I actually started—with the fact that some people felt freer to express themselves. . . .

Adrianne: Hmm.

Patrice: You certainly see things about socialization, and socialization with regard to particular groups, not necessarily when we think of organizational socialization, we usually think that or family socialization.

Adrianne: Oh, yeah.

Patrice: I would say yes, there's family socialization going on, but there's also different kinds of groups that they find themselves in, and cultural socialization, and figuring out what kinds of strategies to use in terms of impression management and self-presentation, you know, in terms of who they want to be with regard to their positions and their jobs and their studies and so on, and with their cohorts. So there's mentoring, there's collaborative comentoring kinds of things, and so on. There may even be—we haven't investigated this, but I would think there's probably some branding going on, too, in terms of what it is that they do very uniquely ... as they're sorting through why people may have responded the way they did to them.

Adrianne: Yeah.

Patrice: As you go back through and you read some of the quotes, there are certainly things about accommodation and aging accommodation and gender and so on. I mean, these are young women, for the most part, who are in this piece, and they're dealing with a variety of people, and they *are* trying to accommodate in a way that would enable them to be successful and gain approval for what they're doing. And yet they realize that they aren't, or cannot, maybe at times, fully accommodate. So in terms of looking at some of these, I think you could go to a variety of different things. You know, you can look at boundaries and boundary management theory. You can look at different, you know, role congruity theories that aren't necessarily interpersonal communication but certainly relate to interpersonal communication from a more psychological sense. There's just a lot that's going on in there that, you know, we really haven't unpacked fully ... in part because what we wanted to do was present the words and present the feelings, the emotions, and the behaviors. So, really integrating those kinds of things has been really important.

Adrianne: Yeah. And actually, that's one of the last questions I was going to ask you, but I'm going to go ahead and skip to that. Crystallization is kind of an analytical way of knowing based on emotions and feelings, and you really captured that in sharing the stories through the quotes, and I really appreciated the narrator as kind of a performance script, as you call it. . . . How did you get to the emotions and the feelings? What did you do to really capture those so that we could see them when we were presented with it?

Patrice: We were very conscious of the fact that we wanted to have concrete details, not necessarily in all of the excerpts from the interviews, but enough for people to kind of get a handle on what the lived experiences are, the material conditions of people's lives. So we wanted to get that, I think, that and the language. Some of the language is very evocative.

So, between those two issues within particular contexts, I think that's how we're really getting at the emotion. We're not simply getting at, oh, this is happiness here; but it's really a very complex . . . maybe sequencing even, in some of these quotes, of emotions. Sometimes we just captured one main idea, but sometimes we captured kind of a sequence as they run through—not only of emotions but also of identity, as they're figuring out how they sort through some of these issues that they're being confronted with and what kinds of strategies they want to use and so on. So, I think that that was helpful. The other thing that's helpful is that you don't lose hope while you're reading it.

Adrianne: Right.

Patrice: And we were being true to our data insofar as there may have been incredible barriers that you look at, and you say, "How could a professor have said that or done some of these things?" . . . Or their colleagues, their peers, you know, the male engineers or some of the other female engineers. And then you go back, and you say, "Well, for everything that has been said, there are also these stories that counteract, maybe not in the same narrative section but maybe in another section." And so that's true to the data, because we got people who are continuing with the program. So even though we as outsiders may look at this and say, "Oh my gosh, that's just horrific. Why would you want to be in this kind of situation?"

Adrianne: Right.

Patrice: There are countervailing forces that really have been set in motion by these women and by other people who are assisting them. So I think that that's part of what's really important about this piece is that it's not just . . . a kind of debilitating and negative narrative.

Adrianne: Right, no, it's not. People often say that writing is a huge part when doing qualitative research. Can you tell me about your specific feelings and experiences when you were writing up this research, like how did the editing process enter in and that kind of thing?

Patrice: Well, the writing process is in bits and pieces and fragments when I do this kind of research. . . . And so sometimes, it's . . . you go out to lunch, and literally, you're just sitting there and chatting about something, and you go, "Oh, wait a second. I have to write this down." And so you start doing that. Or sometimes, it's . . . you know, you wake up in the middle of the night and you're kind of thinking about something but not really actively thinking, but, you know, you've been doing this background thinking on it, and all of a sudden you realize, oh, wait a second, there's something else going on. And so you get on e-mail and you send an e-mail. Or you're just talking through and kind of analyzing and putting together maybe some sort of a table that doesn't show up in the piece but that you're trying to analyze just what's going on there, because sometimes you have to line up—especially if it's around a particular event, you have to line up what people are doing at certain times to see whether or not there's any commonalities and really huge distinctions in terms of how they're approaching and reacting and so on. So there are a lot of different things that are going on, but I would say that, for the most part, it's not a straightforward sit-down-and-write-a-section kind of method. . . . At least not for me.

Adrianne: OK.

Patrice: It might be for other people. You're writing all these different parts simultaneously, and you're also understanding and writing out why you're doing what you're doing and what the criteria are for what you're going to retain in the process. So for every one of these that I write, there's, like, another five pieces that probably could be written.

Adrianne: Yeah.

Patrice: You know, because you move things out as you're realizing you need to explain what you're retaining more.

Adrianne: Mmm-hmm.

Patrice: Because people aren't going to understand, especially when you take out a chunk of something. And since it all interrelates, you've got to keep going back and forth and saying, "OK, what is it that we had assumed, and that we knew based on something else, that just isn't in here anymore?" So it's an evolving process, an iterative process, but it's . . . both inductive and deductive insofar as you're looking at the data to try to come up with . . . what can you do that shows how you made sense of things and also how you integrated other materials, and to present something that might be of interest, but also realizing that what is of interest needs to be unpacked further for them. And you're doing this constantly, this inductive/deductive back and forth, when you're doing these writing stories.

Adrianne: Yeah. Oh, that's fascinating. . . . Well, what advice would you give to somebody who said, "I would like to use a crystallization approach in my work?" What advice would you give?

Patrice: Well, I'd say that the starting point, at least for me, is that there's something that I've seen or heard about, experienced, read, whatever it is, that really makes me pause . . . for one reason or another. I mean, it just . . . you know, there's something in the data, maybe, that I look at, and I think, I want to pull this out and extract it in a way that makes it come to life and that makes this understandable to other people . . . in the way *I* understand it but also in the way the research would tell us to understand it and the way that the person himself or herself . or the group expresses it and expresses their understanding of it. And so, um . . . you know, what got us going with this piece was looking at the incidents in childhood and how those early experiences that fed into their interests in certain kinds of work and career activities and occupations, and then there were changing experiences throughout, you know?

Adrianne: Mmm-hmm.

Patrice: Some encouraging and some discouraging, some that were considered challenges, and some that were major reasons to rethink what one was doing. And the learning part—like, every time I read this piece and also some of the other data, I learn something more about how people maneuver in academe, which is interesting to me. I mean, I still think about some of the quotes in there and think, I just didn't know that; I just didn't think about doing it that way. So I think it's that—the constant learning and relearning from a piece like this. It's this one, and then it's some other of the crystallization pieces I've done, where I go back to it, and I go, "Oh. They have said this or written this, but now I understand what it might mean."

Adrianne: Right.

Patrice: And then I'll come back to it maybe much later, and I'm rereading and going, "Oh, it means something different to me now." So it's that kind of thing, but there's still a hook in there that gets me going. So in this case it was really some of the early childhood experiences and then really their interpersonal interactions, so the workplace, the power displays and interactions and so on, the mentor-mentees. You want to see the professor-student kinds of power dynamics and interactions . . . that you can analyze using all kinds of different theories, interpersonal theories. But it's those kinds of things that I thought, this is just really interesting, and what is it that made these people resilient?

Adrianne: Right.

Patrice: Not them as individuals necessarily but in the communicative context such that they constructed resilience. You know, how did they construct this? . . . And it can be taken at all different levels. And you just kind of look at this data, and you go, there's just a lot in here, you know, for how this communicative construction goes on, so that it's not an individual, but it's the interweaving of a variety of experiences and, to go back to the method itself, the sensemaking about those things that these people in a certain context with other people are doing. That's the kind of thing that makes it just really powerful. . . .

Adrianne: In terms of crystallization as a method, are there things that you could identify that you should definitely *avoid* when you're trying to put this methodology into practice?

Patrice: . . . just as I've said that I think a good starting point is to find a particular incident or something that really grabs your attention that you want to spend this kind of time with— because it takes a long time to put these things together; it's just not easy. So are there things you should avoid? You should avoid the notion that there is a formula to do it.

Adrianne: OK.

Patrice: I think you should look at a variety of different examples, if you're trying to do it, to see how other people do it, because the way one scholar or set of scholars processes these things isn't necessarily how somebody else is going to do it, and you don't want to get caught up on their own way of making sense of some of this work. I think the other thing is you don't want to go into it thinking that you know what the answer is going to be, because part of this is that you're going to be very surprised. . . . You're not going to find what you thought you were going to find, and that's the beauty of it. But having that kind of suspended sense of . . . suspended sense in terms of the process and not closing things off, so kind of making sure that you don't inadvertently achieve closure before it's time. So those are some of things . . . .

Adrianne: Those are great. Those are great tips . . . thank you. So I have one last question that's kind of a huge question. . . . Obviously, most of your work is interpretivist or qualitative. What are some of the things that you've had to consider as you present your studies to a discipline that is often postpositivist or rhetorical in background? What are some of the struggles that you've had to overcome?

Patrice: Well . . . let me backtrack and say that my research has been—I think you're right in characterizing the way you did. It's been kind of a critical postmodern interpretative kind of blend for a lot of it, yet some of my projects right now are construct validation . . . and going back to doing some of that work. And I've always been collecting survey data; I just haven't always been publishing it, but using it for other things.

Adrianne: OK.

Patrice: And so I think I've been really fortunate that I was trained quantitatively, because what it has given me all along has been a suspicion of different kinds of research, just as I'm suspicious of the quantitative research.

Adrianne: Mmm-hmm.

Patrice: I'm suspicious of a lot of research, like I want to see really, really good quality, no matter what it is that I'm doing. And I think that that's part of the reason why my work, especially my feminist work, has gained acceptance: I understand the logics and the argument structure and content or values . . . for the study. And so, in terms of doing this kind of work, my goal is to mainstream my argument. So, with my feminist work, I really didn't have any troubles getting it accepted, maybe in part because I was coming in at a time when people were kind of looking to see how to rethink some of our communication theory and our methodologies and practices and so on. But I think the other part of it is, you know, you understand what people are looking for. You know, you don't make claims without justifying it and that kind of thing, and what are the other kinds of arguments that could be brought into it to support your findings. And where you see any of these methods—it's not just qualitative but any of these methods—getting a bad rap is when, you know, people are doing variable-analytic studies without connecting to, you know, a nomothetical net, and so it's not really that interesting. They just run some statistics and think it's going to be a publication, or somebody hasn't really spent the time with the data to *really* figure out what's of interest. Maybe they take a framework and apply it, and that's all they do.

Adrianne: Right.

Patrice: And sometimes these things are worthwhile because you do want to look at maybe a single construct and see how it's operating. But for the most part, I think that having this kind of suspicion, understanding what the values are and why people would say that they ... there are certain kinds of ways of knowing and understanding data and the world that they ascribe to; I mean, I think that that's helpful. . . .

Adrianne: Well, thank you so much for your responses—they're excellent, and I look forward to writing them up.

Questions for Growth

1. What might be some important considerations for you personally as to whether or not you want to use discourse analysis or narrative analysis? How might this fit into your research plans?

2. Do you buy into the idea that all relationships are stories? Why or why not? How might such a perspective play into your current research studies?

3. What are some of the best ways to collect stories for narrative inquiry? What might be some of the ethics involved?

4. What might be some forms of crystallization you could try? Does this analytical tool appeal to you? Why or why not?

CHAPTER 9

Writing and Presenting Qualitative Interpersonal Communication Studies

FUNCTIONS FOR "GOOD" INTERPRETIVE THEORIZING FROM RESEARCH

We begin our final chapter with a comment we really appreciate from the late and great Harold Lloyd ("Bud") Goodall. He said,

> One fact I love about the field of Communication is that it is large and diverse enough to embrace not only lifetimes of inquiry but also that its citizens have the good sense to recognize that no one method, approach, theory, or writing style can lead us to perfect knowledge. (2004, p. 192)

Of course, research and its methodologies ultimately serve to aid in the creation, testing, supporting, and refutation of theory, the stated accumulation of knowledge that inquiry seeks to explain and understand. Thus, research studies should be designed to match the standards of high-quality theorizing.

As we can easily appreciate Goodall's (2004) words, we might also make a few more considerations about ensuring high qualitative research standards. First, let's say you are finished with your research study and have written it up in a way that matches the unique specifications of your study. Further, you have read through all our suggestions from the relevant chapters of this book. In addition, you have considered the specific methods and analytical tools we have provided and exemplified. Finally, as you look at your manuscript or presentation, you might ask yourself some questions as you consider whether your study has done what you had originally set out to do. Specifically, Griffin (2012) suggests in his popular undergraduate communication theory textbook several "functions" interpretive work should accomplish in terms of qualitative theorizing. Good qualitative work should "create understanding, identify values, inspire aesthetic appreciation, stimulate agreement, reform society, and conduct qualitative research" (p. 31). The importance of each function depends on the researcher's questions or goals, but all are worth considering. Some might question why we would turn to an undergraduate textbook to examine qualitative criteria—but we feel it is an especially good place to look, as textbooks are about translation. They are a primary resource for research to be disseminated and to make a practical difference. Thus, each function is discussed here, with the exception of Griffin's sixth offering, "conduct qualitative research" (because our entire book covers that).

So, first, according to Griffin (2012), ask yourself whether your study provides a new understanding of people. That is, does your research offer "fresh insight into the human condition" (p. 31)? By examining an activity regarded as "uniquely human" (p. 31), like the use of language and symbols, the interpretive scholar can come to new understandings about a particular group of people in a specific communication setting. The interpretive/qualitative scholar is not interested in finding patterns across all human beings but instead in understanding how a specific group of people uses language within its own speech community. For example, in a recent study mentioned earlier, Adrianne and her colleague Suzy D'Enbeau were interested in examining the types of interactions within a domestic violence organization and how those interactions were both simultaneously constraining and enabling for the workers/advocates and the survivors they served. Further, Adrianne and Suzy were quite aware that, as advocates against domestic violence within that same organization, their mere presence and experience shaped the kinds of interactions observed. Thus, as interpretive scholars, Adrianne and Suzy played a role in the kinds of interactions they saw, as they were both observers and active participants in the research process.

Second, according to Griffin (2012), ask yourself whether your study provides a clarification of values. High-quality interpretive works should foreground and highlight the values of the people you are studying. This particular function of qualitative scholarship has to do with morals and ethics. You want the values, beliefs, and attitudes of your participants to be featured and illuminated brightly. One of the only ways a scholar can do this is to ask people directly about their values and then to represent those as carefully and clearly as possible. As qualitative researchers, we can "check" our representations of values by asking the people we are studying if our representations are clear and accurate. If they are, great! But, if not, we have to be willing to change what we have written to be true to our source(s). Qualitative writing and representation must be constantly open to revision. The front end of the paper will undoubtedly change as the back end of the paper (including the results) gets written. The manuscript may go through multiple iterations before it is actually considered "final." This process is true for almost anyone who does top-notch research, but it is particularly true for the qualitative scholar who often goes into his or her data not knowing what he or she might find. A pure, qualitative scholar must be open to writing, rewriting, criticism, starting over, revising, more criticism, and rewriting again. Qualitative research unfolds over time as the data start to make sense. It is rarely linear.

Third, according to Griffin (2012), ask yourself whether your study has aesthetic appeal. As Griffin notes, "The way a theorist presents ideas can capture the imagination of the reader just as much as the wisdom and originality of the theory he or she has created" (p. 32). Indeed, *what* is presented is as important as *how*. Interpretive scholars have room for creativity in their work; they are not constrained like the postpositivist to a traditional, scientific writing style. The rationale and literature review rarely lead to clean-cut hypotheses or research questions. As Griffin further notes, "By artfully incorporating imagery, metaphor, illustration, and story into the core of the theory, the theorist can make his or her creation come alive for others" (p. 32). The qualitative scholar has to be open to rethinking, recrafting, and rewriting his or her research questions. And, as Goodall (2004) aptly articulated,

Personal experience narratives are used to write about the poetics of living; about the communication of beauty and peace and connectedness; to articulate the interplays of aesthetic values in everyday life; of the ability humans have to love, to care for, to hope, to teach, as well as our ability to create friendships, communities, and to perform random acts of creative kindness. For these, too, are personal experiences that are largely under-written in academic journals and so-called professional prose. (p. 188)

In other words, interpretive scholarship allows for the lives we study to be realized more fully, to be contextualized, and to be honored.

Fourth, according to Griffin (2012), ask yourself whether your study fosters a community of agreement. As Griffin argues, "We can identify a good interpretive theory by the amount of support it generates within a community of scholars who are interested and knowledgeable about the same type of communication" (p. 32). The interpretivist scholar must be willing to put his or her ideas out there, under the microscope for like-minded others to view, review, and sometimes reject. Griffin further notes that the "acceptance or rejection [of ideas] is an objective fact that helps verify or vilify a theorist's ideas" (p. 32). Rejection can be just as illuminating as acceptance if the interpretive scholar is open-minded and accepting of others who embrace similar research and methodological commitments. While it hurts a bit, you can learn as much from rejection as you can from acceptance.

Finally, according to Griffin (2012), ask yourself whether your study has the capability of creating or inciting change and possibly generating "fresh alternatives for social action" (p. 33). This function of interpretive work is similar to the critical theorist's goal of generating and exposing "unjust communication practices that create or perpetuate gross imbalances of power" (Griffin, 2012, p. 33). The goal of Adrianne and Suzy's work was to ultimately help an organization dealing with a very serious and potentially deadly issue (i.e., domestic violence) to function more effectively. Indeed, the imperative for that research was to provide the tools and resources to help the organization function better to help survivors of domestic violence. As Goodall (2004) so artfully claims,

In all of these applied contexts, communication is shown to be the meaningful organizing locus for how our worlds are rendered visible, personal, and real. Conversations—or the absence of them—are often foci of how humans learn to make, reveal, and do. Personal narratives are about communication as it is experienced in everyday life, which is always first person, deeply felt, rooted in our past, not always rational, and often messy. By saying so, and by writing about how it is so . . . [we] seek to reclaim the personal experience of everyday life for communication research in ways that challenge existing ways of thinking, writing, and speaking about those issues in our field. Ours is the challenge the subjective makes to the objective. Our goal is not to reject one over the other but to combine what is best about these two ways of being in the world and thinking about it, into a far more powerful tool— memorable stories—for understanding and improving human lives. (p. 188)

We can, with our work, start to make a difference in people's lives. We cannot think of anything more rewarding. Of course to reach beyond the pragmatic, we must also take into account how research gets evaluated.

FINAL THOUGHTS ON VALIDITY AND QUALITATIVE RESEARCH

As noted earlier, providing validity is a constant and ongoing concern in qualitative research. Qualitative researchers, unlike quantitative researchers who aim to make generalizations about large groups of people, are much more concerned about the richness of their data and resulting findings. As Suter (2009) reminds us, there are many different terms to describe validity, such as "trustworthiness" (Lincoln & Guba, 1985), "confirming findings" (Miles & Huberman, 1994), and "evocation" (Ellis, 1995). We prefer to simply equate the term *validity* with the "truth value" of the research findings (Lindlof & Taylor, 2011, p. 273). In addition, validity can be conceptualized in terms of its transactional or transformational quality. Transactional validity is an "interactive process between the researcher, the researched, and the collected data that is aimed at achieving a relatively higher level of accuracy and consensus by means of revisiting facts, feelings, experiences, and values or beliefs collected and interpreted" (Cho & Trent, 2006, p. 321). In contrast, transformational validity is a "progressive emancipatory process leading toward social change that is to be achieved by the research endeavor itself" (Cho & Trent, 2006, pp. 321–322). Transformational validity attempts to change the personal and social condition of the people researched, thus addressing Griffin's (2012) issue of whether research has the possibility of generating change or social action.

Here are the four most prominent ways to assess validity in qualitative research. First, as many qualitative studies feature deep and lasting connections with research participants (e.g., in an ethnography or long-term, multi-interview study), researchers are gifted with a more thorough and complete understanding of the social situation than that found in any quantitative study. And this level of understanding is more valuable than just about any type of traditional validity check. The researcher and the researched co-learn and share in their experiences. Thus, one common method for "checking" validity is to do member checks—to ask participants if their words and voices are represented correctly (Lincoln & Guba, 1985). Share interview transcripts with participants and let them comment, offer suggestions, and make changes as they so desire. Another technique is to ask informants what they think of your data analysis and conclusions. You can also ask participants for follow-up interviews that enable them to "fix" or "adjust" earlier positions that may have changed throughout the research process.

A second validity consideration is the analysis of negative cases or "deviant case analysis" (Lindlof & Taylor, 2011, p. 278). If you find in your analysis process cases that go against your overall categories or codes, try to "understand why they occurred and what circumstances produced them" (Gibbs, 2007, p. 96). As you begin to understand their occurrence and surrounding circumstances, you may develop a revised category or a new category altogether (Lindlof & Taylor, 2011). The negative cases should not be perceived negatively; instead, consider them as opportunities for insight about a different part of the "story" behind the data that will make the results more holistic and meaningful.

A third validity consideration involves triangulation (or comparing "two or more forms of evidence with respect to an object of research interest," Lindlof & Taylor, 2011, p. 274). If the data from the evidence lead to the same conclusions, then validation is enhanced. Unlike traditional senses of triangulation that imply corroborating qualitative and quantitative data sources, triangulation in qualitative research involves collecting data from diverse participants (e.g., interviewing several people about one of your participant's experiences with sexual abuse—including the participant, his or her counselor, one or two of his or her family members, one or two of his or her friends). Triangulation in qualitative research is also achieved using multiple methods (e.g., field notes gathered by the researcher who observes the rape crisis center, interviews with rape crisis advocates, interviews with rape survivors, analysis of rape crisis center documents). And finally, triangulation is achieved in qualitative research by using multiple researchers (e.g., multiple observers and interviewers at a rape crisis center) or multiple analysts working together to code a data set (Lindlof & Taylor, 2011). These researchers will work both independently and together to compare interview transcripts or coding processes (sometimes even working to calculate intercoder reliability or agreement, which is a quantitative assessment of validation).

Finally, a fourth and very common way to enhance (and ensure) validity in qualitative research is to use "constant comparison," which was initially introduced as part of grounded theory by Glaser and Strauss (1967). This iterative process is where researchers "continuously check and re-check emerging categories against raw data as they develop theory" (Suter, 2009, p. 84; see also Lindlof & Taylor, 2011). Continuously checking and rechecking categories helps to yield more valid and meaningful categories and codes within the data analysis process.

DISSEMINATING QUALITATIVE RESEARCH FINDINGS

As we said in the introduction, we knew we had to write this book because, as qualitative scholars who study interpersonal communication and personal relationships, we feel a burden—a burden of proof, a burden of explanation, a burden of instilling understanding, a burden to demonstrate why our research matters and how it can make a difference. Our hope, however, is that once people finish reading this book and savor and take to heart what it offers, their burden will be lessened. As we noted earlier, interpersonal communication, as an area within our discipline, has been especially slow in embracing qualitative studies (Baxter, 2011; Tracy & Muñoz, 2011).

In fact, as Suter (2009) notes in her analysis of the top relationship-oriented research journals, the *Journal of Social and Personal Relationships* (which began in 1984) and *Personal Relationships* (which began in 1994), they have published purely qualitative research at the rates of only 6% and 1%, respectively, during their entire existence. Our hope is that this book demonstrates what qualitative research has to offer for interpersonal communication and relationships studies in general and demonstrates that it does have a place in our top journals. More importantly, we hope it encourages qualitative interpersonal scholars to become more confident about their work and submit it to those journals.

We hope this book is useful to qualitative researchers from other disciplines that study relationships, too. Overall, we hope our book has been inspiring and will ultimately foster a sense of freedom to qualitative interpersonal scholars to focus on the possibilities of their work. We also want to reemphasize that the only way to learn how to use a method is to actually use it. And, as with anything rigorous, it takes time and practice to master a method. Qualitative research involves different assumptions, different styles of inquiry, and different presentational modes. Our hope is that this book provides a sense of validation to scholars who already use qualitative methods and that it will unlock scholars who refuse (or are afraid) to ask questions that might lend themselves to qualitative approaches. Indeed, one should let his or her research question drive the research method.

GOALS OF THE BOOK

We are fairly confident we have accomplished the primary goals set out in writing this book. First, we hope we have offered ideas and solutions to help alleviate translation issues (e.g., methodological choices, analysis techniques). Specifically, we hope we have lessened the need for qualitative scholars to justify and defend the *way* they are working and instead focus on justifying and rationalizing the importance of the research overall. Second, we hope we have generated a sense of intrigue about the immense number of possibilities, situations, and experiences to be explored and uncovered with qualitative research. Carefully examining people's stories and lived experiences can be quite a "messy" process, but it can also be incredibly illuminating and thrilling as the data start to unfold and make sense. And, finally, we hope to foster a sense of community for interpersonal scholars who perform qualitative research (across traditions and methodological paradigms). By creating such a community, we open new doors and possibilities for disseminating research, as we participate in a dialogue with other qualitative researchers in our own discipline and related others.

Reviewing the Experience

After our introduction, Chapter 1 describes and elucidates interpretivism and the many approaches to qualitative inquiry. Not only do we describe what interpretivist-oriented qualitative research is, we also describe what it is *not*. This provides the reader with a fuller and richer picture of the possibilities of qualitative inquiry. In addition, Chapter 1 provides a description of the various research traditions associated with interpersonal qualitative research, as well as the commitments necessary for high-quality, interpretivist-oriented communication studies.

Chapter 2 describes research traditions associated with qualitative relationships research (e.g., narrative, ethnography, grounded theory). It also offers solid advice for analyzing qualitative data and modes for presenting top-notch qualitative research. Finally, Chapter 2 provides an overview of the criteria one might use in evaluating the merits and quality of qualitative research (e.g., S. J. Tracy, 2010), as well as the many procedural, situational, relational, and personal ethical issues and paradoxes with which qualitative researchers must grapple.

The next six chapters offer descriptions of qualitative research methods, as well as specialized analytical tools for examining particular data sets. We present six unique and illustrative relationship-based research studies using specific qualitative analytical tools. Some of the featured scholars are fluent with qualitative methods and approaches, while others are less familiar and not nearly as comfortable taking a qualitative approach. At the end of each of the six research studies, we present scholars' candid thoughts and feelings related to the qualitative research process and the specific data analysis technique used.

In Chapter 3, Laura Ellingson and Patty Sotirin, two scholars quite knowledgeable about qualitative research methods, present an interview study wherein they used a modified version of emotion coding to study "aunting" relationships. In Chapter 4, Laura Stafford and colleagues (all of whom primarily use more postpositivist research methods in most of their other work) present a focus group study of friendship. The Stafford team uses the analytical tool of values coding to try to better understand the phenomenon of "friends with benefits." Erin Sahlstein, a scholar versed and trained in both quantitative and qualitative research methods, provides an open-ended survey study of long-distance friendship in Chapter 5. Sahlstein uses taxonomic coding (or typology development) to better understand how long-distance friendships can grow and change over time. Chapter 6 presents an ethnographic field study by Jennifer C. Dunn. Dunn uses dramaturgical analysis to consider how identity is negotiated and renegotiated for workers at the Moonlite Bunny Ranch. Denise Solomon, a scholar very much rooted in postpositivist methods, and Victoria Jennings-Kelsall, a more qualitatively oriented scholar, provide a discourse analytic study of computer-mediated communication and military spouses in Chapter 7. Solomon and Jennings-Kelsall make use of grounded theory to elucidate the challenges of being in a military marriage. Patrice M. Buzzanell, a qualitative research veteran originally trained using quantitative methods, and her colleagues provide a narrative study of women engineers in Chapter 8. Buzzanell and colleagues use crystallization to unpack and understand how women engineers navigate and make sense of their gendered experiences.

OUR STORIES, YOUR STORIES

After reading this book, we hope you understand that the qualitative scholar

> should be able to sweep the floor, carry out the garbage, carry in the laundry, cook for large groups, go without food and sleep, read and write by candlelight, see in the dark, see in the light, cooperate without offending, suppress sarcastic remarks, smile to express both pain and hurt, experience both pain and hurt, spend time alone, respond to orders, take sides, stay neutral, take risks, avoid harm, be confused, care terribly, become attached to nothing. . . . The nine-to-five set need not apply. (Patton, 1990, p. 143)

In other words, qualitative research involves a lot of work. For those who have not experienced the joys of qualitative research yet, we hope you trust us when we tell you it is as exhilarating as it is fascinating. In the introduction, you learned about our personal stories of how we came to love and appreciate qualitative approaches to inquiry. Those stories were written well over a year before this book was finished. In the spirit of reflexivity encouraged in much qualitative research, we as authors have reflected many times about what we were learning (and how we were learning) in the process of writing this book. During the journey, we have dialogued with each other, attended conferences where we facilitated roundtable discussions, and have discovered and reviewed countless new qualitative research studies that have expanded our understandings of method and theorizing. We have continued to revisit our stories. We hope that at this point you will want to revisit *your* story, too.

Surely you had goals in reading this book. We hope we have helped you to meet them—but if we did not, or if you have other goals we can help you reach, let us know. We hope this is but the first of many editions of this book and our musings about qualitative research and interpersonal communication studies. It has been rewarding to pull together bodies of writing that interpersonal communication scholars previously had to seek out through several sources to use and to help make sense of it as a coherent whole. It has been exciting to offer our own theorizing and insights about how to best use qualitative methods. If you have ideas about where that might go, or if you want to share your own qualitative work, look us up or join our Facebook group, Qualitative Relationships Researchers. We are all about extending a community of qualitative relationships researchers where we can all learn from each other.

References

Adams, T. E. (2011). *Narrating the closet: An autoethnography of same-sex attraction.* Walnut Creek, CA: Left Coast Press.

Afifi, W. A., & Weiner, J. L. (2004). Toward a theory of motivated information management. *Communication Theory, 14,* 167–190.

Albers, P. (2007). Visual discourse analysis: An introduction to the analysis of school-generated visual texts. *Literacy Research Association Yearbook, 56,* 81–95.

Albert, A. (2001). *Brothel: Mustang Ranch and its women.* New York: Random House.

Albrecht, S. L. (1980). Reaction and adjustments to divorce: Differences in the experiences of males and females. *Family Relations, 29,* 59–68.

Allen, B. J., Orbe, M. P., & Olivas, M. R. (1999). The complexity of our tears: Dis/enchantment and (in)difference in the academy. *Communication Theory, 9,* 402–429.

Anderson, L. (2006). Analytic autoethnography. *Journal of Contemporary Ethnography, 35,* 373–395.

Anderson, M., Kunkel, A., & Dennis, M. R. (2011). "Let's (not) talk about that": Bridging the past sexual experiences taboo to build healthy romantic relationships. *The Journal of Sex Research, 48,* 381–391.

Anderson, R., Baxter, L. A., & Cissna, K. N. (2004). Texts and contexts of dialogue. In R. Anderson, L. A. Baxter, & K. N. Cissna (Eds.), *Dialogue: Theorizing difference in communication studies* (pp. 1–17). Thousand Oaks, CA: Sage.

Andrews, M., Squire, C., & Tamboukou, M. (2008). What is narrative research? In M. Andrews, C. Squire, & M. Tamboukou (Eds.), *Doing narrative research* (pp. 1–21). Thousand Oaks, CA: Sage.

Arrington, M. I. (2002). The Louis Farrakhan-Arsenio Hall interview: Apologia and the daytime television mentality. *Florida Communication Journal, 30,* 25–33.

Arrington, M. I. (2005). "She's right behind me all the way": An analysis of prostate cancer narratives and changes in family relationships. *The Journal of Family Communication, 5,* 141–162.

Artz, S. (1994). *Feeling as a way of knowing: A practical guide for working with emotional experience.* Toronto: Trifolium.

Ashcraft, K. L., & Pacanowsky, M. E. (1996). "A woman's worst enemy": Reflections on a narrative of organizational life and female identity. *Journal of Applied Communication Research, 24,* 217–239.

Auerbach, C. F., & Silverstein, L. B. (2003). *Qualitative data: An introduction to coding and analysis.* New York: New York University.

Austin, J. L. (1962). *How to do things with words.* Oxford, UK: Oxford University.

Axelrod, M. (1975). Ten essentials for good qualitative research. *Marketing News, 8,* 10–11.

Babbie, E. (2010). *The practice of social research* (12th ed.). Belmont, CA: Wadsworth/Cengage Learning.

Bartesaghi, M. (2009). Conversation and psychotherapy: How questioning reveals institutional answers. *Discourse & Society, 11,* 153–177.

Bartesaghi, M., & Castor, T. (2008). Social construction in communication: Re-constituting the conversation. *Communication Yearbook, 32,* 3–39.

Baxter, L. A. (2011). *Voicing relationships: A dialogic perspective.* Thousand Oaks, CA: Sage.

Baxter, L. A., & Babbie, E. (2004). *The basics of communication research.* Belmont, CA: Wadsworth.

Baxter, L. A., & Braithwaite, D. O. (2002). Performing marriage: Marriage renewal rituals as cultural performance. *Southern Communication Journal, 67,* 94–109.

Baxter, L. A., & Braithwaite, D. O. (2008). *Engaging theories in interpersonal communication: Multiple perspectives.* Thousand Oaks, CA: Sage.

Baxter, L. A., Braithwaite, D. O., Kellas, J., LeClair-Underberg, C., Normand, E. L., Routsong, T. R., et al. (2009). Empty ritual: Young-adult stepchildren's perceptions of the remarriage ceremony. *Journal of Social and Personal Relationships, 26*, 467–487.

Baxter, L. A., & Montgomery, B. M. (1996). *Relating: Dialogues and dialectics.* New York: Guilford.

Becker, H. S. (1970). *Sociological work: Method and substance.* Hawthorne, NY: Aldine.

Becker, H. S., & Geer, B. (1957). Participant observation and interviewing: A comparison. *Human Organization, 16*, 28–32.

Becker, J. A. H., Johnson, A. J., Craig, E. A., Gilchrist, E. S., Haigh, M. M., & Lane, L. T. (2009). Friendships are flexible, not fragile: Turning points in geographically-close and long-distance friendships. *Journal of Social and Personal Relationships, 26*, 347–369.

Berger, C. R., & Calabrese, R. J. (1975). Some explorations in initial interaction and beyond: Toward a developmental theory of interpersonal communication. *Human Communication Research, 1*, 99–112.

Best, S., & Kellner, D. (1991). *Postmodern theory.* New York: Guilford.

Best, S., & Kellner, D. (1997). *The postmodern turn.* New York: Guilford.

Bingham, W. V. D., & Moore, B. V. (1959). *How to interview* (4th ed.). New York: Harper & Row.

Bisson, M. A., & Levine, T. R. (2007). Negotiating a friends with benefits relationship. *Archives of Sexual Behavior, 38*, 66–73.

Black, W. G. (1993). Military-induced family sepraration: A stress reduction intervention. *Social Work, 38*, 273–280.

Blair, C., Brown, J. R., & Baxter, L. A. (1994). Disciplining the feminine. *Quarterly Journal of Speech, 80*, 383–409.

Blumer, H. (1969). *Symbolic interactionism: Perspective and method.* Berkeley: University of California.

Bochner, A. P. (1985). Perspectives on inquiry: Representation, conversation, and reflection. In M. L. Knapp & J. A. Daly (Eds.), *Handbook of interpersonal communication* (pp. 27–58). Beverly Hills, CA: Sage.

Bochner, A. P. (1994). Perspectives on inquiry II: Theories and stories. In M. L. Knapp & J. A. Daly (Eds.), *Handbook of interpersonal communication* (2nd ed., pp. 21–41). Thousand Oaks, CA: Sage.

Bochner, A. P. (2000). Criteria against ourselves. *Qualitative Inquiry, 6*, 266–272.

Bochner, A. P. (2002). Perspectives on inquiry III: The moral of stories. In M. L. Knapp & J. A. Daly (Eds.), *Handbook of interpersonal communication* (3rd ed., pp. 73–101). Thousand Oaks, CA: Sage.

Bochner, A. P. (2008). Communication's calling: The importance of what we care about. *Spectra* (January 2009), 14–19.

Bochner, A. P., & Ellis, C. S. (2006). Communication as autoethnography. In G. J. Shepherd, J. St. John, & T. Striphas (Eds.), *Communication as . . .: Perspectives on theory* (pp. 110–122). Thousand Oaks, CA: Sage.

Bochner, A. P., Ellis, C., & Tillman-Healy, L. M. (1997). Relationships as stories. In S. Duck (Ed.), *Handbook of personal relationships: Theory, research, and interventions* (2nd ed., pp. 307–324). New York: Wiley.

Bogdan, R. C., & Biklen, S. K. (2007). *Qualitative research for education: An introduction to theories and methods.* Boston: Pearson.

Boje, D. M. (1995). Stories of the storytelling organization: A postmodern analysis of Disney as "Tamara-Land." *Academy of Management Journal, 38*, 997–1035.

Bolster, A. S. (1983). Toward a more effective model of research on teaching. *Harvard Educational Review, 53*, 294–308.

Boyatzis, R. E. (1998). *Transforming qualitative information: Thematic analysis and code development.* Thousand Oaks, CA: Sage.

Braun, V., & Clarke, V. (2006). Using thematic analysis in psychology. *Qualitative Research in Psychology, 3*, 77–101.

Bredo, E., & Feinberg, W. (1982). *Knowledge and values in social and educational research.* Philadelphia: Temple University.

Brooks, M. (2006). Using visual ethnography in the primary classroom. *Journal of Australian Research in Early Childhood Education, 13*, 67–80.

Brown, R. H. (1977). *A poetic for sociology.* Chicago: University of Chicago.

Bruner, J. (1987). Life as narrative. *Social Research, 54*, 11–32.

Bryman, A. (1988). *Quantity and quality in social research*. New York: Routledge.

Buber, M. (1923). *I and thou*. New York: Charles Scribner.

Burgchardt, C. R. (Ed.). (2010). *Readings in rhetorical criticism* (4th ed.). State College, PA: Strata.

Burke, K. (1966). Terministic screens. In K. Burke, *Language as symbolic action: Essays on life, literature, and method* (pp. 44–62). Berkeley: University of California.

Burleson, B. R., & Kunkel, A. (2006). Revisiting the different cultures thesis: An assessment of sex differences and similarities in supportive communication. In K. Dindia & D. Canary (Eds.), *Sex differences and similarities in communication* (2nd ed., pp. 137–159). Mahwah, NJ: Erlbaum.

Burleson, B. R., Kunkel, A. W., Samter, W., & Werking, K. (1996). Men's and women's evaluations of communication skills in personal relationships: When sex differences make a difference—and when they don't. *Journal of Social and Personal Relationships, 13*, 201–224.

Buzzanell, P. M. (Ed.). (2000). *Rethinking organizational and managerial communication from feminist perspectives* (pp. 157–174). Thousand Oaks, CA: Sage.

Buzzanell, P. M., Berkelaar, B., & Kisselburgh, L. (2011). From the mouths of babes: Exploring families' career socialization of young children in China, Lebanon, Belgium, and the United States. *Journal of Family Communication, 11*, 148–164.

Buzzanell, P. M., Berkelaar, B., & Kisselburgh, L. (2012). Expanding understandings of mediated and human socialization agents: Chinese children talk about desirable work and careers. *China Media Research, 8*, 1–14.

Buzzanell, P. M., & D'Enbeau, S. (2009). Stories of caregiving: Intersections of academic research and women's everyday experiences. *Qualitative Inquiry, 15*, 1199–1224.

Byers, P. Y., & Wilcox, J. R. (1991). Focus groups: A qualitative opportunity for researchers. *The Journal of Business Communication, 28*, 63–78.

Cahnmann-Taylor, M. & Siegesmund, R. (2008). *Arts-based research in education: Foundations for practice*. London: Routledge.

Calder, B. J. (1977). Focus groups and the nature of qualitative marketing research. *Journal of Marketing Research, 14*, 353–364.

Calvert, S. L., Rideout, V. J., Woolard, J. L., Barr, R. F., & Strouse, G. A. (2005). Age, ethnicity, and socioeconomic patterns in early computer use. *American Behavioral Scientist, 48*, 590–607.

Carey, M. A. (1994). The group effect in focus groups: Planning, implementing, and interpreting focus group research. In J. Morse (Ed.), *Critical issues in qualitative research methods* (pp. 225–241). Thousand Oaks, CA: Sage.

Castle Bell, G., & Hastings, S. O. (2011). Black and white interracial couples: Managing relational disapproval through facework. *Howard Journal of Communications, 22*, 240–259.

Chalaby, J. K. (1996). Beyond the prison-house of language: Discourse as a sociological concept. *British Journal of Sociology, 47*, 684–698.

Charmaz, K. (1991). Translating graduate qualitative methods into undergraduate teaching: Intensive interviewing as a case example. *Teaching Sociology, 19*, 384–395.

Charmaz, K. (2006). *Constructing grounded theory: A practical guide through qualitative methods*. Thousand Oaks, CA: Sage.

Chase, S. E. (2008). Narrative inquiry: Multiple lenses, approaches, voices. In N. K. Denzin & Y. S. Lincoln (Eds.), *Collecting and interpreting qualitative materials* (pp. 57–94). Thousand Oaks, CA: Sage.

Cheney, G. (1983). The rhetoric of identification and the study of organizational communication. *Quarterly Journal of Speech, 69*, 143–168.

Cho, J., & Trent, A. (2006). Validity in qualitative research revisited. *Qualitative Research, 6*, 319–340.

Christians, C. G. (2000). Ethics and politics in qualitative research. In N. K. Denzin & Y. S. Lincoln (Eds.), *The SAGE handbook of qualitative research* (2nd ed., pp. 133–155). Thousand Oaks, CA: Sage.

Christiansen, R., & Brophy, B. (2007). *The complete book of aunts*. New York: Twelve.

Clair, R. P. (1996). The political nature of the colloquialism, "a real job": Implications for organizational socialization. *Communication Monographs, 63*, 249–267.

Clair, R. P., Chapman, P. A., & Kunkel, A. W. (1996). Narrative approaches to raising consciousness about sexual harassment: From research to pedagogy and back again. *Journal of Applied Communication Research, 24*, 241–259.

Clair, R. P., & Kunkel, A. W. (1998). "Unrealistic realities": Child abuse and the aesthetic resolution. *Communication Monographs, 65*, 24–46.

Clark, M. S., Fitness, J., & Bristette, I. (2004). Understanding people's perceptions of relationships is crucial to understanding their emotional lives. In M. B. Brewer & M. Hewstone (Eds.), *Emotion and motivation* (pp. 21–46). Malden, MA: Blackwell.

Clark, M. S., Fitness, J., & Brisette, I. (2008). Understanding people's perceptions of relationships is crucial to understanding their emotional lives. In M. B. Brewer & M. Hewstone (Eds.), *Emotion and motivation* (pp. 21–46). Malden, MA: Blackwell.

Clarke, M. (1975). Survival in the field: Implications of personal experience in field work. *Theory and Society 2*, 95–123.

Clifford, J., & Marcus, G. E. (1986). *Writing culture: The poetics and politics of ethnography.* Berkeley: University of California.

Clough, P. T. (1995). Beginning again at the end(s) of ethnography: Response to "The Man at the End of the Machine." *Symbolic Interaction, 18*, 527–534.

Coltrane, S., & Adams, M. (2008). *Gender and families* (2nd ed.). Lanham, MD: Rowan & Littlefield.

Conquergood, D. (1991). Rethinking ethnography: Towards a critical cultural politics. *Communication Monographs, 58*, 179–194.

Conquergood, D. (1992). Ethnography, rhetoric, and performance. *Quarterly Journal of Speech, 78*, 80–97.

Conquergood, D. (1998). Beyond the text: Toward a performative cultural politics. In S. J. Dailey (Ed.), *The future of performance studies: Visions and revisions* (pp. 25–36). Annandale, VA: National Communication Association.

Cooley, C. H. (1902). *Human nature and the social order.* New York: Scribners.

Cooren, F. (2010). *Action and agency in dialogue: Passion, incarnation, and ventriloquism.* Amsterdam: John Benjamins.

Corbin, J., & Strauss, A. (1990). *Basics of qualitative research: Grounded theory procedures and techniques.* Thousand Oaks, CA: Sage.

Corbin, J., & Strauss, A. (2008). *Qualitative research* (3rd ed.). Thousand Oaks, CA: Sage.

Corey, F. C. (1996). Personal narratives and young men in prison: Labeling the outside inside. *Western Journal of Communication, 60*, 57–75.

Corsaro, W. A. (1997). *The sociology of childhood.* Thousand Oaks, CA: Pine Forge.

Côte, J. E. (1996). Sociological perspectives on identity formation: The culture-identity link and identity capital. *Journal of Adolescence, 19*, 3–25.

Coupland, J. (1996). Dating advertisements: Discourses of the commodified self. *Discourse & Society, 7*, 187–207.

Cousins, J. B., & Earl, L. M. (1995). *Participatory evaluation in education: Studies of evaluation use and organizational learning.* New York: Routledge.

Craig, R. T. (1999). Communication theory as a field. *Communication Theory, 9*, 119–161.

Craig, R. T., & Muller, H. L. (2007). *Theorizing communication: Readings across traditions.* Thousand Oaks, CA: Sage.

Craig, R. T., & Tracy, K. (1995). Grounded practical theory: The case of intellectual discussion. *Communication Theory, 5*, 248–272.

Cresswell, J. W., & Plano Clark, V. L. (2010). *Designing and conducting mixed methods research.* Thousand Oaks, CA: Sage.

Dainton, M., & Aylor, B. (2009). Patterns of communication channel use in the maintenance of long-distance relationships. *Communication Research Reports, 19*, 118–129.

Dakof, G. A., & Taylor, S. E. (1990). Victims' perceptions of social support: What is helpful from whom? *Journal of Personality and Social Psychology, 58*, 80–89.

Davis, C. A. (1999). *Reflexive ethnography: A guide to research selves and others*. London: Routledge.

Deetz, S. (1973). An understanding of science and a hermeneutic science of understanding. *Journal of Communication, 23*, 139–159.

Deetz, S. (1992). *Democracy in an age of corporate colonization: Developments in communication and the politics of everyday life*. Albany: State University of New York.

Delacoste, F., & Alexander, P. (Eds.). (1998). *Sex work: Writings by women in the sex industry*. San Francisco: Cleis Press.

Dennis, M. R., & Kunkel, A. D. (2004). Fallen heroes, lifted hearts: Consolation in contemporary presidential eulogia. *Death Studies, 28*, 1–29.

Dennis, M. R., Kunkel, A. D., & Keyton, J. (2008). Problematic integration theory, appraisal theory, and the bosom buddies breast cancer support group. *Journal of Applied Communication Research, 36*, 415–436.

Dennis, M. R., Ridder, K., & Kunkel, A. D. (2006). Grief, glory, and political capital in the capitol: Presidents eulogizing presidents. *Death Studies, 30*, 325–349.

Denzin, N. K. (1978). *The research act* (2nd ed.). New York: McGraw-Hill.

Denzin, N. K. (1992). *Symbolic interactionism and cultural studies: The politics of interpretation*. Hoboken, NJ: Wiley-Blackwell.

Denzin, N. K. (2006). Analytic autoethnography, or déjà vu all over again. *Journal of Contemporary Ethnography, 35*, 419–428.

Denzin, N. K. (2010). *The qualitative manifesto: A call to arms*. Walnut Creek, CA: Left Coast Press.

Denzin, N. K., & Lincoln, Y. S. (1994). *Handbook of qualitative research*. Thousand Oaks, CA: Sage.

Denzin, N. K., & Lincoln, Y. S. (2011). Introduction: The discipline and practice of qualitative research. In N. K. Denzin & Y. S. Lincoln (Eds.), *The SAGE handbook of qualitative research* (4th ed., pp. 1–20). Thousand Oaks, CA: Sage.

de Sousa, R. (2010). Emotion. In E. N. Zalta (Ed.), *The Stanford encyclopedia of philosophy* (Spring 2010 Edition). Retrieved September 11, 2011, from http://plato.stanford.edu/archives/spr2010/entries/emotion.

Dey, I. (1999). *Grounding grounded theory: Guidelines for qualitative inquiry*. San Diego, CA: Academic Press.

Dickinson, G., Blair, C, & Ott, B. L. (Eds.). (2010). *Places of public memory: The rhetoric of museums and memorials* (pp. 1–41). Tuscaloosa: University of Alabama.

Diekman, A., Brown, E., Johnston, A., & Clark, E. (2011). Seeking congruity between goals and roles: A new look at why women opt out of science, technology, engineering, and mathematics careers. *Psychological Science, 21*, 1051–1057.

Dilley, P. (2000). Conducting successful interviews: Tips for intrepid research. *Theory Into Practice, 39*, 131–137.

Dowling, R. (2000). Power, subjectivity, and ethics in qualitative research. In H. Iain, *Qualitative research methods in human geography* (2nd ed., pp. 19–29). South Melbourne, Australia: Oxford University.

Drummet, A. R., Coleman, M., & Cable, S. (2003). Military families under stress: Implications for family life education. *Family Relations, 52*, 279–287.

Duck, S. W. (2011). *Rethinking relationships*. Thousand Oaks, CA: Sage.

Eccles, J. S. (2007). Where are all the women? Gender differences in participation in physical science and engineering. In S. J. Ceci & W. M. Williams (Eds.), *Why aren't more women in science? Top researchers debate the evidence* (pp. 199–210). Washington, DC: American Psychological Association.

Eckstein, J. J. (2012). *"Disconnect those bastards!" People we should stigmatize*. Panel presented at Central States Communication Association annual conference, Cleveland, OH.

Eckstein, J. J., & Frey, L. R. (2011). *You all make us baaad! Addressing stigmatizing difference as interpersonally built and manageably housed*. Panel presented at Central States Communication Association annual conference, Milwaukee, WI.

Eckstein, N. J. (2004). Emergent issues in families experiencing adolescent-to-parent abuse. *Western Journal of Communication, 68*, 365–388.

Ellingson, L. L. (2005). *Communicating in the clinic: Negotiating frontstage and backstage teamwork*. Cresskill, NJ: Hampton Press.

Ellingson, L. L. (2008). *Qualitative crystallization: Integrating grounded theory and narrative representation*. Thousand Oaks, CA: Sage.

Ellingson, L. L. (2009). *Engaging crystallization in qualitative research: An introduction*. Thousand Oaks, CA: Sage.

Ellingson, L. L. (2011). Analysis and representation across the continuum. In N. K. Denzin & Y. S. Lincoln (Eds.), *The SAGE handbook of qualitative research* (4th ed., pp. 595–610). Thousand Oaks, CA: Sage.

Ellingson, L. L., & Sotirin, P. (2006). Exploring young adults' perspectives on communication with aunts. *Journal of Social and Personal Relationships, 23*, 499–517.

Ellingson, L. L., & Sotirin, P. (2010). *Aunting: Cultural practices that sustain family and community life*. Waco, TX: Baylor University Press.

Ellis, C. (1995). *Final negotiations: A story of love, loss, and common illness*. Philadelphia: Temple University.

Ellis, C. (2003). Grave tending: With Mom at the cemetery. *Forum: Qualitative Social Research, 4*(2), Article 28. Retrieved from www.qualitative-research.net/index.php/fqs/article/view/701/1521.

Ellis, C. (2004). *The ethnographic I: A methodological novel about autoethnography*. Walnut Creek, CA: AltaMira Press.

Ellis, C. (2007). Telling secrets, revealing lives: Relational ethics in research with intimate others. *Qualitative Inquiry, 13*, 3–29.

Ellis, C., & Ellingson, L. L. (2000). Qualitative methods. In E. F. Borgatta & R. J. V. Montgomery (Eds.), *Encyclopedia of sociology* (Vol. 4, 2nd ed., pp. 2287–2296). New York: Macmillan Library Reference.

Ellis, C., Kiesinger, C. E., & Tillman-Healy, L. M. (1997). Interactive interviewing: Talking about emotional experience. In R. Hertz (Ed.), *Reflexivity and voice* (pp. 119–149). Thousand Oaks, CA: Sage.

Emerson, R. M. (2001). Introduction: The development of ethnographic field research. In R. M. Emerson (Ed.), *Contemporary field research: Perspectives and formulations* (2nd ed., pp. 1–26). Prospect Heights, IL: Waveland.

Emerson, R. M., Fretz, R. I., & Shaw, L. L. (1995). *Writing ethnographic fieldnotes*. Chicago: University of Chicago Press.

Endres, D., & Gould, M. (2009). "I am also in the position to use my whiteness to help them out": The communication of whiteness in service learning. *Western Journal of Communication, 73*, 418–436.

Erickson, E. H. (1968). *Identity: Youth and crisis*. New York: Norton.

Fahy, K. (1997). Postmodern feminist emancipatory research: Is it an oxymoron? *Nursing Inquiry, 4*, 27–33.

Fairclough, N. (1996). A reply to Henry Widdowson's "Discourse analysis: A critical view." *Language & Literature, 5*, 49–56.

Fairclough, N. (2009). *Language and power*. London: Longman.

Fairclough, N., & Wodak, R. (1997). Critical discourse analysis. In T. A. van Dijk (Ed.), *Discourse as social interaction* (Vol. 1, pp. 258–284). Thousand Oaks, CA: Sage.

Farley, M. (2005). Prostitution harms women even if indoors. *Violence Against Women, 11*, 950–964.

Fassett, D. L., & Warren, J. T. (2006). *Critical communication pedagogy*. Thousand Oaks, CA: Sage.

Faulkner, S. L. (2009). *Poetry as method: Reporting research through verse*. Walnut, CA: Left Coast Press.

Faulkner, W. (2009). Doing gender in engineering workplace cultures. I. Observations from the field. *Engineering Studies, 1*, 3–18.

Feldman, M. S. (1995). *Strategies for interpreting qualitative data*. Thousand Oaks, CA: Sage.

Fielding, N. J., & Fielding, J. L. (1986). *Linking data*. Beverly Hills, CA: Sage.

Fine, G. A. (1993). Ten lies of ethnography: Moral dilemmas of field research. *Journal of Contemporary Ethnography, 22*, 267–294.

Fine, M. (1994). Distance and other stances: Negotiations of power inside feminist research. In A. Gitlin (Ed.), *Power and methods* (pp. 13–55). New York: Routledge.

Fine, M., Weis, L., Weseen, S., & Wong, L. (2000). For whom: Qualitative research, representations, and social responsibilities. In N. Denzin & Y. S. Lincoln (Eds.), *Handbook of qualitative research* (2nd ed., pp. 107–132). Thousand Oaks, CA: Sage.

Fisher, W. R. (1989). *Human communication as narration: Toward a philosophy of reason, value, and action*. Columbia: University of South Carolina.

Fitch, K. (1998). Text and context: A problematic distinction for ethnographers. *Research on Language and Social Interaction, 31*, 91–107.

Fitch, K. (2003). Cultural persuadables. *Communication Theory, 13*, 100–123.

Fitness, J., & Duffield, J. (2004). Emotion and communication in families. In A. L. Vangelisti (Ed.), *Handbook of family communication* (pp. 473–494). Mahwah, NJ: Erlbaum.

Floyd, K., & Morman, M. (Eds.). (2006). *Widening the family circle: New research on family communication.* Thousand Oaks, CA: Sage.

Fontana, A., & Frey, J. H. (2000). The interview: From structured questions to negotiated text. In N. K. Denzin & Y. S Lincoln (Eds.), *Handbook of qualitative research* (2nd ed., pp. 645–672). Thousand Oaks, CA: Sage.

Foss, S. K. (2009). *Rhetorical criticism: Exploration and practice.* Long Grove, IL: Waveland.

Foss, S. K., Domenico, M. E., & Foss, K. A. (2013). *Gender stories: Negotiating identity in a binary world.* Long Grove, IL: Waveland.

Foster, E. (2008). Commitment, communication, and contending with heteronormativity: An invitation to greater reflexivity in interpersonal research. *Southern Communication Journal, 73*, 84–101.

Foucault, M. (1972). *The archeology of knowledge.* New York: Pantheon.

Foucault, M. (1979). My body, this paper, this fire. *Oxford Literary Review, 4*, 9–28.

Foucault, M. (1980). *Power/knowledge.* New York: Pantheon.

Foucault, M. (1988). The ethic of care for the self as practice of freedom. In J. Bernauer & G. Rasmussen (Eds.), *The final Foucault* (pp. 1–20). Cambridge, MA: MIT.

Fox, R. C. (2007). Skinny bones #126–774–835–29: Thin gay bodies signifying a modern plague. *Text and Performance Quarterly, 27*, 3–19.

Freedman, M. (1993). *The kindness of strangers: Adult mentors, urban youth and the new Voluntarism* (Reprinted ed.). Cambridge, UK: Cambridge University Press.

Frey, L. R. (2009). What a difference more difference-making communication scholarship might make: Making a difference from and through communication research. *Journal of Applied Communication Research, 37*, 205–214.

Frey, L. R., Botan, C. H., Friedman, P. G., & Kreps, G. L. (1992). *Interpreting communication research: A case study approach.* Englewood Cliffs, NJ: Prentice-Hall.

Gable, R. K., & Wolf, M. B. (1993). *Instrument development in the affective domain: Measuring attitudes and values in corporate and school settings.* Boston: Kluwer.

Gamson, W. A. (1992). *Talking politics.* New York: Cambridge University Press.

Geertz, C. (1973). *The interpretation of cultures: Selected essays.* New York: Basic Books.

Gergen, K. J. (1992). Toward a postmodern psychology. In S. Kvale (Ed.), *Psychology and postmodernism* (pp. 17–30). London: Sage.

Gibbs, G. R. (2007). *Analyzing qualitative data.* Thousand Oaks, CA: Sage.

Glaser, B. (1992). *Basics of grounded theory analysis.* Mill Valley, CA: Sociology.

Glaser, B. G., & Strauss, A. L. (1967). *The discovery of grounded theory: Strategies for qualitative research.* New York: Aldine de Gruyter.

Gleick, J. (2011). *The information: A history, a theory, a flood.* New York: Vintage.

Goffman, E. (1959). *The presentation of self in everyday life.* Garden City, NY: Doubleday.

Goffman, E. (1963). *Stigma: Notes on the management of spoiled identity.* Englewood Cliffs, NJ: Prentice-Hall.

Gold, R. L. (1958). Roles in sociological field observations. *Social Forces, 36*, 217–223.

Goltz, D. B. (2012). Blasphemies on forever: Remembering queer futures. *Liminalities, 8*(2). Retrieved from http://liminalities.net/8-2/blasphemies.html.

Goodall, H. L. (1991). *Living in the rock n roll mystery: Reading context, self, and others as clues.* Carbondale, IL: Southern Illinois University.

Goodall, H. L. (2000). *Writing the new ethnography.* Walnut Creek, CA: AltaMira.

Goodall, H. L. (2004). Narrative ethnography as applied communication research. *Journal of Applied Communication Research, 32*, 185–194.

Graham, C. A., Sanders, S. A., Milhausen, R. R., & McBride, K. R. (2004). Turning on and turning off: A focus group study of the factors that affect women's sexual arousal. *Archives of Sexual Behavior, 33,* 527–538.

Graham, H. (1984). Surveying through stories. In C. Bell & H. Roberts (Ed.), *Social researching: Politics, problems, practices* (pp. 104–124). New York: Routledge.

Grant, D., Keenoy, T., & Oswick, C. (1998). Organizational discourse: Of diversity, dichotomy, and multi-disciplinarity. In D. Grant, T. Keenoy, & C. Oswick (Eds.), *Discourse and organization* (pp. 1–14). London: Sage.

Griffin, E..(2012). *A first look at communication theory* (8th ed.). Boston: McGraw-Hill.

Guba, E. G., & Lincoln, Y. S. (1989). *Fourth generation evaluation.* Beverly Hills, CA: Sage.

Guba, E. G., & Lincoln, Y. S. (2005). Paradigmatic controversies, contradictions, and emerging confluences. In N. K. Denzin & Y. S. Lincoln (Eds.), *The SAGE handbook of qualitative research* (3rd ed., pp. 191–215). Thousand Oaks, CA: Sage.

Gubrium, J. F., & Holstein, J. A. (1998). Standing our middle ground. *Journal of Contemporary Ethnography, 27,* 416–421.

Gubrium, J. F., & Holstein, J. A. (2009). *Analyzing narrative reality.* Thousand Oaks, CA: Sage.

Hallgrimsdottir, H. K., Phillips, R., & Benoit, C. (2006). Fallen women and rescued girls: Social stigma and media narratives of the sex industry in Victoria, B.C., from 1980 to 2005. *The Canadian Review of Sociology and Anthropology, 43,* 265–280.

Harter, L. M. (2009). Narratives as dialogic, contested, and aesthetic performances. *Journal of Applied Communication Research, 37,* 140–150.

Harter, L. M., Leeman, M., Norander, S., Young, S., & Rawlins, W. K. (2008). The intermingling of aesthetic and instrumental rationalities in a collaborative art studio for individuals with development disabilities. *Management Communication Quarterly, 21,* 423–453.

Harter, L. M., Scott, J., Novak, D., Leeman, M., & Morris, J. (2006). Freedom through flight: Performing a counter-narrative of disability. *Journal of Applied Communication Research, 34,* 3–29.

Hatch, J. A. (2002). *Doing qualitative research in education settings.* Albany: State University of New York Press.

Hatfield, E., & Rapson, R. (1993). Love and attachment processes. In M. Lewis & J. M. Haviland (Eds.), *Handbook of emotions* (pp. 595–604). New York: Guilford.

Heary, C. M., & Hennessy, E. (2000). The use of focus group interviews in pediatric health care research. *Journal of Pediatric Psychology, 27,* 47–57.

Heino, R. D., Ellison, N. B., & Gibbs, J. L. (2010). Relationshopping: Investigating the market metaphor in online dating. *Journal of Social and Personal Relationships, 27,* 427–447.

Hequembourg, A. (2004). Unscripted motherhood: Lesbian mothers negotiating incompletely institutionalized relationships. *Journal of Social and Personal Relationships, 21,* 739–762.

Herbert, B. (2007, Sept. 12). Legal prostitution does not empower women. *Columbus Dispatch.*

Hess, J. A. (2002). Distance regulation in personal relationships: The development of a conceptual model and a test of representational validity. *Journal of Social and Personal Relationships, 19,* 663–683.

Holstein, J. A., & Gubrium, J. F. (2011). The constructionist analytics of interpretive practice. In N. K. Denzin & Y. S. Lincoln (Eds.), *The SAGE handbook of qualitative research* (4th ed., pp. 341–357). Thousand Oaks, CA: Sage.

Hughes, M., Morrison, K., & Asada, K. J. (2005). What's love got to do with it? Exploring the impact of maintenance rules, love attitudes, and network support on friends with benefits relationships. *Western Journal of Communication, 69,* 49–66.

Huston, T. L., Surra, C. A., Fitzgerald, N. M., & Cate, R. M. (1981). From courtship to marriage: Mate selection as an interpersonal process. In S. Duck & R. Gilmour (Eds.), *Personal relationships 2: Developing personal relationships* (pp. 53–90). New York: Academic.

Hymes, D. (1962). The ethnography of speaking. In T. Gladwin & W. C. Sturtevant (Eds.), *Anthropology and human behavior* (pp. 13–53). Washington, DC: Anthropology Society of Washington.

Jackson, J. E. (1990). "I am a fieldnote": Fieldnotes as a symbol of professional identity. In R. Sanjek (Ed.), *Fieldnotes: The makings of ethnography* (pp. 3–33). Ithaca, NY: Cornell University Press.

Janesick, V. (1994). The dance of qualitative research design: Metaphor, methodology, and meaning. In N. Denzin & Y. Lincoln (Eds.), *Handbook of qualitative research* (pp. 209–219). Thousand Oaks, CA: Sage.

Janis, I. L. (1982). *Groupthink* (2nd ed.). Boston: Houghton Mifflin.

Jaschik, S. (2012). Confidentiality right rejected. *Inside Higher Ed*. Retrieved from www.insidehighered.com/news/2012/07/09/appeals-court-rejects-researchers-bid-protect-oral-history-confidentiality.

Johnson, A. J. (2001). Examining the maintenance of friendships: Are there differences between geographically close and long-distance friends? *Communication Quarterly, 49*, 424–435.

Johnson, A. J., Becker, J. A. H., Craig, E. A., Gilchrist, E. S., & Haigh, M. M. (2009). Changes in friendship commitment: Comparing geographically close and long-distance young-adult friendships. *Communication Quarterly, 57*, 395–415.

Johnson, A. J., Haigh, M. M., Becker, J. A. H., Craigh, E. A., & Wigley, S. (2008). College students' use of relational maintenance in email in long-distance and geographically close relationships. *Journal of Computer-Mediated Communication, 13*, 384–401.

Jorgenson, J. (2002). Engineering selves: Negotiating gender and identity in technical work. *Management Communication Quarterly, 15*, 350–380.

Jorgenson, J., & Bochner, A. P. (2004). Imagining families through stories and rituals. In A. L. Vangelisti (Ed.), *Handbook of family communication* (pp. 513–538). Mahwah, NJ: Erlbaum.

Jung, E., & Hecht, M. L. (2004). Elaborating the communication theory of identity: Identity gaps and communication outcomes. *Communication Quarterly, 52*, 265–283.

Kahn, R. L., & Cannell, C. F. (1957). *The dynamics of interviewing: Theory, technique, and cases*. New York: Wiley.

Kaler, A., & Beres, M. (2010). *Essentials of field relationships*. Walnut, CA: Left Coast Press.

Kaufman, M. (2000). *The Laramie project*. New York: Vintage.

Kelley, M. L. (1994). The effects of military-induced separation on family factors and child behavior. *American Journal of Orthospyschiatry, 64*, 103–111.

Keyton, J. (2010). *Communication research: Asking questions, finding answers* (3rd ed.). Boston: McGraw Hill.

Kisselburgh, L., Buzzanell, P. M., & Berkelaar, B. L. (2009). Discourse, gender, and the meanings of work: Rearticulating science, technology, and engineering careers through communicative lenses. In C. Beck (Ed.), *Communication Yearbook 33* (pp. 258–299). New York: Routledge.

Knobloch, L. K., & Solomon, D. H. (1999). Measuring the sources and content of relational uncertainty. *Communication Studies, 50*, 261–278.

Knowles, J., & Cole, A. (2008). *Handbook of the art in qualitative research*. Thousand Oaks, CA: Sage.

Koenig Kellas, J. (2008). Narrative theories: Making sense of interpersonal communication. In L. A. Baxter & D. O. Braithwaite (Eds.), *Engaging theories in interpersonal communication: Multiple perspectives* (pp. 241–254). Thousand Oaks, CA: Sage.

Koenig Kellas, J., & Suter, E. A. (2012). Accounting for lesbian-headed families: Lesbian mothers' responses to discursive challenges. *Communication Monographs*, DOI:10.1080/03637751.2012.723812

Krueger, R. A. (1988). *Focus groups*. Newbury Park, CA: Sage.

Krueger, R. A. (1998). *Analyzing and reporting focus group results: Focus group kit 6*. Thousand Oaks, CA: Sage.

Krueger, R. A., & Casey, M. A. (2009). *Focus groups: A practical guide for applied research*. Thousand Oaks, CA: Sage.

Kunkel, A. D., & Dennis, M. R. (2003). Grief consolation in eulogy rhetoric: An integrative framework. *Death Studies, 27*, 1–38.

Kunkel, A. D., Wilson, S. R., Olufowote, J., & Robson, S. (2003). Identity implications of influence goals: Initiating, intensifying, and ending romantic relationships. *Western Journal of Communication, 67*, 382–412.

Kunkel, A. W., & Burleson, B. R. (1998). Social support and the emotional lives of men and women: An assessment of the different cultures perspective. In D. Canary & K. Dindia (Eds.), *Sex differences and similarities in communication* (pp. 101–125). Mahwah, NJ: Erlbaum.

Kunkel, A. W., & Burleson, B. R. (1999). Assessing explanations for sex differences in emotional support: A test of the different cultures and skill specialization accounts. *Human Communication Research, 25*, 307–340.

Kvale, S. (1996). *InterViews: An introduction to qualitative research interviewing.* Thousand Oaks, CA: Sage.

Labov, W., & Waletsky, J. (1967). Narrative analysis: Oral versions of personal experience. In J. Helm (Ed.), *Essays on the verbal and visual arts: Proceedings of the 1996 annual spring meeting of the American Ethnological Society* (pp. 12–44). Seattle: University of Washington.

Langellier, K. M., & Peterson, E. E. (2004). *Storytelling in daily life: Performing narrative.* Philadelphia: Temple University.

Langellier, K. M., & Peterson, E. E. (2006a). Family storytelling as communication practice. In L. H. Turner & R. West (Eds.), *The family communication sourcebook* (pp. 109–128). Thousand Oaks, CA: Sage.

Langellier, K. M., & Peterson, E. E. (2006b). "Somebody's got to pick eggs": Family storytelling about work. *Communication Monographs, 73,* 468–473.

Larson, J. H., & Holmes, T. B. (1994). Premarital predictors of marital quality and stability. *Family Relations, 43,* 228–237. Retrieved from www.jstor.org/stable/585327.

Lave, C. A., & March, J. G. (1975). *An introduction to models in the social sciences.* New York: HarperCollins.

LeCompte, M. D., & Preissle, J. (1993). *Ethnography and qualitative design in educational research.* Waltham, MA: Academic Press.

Ledbetter, A. M. (2010). Content- and medium-specific decomposition of friendship relational maintenance: Integrating equity and media multiplexity approaches. *Journal of Social and Personal Relationships, 27,* 938–955.

Leeds-Hurwitz, W. (1995). Introducing social approaches. In W. Leeds-Hurwitz (Ed.), *Social approaches to communication* (pp. 3–20). New York: Guilford.

Leeds-Hurwitz, W. (2002). *Wedding as text: Communicating cultural identities through ritual.* Hillsdale, NJ: Erlbaum.

Leslie, L. Z. (2010). *Communication research methods in postmodern culture.* Boston: Allyn & Bacon.

Levine, T. R. (2011). Quantitative social science methods of inquiry. In M. L. Knapp & J. A. Daly (Eds.), *The SAGE handbook of interpersonal communication* (4th ed., pp. 25–57). Thousand Oaks, CA: Sage.

Levinson, R. A., Jaccard, J., & Beamer, L. (1995). Older adolescents' engagement in casual sex: Impact of risk perception and psychosocial motivations. *Journal of Youth and Adolescence, 24,* 349–364.

Lincoln, Y. S., & Denzin, N. K. (2003). *Strategies of qualitative inquiry.* Thousand Oaks, CA: Sage.

Lincoln, Y. S., & Guba, E. G. (1985). *Naturalistic inquiry.* Beverly Hills, CA: Sage.

Lincoln, Y. S., Lynham, S. A., & Guba, E. G. (2011). Paradigmatic controversies, contradictions, and emerging confluences, revisited. In Y. S. Lincoln, S. A. Lynham, & E. G. Guba (Eds.), *The SAGE handbook of qualitative research* (4th ed., pp. 97–128). Thousand Oaks, CA: Sage.

Lindlof, T. R. (1995). *Qualitative research methods.* Thousand Oaks, CA: Sage.

Lindlof, T. R., & Taylor, B. C. (2002). *Qualitative communication research methods* (2nd ed.). Thousand Oaks, CA: Sage.

Lindlof, T. R., & Taylor, B. C. (2011). *Qualitative communication research methods* (3rd ed.). Thousand Oaks, CA: Sage.

Littlejohn, S. W., & Foss, K. A. (2008). *Theories of human communication* (9th ed.). Belmont, CA: Wadsworth.

Locke, L. F., Spirduso, W. W., & Silverman, S. J. (1993). *Proposals that work: A guide to dissertation and grant proposals.* Thousand Oaks, CA: Sage.

Lofland, J., Snow, D., Anderson, L., & Lofland, L. (2006). *Analyzing social settings: A guide to qualitative observation and analysis* (4th ed.). Belmont, CA: Wadsworth.

Lucaites, J. L., & Fitch, K. L. (1997). Book reviews. *Quarterly Journal of Speech, 83,* 262.

Madison, D. S. (2005). *Critical ethnography: Method, ethics, and performance.* Thousand Oaks, CA: Sage.

Madison, D. S. (2011). The labor of reflexivity. *Cultural Studies < = > Critical Methodologies, 11,* 129–138.

Madison, D. S. (2012). *Critical ethnography: Methods, ethics, and performance* (2nd ed.). Thousand Oaks, CA: Sage.

Maines, D. R. (1993). Narrative's moment and sociology's phenomena: Toward a narrative sociology. *Sociological Quarterly, 34,* 17–37.

Malin, B. (2001). Communication with feeling: Emotion, publicness, and embodiment. *Quarterly Journal of Speech, 87,* 216–230.

Manning, J. (2009a). Because the personal is the political: Politics and unpacking the rhetoric of (queer) relationships. In K. German & B. Dreshel (Eds.), *Queer identities/political realities* (pp. 1–8). Newcastle, UK: Cambridge Scholars.

Manning, J. (2009b). Introduction: The future of relationships. *Kentucky Journal of Communication, 34*, vii–viii.

Manning, J. (2010a). After the storm: Communication and service learning. *Communication Currents, 4*. Retrieved from www.natcom.org/CommCurrentsArticle.aspx?id=924.

Manning, J. (2010b). "There is no agony like bearing an untold story inside you": Communication research as interventive practice. *Communication Monographs, 77*, 437–439.

Manning, J. (2010c, November). *Virginity contracts as sex education: Efficacies and understandings in family discourses about sexuality.* Paper presented at the Society for the Scientific Study of Sexuality annual meeting, Las Vegas.

Manning, J. (in press-a). Perceptions of positive and negative communicative behaviors in coming out conversations. *Journal of Homosexuality.*

Manning, J. (in press-b). Values in online and offline dating discourses: Comparing presentational and articulated rhetorics of relationship seeking. *Journal of Computer-Mediated Communication.*

Marcia, J. E. (1980). Identity in adolescence. In J. Adelson (Ed.), *Handbook of adolescent psychology* (pp. 159–187). New York: Wiley.

Markham, A. N., & Baym, N. K. (2009). *Internet inquiry: Conversations about method.* Thousand Oaks, CA: Sage.

Mattson, M., Clair, R. P., Sanger, P. A. C., & Kunkel, A. D. (2000). A feminist reframing of stress: Rose's story. In P. M. Buzzanell (Ed.), *Rethinking organizational and managerial communication from feminist perspectives* (pp. 157–174). Thousand Oaks, CA: Sage.

Maxwell, J. A. (2004). Causal explanation, qualitative research, and scientific inquiry in education. *Educational Researcher, 33*, 3–11.

Maxwell, J. A. (2005). *Qualitative research design: An interactive approach* (2nd ed.). Thousand Oaks, CA: Sage.

Maxwell, J. A. (2009). Designing a qualitative study. In L. Bickman & D. J. Rogers (Eds.), *The SAGE handbook of applied social research methods* (2nd ed., pp. 214–253). Thousand Oaks, CA: Sage.

Maxwell, J. A. (2011). *A realist approach for qualitative research.* Thousand Oaks, CA: Sage.

Maxwell, J. A. (2012). *Qualitative research design: An interactive approach* (3rd ed.). Thousand Oaks, CA: Sage.

McAdams, D. P. (2004). Generativity and the narrative ecology of family life. In M. W. Pratt & B. H. Fiese (Eds.), *Family stories and the life course across time and generations* (pp. 235–257). Mahwah, NJ: Erlbaum.

McAdams, D. P., & de St. Aubin, E. (1992). A theory of generativity and its assessment through self-report, behavioral acts, and narrative themes in autobiography. *Journal of Personal and Social Psychology, 62*, 1003–1015.

McAlister, J. F. (2011). Figural materialism: Renovating marriage through the American family home. *Southern Communication Journal, 76*, 279–304.

McCurdy, D. W., Spradley, J. P., & Shandy, D. J. (2005). *The cultural experience: Ethnography in complex society* (2nd ed.). Long Grove, IL: Waveland Press.

McLaughlin, L. (1991). Discourses of prostitution/discourses of sexuality. *Critical Studies in Mass Communication, 8*, 249–272.

Mead, G. H. (1934). *Mind, self, and society from the standpoint of a social behaviorist.* Chicago: University of Chicago Press.

Medford, K. (2006). Caught with a fake ID: Ethical questions about slippage in autoethnography. *Qualitative Inquiry, 12*, 853–864.

Meyer, M. D. E. (2003). "It's me. I'm it.": Defining adolescent sexual identity through relational dialectics in *Dawson's Creek*. *Communication Quarterly, 51*, 262–276.

Milardo, R. (2010). *The forgotten kin: Aunts and uncles.* New York: Cambridge University Press.

Miles, M. B., & Huberman, A. M. (1994). *Qualitative data analysis: An expanded sourcebook* (2nd ed.). Thousand Oaks, CA: Sage.

Miller, K. (2004). *Communication theories: Perspectives, processes, and contexts.* Boston: McGraw-Hill.

Mirivel, J. (2007). Managing poor surgical candidacy: Communication problems for plastic surgeons. *Discourse & Communication, 1*, 309–336.

Mohr, L. B. (1996). *The causes of human behavior: Implications for theory and method in the social sciences.* Ann Arbor: University of Michigan.

Mokros, H. B. (2003). *Identity matters*. Cresskill, NJ: Hampton Press.

Mongeau, P. A., Shaw, C. M., & Knight, K. R. (2009). Friends with benefits. In H. Reis & S. Sprecher (Eds.), *Encyclopedia of human relationships* (Vol. 2, pp. 740–741). Thousand Oaks, CA: Sage.

Morgan, D. L. (1989). Adjusting to widowhood: Do social networks really make it easier? *The Gerontologist, 29*, 101–107.

Morgan, D. L. (1997). *Focus groups as qualitative research* (2nd ed.). Thousand Oaks, CA: Sage.

Mumby, D. K. (1997). Modernism, postmodernism, and communication studies: A rereading of an ongoing debate. *Communication Theory, 7*, 1–28.

Mumby, D. K., & Putnam, L. L. (1992). The politics of emotion: A feminist reading of bounded rationality. *The Academy of Management Review, 17*, 465–486.

Myers, M. D., & Newman, M. (2007). The qualitative interview in IS research: Examining the craft. *Information and Organization, 17*, 2–26.

Nagle, J. (Ed.). (1997). *Whores and other feminists*. New York: Routledge.

National Academy of Engineering (NAE). (2008). *Changing the conversation: Messages for improving public understanding of engineering*. Washington, DC: National Academies Press.

Norris, S. P. (1983). The inconsistencies at the foundation of construct validation theory. In E. R. House (Ed.), *Philosophy of evaluation* (pp. 53–74). San Francisco: Jossey-Bass.

Norton, R. (1983). *Communicator style: Theory, applications, and measures*. Beverly Hills, CA: Sage.

Norwood, K. (2012). Grieving gender: Trans-identities, transition, and ambiguous loss. *Communication Monographs*, DOI:10.1080/03637751.2012.739705

Ochs, E. (1979). Transcription as theory. In E. Ochs & B. B. Schieffelin (Eds.), *Developmental pragmatics* (pp. 43–72). New York: Academic Press.

Ochs, E. (1993). Constructing social identity: A language socialization perspective. *Research on Language and Social Interaction, 26*, 287–306.

Ochs, E. (1997). Narrative. In T. van Dijk (Ed.), *Discourse as structure and process* (pp. 185–207). London: Sage.

O'Hair, D. (2006, May). Work as identity. *Spectra*.

Olson, L. N. (2004). The role of voice in the (re)construction of a battered woman's identity: An autoethnography of one woman's experiences of abuse. *Women's Studies in Communication, 27*, 1–33.

Orbuch, T. L. (1997). People's accounts count: The sociology of accounts. *Annual Review of Sociology, 23*, 455–478.

O'Reilly, A., & Abbey, S. (Eds.). (2000). *Mothers and daughters: Connection, empowerment and transformation*. Lanham, MD: Rowman & Littlefield.

Owen, J., & Fincham, F. D. (2011). The effects of gender and psychosocial factors on "friends with benefits" relationships among young adults. *Archives of Sexual Behavior, 40*, 311–320.

Park, L., Young, A., Troisi, J., & Pinkus, R. (2011). Effects of everyday romantic goal pursuit on women's attitudes toward math and science. *Personality and Social Psychology Bulletin, 37*, 1259–1273.

Parker, I., & Burman, E. (1993). Against discursive imperialism, empiricism, and constructionism: Thirty-two problems with discourse analysis. In E. Burman & I. Parker (Eds.), *Discourse analytic research* (pp. 155–172). London: Routledge.

Parks, M. R. (1998). Where does scholarship begin? *American Communication Journal, 1*. Retrieved from http://ac-journal.org/journal/vol1/Iss2/special/parks.htm.

Patton, M. Q. (1990). *Qualitative evaluation and research methods* (2nd ed.). Newbury Park, CA: Sage.

Paul, E. L., McManus, B., & Hayes, A. (2000). "Hookups": Characteristics and correlates of college students' spontaneous and anonymous sexual experiences. *Journal of Sex Research, 37*, 76–88.

Peington, B. A. (2004). The communicative management of connection and autonomy in African American and European American mother-daughter relationships. *Journal of Family Communication, 4*, 3–34.

Pelias, R. J. (1999). *Writing performance: Poeticizing the researcher's body*. Carbondale: Southern Illinois University.

Pelias, R. J. (2006). A personal history of lust on Bourbon Street. *Text and Performance Quarterly, 26*, 47–56.

Pelias, R. J. (2009). Pledging personal allegiance to qualitative inquiry. *International Review of Qualitative Research, 2,* 351–356.

Pelias, R. J. (2011a). *Leaning: A poetics of personal relations.* Walnut Creek, CA: Left Coast Press.

Pelias, R. J. (2011b). Writing into position: Strategies for composition and evaluation. In N. K. Denzin & Y. S. Lincoln (Eds.), *The SAGE handbook of qualitative research* (4th ed., pp. 645–658). Thousand Oaks, CA: Sage.

Pelto, P. J., & Pelto, G. H. (1978). *Anthropological research: The structure of inquiry.* Cambridge, UK: Cambridge University.

Petronio, S. (2002). *Boundaries of privacy: Dialectics of disclosure.* Albany: State University of New York.

Philipsen, G. (1975). Speaking "like a man" in Teamsterville: Culture patterns of role enactment in an urban neighborhood. *Quarterly Journal of Speech, 61,* 13–22.

Philipsen, G. (1992). *Speaking culturally: Explorations in social communication.* Albany: State University of New York.

Phillips, N., & Brown, J. (1993). Analyzing communication in and around organizations: A critical hermeneutic approach. *Academy of Management Journal, 36,* 1547–1576.

Phillips, N., & Hardy, C. (2002). *Discourse analysis: Investigating processes of social construction.* Thousand Oaks, CA: Sage.

Pike, K. L. (1967). *Language in relation to a unified theory of the structure of human behavior* (2nd ed.). The Hague: Mouton.

Plutchik, R. (1981). *Development of a scale for the measurement of coping styles: A preliminary report.* New York: Einstein College of Medicine.

Plutchik, R. (2001). The nature of emotions. *American Scientist, 89,* 344–350.

Poovey, M. (1998). *A history of the modern fact: Problems of knowledge in the sciences of wealth and society.* Chicago: University of Chicago.

Pratt, M. W., & Friese, B. H. (2004). Families, stories, and the life course: An ecological context. In M. W. Pratt & B. H. Fiese (Eds.), *Family stories and the life course: Across time and generations.* Mahwah, NJ: Erlbaum.

Prus, R. (1996). *Symbolic interaction and ethnographic research.* Albany: State University of New York Press.

Punch, M. (1986). *The politics and ethics of fieldwork.* Beverly Hills, CA: Sage.

Ragin, C. C. (1987). *The comparative method: Moving beyond qualitative and quantitative strategies.* Berkeley: University of California.

Rawlins, W. K. (2007). Living scholarship: A field report. *Communication Methods and Measures, 1,* 55–63.

Reason, P. (1988). *Human inquiry in action: Developments in new paradigm research.* Thousand Oaks, CA: Sage.

Rich, A. (1976). *Of woman born: Motherhood as experience and institution.* New York: Norton.

Richardson, L. (1994). Writing: A method of inquiry. In N. K. Denzin & Y. S. Lincoln (Eds.), *Handbook of qualitative research* (pp. 516–529). Thousand Oaks, CA: Sage.

Richardson, L. (2000). Writing: A method of inquiry. In N. K. Denzin & Y. S. Lincoln (Eds.), *Handbook of qualitative research* (2nd ed., pp. 923–948). Thousand Oaks, CA: Sage.

Richardson, L., & St. Pierre, E. A. (2005). Writing: A method of inquiry. In N. K. Denzin & Y. S. Lincoln (Eds.), *Handbook of qualitative research* (3rd ed., pp. 959–978). Thousand Oaks, CA: Sage.

Riessman, C. K. (1993). *Narrative analysis.* Newbury Park, CA: Sage.

Riessman, C. K. (2007). *Narrative methods for the human sciences.* Thousand Oaks, CA: Sage.

Rohlfing, M. A. (1995). Doesn't anyone stay in one place anymore? An exploration of the under-studied phenomenon of long-distance relationships. In S. Duck & J. Wood (Eds.), *Under-studied relationships: Off the beaten track* (pp. 173–196). London: Sage.

Rossi, A. (Ed.). (2001). *Caring and doing for others: Social responsibility in the domains of family, work, and community.* Chicago: University of Chicago Press.

Rossman, G. B., & Rallis, S. F. (2003). *Learning in the field: An introduction to qualitative research* (2nd ed.). Thousand Oaks, CA: Sage.

Rubin, H. J., & Rubin, I. S. (1995). *Qualitative interviewing: The art of hearing data.* Thousand Oaks, CA: Sage.

Ruby, J. (1982). *A crack in the mirror: Reflective perspectives in anthropology.* Philadelphia: University of Pennsylvania.

Sacks, H. (1992). *Lectures on conversation* (2 vols.; G. Jefferson, Ed.). Cambridge, MA: Blackwell.

Sahlstein, E. (2004). Relating at a distance: Negotiating long-distance and proximal relationships. *Journal of Social and Personal Relationships, 21,* 689–702.

Sahlstein, E. (2010). Communication and distance: The present and future interpreted through the past. *Journal of Applied Communication Research, 38,* 106–114.

Sahlstein, E., & Stafford, L. (2010). Communication and distance: A special issue. *Journal of Applied Communication Research, 38,* 1–3.

Saldaña, J. (1998). Ethical issues in an ethnographic performance text: The "dramatic impact" of "juicy stuff." *Research in Drama Education, 3,* 181–196.

Saldaña, J. (2005). *Ethnodrama: An anthology of reality theatre.* Walnut Creek, CA: AltaMira Press.

Saldaña, J. (2009). *The coding manual for qualitative researchers.* Thousand Oaks, CA: Sage.

Schegloff, E. A., & Sacks, H. (1973). Opening up closings. *Semiotica, 8,* 289–327.

Schiffrin, D. (1994). *Approaches to discourse.* Cambridge, MA: Blackwell.

Scriven, M. (1991). *Evaluation thesaurus* (4th ed.). Newbury Park, CA: Sage.

Searle, J. R. (1979). *Expression and meaning.* Cambridge, UK: Cambridge University.

Shadish, W. R., Cook, T. D., & Campbell, D. T. (2002). *Experimental and quasi-experimental designs for generalized causal inference* (2nd ed.). Belmont, CA: Wadsworth.

Sigman, S. J. (1991). Handling the discontinuous aspects of continuing social relationships: Towards research of the persistence of social forms. *Communication Theory, 1,* 106–127.

Sim, J. (1998). Collecting and analysing qualitative data: Issues raised by the focus group. *Journal of Advanced Nursing, 28,* 345–352.

Simmons, O. E. (2011). Book review: *Essentials of Accessible Grounded Theory. The Grounded Theory Review, 10.* Retrieved from http://groundedtheoryreview.com/wp-content/uploads/2012/06/GT-Review-vol-10-no-2.pdf.

Singleton, R. A., Jr., & Straits, B. C. (2010). *Approaches to social research* (5th ed.). New York: Oxford University Press.

Snow, D. A. (1980). The disengagement process: A neglected problem in participant observation research. *Qualitative Sociology, 3,* 100–122.

Solomon, D., & Knobloch, L. (2004). A model of relational turbulence: The role of intimacy, relational uncertainty, and interference from partners in appraisals of irritations. *Journal of Social and Personal Relationships, 21,* 795–816.

Solomon, D. H., & Theiss, J. A. (2011). Relational turbulence: What doesn't kill us makes us stronger. In W. R. Cupach & B. H. Spitzberg (Eds.), *The dark side of close relationships.* New York: Routledge, Tayor, & Francis.

Solomon, D. H., Weber, K. M., & Steuber, K. R. (2010). Turbulence in relationship transitions. In S. W. Smith & S. R. Wilson (Eds.), *New directions in interpersonal communication research* (pp. 115–134). Thousand Oaks, CA: Sage.

Sotirin, P., & Ellingson, L. L. (2006). The "other" woman in family life: Aunt/niece/nephew communication. In K. Floyd & M. Morman (Eds.), *Widening the family circle: New research on family communication* (pp. 81–99). Thousand Oaks, CA: Sage.

Spradley, J. P. (1970). *You owe yourself a drunk: Adaptive strategies of urban nomads.* Boston, MA: Little Brown.

Spradley, J. P. (1979). *The ethnographic interview.* New York: Holt, Reinhart, & Winston.

Spradley, J. P. (1980). *Participant observation.* Fort Worth, TX: Harcourt Brace Jovanovich.

Stafford, L. (2005). *Maintaining long-distance and cross-residential relationships.* Mahwah, NJ: Erlbaum.

Stafford, L. (2008). Dating relationships. In W. Donsbach (Ed.), *The international encyclopedia of communication* (Vol. 3, pp. 1167–1171). Malden, MA: Blackwell.

Stern, P. N. (1994). Eroding grounded theory. In J. M. Morse (Ed.), *Critical issues in qualitative research methods* (pp. 212–223). Thousand Oaks, CA: Sage.

Stern, P. N., & Porr, C. J. (2011). *Essentials of accessible grounded theory.* Walnut Creek, CA: Left Coast Press.

Stohl, C. (1986). The role of memorable messages in the process of organizational socialization. *Communication Quarterly, 34,* 231–249.

Strauss, A. (1987). *Qualitative analysis for social scientists.* Cambridge, UK: Cambridge University.

Strauss, A., & Corbin, J. (1990). *Basics of qualitative research: Techniques and procedures for developing grounded theory.* Thousand Oaks, CA: Sage.

Strauss, A., & Corbin, J. (1998). *Basics of qualitative research: Techniques and procedures for developing grounded theory* (2nd ed.). Thousand Oaks, CA: Sage.

Sturdy, A. J. (2003). Knowing the unknowable? A discussion of methodological and theoretical issues in emotion research and organizational studies. *Organization, 10,* 81–105.

Sturgis, H. (2004). *Aunties: Thirty-five writers celebrate their other mother.* New York: Ballantine Books.

Sunwolf, & Frey, L. R. (2001). Storytelling: The power of narrative communication and interpretation. In W. P. Robinson & H. Giles (Eds.), *The new handbook of language and social psychology* (pp. 119–135). Chicester, UK: Wiley.

Surra, C. A., Boettcher-Burke, T. M., Cottle, N. R., West, A. R., & Gray, C. R. (2007). The treatment of relationship status in research on dating and mate selection. *Journal of Marriage and Family, 69,* 207–221.

Suter, B. (2009). Validity in qualitative research on personal relationships. *Kentucky Journal of Communication, 28,* 77–96.

Teo, T. (2005). *The critique of psychology: From Kant to postcolonial theory.* New York: Springer.

Thibaut, J. W., & Kelley, H. H. (1978). *Interpersonal relations: A theory of interdependence.* New York: Wiley.

Thompson, J., Petronio, S., & Braithwaite, D. O. (2012). An examination of privacy rules for academic advisors and college student-athletes: A communication privacy management perspective. *Communication Studies, 63,* 54–76.

Tillmann, L. M. (2009). Speaking into silences: Autoethnography, communication, and applied research. *Journal of Applied Communication Research, 37,* 94–97.

Tokic, A., & Pecnik, N. (2010). Parental behaviors related to adolescents' self-disclosure: Adolescents' views. *Journal of Social and Personal Relationships, 28,* 201–222.

Toller, P. W. (2005). Negotiation of dialectical contradictions by parents who have experienced the death of a child. *Journal of Applied Communication Research, 33,* 46–66.

Toller, P. W. (2008). Bereaved parents' negotiation of identity following the death of a child. *Communication Studies, 59,* 306–321.

Toller, P. W. (2011). Bereaved parents' experiences of supportive and unsupportive communication. *Southern Communication Journal, 76,* 17–34.

Tracy, K. (1995). Action-implicative discourse analysis. *Journal of Language and Social Psychology, 14,* 195–215.

Tracy, K. (2002). *Everyday talk: Building and reflecting identities.* New York: Guilford.

Tracy, K. (2005). Reconstructing communicative practices: Action-implicative discourse analysis. In K. Fitch & R. Sanders (Eds.), *Handbook of language and social interaction* (pp. 301–319). Mahwah, NJ: Erlbaum.

Tracy, K. (2008). Action-implicative discourse analysis theory: Theorizing communicative practices. In L. A. Baxter & D. O. Braithwaite (Eds.), *Engaging theories in interpersonal communication: Multiple perspectives* (pp. 149–160). Thousand Oaks, CA: Sage.

Tracy, K. (2010). *Challenges of ordinary democracy: A case study in deliberation and dissent.* University Park: Pennsylvania State University Press.

Tracy, K., & Agne, R. R. (2002). "I just need to ask somebody some questions": Sensitivities in domestic dispute calls. In J. Cottrell (Ed.), *Language in the legal process* (pp. 75–89). Brunel, UK: Palgrave.

Tracy, K., & Craig, R. T. (2010). Studying interaction in order to cultivate practice: Action-implicative discourse analysis. In J. Streeck (Ed.), *New adventures in language and interaction* (pp. 145–166). Amsterdam: John Benjamins.

Tracy, K., & Muñoz, K. (2011). Qualitative methods in interpersonal communication. In M. L. Knapp & J. A. Daly (Eds.), *The SAGE handbook of interpersonal communication* (4th ed., pp. 59–86). Thousand Oaks, CA: Sage.

Tracy, S. J. (2010). Qualitative quality: Eight "big-tent" criteria for excellent qualitative research. *Qualitative Inquiry, 16,* 837–851.

Tracy, S. J. (2012). The toxic and mythical combination of a deductive writing logic for inductive qualitative research. *Qualitative Communication Research, 1*, 109–142.

Traeder, T., & Bennett, J. (1998). *Aunties: Our older, cooler, wiser friends*. Berkeley, CA: Wildcat Canyon Press.

Trix, F., & Psenka, C. (2003). Exploring the color of glass: Letters of recommendation for female and male faculty. *Discourse & Society, 14*, 191–220.

Utz, S. (2007). Media use in long-distance friendships. *Information, Communication & Society, 10*, 694–713.

Valsiner, J. (2000). Data as representations: Contextualizing qualitative and quantitative research strategies. *Social Science Information, 39*, 99–113.

Vanderstaay, S. L. (2005). One hundred dollars and a dead man: Ethical decision making in ethnographic field work. *Journal of Contemporary Ethnography, 34*, 371–409.

van Dijk, T. A. (1987). *Communicating racism: Ethnic prejudice in thought and talk*. Newbury Park, CA: Sage.

van Dijk, T. A. (1997a). *Discourse as structure and process: Volume 1*. London: Sage.

van Dijk, T. A. (1997b). *Discourse as structure and process: Volume 2*. London: Sage.

van Dijk, T. A. (2009). Critical discourse studies: A sociocognitive approach. In R. Wodak & M. Meyer (Eds.), *Methods for critical discourse analysis* (2nd ed., pp. 62–86). London: Sage.

Van Maanen, J. (1988). *Tales of the field: On writing ethnography*. Chicago: University of Chicago.

van Manen, M. (1990). *Researching lived experience: Human science for an action sensitive pedagogy*. Albany: State University of New York Press.

Walker, K. L., & Dickson, F. C. (2004). An exploration of illness-related narratives in marriage: The identification of illness-identity scripts. *Journal of Social and Personal Relationships, 21*, 527–544.

Walther, J. B. (1996). Computer-mediated communication: Impersonal, interpersonal, and hyperpersonal interaction. *Communication Research, 23*, 3–43.

Wax, M. L. (1980). Paradoxes of "consent" to the practice of fieldwork. *Social Problems, 27*, 272–283.

Weick, K. E. (1993). Collapse of sensemaking in organizations: The Mann Gulch disaster. *Administrative Science Quarterly, 38*, 628–652.

Weick, K. E. (1995). *Sensemaking in organizations*. Thousand Oaks, CA: Sage.

Wight, D. (1994). Boys' thoughts and talk about sex in a working class locality of Glascow. *Sociological Review, 42*, 702–737.

Wildermuth, S. M., & Vogl-Bauer, S. (2007). We met on the net: Exploring the perceptions of online romantic relationship participants. *Southern Communication Journal, 72*, 211–227.

Wilkinson, S. (1998). Focus groups in health research: Exploring the meanings of health and illness. *Journal of Health Psychology, 3*, 329–348.

Wilson, S. R., Kunkel, A. D., Robson, S., Olufowote, J. O., & Soliz, J. (2009). Identity implications of relationship (re) definition goals: An analysis of face threats and facework as young adults initiate, intensify, and disengage from romantic relationships. *Journal of Language and Social Psychology, 28*, 32–61.

Wiseman, J. P. (1986). Friendship: Bonds and binds in a voluntary relationship. *Journal of Social and Personal Relationships, 3*, 191–211.

Wodak, R., & Chilton, P. (2007). *A new agenda in critical discourse analysis* (2nd ed.). Amsterdam: John Benjamins.

Wolcott, H. F. (1994). *Transforming qualitative data: Description, analysis, and interpretation*. Thousand Oaks, CA: Sage.

Wood, J. T. (2008). Critical feminist theories: Giving voice and visibility to women's experiences in interpersonal communication. In L. A. Baxter & D. O. Braithwaite (Eds.), *Engaging theories in interpersonal communication: Multiple perspectives* (pp. 323–334). Thousand Oaks, CA: Sage.

Wood, L. A., & Kroger, R. O. (2000). *Doing discourse analysis: Methods for studying action in talk and text*. Thousand Oaks, CA: Sage.

Woodilla, J. (1998). Workplace conversations: The text of organizing. In D. Grant, T. Keenoy, & C. Oswick (Eds.), *Discourse and organization* (pp. 31–50). London: Sage.

Yin, R. (1994). *Case study research: Design and methods*. Thousand Oaks, CA: Sage.

Index

About the Authors

Jimmie Manning (PhD, University of Kansas) is an associate professor of communication at Northern Illinois University. His research program focuses on meaning-making in relationships. This research spans interpersonal, mediated, organizational, and political communication to understand how individuals, couples, families, organizations, and other cultural institutions attempt to define, support, control, limit, encourage, or otherwise negotiate relationships. He explores these ideas through three distinct contexts: relational discourses (such as those about sexuality, gender, love, rituals, legitimacy, identity, and expectations); organizational culture and workplace interaction; and digitally mediated communication contexts (such as social media). His research has been supported by a number of funding agencies, including the National Science Foundation and Learn & Serve America, and has resulted in over 50 publications, including the coedited *Case Studies of Communication About Sex* and journal articles in outlets such as *Communication Monographs* and *Journal of Computer-Mediated Communication*. His research has won numerous awards, including the Society for the Scientific Study of Sexuality Early Professional Leadership Award and ten different top-paper awards from regional, national, and international professional organizations. He teaches classes exploring relational communication, qualitative research methods, social media, communication theory, and cultural studies. Professor Manning's teaching and mentoring have been honored with the National Communication Outstanding Mentor in Master's Education Award, the Central States Communication Association's Outstanding New Teacher Award, and the Organization for the Study of Communication, Language, and Gender's Outstanding Feminist Teacher-Mentor Award. Recently he founded and serves as editor for the journal *Sexuality & Communication*. He resides in Chicago.

Adrianne Kunkel (PhD, Purdue University) is an associate professor at the University of Kansas. Her research interests include emotional support/coping processes in personal relationships and support group settings, romantic relationship (re)definition processes, sex/gender similarities and differences, and sexual harassment and domestic violence intervention. She has received grants to study how people cope with distressing events through narrative, how participation in support groups affects breast cancer survivors, how technology shapes satisfaction and perceived support in doctor-patient interaction, and how domestic violence survivors and advocates pursue freedom from abuse. Along with several book chapters, Professor Kunkel has published in a variety of journals, including *Human Communication Research*, *Communication Monographs*, *Journal of Applied Communication Research*, *Journal of Social and Personal Relationships*, *Health Communication*, *Death Studies*, *Journal of Family Communication*, and *Journal of Language and Social Psychology*. Professor Kunkel teaches courses in interpersonal communication, communication and gender, research methods, and social support. She has been named the Outstanding Woman Educator of the Year and received both the Silver Anniversary Award for Excellence in Teaching and the John C. Wright Mentor Award at the University of Kansas. She was also recognized nationally with the Central States Communication Outstanding New Teacher Award. She resides in Lawrence, Kansas.

⑤SAGE research**methods**
The Essential Online Tool for Researchers

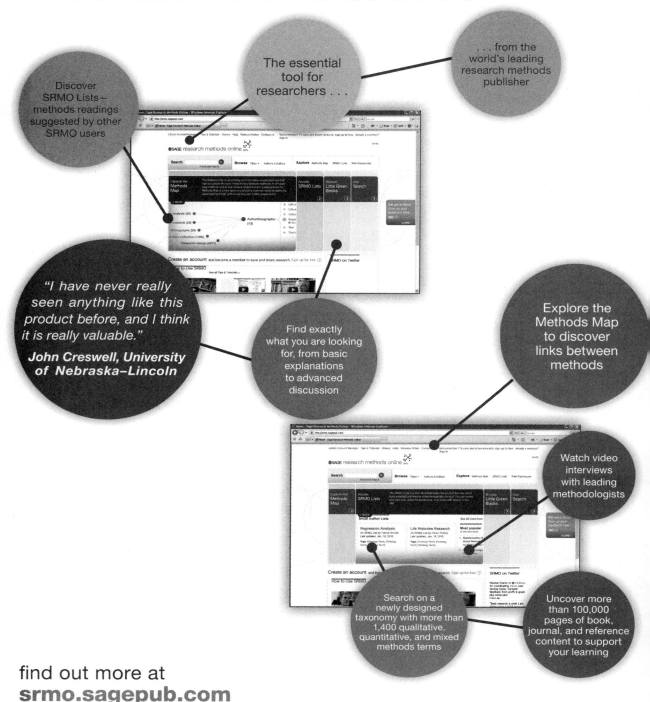

The essential tool for researchers . . .

. . . from the world's leading research methods publisher

Discover SRMO Lists—methods readings suggested by other SRMO users

"I have never really seen anything like this product before, and I think it is really valuable."

John Creswell, University of Nebraska–Lincoln

Find exactly what you are looking for, from basic explanations to advanced discussion

Explore the Methods Map to discover links between methods

Watch video interviews with leading methodologists

Search on a newly designed taxonomy with more than 1,400 qualitative, quantitative, and mixed methods terms

Uncover more than 100,000 pages of book, journal, and reference content to support your learning

find out more at
srmo.sagepub.com